# SPEED, TIME, DISTANCE CALCULATIONS

## TO FIND SPEED

Place one point of dividers on nautical miles run, the other point on the minutes run. Lift dividers without changing the spread and place the upper point on 60. The lower point will fall on the speed in knots.

## TO FIND TIME

Place one point of dividers on nautical miles run, the other point on the speed in knots. Lift dividers without changing the spread and place one point on 60. If speed exceeds distance, swing the other point down and read time in minutes. If distance exceeds speed, swing up and read time in minutes. For very long distances place the first point on 1.0, swing up and read the time in hours.

## TO FIND DISTANCE

Place the lower point of dividers on 1.0, the upper end on the speed in knots. Without changing the spread, lift the dividers and place the upper point on 60. Prick the other point of the dividers on the scale and swing the dividers about it. Reset the other point (which has now become the lower) on 1.0. Without changing the new spread, lift the dividers and place the upper end on the time run in minutes. The lower end will fall on the distance run in nautical miles.

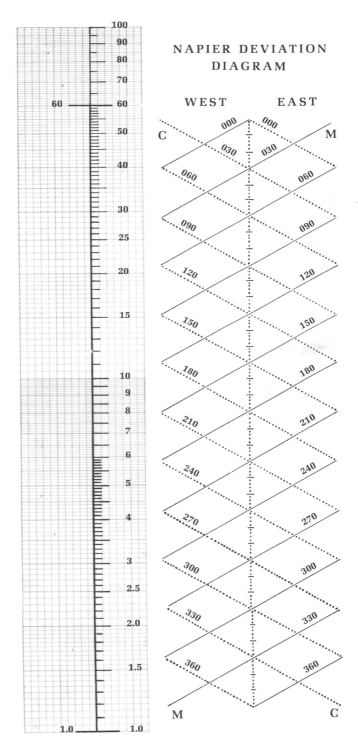

NAPIER DEVIATION DIAGRAM

# Basic Boating:
## PILOTING
## AND
## SEAMANSHIP

# Basic

# Boating:
## PILOTING
## AND
## SEAMANSHIP
### REVISED EDITION

HOWARD L. ANDREWS, N

Navigator, United States Power Squadrons
Greenwich Bay Squadron

DR. ALEXANDER L. RUSSELL, N

Navigator, United States Power Squadrons
Potomac River Squadron

PRENTICE-HALL, INC., Englewood Cliffs, N.J.

*Basic Boating: Piloting and Seamanship,* Revised Edition,
    by Howard L. Andrews and Alexander L. Russell
Copyright © 1974, 1964 by Prentice-Hall, Inc.
All rights reserved. No part of this book may be
reproduced in any form or by any means, except
for the inclusion of brief quotations in a review,
without permission in writing from the publisher.
Printed in the United States of America
Prentice-Hall International, Inc., London
Prentice-Hall of Australia, Pty. Ltd., North Sydney
Prentice-Hall of Canada, Ltd., Toronto
Prentice-Hall of India Private Ltd., New Delhi
Prentice-Hall of Japan, Inc., Tokyo

Library of Congress Cataloging in Publication Data
Andrews, Howard Lucius.
    Basic Boating.
        1.   Motor-boats.        2.   Boats and boating.
I.   Russell, Alexander L., joint author.     II.   Title.
GV835.A67   1974              797.1              73-9631
ISBN  0-13-057075-3

10  9  8  7  6  5  4  3  2  1

# Preface to the
# Second Edition

The high level of interest in recreational boating in evidence at the time of the first edition of this book has continued. Year by year the congestion on our waterways continues to increase as more and more people join those already enjoying the benefits and pleasures of a life afloat.

This book is designed to provide the prospective or beginning boatman with a concise, comprehensive text that will give him the information needed to operate a boat safely on our crowded waterways. The basic material presented in the first edition has been retained but brought up to date to conform to legislative changes. Safety is emphasized throughout. This emphasis may convey to some the feeling that all boats operate under the constant threat of disaster. This is far from the case. To these people we would point out that adverse conditions, caused either by a deterioration of the weather or by an equipment or personnel failure must be anticipated and planned for before they occur.

Safe small-boat operation becomes more demanding every year because of the mounting traffic, the continued trend toward higher speeds, and the increasing number of skippers inadequately prepared to cope with the problems that are bound to arise. With a greater proportion of boats being trailered to distant points, more boatmen are cruising in unfamiliar areas, where an understanding of the principles of piloting and the use of navigational aids must replace detailed knowledge of home waters.

Many beginners caught up in a wave of enthusiasm enter into the acquisition and operation of a vessel without the knowledge required for safe and enjoyable use. Financial loss and emotional disappointment all too frequently follow the belated recognition that boat ownership carries serious responsibilities as well as rich rewards.

The United States Coast Guard is increasing its controls to make certain that boats are seaworthy and are being operated with the equipment deemed necessary to insure safety afloat. Examination and licensing of small-boat operators is not now required, but prompt and effective use of educational programs appears to be the only alternative to the enactment of more restrictive legislation than is now in effect.

The national fight against environmental pollution is intensifying, and the recreational boatman must be informed and prepared to comply with regulations designed to improve and preserve this priceless heritage.

This book is suitable for self-study, but as in any educational effort, greater progress will be made by joining a well-organized group with competent instruction. Two organizations, the United States Coast Guard Auxiliary and the United States Power Squadrons, through its local squadrons, conduct extensive educational programs providing highly qualified instruction which is either free or is nominally priced. These programs have been very effective in raising the standards of boating throughout the United States. The beginner is urged to participate in one or both of them. As in no other avocation, progress toward professional competence through education is accompanied by an increased confidence and more and more pleasure afloat.

In preparing this material we have relied heavily on the publications of those federal agencies whose activities contribute to better and safer boating. We are particularly grateful to the representatives of the Coast Guard, the National Oceanic and Atmospheric Administration, and the National Weather Service for providing illustrative material and offering many valuable suggestions.

H.L.A.
A.L.R.

# The United States Power Squadrons

by R/C W. Clinton Weitmann, N, Historian

On 2 February 1914, at the New York Yacht Club, representatives of 20 yacht clubs and associations from Maine to Chesapeake Bay met and launched The United States Power Squadrons. On 18 January 1969, at the annual meeting in Florida, there were present 929 representatives from 378 Squadrons, with a total membership of 76,210 extending from Maine to Yokohama and from Key West to Alaska.

Between these two dates an idea became a reality, grew and almost died, and was reborn to reach a zenith of unparalleled service to the boating world. In the early spring of 1912 when Roger Upton, Vice Commodore of the Boston Yacht Club, conceived the idea of a "club within a club" for development of new forms of cruising and racing for motor-driven yachts and for the nautical education and training of motorboatmen, it is not likely that he foresaw the tremendous ultimate expansion of the USPS from coast to coast and beyond the limits of the continental United States. Upton's organizational plan for motorboat cruises modeled on Naval fleet maneuvers, with annual drill requirements, together with the development of flag signals, a fairly stiff examination in piloting in order to fly a distinguishing pennant and the regular educational sessions, envisioned greater respect for the sport of motor boating.

Our early history is replete with the illustrious names of men who gave unstintingly and enthusiastically of their resources in time, energy and initiative to stimulate this new movement. In June 1913, Charles F. Chapman, Editor of *Motor Boating*, helped to inspire the organization by giving a full-page display to the movement. Captain DeWitt Coffman, USN, a member of the original governing board, represented the Navy Department and was keenly interested in Squadron activities. The Honorable A. J. Tyrer, deputy commissioner of navigation of the Department of Commerce, another active member, helped to maintain excellent relations between the Department of Commerce and the squadrons. N. L. Stebbins was largely responsible for the building of friendly relations with the steamboat inspection service personnel, which resulted in overcoming sentiment for requiring small-boat operators to pass examinations and hold licenses similar to those men in charge of large merchant ships.

In World War II over 3,000 members served full time in the U.S. armed forces. Many taught navigation and allied subjects in Navy and Coast Guard schools. The original Coast Guard Auxiliary was organized with the help of USPS, and the majority of the original auxiliary were USPS members.

When in 1919, interest in USPS began to wane after World War I, due to the passing of the emergency, two men of vision and extraordinary energy proposed and brought about constitutional changes that served as the foundation on which USPS was rebuilt. These men were Vice Commander A. B. Bennett and Rear Commander Henry A. Jackson. The changes they proposed still remain the corner stone of our strength.

Their recommendations were that a man should first be a member of USPS, and then a member of a local squadron. And that the USPS should stress nautical education, nothing else.

While our educational organization was being revised, expanded, and improved every year, it was not until the 1930s that our present educational system was developed and standardized. The modern system insists on a full knowledge of fundamentals as well as of shorter methods. It produces men whose nautical education surpasses that of many professional schools and is equal in all ways to that of the best.

Our cooperation with governmental agencies and the armed forces has grown both in importance and in service rendered. Among these cooperative ventures are annual visits by our educational department personnel to the service academies in Annapolis and New London; work with the National Ocean Survey in drafting and correcting of charts; attendance at, and work with, the Geneva Conference on International Communications; mutual visitations and cooperation with the Canadian Power Squadrons, which was patterned after the USPS; and many other local and national consultations with governmental bodies to the end that boating may become a safer and more enjoyable recreational activity.

# Coast Guard

by Captain John D. McCann,
Chief Director,
Coast Guard Auxiliary

As a civilian component of the U. S. Coast Guard, the Auxiliary represents a vital link between the parent organization and the boating public.

The Coast Guard itself as this country's primary maritime law enforcement agency deems itself extremely fortunate to have had for thirty years the dedicated services of these civilian volunteers. For while the Auxiliary has no law enforcement power, its very existence presents a unique opportunity for a group of 25,000 volunteers to assist the boating public by example and by education with the complete endorsement of a federal agency.

The actual purpose of the Auxiliary is succinctly stated in Title 14 of the U. S. Code; sic: "to assist the Coast Guard: (a) to promote safety and to effect rescues on and over the high seas and on navigable waters; (b) to promote efficiency in the operation of motorboats and yachts; (c) to foster a wider knowledge of, and better compliance with, the laws, rules, and regulations governing the operation of motorboats and yachts; and (d) to facilitate other operations of the Coast Guard."

In carrying out its mission, the Auxiliary assists the Coast Guard operationally by conducting regatta patrols, supporting missions, and search and rescue missions.

Additionally, and perhaps of even greater importance, they present to the novice boatman major courses of instruction in boating safety.

Our Auxiliarists provide a practical form of instruction for the boatman when they examine his boat, at his request, to determine if his vessel meets the Auxiliary safety standards. If it does, the Seal of Safety decal is awarded.

We in the Coast Guard are extremely proud of our Auxiliary. Throughout its history it has continued to receive more and more recognition for its achievements for us and hence for the public.

We are also quite proud of those in the U. S. Power Squadrons, Boy Scouts, State Agencies, etc., who through courses and texts such as these endeavor to preach the gospel of safety through education. I suggest that you consider membership in the Auxiliary, the Squadrons, or both. You should find it well worthwhile.

# Contents

Preface to the Second Edition      v

The United States Power Squadrons      vii
    *by R/C W. Clinton Weitmann, N, Historian*

The United States Coast Guard Auxiliary      ix
    *by Captain John D. McCann, Chief Director,*
    *Coast Guard Auxiliary*

1. **Choosing a Boat**      1

    1.01      Any Choice a Compromise      1
    1.02      Modes of Propulsion      2
    1.03      Power Plant Options      4
    1.04      Wood in Boat Construction      5
    1.05      Glass-Reinforced Plastics      8
    1.06      Metal Boats      10
    1.07      Ferro-Cement      11
    1.08      Fastenings      11
    1.09      Displacement      12
    1.10      Stability      13
    1.11      Lateral Stability      14
    1.12      Hull Shapes      16
    1.13      Houseboats      18
    1.14      Multihulls      19
    1.15      Hull Speed      19
    1.16      Used Boats      21

2. **Maintenance**      22

    2.01      Sun and Salt      22
    2.02      Dry Rot      22
    2.03      Above-Waterline Paint      23
    2.04      Bright Work      25

2.05    Antifouling Paints                                    26
2.06    Paint Removers                                        27
2.07    Caulking                                              28
2.08    Rope                                                  29
2.09    Engine Maintenance                                    30
2.10    Electrical Ignition System                            32
2.11    Gasoline Fuel Systems                                 34
2.12    Diesel Engines                                        35
2.13    The Submerged Engine                                  36
2.14    Winter Storage                                        37

3.    Equipment and Regulations                               39

3.01    The Need to Know                                      39
3.02    Applicable Regulations                                40
3.03    Numbering and Documentation                           46
3.04    Passengers for Hire                                   47
3.05    Required Equipment                                    48
3.06    Flotation Gear                                        51
3.07    Fire Extinguishers                                    52
3.08    Audible Signaling Devices                             54
3.09    Optional Equipment                                    55

4.    Manners and Customs                                     58

4.01    Nautical Language                                     58
4.02    Seagoing Clothing                                     59
4.03    The Maritime Services                                 60
4.04    The National Ensign                                   62
4.05    The Yacht Ensign                                      63
4.06    The Burgee                                            64
4.07    Private Signals                                       64
4.08    Special Purpose Signals                               65
4.09    International Code Signals                             65
4.10    The Ship's Log                                        66
4.11    Garbage and Sewage                                    67
4.12    At Anchor                                             68

5.    Small-boat Handling Under Power                         69

5.01    Propellers                                            69
5.02    Propeller Handedness                                  70
5.03    Rudder Action                                         70
5.04    Steering the Outboard Motor and Outboard Drive        71
5.05    Propeller Side Thrust                                 72
5.06    Propeller Slip                                        74
5.07    Twin-Screw Maneuvering                                75
5.08    Docking                                               75
5.09    Leaving a Dock                                        79

| 5.10 | Cycloidal Waves | 80 |
| 5.11 | Heavy Weather | 82 |
| 5.12 | Running Narrow Inlets | 85 |
| 5.13 | Heavy Weather Procedures | 87 |

## 6.   Deck Seamanship                                              89

| 6.01 | Nautical Arts and Skills | 89 |
| 6.02 | Rope | 89 |
| 6.03 | Strength of Rope | 90 |
| 6.04 | Permanent Moorings | 92 |
| 6.05 | Mooring at a Dock | 93 |
| 6.06 | Ground Tackle | 94 |
| 6.07 | Anchors | 95 |
| 6.08 | Setting and Weighing Anchor | 99 |
| 6.09 | Deck Hardware | 100 |
| 6.10 | Whipping | 101 |
| 6.11 | Knots, Hitches, and Splices | 102 |
| 6.12 | Stopper Knots | 103 |
| 6.13 | Square or Reef Knot | 104 |
| 6.14 | The Bowline | 105 |
| 6.15 | Bends | 106 |
| 6.16 | Hitches | 106 |
| 6.17 | The Short Splice | 108 |
| 6.18 | The Long Splice | 108 |
| 6.19 | The Eye Splice | 110 |
| 6.20 | Towing | 111 |
| 6.21 | Towing the Dinghy | 112 |

## 7.   Rules of the Nautical Road                                   113

| 7.01 | Applicable Rules | 113 |
| 7.02 | Some Definitions | 113 |
| 7.03 | Relative Bearings | 116 |
| 7.04 | Keep to the Right | 118 |
| 7.05 | Audible Signals | 121 |
| 7.06 | Danger Sector | 122 |
| 7.07 | Overtaking | 123 |
| 7.08 | Points of Sailing | 124 |
| 7.09 | Sailboat Rules | 125 |
| 7.10 | Low Visibility | 126 |
| 7.11 | General Requirements | 128 |

## 8.   Accident Prevention                                          130

| 8.01 | Command Responsibility | 130 |
| 8.02 | Accident Reporting | 131 |

| | | |
|---|---|---|
| 8.03 | Accident Patterns | 131 |
| 8.04 | Loading and Trim | 132 |
| 8.05 | Fueling | 133 |
| 8.06 | Galley Safety | 135 |
| 8.07 | Fire-fighting Equipment | 138 |
| 8.08 | Safety Under Way | 138 |
| 8.09 | Man Overboard | 140 |
| 8.10 | Groundings | 144 |
| 8.11 | Distress Signals | 145 |
| 8.12 | Seasickness | 147 |
| 8.13 | Resuscitation | 149 |
| 8.14 | Sunburn | 150 |
| 8.15 | Shock | 151 |
| 8.16 | Food Poisoning | 152 |
| 8.17 | Alcohol on Board | 153 |
| 8.18 | Trailer Safety | 153 |

**9.   Aids to Navigation                                    155**

| | | |
|---|---|---|
| 9.01 | History | 155 |
| 9.02 | The Buoyage System | 156 |
| 9.03 | Color, Number, Shape | 157 |
| 9.04 | Complications | 159 |
| 9.05 | Whistle, Gong, Bell, and Horn | 160 |
| 9.06 | Buoy Lighting Conventions | 160 |
| 9.07 | Candlepower and Range | 163 |
| 9.08 | Optical Bearing Beacon | 164 |
| 9.09 | Lighthouses and Lightships | 166 |
| 9.10 | Daymarks | 168 |
| 9.11 | Aids on the Intracoastal Waterway | 168 |
| 9.12 | Western Rivers and State and Private Waters | 169 |
| 9.13 | The Light List | 169 |
| 9.14 | Tide Tables | 169 |
| 9.15 | Tidal Current Tables | 172 |
| 9.16 | *United States Coast Pilot* | 175 |
| 9.17 | Notices to Mariners | 176 |
| | Exercises for Chapter 9 | 176 |

**10.   Charts and Maps                                    178**

| | | |
|---|---|---|
| 10.01 | Charts and Maps | 178 |
| 10.02 | Earth Coordinates | 180 |
| 10.03 | Sphere, Plane, and Projection | 181 |
| 10.04 | Mercator Projection | 182 |
| 10.05 | Conic Projections | 184 |
| 10.06 | Gnomonic Projection | 184 |
| 10.07 | Great Circles and Rhumb Lines | 186 |

| | | |
|---|---|---|
| 10.08 | Chart Types and Scales | 187 |
| 10.09 | Chart Symbols and Abbreviations | 190 |
| 10.10 | Compass Rose | 192 |
| 10.11 | Distance Measurements | 192 |
| 10.12 | Chart 1210 Tr | 193 |
| 10.13 | Chart Reading | 195 |
| | Exercises for Chapter 10 | 195 |

**11. The Mariner's Compass**    **197**

| | | |
|---|---|---|
| 11.01 | The Need | 197 |
| 11.02 | The Earth's Magnetic Field | 198 |
| 11.03 | The Mariner's Compass | 200 |
| 11.04 | Compass Construction | 201 |
| 11.05 | Compass Cards | 204 |
| 11.06 | Compass Card Displacement | 205 |
| 11.07 | Variation | 207 |
| 11.08 | Deviation | 208 |
| 11.09 | Direction of Compass Displacements | 210 |
| 11.10 | Compass Conversions | 212 |
| 11.11 | Determining Deviation | 213 |
| 11.12 | Swinging Ship | 214 |
| 11.13 | Deviation with the Pelorus | 217 |
| 11.14 | Deviation Tables and Graphs | 218 |
| 11.15 | Deviation by Shadow Pin | 220 |
| | Exercises for Chapter 11 | 222 |

**12. Small-boat Piloting**    **224**

| | | |
|---|---|---|
| 12.01 | Art and Science | 224 |
| 12.02 | Speed, Time, and Distance | 225 |
| 12.03 | Speed-measuring Instruments | 227 |
| 12.04 | Speed Curves | 229 |
| 12.05 | Position Finding by Cross Bearings | 232 |
| 12.06 | Relative Bearings | 234 |
| 12.07 | Compass, Magnetic, and True Bearings | 236 |
| 12.08 | Distance to Visible Objects | 237 |
| 12.09 | Position by Soundings | 237 |
| 12.10 | Plotting Courses and Bearings | 238 |
| 12.11 | Position Fix | 240 |
| 12.12 | Dead Reckoning | 240 |
| 12.13 | Estimated Position | 241 |
| 12.14 | Running Fix | 242 |
| 12.15 | Labels and Symbols | 244 |
| 12.16 | Current | 245 |
| 12.17 | Model Cruise | 247 |
| | Exercises for Chapter 12 | 253 |

13.   Electronic Aids to Navigation                                255

      13.01   Technical Developments                                255
      13.02   Radio Waves                                           255
      13.03   Frequency Bands                                       257
      13.04   Radio Broadcast Receivers                             259
      13.05   Radio Direction Finding                               260
      13.06   Radiobeacons                                          263
      13.07   Electronic Fathometers                                265
      13.08   Radiotelephone                                        266
      13.09   Marine VHF-FM                                         267
      13.10   MF Marine Band                                        268
      13.11   Radiotelephone Operation                              270
      13.12   The Citizen's Band                                    271
      13.13   Automatic Pilots                                      272
      13.14   Small-boat Radar                                      272
      13.15   Loran                                                 276
      13.16   Omega                                                 280
      13.17   Aeronautical Aids                                     280
      13.18   Time Signals                                          281
      13.19   Medical Advice Afloat                                 281

14.   Lighting Requirements                                         282

      14.01   Sunset to Sunrise                                     282
      14.02   Applicable Rules                                      283
      14.03   Required Lighting While Under Way                     285
      14.04   Anchor Lights                                         289
      14.05   Unmaneuverable Vessels                                289
      14.06   Towing Situations—International Rules                 294
      14.07   Towing Situations—Inland Rules                        295
      14.08   Special Lighting Requirements                         297
      14.09   General Considerations                                298
      14.10   Day Signals                                           299

15.   Electricity Afloat                                            301

      15.01   More Power to You                                     301
      15.02   The Lead-Acid Storage Cell                            302
      15.03   Storage Battery Installations                         303
      15.04   Battery Maintenance                                   305
      15.05   Battery Charging Devices                              306
      15.06   Power Priorities on Board                             308
      15.07   Electrical Distribution Systems                       309
      15.08   Electrical Grounds                                    311
      15.09   Protection Against Lightning                          311

16.  Boats Under Sail                                          313

     16.01    An Ancient Art                                   313
     16.02    Types of Sailing Craft                           313
     16.03    Leeway and Heel                                  316
     16.04    Rigging                                          317
     16.05    Sails and Their Parts                            318
     16.06    Sailing Off the Wind                             320
     16.07    Reaching                                         321
     16.08    Close-hauled                                     323
     16.09    Tacking                                          324
     16.10    Heavy-weather Sailing                            325

17.  Weather Forecasting                                       328

     17.01    Information and Observation                      328
     17.02    Insolation                                       329
     17.03    Humidity                                         331
     17.04    Radiation Fog                                    333
     17.05    Wind Strengths                                   334
     17.06    Cold Front                                       336
     17.07    Warm Front                                       337
     17.08    Uplift Thunderstorms                             338
     17.09    Cloud Identification                             339
     17.10    Barometric Pressure                              342
     17.11    Low-pressure Systems                             344
     17.12    High-pressure Systems                            345
     17.13    Cyclones                                         346
     17.14    Cyclonic Passage                                 347
     17.15    Advection Fog                                    348
     17.16    Tropical Cyclones                                350
     17.17    Marine Weather Service on the Great Lakes        352

Appendix   I—Glossary                                          354

Appendix   II—Coast Guard Districts—Reports                    363

Appendix  III—Calculating the Effect of Current                365

Appendix  IV—Special Piloting Methods                          368

Appendix   V—Compass Compensation                              372

Appendix  VI—Morse Code Characters                             374

Index                                                          375

CHAPTER **1**

# Choosing a Boat

## 1.01   Any Choice a Compromise

As leisure time has become more generally available, recreational boating is attracting an ever-increasing fraction of our population. Interest in boats and boating may start with the floating toys in the baby's bath and end only with the failing faculties of old age. Boats are for all, and there are boats for all.

The very definition of *boat* implies a vast array of types and sizes. "Boat: A vessel for transport by water, constructed to provide buoyancy by excluding water and shaped to give stability and permit propulsion." * There are really only three requirements in the definition: buoyancy, stability, and mobility. No material, size, shape, or other characteristic is specified.

For centuries wood was the only material used in the construction of buoyant hulls. Today aluminum, glass-reinforced plastics, steel, and steel-reinforced cement are in wide use. Noncorrosive alloys such as the stainless steels and even the exotic element titanium provide metal fittings that have a reliability and a freedom from maintenance undreamed of only a few years ago. Because of their great strength and resistance to damage from mildew, synthetic fibers such as nylon and Dacron are displacing natural materials for the production of ropes and sails.

Improvements in marine propulsion engines have closely followed the improvements in automobile engines, with corresponding increases in reliability and life expectancy. Many of the developments in the automotive field have been carried over to the outboard marine engine, which has been responsible for a near-revolution in boating.

Only a few years ago each boat was a hand-made, custom item. Even the so-called stock boats of the past were expensive, individual products, even though built to standard specifications. Many boats are built by these methods

* *Random House Dictionary of the English Language,* Random House, New York, 1967.

1

today, but in addition production-line techniques have been introduced, a trend that has been accelerated by the introduction of some of the new construction materials. A large number of sizes and styles at relatively modest prices now confronts the prospective customer. Small wonder that many newcomers to the sport are bewildered by the offerings and may make choices later regretted.

Only general advice can be offered to the novice. A boat is a highly personalized thing, meaning something different to each individual. Detailed advice is as futile as is advice on the choice of a husband or wife. Fortunately mistakes in boat choices are easily rectified, as is demonstrated by the active market in used vessels.

Any boat is certain to be a compromise, in spite of glowing advertisements promising racing-cruising designs with the best features of each or the greatest amount of room in the smallest outside dimension. Compromise is inevitable when a vessel is to be used by a group or a family. Something less than perfection can be accepted in accommodations and performance, but safety is a feature that cannot be abridged. Boating is not an inherently dangerous sport, but it can be made so by inferior equipment and irresponsible operation. Hence the emphasis on safety throughout this book.

## 1.02   Modes of Propulsion

In choosing a boat the first major decision will be between sail, power, and manual propulsion. With our present emphasis on size and speed, we are apt to overlook manual propulsion as a pleasant and important part of recreational boating. Rowboats and paddle boats of various types, obtainable with only a modest financial involvement, can provide many hours of pleasure. Every skipper under either power or sail should master the art of rowing and maintaining a course under a variety of conditions of wind and current. Some of the techniques seen around boat anchorages make rowing seem like a lost art.

A powerboat must be the choice when speed and the maintenance of a predetermined schedule are of prime importance. A sport fisherman can travel at high speed to offshore fishing areas, throttle down for trolling, and return her passengers to the dock at a scheduled time. Only power—and lots of it—can provide the speed needed for water skiing.

Powerboats usually have a cruising range decidedly shorter than that of sailboats of comparable size. Space for fuel tanks is strictly limited, and when fuel is exhausted a powerboat becomes dead in the water. On the other hand Robin Knox-Robinson sailed a 32-foot auxiliary ketch around the world nonstop and had food and supplies in hand at the end of the 30,000 mile voyage.

Motor noise from powerful engines and the vibration from high-speed travel over water can lead to fatigue in a run of several hours. However, a powerboat can have a relatively large electric generating capability, and it is thus able to offer shoreside comforts such as refrigerators, toasters, and even electric stoves. These devices are out of the question on sailboats of moderate size.

A power cruiser, particularly the roomy stern type with a high, wide transom is not well adapted for operating far offshore in heavy weather. On the other hand, a power-driven vessel, forced to seek shelter from a storm may be able to safely negotiate narrow inlets into sheltered waters that would be impassable to a sailboat. Even with auxiliary power the latter might have no choice but to lay offshore until the weather cleared.

Except for small day-sailers, almost every sailboat will have an auxiliary engine, usually of modest power, used for entering and leaving crowded harbors and for maintaining progress when the wind has utterly failed. Top speed in a sailing auxiliary will depend somewhat upon the size and design of the hull, but will rarely exceed six to eight knots under either sail or power.

Under sail even the top speed may not be exactly in the direction of the ultimate destination. Sailboats cannot go directly against the wind; they must tack back and forth in order to make progress to windward. If the wind is brisk a boat *beating* to windward may heel 20 degrees or more from the upright position, frightening some novices, annoying others, but bringing delight to the skipper who appreciates the performance of a well-designed vessel with water rushing past the lee rail.

A modern powerboat can be driven much like an automobile, or even more casually, when steering is put on automatic pilot. A prudent skipper, however, will enjoy developing and applying the numerous skills required to take his vessel over a surface unmarked with traffic lanes and without detailed driving instructions. As speeds and congestion on our waterways increase, more and more attention must be paid to the exercise of these skills, if safety in boating is to be insured.

When under sail constant attention to detail is needed if one is to extract the most forward motion from a fickle, changeable driving force. Except in racing situations, however, sailing can be attention and not tension. Few human activities can bring the relaxation and satisfaction that can be derived from the performance of a well-balanced sailing vessel as she quietly responds to the skipper's adjustments as he meets the changing requirements of wind and sea.

Power-sail compromise designs are available and have their uses, but their performance is necessarily a compromise between sets of conflicting requirements. A motor sailer will have the power and some of the speed capability of a powerboat, and she can also be sailed. She will lack some ability to go to windward and will not have the crisp response of a true sailboat. And so to each his own.

## 1.03   Power Plant Options

There are presently a good many choices to be made within each of the general propulsion classes. Sailboat rigs require a detailed discussion that will be found in Chapter XVI.

Marine engine types can be divided into *inboards, outboards* and *inboard-outboards* (*IOs*). For a good many years powerboats used inboard engines exclusively. The power plant was firmly bolted to an engine bed and drove the propeller through a long shaft. The shaft passed through a *stuffing box* containing packing material and a compression nut to prevent water leakage around the shaft.

Outboard engines are relatively small and lightweight for their horse-power, which makes possible the easy land transport of boats and engines. Since propeller and rudder move together, the outboard engine provides a degree of maneuverability that is impossible with inboard power.

Outboards are predominantly *two-cycle* engines in which a fuel charge is burned each time a piston comes to the top of its stroke. Two-cycle engines require no moving valve mechanism to admit the fuel and discharge the products of the combustion. Fuel economy is not equal to that achieved by *four-cycle* inboard engines in which a fuel charge is fired every *second time* a piston comes to the top of its stroke. Two-cycle engines have special lubrica-tion problems that are solved by adding lubricating oil to the gasoline fuel. Considerable concern has been expressed over the amount of pollution pro-duced by unburned fuel and lubricating oil exhausted from two-cycle engines.

Outboard engines have outgrown their modest origin and are now avail-able in multicylinder units developing well over 100 horsepower. These giants are no longer easily portable and are so heavy that special vessel designs are needed to carry them.

Inboard-outboard installations attempt to combine the best features of each of the other two types. An efficient inboard engine is coupled by a through-transom gear train to an outboard-type propulsion unit. The latter provides the good maneuverability of the outboard's directed propeller thrust and the ability to be lifted over obstructions and shallow bottoms.

Inboard diesel engines are now available in sizes ranging up from single-cylinder six horsepower units intended primarily for auxiliary sailboat power. Diesel engines are heavy and are expensive when first cost alone is considered. They operate on cheap fuel oil instead of gasoline, but even though they are more efficient than a gasoline engine, it is doubtful that savings in fuel costs can make up the difference between the original purchase prices.

The high efficiency of a diesel will give a cruising range almost double that obtained with a gasoline installation of equal power and tankage. Most important, diesel fuel has few volatile components, so that essentially no flammable vapors are released during fueling or normal operation. Any flam-mable fuel must be handled with caution, but diesel oil presents a fire hazard very much less than that associated with gasoline. This fact must be weighed heavily when a power plant for marine propulsion is being selected.

## 1.04   Wood in Boat Construction

Wood has been used in boat construction for centuries, and it has given names to various parts of the hull that are in use today, even though they may now be made of quite different materials. The many varieties of wood available permit an adaptation of particular characteristics to particular requirements. Strong, tough woods such as white oak are used in the keel, frames, and other strength members (Fig. 1-1). Some of the complex forms re-

**FIGURE 1-1**  The main strength members and framing details of a wooden hull. (A) Longitudinal section, (B) transverse cross section, (C) deck.

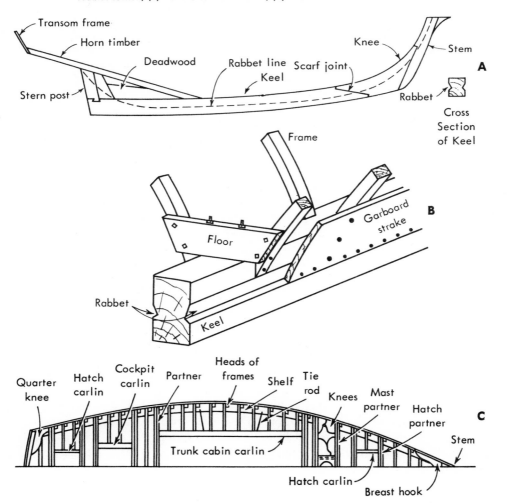

quired are obtained by sawing; others are produced by bending thoroughly steamed wood. The skeleton structure may be *planked* with any one of several suitable woods. Cedar may be used in boats where light weight is of prime importance; pine is somewhat heavier but is more resistant to abrasion. "Mahogany" is the wood most commonly used for planking and finishing cruising boats, but in fact little of this wood is true mahogany. The rules of the Federal Trade Commission require the use of qualifying adjectives unless the reference is to true mahogany. "Philippine Mahogany" may thus refer to a variety of woods native to the Philippines and "African Mahogany" may be used to describe wood of the *genus Khaya*. Teak is very heavy but has a high resistance to attack by marine organisms; it swells only slightly upon immersion. Selected spruce is the most satisfactory wood for masts and other spars. Boats built in Asia or Europe may contain one or more local woods little known outside of the country of origin.

The development of truly waterproof glues has led to the widespread use of marine plywood. Plywood can be used in large sheets on surfaces of moderate, single curvature, but these sheets cannot be made to conform to the surfaces of double curvature found in many hull designs. These surfaces must be planked with narrow strips rather than with wide sheets. The advantages of plywood have led to many hull designs specifically for its use. First-quality plywood construction may be as expensive as that using solid wood, but it may produce a hull of superior strength and smoothness. Only plywood specifically produced for marine use should go into a boat, either above or below the waterline. Ordinary plywoods will deteriorate very rapidly in marine service.

Three types of planking must be distinguished (Fig. 1-2). The smooth planking known as *carvel* must be applied with regard for the swelling that will inevitably take place after immersion in water. Carvel planking is applied with wedge-shaped seams (Fig. 1-3) to hold caulking material and seam compound. A properly planked carvel boat may leak for a day or so after launching, until the planks tighten up on the caulking. If a carvel boat is too tightly planked hard contact between adjacent planks will set up enormous stresses. Frames may be pulled apart by the tension (Fig.1-4), or the planks may cup away from the frames.

Water-tight seams on a *lapstrake* or *clinker-built* hull are obtained by the pressure of one strake against another, produced by the pull of the *fastenings*. Lapstrake boats are not caulked with cotton and compound, because the lapped seams cannot exert the strong squeezing forces on the caulking that are developed in carvel planking. The new polymerizing caulking compounds with high adhesive qualities have proved useful in clinker construction.

The replacement of a damaged strake in a lapstrake hull is a very difficult job compared to a similar operation on a carvel hull. In the latter case each damaged plank can be removed from the frames independently, whereas each strake in a clinker hull is riveted to its neighbors and has a precise bevel for achieving a tight joint.

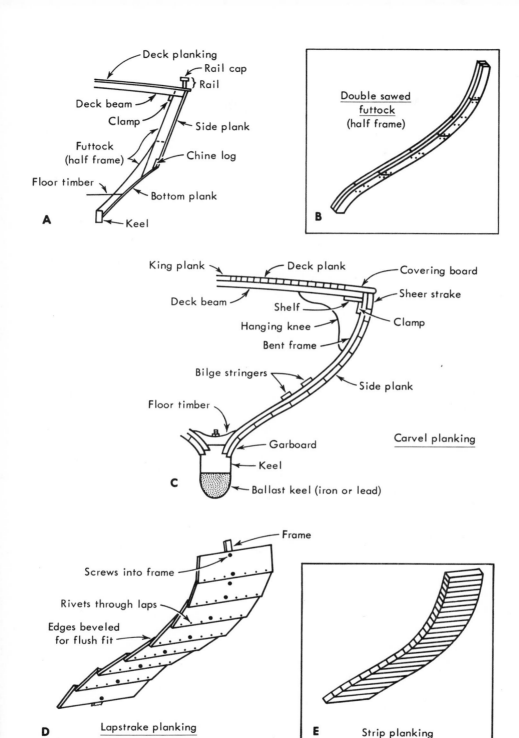

**A**

Deck planking
Rail cap
Rail
Deck beam
Clamp
Side plank
Futtock (half frame)
Chine log
Floor timber
Bottom plank
Keel

**B**

Double sawed futtock (half frame)

**C**

King plank
Deck plank
Covering board
Deck beam
Shelf
Sheer strake
Hanging knee
Clamp
Bent frame
Bilge stringers
Side plank
Floor timber
Garboard
Keel
Ballast keel (iron or lead)

Carvel planking

**D**

Frame
Screws into frame
Rivets through laps
Edges beveled for flush fit

Lapstrake planking

**E**

Strip planking

FIGURE 1-2  Framing and planking details of wooden hulls.

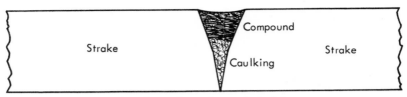

Interior surface of carvel planking

**FIGURE 1-3** A wedge-shaped seam in carvel planking is caulked and compounded.

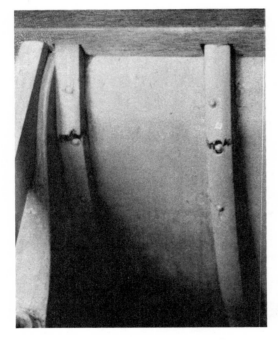

**FIGURE 1-4** Frames broken in tension at the planking rivets by overly tight planking.

*Glued-strip* planking produces a hull with seams that do not open up as a hull dries out after hauling. A glued-strip hull is very rigid, being held by both the adhesion and the fastenings. Careful design and construction are required to insure that destructive stresses are not set up in planking and frames from repeated cycles of drying and swelling. These stresses will not develop if the glued-strip hull is kept in wet storage during the winter months.

## 1.05   Glass-Reinforced Plastics

It has long been known that glass, particularly in the form of small fibers, is extremely strong. In the past the chief obstacle to utilizing glass in construction lay in the lack of suitable binders to hold the glass in the proper load-bearing position. This obstacle has been largely removed by the development of a series of polymerized resins, of which *polyester* and *epoxy* have proved to be most useful in marine construction.

The load-carrying glass is usually produced as thin threadlike fibers although small glass spheres have also been used. Glass cloth is produced from the threads with a coarse weave permitting a thorough penetration by the bonding resins. Most marine construction utilizes glass cloth weighing six to twenty ounces per square yard. A heavier weave known as roving is used for heavy structural members. Glass is also supplied as a heavy matting made up of random short lengths of the fibers. Fibers may be chopped into short lengths, mixed with resin, and blown into a mold with a special gun.

Bonding resins are mixed with a catalyst or *activator*, which causes them to polymerize or harden to the desired degree. The hardening process takes place rapidly and is accelerated at high temperatures. The final product is almost immune to attack by marine organisms and many solvents.

Polyester resin is used most extensively in boat construction. At ordinary working temperatures, polyester sets in 20 to 30 minutes, although complete curing takes somewhat longer. Epoxy resin is more expensive and will be used where extreme adhesion is required as in bonding to metal or to some species of wood such as oak. The high cost and long setting time of epoxy make it less popular than polyester for routine production.

Reinforced plastic hulls are produced by applying alternate layers of resin and glass to either a male or female mold to form a *fiberglass* structure. Techniques for producing large components have been developed so that a hull, molded as a single unit, may be joined to a deck and cabin molding by a single joint along the shear line. Large rigid sections are made by covering internal stiffeners of metal, wood, or plywood with the glass-resin mixture. Although a good bit of the material in a fiberglass boat is neither glass nor resin, with good construction the less permanent components will be protected from the hostile environment by complete enclosure in glass and resin.

As with any other type of construction, the quality of a fiberglass boat depends on the quality of the workmanship going into it. Defects in fiberglass structures may be very difficult to detect. An outside hull surface may come from the mold smooth and polished but careless *layup* may have left voids in critical areas where strength is needed. Much reliance must be placed in the reputation of the manufacturer.

Although fiberglass is gaining wide acceptance, it does have a few draw-backs that should be known before a final hull choice is made. Wave action produces more noise on fiberglass than on wood, to a level that sometimes disturbs light sleepers. Fiberglass transmits heat and cold more readily than wood, and this can lead to a disagreeable condensation of moisture on the inner surface of the hull. In all-fiberglass construction, the convenience of attaching accessories with woodscrews will be missed. Through-bolts or adhesives will be required for fastening to the relatively thin fiberglass sections.

Fiberglass boats are frequently called "minimum maintenance" boats, which is somewhat misleading because any vessel will require a substantial amount of maintenance if she is to be kept in top condition. Fiberglass structures may suffer less when neglected, but hull colors will fade and will require repainting, outer gel coats may craze, and barnacles will flourish on any unprotected underwater surface, be it wood, metal, or fiberglass.

All wood used in boat construction has a density less than that of seawater. As a consequence an unloaded hull will float, even when filled with water, and may even support a considerable weight. Fiberglass and all metals have a density substantially greater than that of seawater, and all of these hulls will sink promptly when filled. Whenever possible these hulls should be provided with some built-in flotation.

Some plastics polymerize into large volumes of foam, in which myriads of small gas bubbles are enclosed in the solidified polymer. Foam is an excellent material for providing buoyancy. It can be developed directly in remote, inaccessible parts of a hull, or it can be installed in individual blocks of preformed foam. In either case it will be as indestructible as the fiberglass hull structure.

## 1.06    Metal Boats

Steel is the hull material of choice for large seagoing vessels and for some of the larger pleasure boats, but it does not appear to be a practical material for the smaller hulls. Steel hulls can be made very strong, but the ratio of strength to weight is not favorable for the hull sizes commonly used in recreational boating. Steel hulls must be constantly protected from destruction by corrosion or electrolysis with intact coats of paint. Below the waterline the outer layers of antifouling paint must be applied over undercoats, which are electrical nonconductors, to prevent electrolytic action through the paint to the base metal. Breaks in the protective coatings over steel are more serious than with a nonconducting hull, because corrosion can start at a pinhole and spread underneath layers of paint to produce widespread destruction.

Pure aluminum corrodes rapidly in seawater but some of its alloys have been used successfully for many years in small boat hulls. As the general use of aluminum in the construction industry increased, new techniques applicable to boat construction were developed, and many new structural forms and alloys became available. These techniques and alloys have been applied to larger and larger sizes, until now there are a good many ocean-going vessels built on aluminum hulls. In many respects the details of construction follow the methods used with wooden hulls, modified to take advantage of the particular properties of the metal. As with steel, all aluminum underwater surfaces must be protected with electrically nonconducting paint to reduce the chance of destruction by electrolytic action.

## 1.07 Ferro-Cement

Reinforced concrete has been known for many years as a cheap structural material in the production of a relatively few commercial hulls. New techniques designed to distribute the stresses more uniformly between steel and cement have been applied to the construction of *ferro-cement* hulls. A variety of designs in the 25- to 40-foot range have been used successfully, and the methods are being extended to even larger sizes.

Few people have the skills and the facilities to build a first-class hull out of either wood or fiberglass. Ferro-cement has been advocated as a material suitable for home construction by people with only ordinary abilities and facilities, and its use represents a considerable financial saving. Prospective builders should be aware that a high order of competence is required to build even a ferro-cement boat that has the proper strength and symmetry required for a safe high-performance hull. All phases of ferro-cement construction should be thoroughly investigated before embarking on the construction of even a small hull. As with any composite construction, even serious internal defects may go undetected by the ordinary methods of boat inspection.

## 1.08 Fastenings

A wide variety of metal *fastenings* is required for holding together the component members of a wooden hull. Even in plastic construction, a considerable number of screws and bolts are required, and it can be truly said that no boat is in better condition than its fastenings.

Before the advent of the alloys that are now available *galvanized* (zinc-coated iron) screws, bolts, and boat nails were the most commonly used marine fastenings. Galvanized fastenings are still used extensively, and with proper protection they may last for decades. Eventually, however, corrosion will take its toll, and if the galvanized parts are not replaced, both the metal and some of the wood around it will be destroyed. A boat in this condition, which is said to be *nail-sick,* may require extensive reconstruction to be made seaworthy. Whenever possible the new fastenings should be made from one of the corrosion-resistant alloys now available.

Copper is highly resistant to corrosion in either fresh or salt water, but it is too soft for the production of satisfactory nails or threaded fastenings. Pure copper is used either as small tacks or brads or as rivets headed over onto copper burrs or *rooves.*

Brass is an alloy of copper with 10 to 40 percent of zinc, sometimes with traces of other metals. Brass is hard enough to permit the production of good threaded forms such as wood and machine screws. Brass has a considerable resistance to corrosion, and it is quite satisfactory for fastenings above the waterline. Below the waterline electrolytic action can quickly remove the zinc component to leave only a spongy copper matrix with little or no holding power. Brass fastenings should not be used below the waterline.

Bronzes are alloys of copper and tin with other metals sometimes added to obtain special properties. Tin is not electrolyzed out of bronze alloys, and hence they are quite satisfactory for use below the waterline in salt water. Some bronze alloys, however, may contain zinc as well, and these may be seriously weakened by saltwater corrosion. The dismasting, and ultimate destruction of the yacht *Vignette* in the 1967 Annapolis-Newport race was laid to the loss of zinc from a backstay fitting.[*]

Silicon bronze is a tough, corrosion-resistant alloy of copper, tin, and silicon suitable for use in saltwater. Another popular alloy with outstanding properties is made of copper, tin, and manganese. This allow is used to produce fastenings sold under the name of *Everdur*.

A wide variety of fastenings are now made from some of the corrosion-resistant alloys of iron known generically as stainless steels. The most satisfactory alloy for marine use appears to be the so-called 18-8 composition of chromium and nickel. Some alloys sold as stainless steel are poorly suited to marine use and should not be installed where they will be in direct contact with salt water or highly stressed.

Although some aluminum bronzes may be suitable for use aboard ship, many aluminum alloys are undesirable for fastenings. Even when supplied with a protective plated coating, these fastenings may be weakened through corrosion. A screw may fail when stressed, or it may shear off on an attempted withdrawal, leaving a stub difficult to remove.

## 1.09   Displacement

The choice of a hull shape is a complicated matter depending on many factors. Before considering the most important of these factors, stability, we must understand the meaning of *displacement*.

A boat and her equipment, out of water, will have a certain weight, customarily expressed in pounds or in long tons of 2,240 pounds. When afloat this weight will be exactly balanced by the upward thrust of the water on the submerged portions of the hull. Like any other floating object, the boat will sink in the water until it has pushed aside or *displaced* an amount of water equal to its own weight. Seawater has an average density of 64 pounds per cubic foot, which requires that any floating object displace one cubic foot for each 64 pounds of weight. This relation must be maintained under all floating conditions, whether she be upright or heeled.

Consider a vessel weighing 6,400 pounds. This boat will settle in salt water until a volume of 6,400/64 = 100 cubic feet of the hull is submerged. The boat has pushed aside 6,400 pounds of water and hence has a *displacement* of 6,400 pounds or 6,400/2,240 = 2.9 tons. A solid object such as a block of

[*] *Yachting*, v. 123, p. 82, April 1968.

concrete weighing 6,400 pounds will not have the required volume of 100 cubic feet, and hence it will sink before the necessary buoyant force can be established. Fresh water weighs only 62.4 pounds per cubic foot, so here our boat will have to displace $6,400/62.4 = 103$ cubic feet. She will ride lower in the water, but her displacement will still be 6,400 pounds.

The depth submerged, or the *draft*, depends on the shape of the underwater portions of the hull. In addition, underwater shape is of great importance in determining the *stability*, or resistance of the hull to tipping.

Some underwater shapes, notably those with rounded cross sections, produce *displacement* hulls, which are driven forward at relatively slow speeds by forcing the bow through the water. Designs with relatively flat underwater surfaces may be *planing* hulls, which at high speeds tend to rise at the bow and glide on rather than push through the water.

## 1.10   Stability

Any seaworthy vessel must show a strong tendency to return to a level position when disturbed by wind, waves, or by the movement of passengers or cargo. *Lateral stability* is a measure of a boat's ability to resist *roll* or *heel*, which is the tipping to one side or the other from an *even keel*. *Longitudinal stability* is a measure of the resistance to *pitch*, which is a fore-and-aft rocking motion.

Longitudinal stability is attained by designing reserve buoyancy into the bow and stern sections. In most powerboats this is achieved by providing wide after sections and *flared* bows. With these hull shapes the volume of water displaced increases rapidly as either bow or stern is depressed, thus bringing large corrective forces into play.

Pitch is strongly influenced by weight distribution as well as by the shape of the hull. In boats having a heavy power plant well aft, the longitudinal rotation associated with pitch will be centered near the stern. A violent pitch may throw the bow high in the air and bury the stern. Rapid flooding may then take place if the transom is low or notched, as is the case on some outboard hulls.

When operated at high speeds, planing hulls have a tendency to *porpoise*, a particularly unpleasant type of pitch. A porpoising hull will bounce from one wave to another, spanking the water as the boat oscillates around its center of longitudinal stability. Only a relatively short length of hull near the stern will be submerged, making the boat susceptible to being flipped over by a wave of only moderate height. Reducing speed will increase the wetted surface and will rapidly reduce the tendency to porpoise.

The longitudinal stability of high-speed hulls can be increased by the use of *trim tabs* (Fig. 1-5). Located below the waterline, these adjustable surfaces are in the slipstream just aft of the transom, where they can exert powerful leveling and stabilizing forces on the hull.

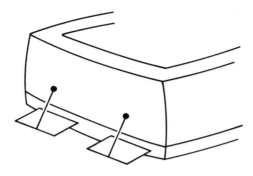

**FIGURE 1-5** Adjustable trim tabs control longitudinal trim when under way.

## 1.11    Lateral Stability

Lateral stability depends in a complicated way on the underwater shape of the hull and on the center of gravity of the vessel and its cargo. If we disregard the transient bouncing motion due to wave action, a vessel will ride with a constant volume submerged, since the amount of water displaced must always equal the weight of the boat. The pull of gravity, actually distributed over the entire structure, can be considered to act at a single point, the *center of gravity*. The balancing upward thrust will be distributed over the entire *submerged* portion of the vessel, but can be considered to act at a single point, the geometrical center of the submerged portion. This point is known as the *center of buoyancy*. If a vessel is to have any lateral stability, a roll or heel must change the *shape* of the submerged portion in such a way as to shift the center of buoyancy and produce a *righting moment,* which attempts to return the vessel to its original level position.

A perfectly round log will have no lateral stability, because the shape of the submerged portion will not change with any angle of roll. In any hull with a perfectly round cross-section, the center of gravity and the center of buoyancy will always lie on the same vertical line (Fig. 1-6A), and hence no righting moment can be created.

A vessel with a rectangular cross-section, such as the barge shown (Fig. 1-6), will have great lateral stability. When evenly loaded (Fig. 1-6B), she will ride in level equilibrium. When heeled (Fig. 1-6C), the submerged volume will become unsymmetrical, and the center of buoyancy will move away from the line on which the center of gravity is located. The righting moment thus created will tend to restore the hull to its original position.

Up to a certain critical angle, the righting moment created in a rectangular hull will increase as the heeling angle increases. Beyond this critical angle, the center of buoyancy will begin to move back toward the center of gravity (Fig. 1-6E). At this point the righting moment begins to decrease, and the vessel will continue to roll over into a complete capsize. A rectangular hull shape

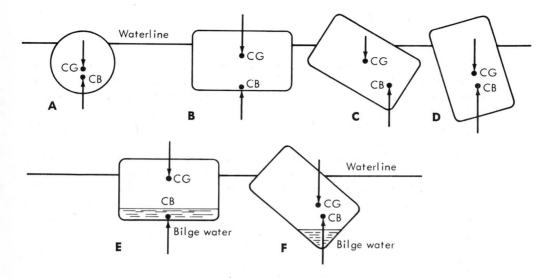

FIGURE 1-6 A circular hull section (A) has no stable lateral position. (B-C-D) Lateral stability is developed and then is lost as the center of buoyancy moves with heel. (E-F) Stability is sharply reduced when the center of gravity also moves with the heel.

has, then, a high *initial stability,* but a low *reserve,* or *ultimate,* stability. A vessel in which large restoring forces are developed at small angles of heel is said to be *stiff.* When the restoring forces develop slowly with heel, the vessel is *tender.*

A deep-keel boat (Fig. 1-7) may be tender for small angles of heel, because her approximately circular bilges do not quickly generate a large restoring moment. As the angle of heel increases, however, the upper parts of the

FIGURE 1-7 (A) Righting tendency in a deep keel boat at a small angle of heel. (B) A powerful righting tendency is present even in a knockdown.

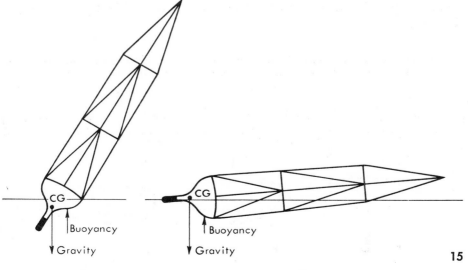

hull start to submerge, and the center of buoyancy moves well out from its normal position to create a powerful restoring force. In a hull of this type, the center of gravity will be determined to a large extent by the heavy keel of lead or iron. The result is a very stiff hull at large angles of heel. A boat of this type will right herself even after a *knockdown* (Fig. 1-7B), unless she has filled and lost all reserve buoyancy.

A low center of gravity contributes to the lateral stability of any hull form. *Internal ballast* of iron, lead, or concrete may be placed deep in the bilges to keep the center of gravity low. *External ballast* may be added to an already heavy keel. Lateral stability can be decreased to the danger point by adding weight or areas of superstructure against which the wind can act, well above the center of gravity. A flying bridge, tuna tower, or other superstructure may be properly incorporated into a unified design, but such structures should be added to an existing hull only with the approval of a competent naval architect, who can evaluate the effect they will have on the lateral stability. Lateral stability in a small boat may be reduced or lost by a few people sunbathing on the cabin top, well above the center of gravity.

The *period* of a vessel is the time required for her to make one complete cycle of roll or pitch. An initially stiff boat may have a short period, each roll being checked sharply as restoring forces come rapidly into play. A vessel that is tender initially, but in which the stiffness increases with the angle of heel, will have a longer period and a softer check at the end of each roll. Such a boat may roll through a greater angle than one with a greater initial stiffness, but the longer period will make for more crew comfort and for less strain on the vessel and its rigging.

## 1.12   Hull Shapes

Innumerable hull shapes have been proposed and constructed, but most of the complex forms are variations or combinations of a few basic types (Fig. 1-8).

**FIGURE 1-8**  (A) Flat bottom, (B) Vee bottom, (C) arc bottom, (D) round bottom, (E) round-bilge keel boat, (F) bulb keel, (G) centerboard retractable into a centerboard trunk.

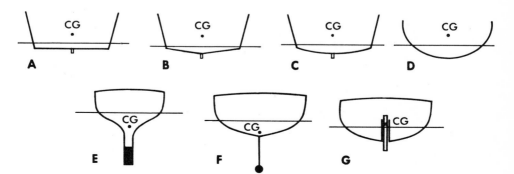

A simple flat-bottom hull (Fig. 1-8A) is commonly used on rowboats, work boats, and on small sailing craft, but the design is rarely extended to larger sizes. A flat-bottom hull may porpoise badly when driven at high or even moderate speeds, producing a wet bumpy ride as the forward flat section smacks into the wave tops. Flat-bottom hulls are relatively inexpensive, and they are more suitable for home construction than are some of the more complicated shapes.

Vee-bottom sections range from the almost flat bottom (Fig. 1-8B) to the sharp, narrow V of Fig. 1-9-1. The latter is typical of the bow sections of many powerboats designed for an easy entry into the water. The junction between the bottom and sides of a V-bottom hull is called the *chine*. When there is a sharp, well-defined angle at the junction the hull has a *hard chine;* a more gradual transition is a *soft chine. Deadrise* is the vertical distance from keel to chine.

Many powerboats show a transition from a relatively sharp V *forebody* to an almost flat, wide *afterbody* (Fig. 1-9A, 1-6). This construction combines the low wave-producing characteristic of the sharp V with the load-carrying ability of the flat afterbody. Flat after sections permit the vessel to plane and reach speeds unattainable with a more rounded hull form.

Round-bottom boats do not have a well-defined chine. Usually however, there is a point where the bottom turns upward more sharply, to form the *turn of the bilge* (originally bulge). Like hard-chine boats, round-bottom designs tend to sharpen up near the bow, to present a better entrance form (Fig. 1-9B). A round-bottom hull will pound less than a hard-chine boat when heading into a sea, and it will usually have an easier roll than the more abrupt motion of the flatter cross-section.

**FIGURE 1-9** (A) Sections of a typical power-driven hull. The sharp Vee near the bow (1) broadens into a nearly flat after section (6). In some designs the stern sections will have a greater deadrise than is shown. (B) A typical sailboat also has a sharp bow section (1) which broadens amidships and retains its rounded shape clear back to the stern (6).

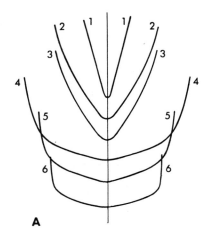

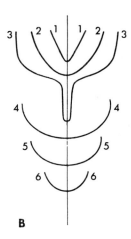

A                                    B

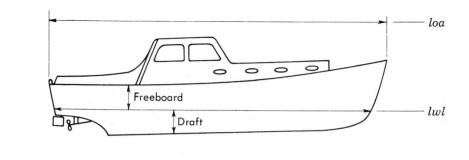

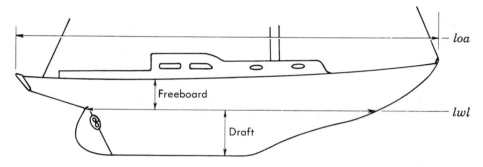

**FIGURE 1-10** Hull shapes of a typical power cruiser and a keel sailboat. Racing sailboat hulls may have a smaller keel area and an independently hung, or spade rudder.

The amount of pitch produced in a seaway will depend upon the hull shapes at bow and stern and upon the amount of *overhang* (Fig. 1-10). Powerboats have little or no overhang, but many sailboats have a loaded waterline length, *lwl*, not more that 70 percent of the length overall, *loa*. With a long overhang the submerged volume, and hence the restoring force, increases rapidly with either pitch or heel. An excessive overhang may lead to a disagreeable pounding motion when the boat pitches. As in other features of boat design, the most desirable overhang for general use will be a compromise between conflicting requirements.

Every hull design is also a compromise between maneuverability and the tendency to swerve or *yaw*. A boat with a long deep keel will hold her course well, but she will not respond rapidly to the helm because of the great resistance of the keel to turning in the water. A short shallow keel, on the other hand, permits more rapid turns, but it has less resistance to the yaws produced by overtaking or quartering seas.

## 1.13 Houseboats

For sheer livability the more-or-less rectangular houseboat exceeds any other hull form. Generally a houseboat is a light boxlike structure on pontoons or a single flat-bottom hull. Within their overall dimensions, these designs provide the greatest possible amount of living quarters and deck space. Houseboat accommodations may be quite similar to those of an apartment ashore, and there are usually spacious high sundecks. Unfortunately no design lends itself more readily to overloading, particularly on the upper decks, with a consequent decrease in stability.

The large flat areas on a houseboat hull make steering difficult in strong winds, although this can be partially overcome by the use of twin power plants.

These are fair weather boats intended for operation in protected waters close to harbors of refuge. Only the foolhardy would tempt fate by subjecting a houseboat to the stresses likely to be encountered offshore.

## 1.14   Multihulls

Several primitive peoples sailed and paddled watercraft having canoelike center sections to which outriggers were attached. Very large initial lateral stability results when a boat's buoyancy is divided between two separated, parallel hulls. Boats so constructed carry no ballast, and hull forms are designed for speed only.

A *catamaran* or *cat*, driven either by power or sail has a pair of identical hulls connected by cross beams. The parallel hulls are usually separated by about three quarters of their length. Small cats may have only a platform over the beams connecting the hulls, while large cruising cats may have elaborate cabin accommodations. Usually either hull of a sailing cat can support the boat's entire weight. The very popular small racing cats may sail with one hull completely out of the water, thrilling but just short of a capsize.

The *trimaran* or *tri* consists of a central hull to which pontoons or outriggers are attached on either side. The pontoons do not have sufficient buoyancy to support the entire boat and will bury when hard pressed. There is, however, quite enough buoyancy in the pontoons to provide an enormous initial lateral stability.

All multihulls are subject to very large stresses in their cross-members. Many have broken apart. Despite their large initial stability, they lose stability with large angles of heel. In addition, when running fast they are subject to tripping over the forward end of the depressed hull, which leads to a very fast complete capsize. In spite of these characteristics many multihulls have made long, fast ocean passages under experienced, competent command.

## 1.15   Hull Speed

In any hull design the speed attained represents a balance between the forward driving thrust and retarding forces developed by the movement through the water. There are two main retarding forces: frictional resistance of the water moving back along the submerged portions of the hull; and the forces required for wave production at the bow and stern.

Frictional resistance can be reduced by keeping the wetted area of the hull as small as possible, consistent with the requirements of stability and maneuverability. Some racing-sailboat designs have gone to extreme lengths to reduce the wetted area, sacrificing some ease in handling for speed. The condition of the underwater surface is of course most important in determining the amount of frictional resistance. Barnacles and other marine growths can greatly increase the resistance over that obtainable with a smooth hull surface.

A displacement hull simply sits in the water and is pushed through it by power or sail. Such a hull sets up a wave motion at the bow and the stern, as it pushes aside water and then allows it to return after the passage. At very low speeds only small waves are created, and the energy required to do this is small. Energy required for wave production increases rapidly with speed up to a point at which the bow and stern waves combine to produce a large drag on the hull. This *hull speed* represents a practical limit to the speed attainable with a displacement hull. Somewhat higher speeds can be attained but only with a very large expenditure of power (Fig. 1-11).

Hull speed depends primarily upon the square root of the wetted length of the hull with a slight dependence on some other hull dimensions. For an average design

$$\text{Hull speed in knots} = 1.2\sqrt{L} \qquad (1\text{-}1)$$

in which L is the wetted hull length in feet. For example, a displacement boat with a waterline length of 36 feet will have a hull speed of $1.2\sqrt{36} = 1.2 \times 6 = 7.2$ knots.

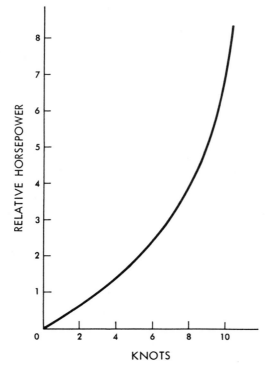

FIGURE 1-11 Typical power-speed curve for a displacement boat with a hull speed of about 10 knots.

RELATIVE HORSEPOWER

KNOTS

A sailboat with long fore and aft overhangs will increase her wetted length when sailing sharply heeled in a stiff breeze. Under this condition the increase in hull speed of a displacement hull is appreciable.

The concept of hull speed, and Equation 1-1 do not apply to planing hulls. At low speeds these hulls may behave like a displacement vessel, but at higher speeds, the bow lifts and the boat rides or planes on her flat after sections. Planing hulls readily attain speeds much higher than those predicted by the simple displacement formula.

## 1.16   Used Boats

Many complex considerations, most of them requiring some compromising, enter into the acquisition of a new boat. The vessel's quality can be reasonably estimated, however, from the reputation of the builder and from the purchase price. Purchasing a used boat may have distinct financial advantages, but great care must be taken to avoid inheriting a series of woes that has prompted the previous owner to sell.

Given proper care, a hull 50 years old may be in good condition and fit for more years of active service; another hull neglected and abused for only a few seasons, may be seriously weakened in some vital points. Paint and varnish can only temporarily conceal defects that may soon appear to plague the new owner.

No used boat should be purchased without a thorough inspection by a competent, disinterested *marine surveyor*. Even old hands, carried away with enthusiasm for a proposed purchase, may fail to notice defects that become only too obvious later on. A knowledgeable surveyor will make an unemotional appraisal of the vessel and may save his fee many times over by the avoidance of later grief.

The value of a new boat is closely related to the cost of its construction. In the used market *value* is highly indeterminate, depending as much on the emotions of buyer and seller as on the condition of the vessel itself. Under these conditions it is not surprising to find a rather flexible price structure. Asking and offering prices may be initially far apart, with the final figure established after detailed negotiations.

# CHAPTER **2**

# Maintenance

## 2.01   Sun and Salt

We have emphasized the need for a boat to be in the best of condition if it is to cope successfully with the stresses set up by high winds and heavy seas. In these days of stainless steel, synthetic fibers, and epoxy resins, maintenance is far and away easier than in the old days of galvanized iron, manila lines, red lead, and linseed oil. Maintenance is, however, still an important factor in safe and efficient boat operation. Even with modern materials neglect can lead to dangerous conditions and can drastically shorten the life of the best designed and constructed boat.

Every boat lives in a very adverse environment. In tidewater areas salt, either in the water or in all-permeating spray, speeds the corrosion of metal parts. The sun, with a strong component of ultraviolet radiation, fades pigments and hastens the deterioration of lines and fabrics.

Water inevitably collects in the bilge of every boat. With the usual pattern of weekend cruising, the boat will be closed more or less tightly from Sunday night to the next Saturday morning. High cabin temperatures will speed the evaporation of bilge water during the day. Night-time cooling may condense water at any and all parts of the interior.

Hulls of resin-bonded fiberglass withstand these extreme conditions well. The new materials are still too new to permit estimates of ultimate life, but it will undoubtedly be long. Wooden hulls are more easily injured by neglect, but with proper care they will last for a surprising length of time. A good many wood hulls are in good condition after 40 years of service, and with proper maintenance 50 years is not unknown.

## 2.02   Dry Rot

Dry rot is the chief destructive agent of wood above the waterline. The term is misleading, because the condition is not rot in the ordinary sense, and it flourishes in a high humidity instead of in a dry atmosphere. The decay known as dry rot is actually caused by the growth of any one of several species of fungus, comparable to the large toadstool growths that attack and destroy standing trees.

These fungi are propagated by spores which germinate in the presence of high humidity. Germination does not take place if the spore-bearing timber is immersed in water. In a dry atmosphere the spores become dormant but are not killed.

Any spores which have gained entrance into wood will germinate in a moist atmosphere, sending out plant bodies as threads or mycelia. These threads will penetrate to all parts of the wood that have a sufficient moisture content. As the fungus feeds on the wood, it destroys the normal fiber structure, leaving a skeleton structure with no strength.

When dry rot is discovered, the affected parts must be completely removed and replaced with new wood to restore strength and prevent reinfection. Drying will stop the infiltration of the fungus, but the spores will remain, ready to resume growth as soon as the moisture content is restored.

Dry rot can best be combated by thorough ventilation, thus preventing the moisture content from rising to the point at which fungus activity can set in. Unfortunately, adequate ventilation of the usual boat hull is almost impossible. As a consequence, dry rot will start to form in the most inaccessible regions where dead, moist air is pocketed. Dry rot may not be suspected until there is a sudden and perhaps a major failure.

Well-seasoned timber can be impregnated before installation with metal-bearing compounds, inhibiting growth of the fungus. Entrance of the spores into timber can be prevented by maintaining intact painted surfaces. Unfortunately, it may be impossible to keep all surfaces painted in a structure as complex and inaccessible as a boat.

The prospective purchaser of a used boat must be on the lookout for dry rot. A thorough survey by an expert is essential. If the boat is one of a class, the survey should be supplemented by inquiry as to the condition of others in the class. Point-blank questions about dry rot must be put to the vendor. Consider areas in the forepeak, around the transom, and any poorly ventilated space as suspect until proved otherwise.

## 2.03   Above-waterline Paint

Recent advances in paint chemistry have provided yachtsmen with a host of new products in colors unavailable a few years ago. Old-fashioned paints formed a protective film by the evaporation of the solvents or vehicle, which was followed by an oxidation and hardening of the pigment. Today synthetic pigments have replaced some of the older ingredients. Some of the new products depend on solvent evaporation to produce a tough, wear-resistant film. Others depend upon a *catalyst* to promote *polymerization*, which means the joining together of the small molecules of a liquid resin pigment into a solid structure composed of much larger molecules. If, while still liquid, the resin has been brushed or sprayed in a thin layer over a surface, it will form a tough, wear-resistant film on polymerization.

Two-component finishes consist of the film-forming resin in liquid form with a catalyst supplied in a separate container. After the two are mixed in the proper proportion, polymerization and hardening will proceed at a rate determined by the temperature. On a hot dry day hardening will be rapid. At low temperatures or high humidity incomplete curing may result. Polymerization hardening does not depend upon an evaporating solvent; once mixed, hardening will proceed in a closed container as readily as in the open. Useful life or *pot life* is strictly limited; once hardening is well advanced, the mixture cannot be applied advantageously. Pot life can be extended in some cases from hours to days by storing the mixed material at deep freeze temperature.

It is not our purpose here to weigh the relative merits of lead pigments, vinyls, urethanes, and epoxys; each has its particular area of usefulness. There is no such thing as a universally best finish. In picking a finish one must remember that a wooden boat is far from a rigid structure. Carvel planks work against one another as the hull is subjected to stress. Spars such as masts and booms bend appreciably when heavily loaded. A rigid finish on such flexible structures is bound to crack, leaving faults for the penetration of water into the basic material. Polymerization of a liquid resin can be carried to various degrees of hardness. Resistance to wear increases with hardness, but flexibility decreases. A delicate compromise is required to balance satisfactorily the opposing requirements.

The decision as to when to paint is as important as the choice of the paint to be used. Many good products are on the market, and expert opinions are available as to the types best suited to local conditions. As for when to paint, it is too easy to postpone needed maintenance until dry rot is well established, or until painted surfaces have deteriorated to the point at which a major effort is required for restoration. This statement applies with equal force to wooden and to reinforced plastic hulls. The latter are not maintenance free, even though pigments may have been incorporated into the hull structure. Eventually the outer surface will discolor, with perhaps an accompanying surface crazing that does not reduce the structural strength but spoils the previously intact smooth finish. This finish can only be restored by glazing and painting, as with a wooden hull.

In the spring everyone is anxious to get under way as soon as possible. There is a great temptation to paint too early, with too little surface preparation. Once afloat poor adhesion, peeling, scrapes, and scuffs go neglected in the interests of maximum usage. At the end of the season the owner may be dismayed to see the extent of finish damage. Without time-consuming treatment, a mottled effect will be obtained at the next refinishing.

Protection of structure is not achieved through the application of great masses of paint. When a repaint job is really needed, the surface should be thoroughly prepared. All chalked pigment should be sanded off; bare spots must be sanded on a gradual taper into the surrounding level to avoid abrupt changes in thickness. An adequate but thin coat of the chosen finish is applied to the prepared surface. Too thick a coat or a coat applied over an already thick base will cause internal stresses that may lift the entire mass off the surface to be protected. Overpainting can thus be as serious as underpainting. Strike a happy medium, and give the surfaces just the care they deserve. You will be well repaid in a longer hull life with less total effort and expense in the long run.

## 2.04    Bright Work

Nothing can equal the beauty of a finely grained piece of wood protected by several coats of clear varnish, giving true meaning to the term *bright work*. Yet too often we see faded or discolored wood more deserving of the name of black work. After a few half-hearted attempts to restore the lost beauty, the disgusted owner covers the whole mess with a coat of paint, and a handsome craft becomes just another boat.

The luminosity of varnished surfaces is obtained because the clear resins permit sunlight to penetrate the film, to be reflected at the lower surface. By the same token the surfaces of wood under clear resin films are exposed to more of the sun's radiation than are surfaces protected by paint. In most cases the wood has been stained prior to varnishing. Stain fading may result from the absorption of ultraviolet light through an intact resin film. An even fading might go unnoticed, but uneven fading will result if portions of the film wear thin or are removed. Prompt action is needed to restore films before uneven fading becomes noticeable.

Recently ultraviolet-absorbing materials have been added to varnishes without seriously reducing the visible transparency of the film. These absorbers reduce the amount of ultraviolet light reaching the basic surfaces, thus maintaining the original color for a much longer period of time.

Water, as well as exposure to the sun, will inevitably discolor exposed wood. Because spot refinishing will always show, the entire piece must be *wooded* by removing all old varnish. Discolorations are then removed by *bleaching* with a dilute solution of oxalic acid. These solutions must be handled with care, because oxalic acid is a dangerous chemical when taken internally. It may be noted in passing that an oxalic acid wash is very effective in removing stains from above-waterline, white-painted surfaces.

Good varnishing can only be learned by doing. Careful surface preparation, meticulous attention to cleanliness, the use of good materials and brushes are mandatory. With these essentials a bit of practice will yield professional-looking surfaces well worth the effort required to produce them. Above all, read the instructions on the products before using them. As with paints, some of the modern varnishes are handled quite differently from the older products. Directions are not intended to show where you went wrong. Read them first.

## 2.05   Antifouling Paints

Below-water surfaces on boats kept in salt water are subject to attack by a wide variety of organisms. Many forms of algae, from thin coats of slime to long streamers of vegetation, will attach themselves to unprotected underwater surfaces. Algae do not destroy the surfaces on which they grow, but their roughness slows a hull appreciably. Barnacles also grow in all unprotected surfaces that are underwater at least part of the time. Like algae, barnacles do not consume the material to which they attach, but their effect on boat speed is considerable. In addition to increasing the frictional drag on the hull, barnacles spoil the smooth surfaces of propeller blades, thus reducing useful thrust.

*Teredo* or shipworm is probably the most destructive agent to wood below or just above the waterline. An attack by teredo can in a few months reduce even the stoutest planking to a skeleton structure comparable in looks and in strength to a Swiss cheese. Teredo is most prevalent in Southern waters, but it is far from unknown in the cold waters of New England. Teak appears to be the only wood immune to teredo attack.

For many years paints heavily loaded with either copper oxide or mercury oxide have been used to prevent underwater damage from marine organisms. Formulations based on organic compounds of tin appear to have a somewhat longer life and, possibly, smoother surfaces than the older types. In maintaining a toxic surface, the outer layers of the paint slowly dissolve or leach into the seawater, exposing fresh material from underneath. The paint thus wears thin and must be renewed at intervals. Some paints may present a sufficiently toxic surface for a year; others may be exhausted in half that time. More than one year's service is not to be expected in normal conditions.

Originally all bottom paints were soft and were still wet when launched. As racing skippers pressed for smoother underwater surfaces, toxic chemicals were added to some of the newer types of paints to produce antifouling surfaces with reduced friction. For a short racing series, antifouling paint may be omitted in favor of a hard, enamel finish.

Antifouling paints can be applied directly over wood bottoms but must not be in intimate contact with metals. Electrolytic action between the metal structure and the high metal content of the antifouling layer will destroy the latter and pit the former. All metal surfaces must be given several coats of an insulating paint known as anticorrosive, before applying antifouling. Successive renewal coats of antifouling can be applied as long as the barrier layers underneath are intact.

Great care must be taken in working with antifouling paints. The active ingredients are highly toxic to man as well as to marine organisms. Some of the toxic effects are delayed and are cumulative so that one may be overexposed before serious symptoms develop. Respirators should be worn whenever old chalky surfaces are being prepared for repainting. Some of the toxic compounds can be absorbed even though the unbroken skin, so contact with the fresh paints should be kept to a minimum.

There is a growing concern for the effects of leaching poisonous paints on marine ecology. Some jurisdictions have outlawed the use of certain products and have prepared lists of acceptable antifouling paints. Experience may show that more frequent haulouts and renewal of bottom paints may be necessary.

Antifouling paints are one of the most expensive items required for maintaining a boat, and one whose efficacy is greatly reduced by faulty application. Various brands differ widely in their methods of application. Read the directions carefully before using.

## 2.06   Paint Removers

A time comes to every boat when she must be *wooded,* or completely stripped of paint and varnish down to the underlying structure. This is a sad time for the owner, for even with all of our modern technology, there is no easy and completely safe method for removing paint; as longer lasting finishes are developed, the problems of removal may arise less often but become more difficult.

Burning off paint with a blowtorch flame is the time-honored method of the expert. Considerable skill is required to work in the narrow temperature margin where the paint is softened without seriously charring the wood or canvas below. The threat of a serious fire is always present, causing many boatyards to ban paint burning by the amateur. Various sources of electric heat are now available for paint burning, but these are too slow for use over an extended area. Paint burning is now little used even by experienced boatyard hands. The best advice to the amateur is that given by the suspicious hotel keeper to the young couple who had registered as man and wife: "If you ain't done it, don't do it."

Chemical finish removers may be either solvents or strong acids or alkalies. These destructive acids and alkalies have no place in the boating field. When properly used, the solvent removers soften the paint layers so that they can be peeled from the underlying structure. Care must be taken to avoid nicks in the planking by the careless use of the putty knife. Even more serious damage can be done to canvas deck coverings by cutting with a putty knife blade during paint removal. When softened the old paint or varnish can be safely taken off with a hook scraper and bronze wool. Never use steel wool on a boat. It is impossible to remove the minute particles of steel that will ultimately rust and stain refinished surfaces.

One class of solvent-type remover is based on benzene or toluene as the active ingredient. Since these are thin liquids at ordinary temperatures, thickening agents must be added to permit use on vertical surfaces. A consistency about like that of thick cream is best suited to marine use. Other additives are required to slow evaporation of the volatile solvents and to form a protective outer film while the solvents penetrate into the paint layers below. When wax is used as the thickening agent, it will leave a film on the stripped wood. Unless this film is removed with a solvent such as turpentine, poor adhesion of the new surface finishes will result.

Benzene and toluene are highly flammable, with flash points lower than that of gasoline. Great care must be taken to avoid fire, not only in the material itself, but also in the paint scrapings after they are peeled off. Benzene and toluene are toxic to human beings, if the vapors are breathed over a prolonged period. Large removal jobs should be done in the open air. Ventilation should be provided even for small jobs done indoors.

Methylene chloride has been introduced as the active ingredient in a solvent-type remover that is nonflammable and somewhat less toxic than those based on benzene or toluene. Note that the reduced toxicity is only relative; prolonged breathing of the vapors from any solvent used in a remover should be avoided. Methylene chloride removers are expensive but have the advantage of being effective on the newer finishes such as urethanes and epoxys.

Either type of solvent remover can be used on a wooden or a metal hull without injury to the hull itself. Special care must be taken when using solvent removers on fiberglass. Strong solvent action may attack the resins in the fiberglass to pit the surface. For the same reason solvent-type removers must be used cautiously over polysulfide caulking materials.

Follow instructions exactly, whatever remover is used. Each remover has been formulated to be most effective when used as directed. The method of application and the time between application and removal are very important. Failure at either of these two points will greatly increase the labor involved in a job which is hard enough at best.

## 2.07   Caulking

Any wooden planking, no matter how well painted, will absorb some water and swell when immersed in water. The forces of expansion are so tremendous in carvel construction that too tightly planked frames may be broken in tension or planks may buckle. To avoid these mishaps carvel planking is left with seams, which will take up more or less completely as the boat swells. The planks are beveled to provide a space for caulking material (Fig. 1-3).

In the old days threads of tarred hemp rope or *oakum* were used for caulking. Today small boats will be almost universally caulked with cotton. Caulking cotton comes in soft, untwisted strands, which are driven into the seams with a caulking iron. After a seam is caulked, it is *payed* or sealed with one of the many seam compounds now available. These compounds have replaced the hot pitch used in old sailing days.

Except in an emergency, the amateur sailor will do well to leave the caulking of underwater seams to his boatyard. There are few things that sound easier than driving cotton caulking into an open seam with an iron and a mallet. In practice considerable skill is required to estimate the amount of caulking required. It is quite possible to overcaulk a boat to the point where planks will buckle or spring upon swelling. The seam between the keel and the garboard strake is a favorite place for leaks to develop. Overcaulking here may loosen or *start* the garboard strake, creating a condition much worse than the original leak.

Small seams either above or below the waterline can be made tight without the use of cotton by forcing in a puttylike material or *caulking compound*. This process, without cotton, is now commonly referred to as caulking or *compounding*. Three classes of caulking compounds are now available.

One type of caulking compound is based on the use of mixtures of oxides of lead with a solvent to form puttylike materials with various degrees of hardness and elasticity. These compounds can be made soft enough to squeeze out of seams as the planking swells, but they may lack sufficient adhesive power to stick to the wood during the next drying period. Stiffer mixtures are used for *bedding* fastenings to decks to prevent the entrance of water between surfaces impossible to paint (Fig. 2-1).

A second type of compound is based on artificial rubber with a suitable solvent. The surface tension of these relatively thin liquids tends to pull them into small cracks and seams, producing a soft, yielding filling when the solvent evaporates. Rubber-based compounds expand and contract with swelling and drying, but they lack really strong adhesion to surfaces.

Two-component mixtures of polysulfides and a catalyst have recently been introduced as caulking compounds. Most of these must be mixed just prior to use as they stiffen by polymerization. They retain considerable elasticity when cured and have a high degree of adhesion to all types of surfaces. They are much more expensive than the older types of caulking compounds, but in many cases the improved characteristics may justify the added expense.

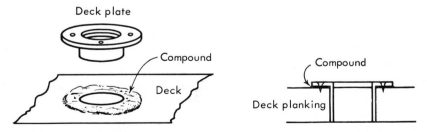

FIGURE 2-1   All deck and through-hull fittings must be bedded in compound to prevent the entrance of water.

## 2.08   Rope

No compromise can be tolerated in keeping all rope used on board in the best of condition. Rope *must* be discarded before it fails, if awkward or dangerous situations are to be avoided. The cost of even the best rope is such a small fraction of the total cost of operation that it is surprising so many owners take chances with inferior materials and continue to use ropes long after their strength has gone.

Rope deterioration can result from mechanical wear or from the biological action of fungi or marine organisms. Surface wear on a rope is produced by friction on pilings, chocks, sheaves, and cleats, or wherever chafing will break the outer fibers. Surface wear can be minimized by always using sheaves of the proper size and by wrapping wear points with *chafing gear* of canvas or pieces of rubber hose.

Internal friction, created as the rope bends and works around sheaves and chocks, can break inner fibers to produce a hidden weakness. Internal conditions should be frequently checked by opening the strands for inspection. Both external and internal wear are enhanced by sand or dirt of any kind. The hard particles are very effective grinding agents, cutting fibers, and insidiously shortening the life of the rope. Some feel that salt crystals have a sufficient abrasive action to cut small fibers as the rope works. Frequent washings with fresh water will remove most of the abrasive particles. Particular attention should be given to the anchor warp if it has lain on a muddy bottom.

Natural fibers, such as cotton or manila, are subject to destruction by mildew, dry rot, and the penetration of marine organisms. If manila mooring lines dip even occasionally into the water, life can be considerably extended by using treated rope. Impregnating with toxic compounds similar to those used in antifouling paints will reduce the activity of the marine organisms and also inhibit some of the damaging fungus growths.

Lines of natural fibers are subject to dry rot, just like a piece of wood, if stored wet or in a poorly ventilated compartment. As with wood, a fungus attack promptly destroys the strength of the fibers. The remedy is to dry all natural fiber lines before storing and to store in as dry a place as possible. Flat, tight coils of manila on deck may look nautical, but they will trap moisture, adversely affecting both the rope and the deck beneath. Loose coils are less impressive but are more sparing of rope and deck.

Synthetics such as nylon and Dacron are equally susceptible to mechanical damage but are quite resistant to attack by fungi and other living organisms. It is good practice to dry the synthetics before storing, but the penalties for not doing so are less severe than with the natural fibers.

With either type of fiber, natural or synthetic, frequent inspections at wear points will prevent an unexpected failure in time of stress. Proper care and working conditions will insure maximum dependable service from one of the most vital elements of boat operation.

## 2.09   Engine Maintenance

Today almost every pleasure boat depends to some extent on an internal combustion engine. In a power cruiser, for example, where dependence is 100 percent, the result of an engine failure could range from a minor inconvenience to a complete loss of control in a heavy sea or the inability to reach port before bad weather. Loss of power in a sailing auxiliary is usually more of an inconvenience in getting in and out of a slip, but even here engine failure can under some circumstances put a boat in jeopardy.

The power plant is frequently the most neglected part of the boat. Inboard engines are usually buried deep in the bilges, to keep them out of sight and to reduce the propeller shaft angle. Inaccessibility makes work on many components uninviting and difficult. As a result much preventive maintenance is put off until a failure forces positive action.

For example, dirty oil can be removed from an automobile engine by removing a drain plug and allowing the crankcase to drain. The lowest point of a marine engine crankcase is seldom accessible. Oil must be removed by pumping, a messy procedure which at best leaves an appreciable fraction of the old, dirty oil. Regular crankcase drainage is essential for prolonging the life of any marine engine. With an unlimited amount of cooling water available, direct cooled engines will usually run too cool unless they are properly thermostated. In a cold engine products of combustion in the form of corrosive acids will accumulate in the crankcase and hasten the engine's destruction. When the engine is run at the proper temperature, most of these corrosive products will be volatilized and escape from the engine. At best, however, the crankcase environment is more destructive than that in an automobile engine.

Even the simplest maintenance items may escape attention. With the trend toward higher horsepowers, it is more imperative than ever to keep engines tightly bolted to their beds. A loose engine is excessively noisy, and the continued impact of pounding against the beds may open seams or crack frames. The time required for a checkup of holdown bolts a few times each season may be well repaid.

When properly mounted, an inboard engine is rigidly attached to the hull through the engine bed. This rigidity fixes the orientation of the power take-off to the propeller, usually made through a flange at the after end of the gearbox. The propeller shaft, oriented by a stuffing box, terminates in a mating flange (Fig. 2-2). If shaft and engine are in exact alignment, the two flange faces will mate perfectly. Flange faces of misaligned shafts can be pulled together with the bolts, but heavy stresses will be introduced into stuffing

FIGURE 2-2  Whenever a boat is hauled the bolts on the flange coupling should be loosened to prevent excessive strains on the gearbox and engine.

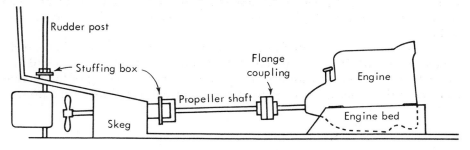

box, shafting, after gear-box bearings, and the gear-box casing. Excessive friction will result in the loss of useful power, excessive heating, and unnecessary wear on bearings.

When a boat is hauled, no matter how gently, hull strains are introduced, and shaft misalignment can be severe until the boat is returned to the water and swells to its original state. It is good practice to loosen the coupling bolts before hauling to avoid abnormal stresses in the entire power transmission system. Flange alignment should be checked after the hull has been returned to the water and has come to equilibrium, before the coupling bolts are tightened. The flange bolts may be highly inaccessible, but this does not lessen the need to relieve the stresses associated with hauling.

Spare engine parts are a necessity on the water. Here the engine manufacturer's advice should be followed, adding to his specific recommendations items of general usefulness. Spare gasket material, bolts and nuts, extra oil and grease will eventually be put to good use.

Be inquisitive; know your engine. It is not recommended that a new engine be disassembled to see how it is made. On the other hand, foreknowledge of some constructional details may save embarrassment and delay when underway. For example, a detailed examination, in port, of a water pump impeller disclosed an ingeniously located, but well-concealed set screw, requiring a special wrench. When the impeller failed in a moderate blow, a spare was installed in a matter of minutes, because knowledge and the needed tools were at hand.

The examples cited by no means complete the items of maintenance required to insure reliable engine operation. Much thought should be given to the power plant and its accessories. Various plausible failures should be imagined for planning repair methods. Some substitution and extemporizing is possible, but most engine failures require exact replacement parts. The most essential parts are neither expensive nor bulky. Attempt to visualize the needs and have the necessary parts on board.

## 2.10    Electrical Ignition System

Every gasoline engine will have a high-voltage electrical system to provide the sparks required to ignite the combustible mixture in the cylinders. Small, hand-cranked engines without a battery-generator will use a magneto, usually built into the flywheel, to supply the high voltage (15,000-30,000 volts) to the spark plugs. Larger engines almost universally use battery power with a breaker point-ignition coil circuit (Fig. 2-3), exactly comparable to that used in automobiles.

A pair of contacts or *breaker points* is operated by a cam driven from the engine crankshaft. When the points close, a current of a few amperes will flow through the relatively few turns making up the *primary* winding of the ignition coil. When the points are opened by the cam, current flow through the primary

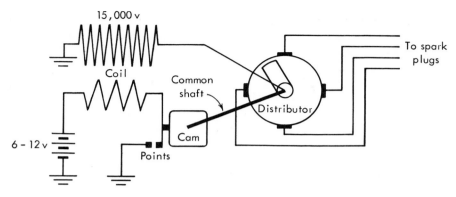

15,000 v

Coil

Common
shaft

Distributor

To spark
plugs

6 - 12 v

Cam

Points

**FIGURE 2-3**   Schematic circuit of a typical four-cylinder ignition system.

winding ceases abruptly, and a high-voltage pulse is produced in the thousands of turns of fine wire comprising the *secondary* winding of the coil. The high-voltage pulse is sent to the *distributor* which directs it to the spark plug of the cylinder ready to be fired. At the plug the high voltage jumps across the gap to ground and ignites the fuel-air mixture.

Proper operation of the system requires that an adequate current flow in the primary winding when the contacts are closed, and that this current be interrupted very rapidly. All connections in the primary circuit must be tight and the breaker points maintained, so that they will make a low-resistance contact. Arcing at the breaker points can rapidly pit them to an unsatisfactory condition or may actually weld them together.

Arcing is suppressed by connecting an electrical condenser across the points (omitted from Fig. 2-3 for simplicity). A defective condenser will lead to the rapid deterioration of the points, but fortunately condensers are simple, rugged devices that rarely become defective. Breaker points must be kept smooth by filing or honing off the sharp points and pits that eventually form in spite of arc suppression by the condenser. Special tools are needed for point maintenance, because the metal alloy is very hard. Some experience is needed to keep points in proper condition. Sandpaper or emery paper must never be used on breaker points. A small grain of nonconducting material is almost certain to lodge between the contacts and make them inoperative.

The high-voltage portion of the ignition system is most vulnerable. The current flow in the secondary circuit is small, but all insulation must be maintained in good condition to insure that the current does not find a leakage path to ground instead of being forced to jump the gap at the spark plug. Moisture, particularly when salt-laden, can collect on parts of the secondary circuit and create low-resistance leakage paths. The coil terminal, distributor cap, high-tension wiring, and the spark plug insulator are all suspect. Sometimes sparks may be seen and heard jumping across leakage paths to ground. More usually the leakage point cannot be detected, and the whole system must be carefully cleaned and dried. Careful wiping with dry clean cloths may remove some of the low-resistance path. Drying with a good water absorber such as high-proof alcohol is also helpful.

The secondary winding of the coil is wound with very fine wire, since it carries little current. Breaks in this wire can occur and reduce the intensity of the spark at the plugs. Internal sparking at the site of the break will destroy the insulation of adjacent turns, quickly rendering the coil ineffective. A spare coil is seldom needed, but when it is, there is no substitute.

Spark plug insulators are brittle ceramic materials, which may be shattered by a blow as from an ill-fitting wrench. The high-voltage spark will usually go across the most minute crack in the insulator in preference to the normal path across the gap. Handle all tools in the vicinity of the plugs and the distributor cap with care. Carry a set of spare plugs, together with a proper wrench.

All powered boats, except those with small, magneto-fired engines, will have an extensive battery-generator system. This provides the low-voltage power for lights and a variety of electrical devices as well as to the ignition system. Maintenance on the main electrical system is discussed in Chapter 15.

## 2.11   Gasoline Fuel Systems

In a gasoline engine, gasoline and air are mixed in proper proportions in the carburetor from which they are drawn into the cylinders for burning. Even the simplest carburetor is called on to perform complicated functions under a wide variety of operating conditions. It is expected to provide a proper fuel-air mixture in the coldest weather, using air from a moist bilge, yet must also operate at temperatures near to the boiling point of the fuel. It must furnish proper mixtures at idling speeds, at full throttle, and during rapid accelerations.

To perform these functions the carburetor is provided with two or more jets or metering orifices which regulate the amount of fuel picked up by the entering air stream. Carburetor jets are accurately drilled and are small, except on the largest engines. Foreign deposits can reduce jet size, partially or completely closing them. Solid particles may be pulled into the jets, blocking them more or less completely. Even the larger openings in the flame arrestor can become partially clogged, restricting air flow and reducing power.

Carburetors are complicated devices, precisely made, and should be left strictly alone unless one is familiar with their construction details. Before proceeding with carburetor disassembly, one should be certain that the symptoms definitely implicate it. Failure of all other parts of the fuel system should be first ruled out. The air vent to the tank may be blocked, preventing the free flow of fuel to the carburetor. A fuel pump may be defective, or perhaps the filter, long neglected, is clogged with solid particles or with gum.

Although all properly installed fuel lines emerge from the top of the tank, they draw from near the bottom (Fig. 8-1), where water and gum may collect.

Water may be mixed with the fuel when it is delivered, or it may enter as temperature changes draw moisture-laden air into the tank, where the water condenses and collects on the bottom. Some fuel filters do not remove water from the lines. Others require regular emptying of a settling bowl to remove trapped water. Water is completely unmixable with gasoline, and so it may be seen in a filter as an isolated drop at the bottom of the bowl.

The average boat is used less frequently than is the family automobile, and consequently fuel is stored for longer periods of time in the boat tanks. During this storage gasoline not specifically designed for marine use may *oxidize* to form a gum, which may clog carburetor jets or fuel lines or cause sticky intake valves in the engine. The rate of gum formation depends primarily on the temperature and on the nature of the metals with which the gasoline is in contact. Copper is a *catalyst* for gum formation, greatly speeding up the oxidation without itself being consumed or weakened. Since copper was extensively used for fuel tanks and is still the most common material for fuel lines, gum formation in unprotected gasolines may proceed rapidly.

True marine gasolines are specially treated to reduce the sulphur content and are then *stabilized* against oxidation with additives, which destroy the catalytic action of copper and greatly slow oxidation. These stabilizers are present in addition to any tetraethyl lead that may have been added to permit obtaining the proper octane rating.

If oxidation gum is present, it may be removed by adding *acetone* to the tank, about 1 part of acetone to 20 parts of gasoline. After mixing, the engine is run until the mixture has certainly reached the fuel pump and the carburetor. After one or two days standing, most or all of the gum will be dissolved. Running the engine on the mixture will then clean up the affected parts of the fuel system.

If emergency inspection of the carburetor is indicated, it should be done with the greatest of care. Each of the small bushings, gaskets, and other oddments must go back exactly as it was originally placed. Disassembly should be done over a solid surface or a container of some sort. The loss of one tiny part deep in a bilge or under a grating can completely prevent carburetor function. A low-power magnifier or jeweler's loupe is an invaluable aid in examining the small parts. Fine wire may be needed for clearing tiny passages. Clearing must be done with care; a wire broken and lodged in a jet may present more of a problem than that originally prompting the investigation. In cleaning jets, remember that the size and shape are important. Vigorous cleaning may destroy either.

## 2.12   Diesel Engines

The previously mentioned advantage of using a fuel that is less easily ignited than gasoline is one of the compelling reasons for choosing diesel power for a boat. Other advantages include a greater power output per fuel gallon, a generally lower fuel cost, and in most cases a longer engine life.

Though many have tried, diesel fuel cannot be successfully vaporized in a carburetor and ignited by a spark plug. Diesel ignition depends on the heat of the air compressed in the combustion chamber. To attain this temperature, compression must be high compared to that in gasoline engines. Diesel engines have no ignition system as such, but some may have a *glow plug* to use for starting only.

The principal fuel problem in a diesel engine involves the delivery under high pressure of metered amounts of liquid fuel to the fine spray jets located in the combustion chambers. In most pleasure-boat diesels, the nozzle openings are small and hence easily clogged. Fuel filtering is at least as important as in a gasoline engine.

In some cases the engine manual will give directions for removing and cleaning the nozzles. These directions should be followed exactly. Low-power magnification will be useful, as with carburetor jets. Care must be taken that a cleaning wire is not broken off in one of the fine passages.

Most diesel fuels have a higher sulphur content than gasoline. Since copper has a high affinity for sulphur, tinned rather than copper tanks must be used for diesel fuels. Lubricating oils for diesel service must also be selected with the sulphur content of the fuels in mind. The high sulphur content also precludes the use of copper exhaust lines for diesel service.

## 2.13   The Submerged Engine

A variety of accidents can lead to a sinking and the complete submersion of the engine. All is not lost if this occurs, but treatment must be correct and thorough if the engine is to be salvaged. Salt water alone is not particularly damaging to metals over a short period of time. It will, however, promote rapid oxidation or rusting when the engine is raised and reexposed to the air. Engine injury can be minimized by allowing it to remain submerged, away from contact with the air, until it can be given the full attention needed to restore it to service. Once the engine is raised, overhauling must proceed rapidly to completion.

As soon as the engine is removed from the boat, all accessories, covers, cylinder head and attachments should be removed. The entire collection of parts should be rinsed thoroughly with several changes of fresh water, or by direct washing with a hose. When all salt has been removed, parts can be dried and coated with a film of oil or antirust compound for future use.

Electrical parts may be damaged beyond repair, but they should not be discarded without a thorough drying and test. Electrical parts may be dried with a gentle heat applied for several hours to insure drying of the interior of each winding. High drying temperatures may damage the insulation.

Without exception every part of the engine must be thoroughly cleaned. The future life of the engine depends on the care taken at this time. An engine only partially restored after submersion may run well for a time, but hidden corrosion will take its toll and lead to a premature failure. With careful cleaning an engine may be no worse off after immersion, except for some electrical parts that defy restoration.

## 2.14    Winter Storage

With the end of the active season, boats in Northern waters must be prepared for winter storage. The engine and its accessories will require the most attention and will require it well in advance of the first hard freeze.

The first step is to run the engine under load until it is thoroughly warm to thin the oil for more complete removal, and to bring into suspension as many dirt particles as possible. When warm, the engine is shut off and the oil pumped off as completely as possible. The full amount of fresh oil is added, and the engine is run for a few minutes to distribute the new oil over all surfaces. When this is done, the engine is killed by pouring engine oil into the carburetor air intake until the engine stops. This treatment will cause considerable smoke when restarting in the spring, but it will leave a coating of oil on many otherwise unreachable surfaces throughout the winter.

Drain water from all parts of the water jacket and exhaust cooling system. Go slowly here. Omission of one drain is almost certain to lead to a frozen and cracked fitting in the spring. Close all drains and fill the entire cooling system with some antifreeze to exclude air and reduce rusting. Kerosene or fuel oil is satisfactory for this purpose. Permanent antifreeze solutions for automobile use such as ethylene glycol are more expensive, but they are less damaging to rubber hose connections. If the boat is in wet storage, be sure that the antifreeze solution gets clear down *into* the closed sea cocks.

Remove spark plugs, pour several teaspoonsful of engine oil in each cylinder, and crank the engine several revolutions *with the plugs out*. Replace the plugs, snug but not compression tight, and do not turn the engine over again until it is recommissioned in the spring.

Drain all fuel from tank, carburetor, and lines to reduce the accumulation of moisture by condensation. Some recommend storage with the fuel system completely full to reduce condensation. This increases the fire hazard, leads to the deposit of unwanted gums, and loses some of the more volatile fuel components needed for starting.

Drive soft wood plugs into the exhaust and cooling water lines. They should be driven gently to avoid injury to the through-hull fittings. These plugs will reduce the moisture entering from the outside by repeated condensations.

Remove ignition coil, high tension wires, and the storage battery, for storage in a dry place at home. See that the battery receives some charge at least once a month, but avoid vigorous overcharging.

Clean rust from all exposed engine surfaces and apply metal primer and paint. Nuts showing rust in the fall may be loosened and oiled; by spring they may be immobile.

Cover the engine to keep out rain and snow, but allow as much circulating air as possible. This will reduce condensation.

With the engine winterized, attention can be turned to the rest of the boat. If in dry storage, all sea cocks can be opened and the lines leading to them drained. In wet storage all sea cocks must be closed after some antifreeze has been run into them. A frozen sea cock can lead to a sinking during a subsequent thaw.

A boat cover will keep out the weather, but it must not fit too tightly. Without ventilation condensation is inevitable, keeping the interior at a high humidity throughout the winter. With free air circulation the chance of dry rot will be substantially reduced.

If a boat is in wet storage, leave a bilge pump on board. With some deep narrow bilges water may accumulate to the point where it may freeze hard enough to spring a plank. Antifreeze should not be added to the bilges; keep them pumped, and remember to drain the pump after each use.

CHAPTER **3**

# Equipment
# and Regulations

## 3.01 The Need to Know

The boat owner and operator must conform to an imposing array of rules and regulations. The basic intent of these requirements is to promote safety: by assuring that vessels shall be operated so as to avoid collision, and by assuring that vessels are equipped to assist in this avoidance or to reduce the hazards if disaster strikes. Every skipper should have a thorough understanding of the rules regarding operation and equipment, and he should operate his boat at all times in conformity with these requirements. In case of accident and legal action, he can expect the rules to be applied precisely to establish fault.

Nearly all situations can be handled by an understanding of a relatively few rules, together with a knowledge of the behavior of boats in various combinations of wind and sea. Strict adherence to the rules, combined with a consideration for the safety and comfort of others, will greatly reduce, if not completely eliminate, the chance of collision at sea.

Legal jurisdiction over collisions between vessels on public waters (excluding a lake wholly within a single state) rests with federal courts sitting as courts of admiralty. Two principles of importance to all boat owners have been established by the admiralty courts:

(1) Although criminal proceedings may lie against the operator, responsibility for damages lies with the vessel itself. Court actions are usually between vessels, and a vessel may be held until all claims against her have been satisfied.

(2) Admiralty courts in the United States have repeatedly upheld the doctrine of equal responsibility for unequal fault. According to this doctrine, in a collision in which both vessels have been found at fault, *each will be held liable for one half of the* total *loss, regardless of the relative degrees of fault or the relative damages sustained by the two vessels.* Should only one vessel be at fault, she will be held liable for the total damages to the other, limited,

39

however, to her own value after the collision. In the most unlikely event of a collision with neither vessel at fault, each is responsible for her own damage only.

Although there is a heavy weight of precedence behind the doctrine of equal responsibility, it is not a mandatory finding and may not apply to all cases.

## 3.02   Applicable Regulations

For many years travel on international waters was governed by the *International Rules of the Road,* put into effect in 1897. Changing conditions required regulatory changes, and in 1948 an International Conference on Safety of Life at Sea proposed a revised set of rules specifically known as the *International Regulations for Preventing Collisions at Sea of 1948.* These regulations, adopted by Congress in 1953, were supplemented by the *International Rules of 1960,* which became effective September 1, 1965.

As a part of the adoption procedure, the United States Coast Guard * established boundary lines separating the high seas, where *International Rules* apply, from the inland waters of the United States. These boundaries are important to the skipper whose craft may have crossed them, because different rules apply in the two areas. Vessels have been found at fault for sounding improper signals only because a slight error in navigation had placed them unknowingly across the boundary. Figs. 3-1, 3-2, and 3-3 show these boundary lines established, for the most part, between prominent aids to navigation. The importance of distinguishing between the high seas and inland waters may diminish in the future.

Along with the adoption of the *International Rules,* Congress approved in 1953 *Inland Rules* governing the operation of vessels on inland waters of the United States, except the Great Lakes, the Mississippi River above the Huey P. Long Bridge, and certain other rivers. Operation in these waters is regulated by Great Lakes Rules and Western Rivers Rules, respectively (7.01).

In addition to the statutory *Inland Rules,* vessels in inland waters come under the Pilot Rules, established by the Coast Guard. These rules, covering such operational items as crossing and passing signals and fog signals and lights, are consistent with the provisions of the Inland Rules. Pilot Rules must be prominently displayed in the wheelhouse of any vessel carrying passengers for hire and should be aboard all pleasure boats.

Required equipment is specified in the *Motorboat Act of 1940.* This Act also established motorboat classes, prescribed lights, and provided penalties for negligent operation of any type of vessel.

The *Federal Boating Act of 1958* became effective in March 1959. This act established a new numbering system, applicable to nearly all vessels not

---

* Future reference will omit *United States* as understood.

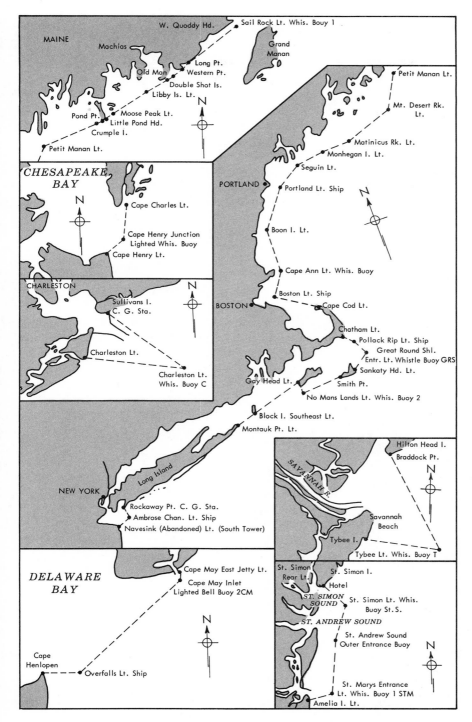

**FIGURE 3-1** Boundary lines, international-inland waters, Atlantic Coast of the United States. Courtesy of the United States Naval Institute.

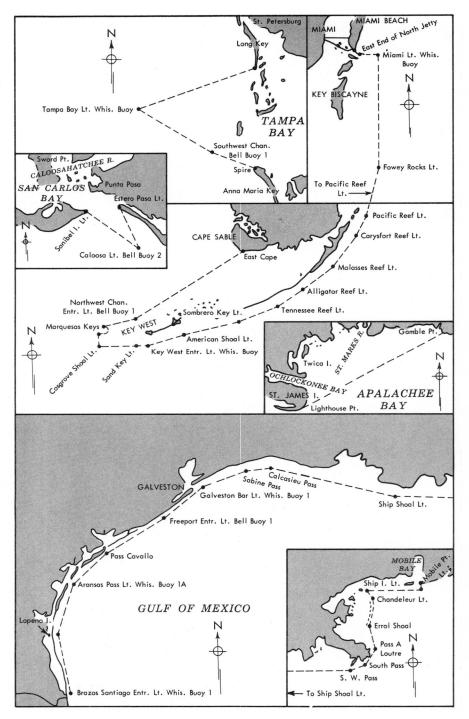

**FIGURE 3-2** Boundary lines, international-inland waters, Gulf Coast of the United States. Courtesy of the United States Naval Institute.

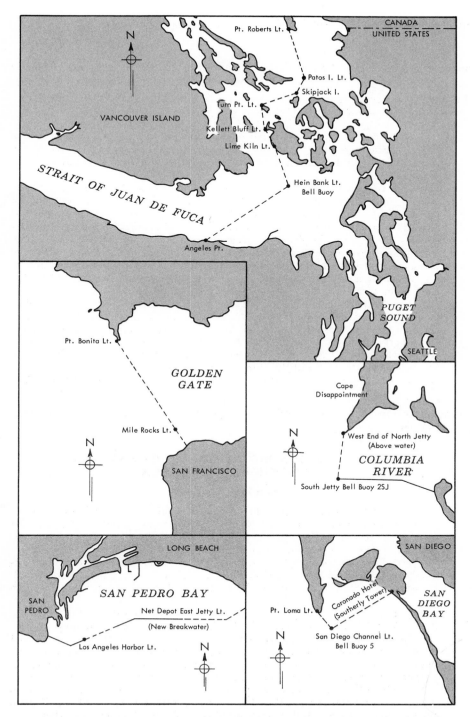

**FIGURE 3-3** Boundary lines, international-inland waters, Pacific Coast of the United States. Courtesy of the United States Naval Institute.

documented by the Coast Guard. Reporting marine accidents became mandatory, and the Coast Guard was empowered to board vessels for inspection and to proceed against violators of rules prohibiting negligent operation.

Section 13 of the *FBA* is of interest in connection with accident reporting:

> SEC. 13. (a) No person shall operate any motorboat or any vessel in a reckless or negligent manner so as to endanger the life, limb, or property of any person. To "operate" means to navigate or otherwise use a motorboat or a vessel.
>
> (b) In the case of collision, accident, or other casualty involving a motorboat or other vessel subject to this Act, it shall be the duty of the operator, if and so far as he can do so without serious danger to his own vessel, or persons aboard, to render such assistance as may be practicable and necessary to other persons affected by the collision, accident, or casualty in order to save them from danger caused by the collision, accident, or casualty. He shall also give his name, address, and identification of his vessel to any person injured and to the owner of any property damaged. The duties imposed by this subsection shall be in addition to any duties otherwise provided by law.
>
> (c) In the case of collision, accident, or other casualty involving a motorboat or other vessel subject to this Act, the operator thereof, if the collision, accident, or other casualty results in death or injury to any person, or damage to property in excess of $100, shall file with the Secretary of the Department within which the Coast Guard is operating, unless such operator is required to file an accident report with the State under section 3 (c) (6) of the Federal Boating Act of 1958, a full description of the collision, accident, or other casualty, including such information as the Secretary may by regulation require.

These provisions have been made more specific by implementing regulations issued by the Coast Guard:

### PART 173—BOATING ACCIDENTS, REPORTS, AND STATISTICAL INFORMATION
#### Boating Accidents

§ 173.01-1  *General.* (a) The provisions of this subpart shall apply (1) to all uninspected motorboats and (2) to all other uninspected vessels used for pleasure or recreational purposes. Uninspected vessels, other than motorboats, used for commercial purposes are not included.

(b) The provisions in this subpart are applicable in the United States, its Territories, and the District of Columbia, as well as to every such vessel which is owned in a State, Territory, or the District of Columbia and using the high seas.

§ 173.01-5  *Reportable boating accidents.* (a) Subsection 13 (c) of the Act of April 25, 1940, as amended (46 U.S.C. 526*l*), reads as follows:

In the case of collision, accident, or other casualty involving a motorboat or other vessel subject to this Act, the operator thereof, if the collision, accident, or other casualty results in death or injury to any person, or damage to property in excess of $100, shall file with the Secretary of the Department within which the Coast Guard is operating, unless such operator is required to file an accident report with the State under section 3 (c) (6) of the Federal Boating Act of 1958, a full description of the collision, accident, or other casualty, including such information as the Secretary may by regulation require.

(b) For the purpose of this subpart a "boating accident" means a collision, accident or other casualty involving (1) an uninspected motorboat or (2) any other uninspected vessel used for pleasure or recreational purposes.

(c) A vessel subject to this subpart is considered to be involved in a "boating accident" whenever the occurrence results in damage by or to the vessel or its equipment; in injury or loss of life to any person, or in the disappearance of any person from on board under circumstances which indicate the possibility of death or injury. A "boating accident" includes, but is not limited to, capsizing, collision, foundering, flooding, fire, explosion, and the disappearance of a vessel other than by theft.

(d) A report is required whenever a vessel subject to this subpart is involved in a "boating accident" which results in any one or more of the following:

(1) Loss of life.

(2) Injury causing any person to remain incapacitated for a period in excess of 24 hours.

(3) Actual physical damage to property (including vessels) in excess of $100.

§ 173.01-10  *Written report required.* (a) Whenever death results from a boating accident, a written report shall be submitted within 48 hours. For every other reportable boating accident a written report shall be submitted within five (5) days after such accident.

(b) The operator(s) of the boat(s) shall prepare and submit the written report(s) to the Coast Guard Officer in Charge, Marine Inspection, nearest to the place where such accident occurred or nearest to the port of first arrival after such accident, unless such operator is required to file an accident report with a State under subsection 3 (c) (6) of the Federal Boating Act of 1958.

(c) Every written report shall contain all of the following and much additional information:

(1) The numbers and/or names of vessels involved.

(2) The locality where the accident occurred.

(3) The time and date when the accident occurred.

(4) Weather and sea conditions at time of accident.

(5) The name, address, age, and boat operating experience of the operator of the reporting vessel.

(6) The names and addresses of operators of other vessels involved.

(7) The names and addresses of the owners of vessels or property involved.

(8) The names and addresses of any person or persons injured or killed.

(9) The nature and extent of injury to any person or persons.

(10) A description of damage to property (including vessels) and estimated cost of repairs.

(11) A description of the accident (including opinions as to the causes).

(12) The length, propulsion, horsepower, fuel, and construction of the reporting vessel.

(13) Names and addresses of known witnesses.

(d) The Coast Guard Form CG-3865 Revised (Boating Accident Report) should be used for the written report required by this section.

All noncommercial and pleasure boats not carrying passengers for hire are subject to the *Federal Boating Safety Act of 1971* which among other things empowers the Coast Guard to promulgate safety standards for boats and associated equipment—"stated in so far as practicable in terms of performance." In addition to boats as such, regulations cover—"fuel systems, ventilation systems, electrical systems, navigational lights, sound producing devices, fire fighting equipment, lifesaving devices, signaling devices, ground tackle, life and grab rails, and navigational equipment." To make, sell, or *use* boats or equipment that do not conform to the regulations is illegal. This, then, goes beyond the regulation of manufacturing and sale of selected marine supplies to give Coast Guard officers authority to enforce the safe use of approved products by the boat operator.

Federal regulations provide for boarding for inspection by officers of the Coast Guard. Any vessel under way when hailed by a vessel flying the Coast Guard ensign or by a vessel recognized as representing state authority shall stop immediately, lay to, or otherwise maneuver to permit an inspecting officer to come on board. Failure to so maneuver makes the owner or operator liable to penalty:

> SEC. 13. If a Coast Guard boarding officer observes a boat being used without sufficient lifesaving or firefighting devices, or in an overloaded or other unsafe condition . . . he may direct the operator to take whatever immediate and reasonable steps would be necessary for the safety of those aboard the vessel, including directing the operator to return to mooring and to remain there until the situation creating the hazard is corrected or ended.

Several changes in the International Rules of 1948 were proposed at the 1960 International Conference on Safety of Life at Sea. These changes have now been adopted by the United States and over 30 other maritime nations which together control more than 80 percent of the world's merchant marine. The 1960 regulations, which became effective September 1, 1965, apply to all vessels on the high seas and on any connecting waters navigable by seagoing vessels.

## 3.03   Numbering and Documentation

Federal regulations require the numbering of all undocumented vessels propelled by machinery of any kind, whether or not machinery is the principal propulsion source. A sailing vessel with auxiliary power must be numbered. The Coast Guard may permit a dinghy or a tender attached to a large numbered vessel to carry the same number as the larger vessel.

A considerable portion of the numbering authority may be assumed by individual states. Most states have adopted regulations of their own. Also: ". . . When a vessel is actually numbered in the state of principal use, it shall be considered as in compliance with the numbering system requirements of any state in which it is temporarily used." But: "When a vessel is removed to a new state of principal use," renumbering by the new state may be required after 60 days.

The numbering requirements do not apply to vessels *documented* by the Coast Guard. Documentation is a higher order of certification imparting the rights and privileges of a U.S. flag-carrying ship when in foreign waters. Documented vessels must, however, comply with all rules governing accident reports, operation, and equipment.

A vessel of more than five net tons may apply for documentation. Following application to the Coast Guard, net tonnage is determined by measurement. All vessels applying for documentation are subject to inspection to judge seaworthiness. A clear title established by certification of ownership from the date of the carpenter's certificate issued by the builder must be presented before a documentation number will be issued. This number and the net tonnage must be deeply engraved into one of the main timbers of the vessel.

Documentation confers certain important privileges and adds some corresponding responsibilities:

(1) Documented yachts may sail for a foreign port without formally clearing customs.

(2) If less than 15 tons, a documented vessel may enter a U.S. port from a foreign port without formal customs entry; however, all dutiable goods must be declared.

(3) Since the title status of the vessel must be known to the Coast Guard, a documented vessel becomes a preferred mortgage risk.

(4) Commercial documented vessels must notify the Captain of the Port at each port of call 24 hours before arrival. Documented yachts are exempt from this requirement.

(5) By law, only documented yachts are authorized to fly the yacht ensign (4.05). This law is generally ignored, and enforcement seems unlikely.

The term *net tonnage* is only one of several measures commonly used to specify the size of a boat. In fact it is not a direct measure of tonnage; it is, rather, a measure of the cubic contents of the vessel. This volume can be translated into tonnage using figures obtained from average types of commercial cargoes. *Gross tonnage* is obtained from a measurement of the total enclosed space on the vessel, allowing a volume of 100 cubic feet for every ton. *Net* or *registered* tonnage is a measure of the space actually available for cargo. Net tonnage is determined by subtracting from the gross tonnage those spaces such as engine room and fuel tanks that cannot be used for cargo stowage. Neither gross nor net tonnage is directly related to *displacement* tonnage, which is the actual weight of the vessel in tons of 2,240 pounds.

## 3.04   Passengers for Hire

Vessels of less than 300 gross tons, used only for recreational boating and not carrying passengers for hire, may be owned and operated by nonlicensed personnel. The vessel itself is not subject to inspection for seaworthiness.

Legally, the operator need have no knowledge of seamanship, navigation, or the Rules of the Road.

A specific license must, however, be obtained from the Coast Guard by a person operating a motorboat carrying passengers for hire. This license is issued only after submitting proofs of character, evidence of boat operating experience, and passing an examination in seamanship and regulations. A physical examination is also required.

The importance of this license requirement lies in the fact that many yachtsmen may be carrying passengers for hire within the interpretations of the regulations. Most of these violations are unwitting and go unrecognized. In case of accident or injury the exact status of each person on board is of great importance.

A prearranged agreement by which a passenger pays a share of the expenses, as for fuel and food, constitutes carrying passengers for hire. There are many borderline situations, including the offer of a gift of appreciation, where the status of the passenger is not clear. Under some circumstances an owner chartering a vessel can be considered as carrying passengers for hire. Any arrangement by which an owner receives gifts or compensation for the use of his vessel must be carefully considered in terms of the regulations and a series of administrative interpretations. Carrying passengers for hire is the subject of publication CG-323, available from the Coast Guard. This should be consulted whenever there is any question of carrying passengers for hire.

## 3.05   Required Equipment

The equipment, exclusive of lights, that is required by law is specified in the Motorboat Act of April 25, 1940, ". . . to Regulate the Equipment of Certain Motorboats on the Navigable Waters of the United States. . . ." The act defines a motorboat as every vessel propelled by machinery and not more than 65 feet in length, except tugboats and towboats propelled by steam. A sailboat with an auxiliary engine comes under the act, since she is sometimes propelled by machinery.

The act is silent on equipment requirements for vessels propelled at all times by sails or manual efforts. These vessels need not carry the items specified for motorboats, but they would be well advised to have on board those which are applicable. *All* vessels must comply with the lighting requirements governing the waters in which they operate and must be prepared to sound the required audible signals.

The act specifically designates responsibility for the required equipment and provides penalties for noncompliance. The owner or operator, or *both,* shall be liable to a penalty of $100 for any violation of the equipment regulations unless the vessel is carrying passengers for hire, when the penalty shall then be $200. According to this provision an operator of a boat borrowed with

A    B    C    D

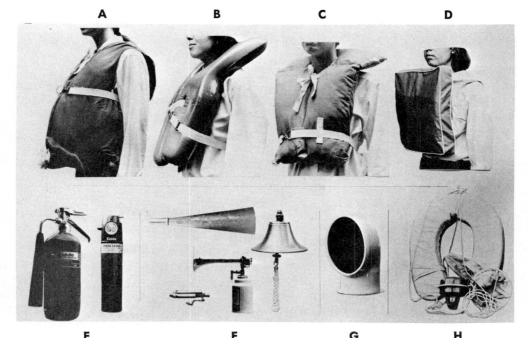

E    F    G    H

**FIGURE 3-4** Typical items of equipment required for motorboats not carrying passengers for hire. Personal flotation gear: A and B, life preservers; C, buoyant vest; D, buoyant cushion. E, carbon dioxide and dry chemical fire extinguishers. F, sound making equipment: mouth horn; whistle; compressed gas horn; bell. G, ventilator. H, horseshoe preserver with strobe light, whistle, and sea anchor.

the owner's consent shall be held liable with the owner for faulty equipment. Similarly the owner of a rented boat can be held liable along with the operator should inspection reveal an equipment violation.

The act recognizes four classes of motorboats:

Class A. Less than sixteen feet in length.
Class 1. Sixteen feet or over and less than twenty-six feet in length.
Class 2. Twenty-six feet or over and less than forty feet in length.
Class 3. Forty feet or over and not more than sixty-five feet in length.

Special provisions apply to larger vessels and to vessels carrying passengers for hire. The equipment prescribed in the motorboat act is in addition to lighting requirements. Boat lighting is so important and so complex that it is discussed separately in Chapter 14.

Requirements by class are as follows:

*Class A.* a. One approved life preserver, buoyant vest, buoyant cushion, or ring buoy for each person on board.

b. One approved hand-portable fire extinguisher of Class B-I (see 3.07 below), unless a fire extinguisher system is installed in the machinery space. Outboard-powered motorboats less than twenty-six feet in length, of open construction, not carrying passengers for hire, need not carry a fire extinguisher. Open construction requires that any decking not form a closed compartment where gases might accumulate.

c. At least two ventilators fitted with cowls or the equivalent for ventilating the bilge of each machinery and fuel tank compartment on boats decked over after April 25, 1940, which use gasoline or any other fuel with a flash point less than 110° F.

d. An approved backfire flame arrestor on every carburetor on engines installed after April 25, 1940, except outboard engines.

e. A whistle is not required by the Motorboat Act, but International Rules, Inland Rules, and the Pilot Rules all require the sounding of whistle signals, without exempting any boat class. A whistle equal to that required for Class 1 should be carried.

f. A bell is not required by the Motorboat Act, but International Rules, Inland Rules, and the Pilot Rules all require an anchored vessel to ring a bell during periods of low visibility. A bell equal to that required for Class 2 should be carried.

*Class 1.* a. Life preserver requirements are identical with those of Class A.

b. Fire extinguisher requirements are identical with those of Class A.

c. Ventilator requirements are identical with those of Class A.

d. Flame arrestor requirements are identical with those of Class A.

e. One hand, mouth, or power-operated whistle capable of producing a sustained blast of two seconds duration, audible at least one-half mile.

f. Situation identical with *f*, Class A.

*Class 2.* a. Life preserver requirements are identical with those of Class A.

b. At least two Class B-I (see 3.07) approved hand-portable fire extinguishers or at least one approved Class B-II hand-portable extinguisher. If an approved fixed fire-extinguishing system is installed in the machinery and fuel tank space, the requirement is reduced to one approved hand-portable Class B-I extinguisher.

c. Ventilator requirements are identical with those of Class A.

d. Backfire flame arrestor requirements are identical with those of Class A.

e. One hand or power-operated whistle capable of producing a sustained blast of two seconds duration, audible at least one mile.

f. One bell which, when struck, produces a clear, bell-like tone.

*Class 3.* a. One approved life preserver or ring buoy for each person on board. Buoyant cushions and buoyant vests are not acceptable in this class.

b. At least three approved hand-portable fire extinguishers of Class B-I (see 3.07) or one Class B-I together with one Class B-II. If an approved fixed fire-extinguishing system is installed in the machinery and fuel tank spaces, the hand-portable requirement is reduced to at least two Class B-I or one Class B-II.

c. Ventilator requirements are identical with those of Class A.

d. Backfire flame arrestor requirements are identical with those of Class A.

e. One power-operated whistle capable of producing a sustained blast of two seconds duration, audible at least one mile.

f. Bell requirements are identical with those of Class 2.

The word *approved,* as used above, refers to an approval by the Commandant, U.S. Coast Guard, which is issued only after demonstration that the equipment complies with Coast Guard specifications covering construction and performance. Names of manufacturers of approved equipment, and the approval numbers assigned to them, are published annually in publication CG-190, *Equipment Lists*.

In general, equipment which has once been approved will be accepted as legal equipment as long as it is in serviceable condition and the approval stamp is legible even though approval may have been withdrawn at a later date.

## 3.06    Flotation Gear

A case of extended approval involves life preservers, buoyant vests, and cushions containing pads of kapok or fibrous glass. Since January 1, 1965, approval has been granted only when the flotation pads have been plastic covered. Approved equipment, previously purchased, will continue to be accepted as legal equipment as long as it meets the "serviceable" requirement.

The term *life preserver*, as used in the regulations, refers to a jacket design with flotation provided by pads of kapok, fibrous glass, cork, unicellular plastic foam, or balsa wood. These materials shall either be in a cloth covering fitted with the necessary straps and ties, or the plastic foam type may have a vinyl dip covering. Since 1949 only the colors Indian Orange or Scarlet Munsell Red have been approved.

An approved life preserver has two markings, one by the manufacturer and the second by a Coast Guard inspector, indicating that it has been "inspected and approved" at the factory. Markings take the form:

LIFE PRESERVER
Adult (or child)
Manufacturer's name and address
U.S. Coast Guard approval No._____
Inspected and passed
Date
Place
Inspector's initials

A *buoyant vest* has pads of kapok or fibrous glass, cloth covered, of vest design, with straps and ties attached, or unicellular plastic foam flotation material with either a vinyl dip or a cloth cover. They are available in three sizes. There is no color requirement for approval. Approved vests are marked with a cloth tag carrying the following information:

BUOYANT VEST
Model
Adult (or child)
Approved for use on motorboats of Class A, 1, or 2 not carrying passengers
    for hire
U.S. Coast Guard approval No._____
Lot No._____
Instructions for care of the vest
Manufacturer's name and address
Weight ranges for child sizes

Approved *buoyant cushions* have kapok, fibrous glass, or unicellular plastic foam as the flotation material. They may be covered with fabric or plastic materials and are fitted with grab straps. No specific shape or color is required for approval. Approved buoyant cushions are marked with a cloth tag carrying the following information:

BUOYANT CUSHION

Size (length, width, thickness)
Contains _____ oz. (kapok or fibrous glass) or _____ cu. in. of unicellular
    plastic foam
Approved for use on motorboats of Class A, 1, or 2 not carrying passengers
    for hire
U.S. Coast Guard approval No._____
Lot No._____
WARNING: DO NOT WEAR ON BACK
Instructions for the care of the cushion
Manufacturer's name and address

Approved *ring buoys* are available in diameters of 20, 24, or 30 inches. They may be made of cloth-covered cork or balsa wood or a specially surfaced plastic foam. All buoys are fitted with a grab line. Indian Orange and white are optional colors. Cork or balsa wood buoys bear two stamps similar to those used on life preservers. Plastic foam buoys have an attached metal tag with the following information:

Manufacturer's name and address
Size of buoy
U.S. Coast Guard approval No._____
Date
Inspector's initials

Smaller ring buoys are sometimes carried for decorative purposes. These might be of some small help in a man-overboard situation, but they cannot be counted as approved flotation gear.

Approved *horseshoe buoys* are favored by the Cruising Club of America and other groups sanctioning ocean sailboat races. They are plastic foam shapes covered with a removable plastic jacket. These buoys are much easier to get into than a ring buoy. They are labeled with the following information:

HORSESHOE BUOY

Manufacturer's name and address
U.S. Coast Guard approval No._____
Date
Inspector's initials

## 3.07    Fire Extinguishers

Fire extinguishers are classified by a letter, which gives the type of fire for which it is suitable, and a number specifying the minmum contents.

Class A—Ordinary combustible materials
Class B—Gasoline, oil, and grease fires
Class C—Fires in electrical equipment

The three classes are not mutually exclusive. Carbon dioxide, for example, is a Class B extinguisher, and it also qualifies as Class C, since it is quite satisfactory for electrical fires.

Extinguishers approved for motorboat use must be of Class B, which means either carbon dioxide ($CO_2$), foam, or dry powder. Some rather toxic liquids such as carbon tetrachloride or chlorobromethane were formerly approved. Approval of existing extinguishers of these types expired January 1, 1962. They can no longer be counted as legal equipment and should not be on board.

Comparative sizes of the three acceptable types are given in Table 3-1.

Carbon dioxide is available in cylinders under a pressure of 800-900 pounds per square inch. All cylinders are built to withstand this pressure with a large margin of safety, but this margin may be reduced or lost completely by abuse or heavy rusting.. A $CO_2$ cylinder must be treated with respect, for the explosion of a large weakened cylinder is quite capable of destroying a boat.

**TABLE 3-1**

Relative Extinguisher Sizes

| Type Size | Carbon Dioxide Pounds | Foam Gallons | Powder Pounds |
|---|---|---|---|
| B-I | 4 | 1.25 | 2 |
| B-II | 15 | 2.50 | 10 |

Weighing is the only feasible method of checking for cylinder leakage. All new $CO_2$ extinguishers should be weighed and recorded, with repeated weighings at least every six months. Inspection and recharging by a qualified expert is indicated if a weight loss exceeds 10 percent of the weight of the contents.

Carbon dioxide systems are well adapted for fixed installations in engine or fuel tank compartments. Operation may be manual from a remote location as at the engine controls, or automatic as by the failure of a fusible element. A properly installed system permits a reduction in the number of hand-portable extinguishers required.

Foam extinguishers operate by producing a tough layer of foam which spreads over surfaces to cut off the supply of oxygen to the fire. Foam extinguishers contain water which may freeze during winter storage and rupture the outer container. Foam extinguishers are not under pressure prior to use, so leakage tests are not required.

Dry powder extinguishers contain the effective chemical along with a propellant gas under pressure. To be eligible for Coast Guard approval, tanks manufactured after June 1, 1965, must have a pressure-indicating gauge. Older approved units are acceptable if they are serviceable, but they should be checked by frequent weighing. Powder extinguishers are very effective for their weight, but like foam leave a messy residue. Extensive engine cleaning may be required after foam or powder has been used near the carburetor air intake.

Backfire flame arresters are a form of fire extinguisher, since they are designed to quench the flames of engine backfires before they escape from the carburetor into the engine compartment. The final metal grid in the arrester quenches the flames by cooling. A flame arrester requires no attention beyond an occasional cleaning. Dirt accumulating in the grid can cut down the air intake to the engine and seriously reduce power.

## 3.08  Audible Signaling Devices

All sets of rules and many court decisions are explicit about the types of equipment to be used for audible signaling in a given situation. A whistle signal is not to be sounded on a foghorn, and vice versa. A vessel may use an audible signaling device more effective than the one prescribed but may still be liable in a collision. There are substantial differences between the various sets of rules, so the equipment purchased should be acceptable to the areas in which the vessel will be operated.

The distinction between the equipment requirements of the Motorboat Act of 1940 and those of the various sets of rules must be clearly understood. Equipment specified by the Motorboat Act must be on board the vessel when she is on the navigable waters of the United States, and the Coast Guard is empowered to make inspections to ascertain compliance. The various rules specify the type of equipment that must be used in sounding warnings to other vessels. In case of a conflict between rules, a vessel must signal on the equipment prescribed for the waters in which she is sailing.

Excerpts from the Rules:

International Rule 15. (a) A power-driven vessel shall be provided with an efficient whistle, sounded by steam or by some substitute for steam, so placed that the sound may not be intercepted by an obstruction, and with an efficient foghorn, to be sounded by mechanical means, and also with an efficient bell. A sailing vessel of 20 tons or upwards shall be provided with a similar foghorn and bell.

Inland Rule 15. (a) A power-driven vessel of 40 feet or more in length shall be provided with an efficient whistle, sounded by steam or by some substitute for steam, so placed that the sound may not be intercepted by any obstruction, and with an efficient foghorn and also with an efficient bell. A sailing vessel of 40 feet or more in length shall be provided with a similar foghorn and bell. Both Rules. (b) All signals prescribed in this rule for vessels under way shall be given:

(i) by power-driven vessels on the whistle;
(ii) by sailing vessels on the foghorn;
(iii) by vessels towed on the whistle or foghorn.

The term *efficient,* used throughout these rules, includes, by court decisions, a recognition that the equipment must be compatible with the vessel's size. A good quality bell eight inches or so in diameter would thus be acceptable under any rule for a motorboat of Class A, 1, 2, or 3. Such a bell would be considered unacceptable on a large liner or on a commercial vessel where machine noises might override the noise of a small bell.

If equipment fails at sea and cannot be repaired, a vessel may use a substitute without becoming in violation. This concession does not apply if the failure was known in a previous port of call and if satisfactory repairs were not made prior to sailing.

## 3.09   Optional Equipment

When a boat, be it a dinghy or a Class 3 power cruiser, is under way, she is on her own. Trouble may come quickly and help may come too late, or a sudden decrease in visibility may conceal the plight of a boat from those who might have rendered assistance. *No conservative skipper would leave a dock or mooring without many items beyond those required by the regulations.* Many boats do indeed sail without adequate equipment, and many tragic accidents can be traced directly to the lack of some essential item.

Listing necessary equipment for all boats and all types of cruises is impossible. Needs vary tremendously with the size and type of boat and with the intended use. The latter factor must be carefully considered, because the actual use may be quite different from that intended. For example, many small craft operate without even the required lights on board on the assumption that they will never be under way after sunset. These boats are taking advantage of the wording of the Motorboat Act: "SEC. 23. Every motorboat in all weathers from sunset to sunrise shall carry and exhibit the following lights while under way . . . ."

Any number of minor mishaps can keep a small unequipped boat out after sunset, putting her in direct violation of the rules. The possible consequences go far beyond a rule violation. Anyone who has spent a night in a disabled, unlighted boat in or near a busy steamer lane becomes a firm believer in complete equipment at all times.

A few equipment suggestions amounting almost to "musts" can be made:

(1) Two anchors of adequate weight and holding power should be on board. These anchors should have matching anchor lines of sufficient length (see 6.07) to be satisfactory in a heavy blow.

(2) Up-to-date charts of all areas where the boat is to be operated are most

important. Local knowledge is an invaluable asset, but adverse conditions may create a need for detailed information obtainable only from a chart.

(3) Small open boats should carry at least two devices for bailing. In larger boats these devices may be bilge pumps, hand operated, and kept in good operating condition at all times. Power-driven pumps will remove large quantities of water with a minimum expenditure of energy, but they should not be depended upon as ultimate bailing devices. Substantial leaks can be controlled for some time by efficient hand pumps after all power has failed.

(4) A good many skippers rely upon local knowledge instead of a compass. This practice is satisfactory in many situations, but it is decidedly unsafe during fog or other periods of low visibility. The compass need not be large, but it should be of good quality, and should have an up-to-date deviation table (see 11.08, 11.11).

The number of incidentals on a well-found boat is legion. Spare engine parts, reserve fuel, engine oil, course plotting equipment, self-contained emergency lights, fenders, and cleaning gear are only a few of the needed items.

Reserves of food and drinking water should be available. The discomfort of an enforced delay in returning to port is greatly mitigated if emergency rations are on hand. The contents of the first-aid kit should be checked frequently. Remedies against seasickness, sunburn protectants, and dark glasses may not be needed by the hardy captain and his crew, but may be welcomed by guests.

The following equipment lists are far from all-inclusive but will serve as checklists for the more important items:

### ESSENTIAL EQUIPMENT
Anchors—at least two, one a heavy storm anchor
Anchor lines—of adequate length and strength
Barometer
Boat hook
Charts
Compass with deviation table—Chapter 11
Course plotting equipment
Distress signals—flares, smoke signals, dye markers, mirrors
Emergency rations and drinking water
First-aid kit—Chapter 8
Lead line
Light list
Oil and grease
Ring buoy
Spare engine parts—manufacturer's recommendations
Spare fastenings—bolts, nuts, cotterpins, screws, nails, wire
Tools—kept free of rust and in good order

### DESIRABLE EQUIPMENT
Binoculars—not more than 6 power
Cleaning gear
Engine crank
Fenders
Fire extinguisher—at least one above minimum requirement

Heaving line
Insect repellent
Log—taffrail or other
Pelorus
Radio direction finder
Radiotelephone—on boats with sufficient power
Searchlight
Spare battery

Skimping on equipment for survival or for comfort under adverse circumstances is poor economy, which may on occasion lead to an unpleasant or dangerous situation. Fire-fighting equipment provides a good example. A fire may be 99 percent extinguished but, if all of the extinguishers are exhausted, the flames may rapidly revive as if no reduction had been achieved. The legally required complement of extinguishers should be considered as a barely adequate minimum to be supplemented for added protection.

Space on the ordinary pleasure boat is scarce, and every item brought on board must be there to serve a good purpose. This is particularly true when a boat is used for protracted cruising, which requires carrying substantial supplies of food and water.

There is a tendency to stow as much equipment as possible into the relatively inaccessible small compartments which usually abound on a small boat. This practice is acceptable provided that a proper inventory is kept of the stores. Memory cannot be trusted, and much time can be saved by use of a proper inventory-location list.

Most careful attention must be given to the location of those items that may be needed in an emergency. Again fire extinguishers are a case in point. They must be so located that they are immediately obtainable, no matter where the fire may be.

# CHAPTER 4

# Manners and Customs

## 4.01 Nautical Language

Over the years a rich and picturesque vocabulary has developed around boats and boating, a vocabulary unequaled by that of any other recreational activity. Much of the language must become a part of, rather than be learned by, anyone who desires more than a casual contact with boats and boating. Although glossaries are available, correct usage of many words and phrases will only come with long experience. Local meanings are a complicating factor, as are some complete separations of spelling and pronunciation, as *leeward* and *sheave*.

The best advice to the newcomer to the field is "proceed with deliberate speed." There is no need to rush into the job of acquiring a salty touch to your conversation. For some time your docking and generally uncertain boat handling will stamp you as a newcomer to an extent not capable of being masked by seagoing talk.

The first step is to learn the anatomy of your boat in proper terms. Among other things this will let you discuss intelligently with your boatyard personnel any necessary work to be done. The word *floor*, for example, must have the same meaning to owner and workman if a proper job is to be done.

Make a conscious effort to increase your vocabulary, but do not force it. Affectation and overuse are as lubberly as ignorance and misuse. Use terms as they begin to come to you naturally without consciously searching for a nautical term to replace a landlubber's expression that would do just as well.

The origin of many nautical terms has been lost over the years; other expressions are logically derived from presently well-known words. Most of the words and phrases were developed so that unmistakable orders could be given to the old-time seaman. Many of these men had no education, and some had a limited capacity to learn. Frequently commands had to be obeyed promptly and exactly. A terse and expressive but precise language thus developed. A command such as "trim the jib sheet" conveys an exact meaning in four words. The need to trim would probably be long gone if the command had to be given in landlubber's language.

Excessive profanity has long been mistaken as the mark of the sailor. Rather, it is an indication of a limited vocabulary, lacking in the appropriate words of meaningful conversation. Profanity has no more place on board a boat than it has in a cultured home. Concentrate on learning the colorful language of the sea, and there will be no need for the other.

## 4.02   Seagoing Clothing

In the days of paid hands and generally more formal living, yachting dress for the owner's party was strictly prescribed for every occasion. In the summer white shoes, trousers, and shirt with black four-in-hand tie were in order. The yachting cap with white cover carried insignia denoting the wearer's status in his yacht club. In early spring and late fall black shoes, dark blue trousers, and blue cap cover replaced the whites.

Today, as boating has become much more of a participation sport, nautical clothing has become more functional and informal. Clothing modeled after naval uniforms may be on board for formal functions at the yacht club; such clothing will rarely be worn while under way. Only the two ends of the yachtsman deserve special consideration. He may cover the intervening portions with shorts, slacks, or whatever suits his fancy and the prevailing weather.

Proper footwear is probably the most important single item in the boatman's wardrobe. Above all, it must be as skidproof as possible to reduce the possibility of a bone-breaking fall or going overboard. An acceptable shoe sole must not pick up grains of sand ashore and bring them on board to scratch carefully finished bright work. Ladies' high heels must never be worn on board.

Bare feet are definitely not safe on a wet deck, and the ordinary rubber-soled sneaker is even worse. Specially designed treads and materials are available and should be worn while under way. Cork soles or special designs in rubber are satisfactory.

The traditional yachting cap, although heavy, has the advantage of a well-designed bill or visor, which is most effective in shading the eyes from extreme light intensities. A baseball type of cap is more practical while under way. The baseball cap provides adequate shielding, is lighter, and is more easily replaced should it be blown overboard.

Sunglasses are such an important part of a sailing outfit that one or two spares should be kept on board. A bright summer sun, with strong reflections from the water, can produce dangerously high light intensities. A forgotten pair of sunglasses can spoil a cruise, or even force an early return to port for medical attention.

Before leaving the subject of clothing, a few words about foul-weather gear are in order. Boating is now almost an all-weather sport, and certainly the warm rains of summer (except for heavy thunderstorms) should not curtail boating activities. Old-fashioned oilskins have been largely replaced by light-weight rubber or synthetic materials. These are available in a variety of colors, including the high-visibility orange.

It is important to put on foul-weather gear *before* getting wet. Too often there is a childlike faith that the rain will not amount to much, certainly not enough to go to the trouble of donning the gear. In a few minutes all clothing may be soaked, and there will be no need for protective measures. Effective foul-weather gear will keep moisture in as well as out, and the wearer will become damp from perspiration soon enough without starting out soaked. Skin that is kept moist for any length of time becomes soft and susceptible to abrasion and fungus attack.

## 4.03   The Maritime Services

Sooner or later most boatmen will encounter personnel from one of the four uniformed services responsible for various phases of maritime operations in the United States. The functions of the Coast Guard have been mentioned in previous chapters; its vessels are frequently seen as they go about their duties of servicing aids to navigation. Coast Guard vessels range from seagoing cutters and weather patrol vessels to small harbor craft for local patrol and rescue.

Contacts with vessels and men of the United States Navy are apt to be less frequent since the primary mission of this service lies off-shore rather than in the waters more accessible to recreational boats. Personnel of the National Ocean Survey, formerly the U.S. Coast and Geodetic Survey, are seldom seen afloat, in spite of their responsibility for maintaining up-to-date information needed for preparing charts. Much of the survey work is done from shore stations, supplemented by a surprisingly small number of vessels. Doctors of the United States Public Health Service will be encountered when entering the country from a foreign port, for this service is responsible for enforcing quarantine regulations. In major ports this service maintains small boarding vessels which meet large incoming passenger ships. In addition, doctors of the Public Health Service may give medical advice by radio when acute situations develop at sea.

Officers of the four services wear basically similar uniforms, dress or working blues in cold weather, dress whites or working khakis when the temperature permits. Each service is identified by a *corps device* (Fig. 4-1), worn on the jacket sleeve or shoulder. Each service also has a distinctive device worn on the uniform cap.

Service rank is indicated by gold braid or *stripes* worn on the sleeves of the blue uniform jacket or on the shoulders of the khaki jacket (Fig. 4-2). The summer yachtsman is more apt to encounter these officers in working summer uniforms, without jackets. The service will then be identified by the cap device, and rank by a pin-on device on the right-hand shirt collar tip, according to the following schedule:

| Grade | Pin-on Device |
|---|---|
| Fleet Admiral | Five silver stars |
| Admiral | Four silver stars |
| Vice Admiral | Three silver stars |
| Rear Admiral | Two silver stars |
| Commodore | One silver star |
| Captain | Silver spread eagle |
| Commander | Silver oak leaf |
| Lieutenant Commander | Gold oak leaf |
| Lieutenant | Two silver bars |
| Lieutenant (jg) | One silver bar |
| Ensign | One gold bar |

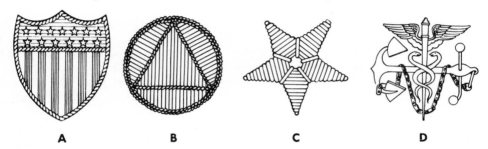

**A**          **B**          **C**          **D**

FIGURE 4-1  Corps devices worn by commissioned officers of the maritime services. (A) Coast Guard, (B) National Ocean Survey, (C) USN line officer, (D) Public Health Service. Each photograph furnished by courtesy of the corresponding service.

FIGURE 4-2  Grade markings used by the four maritime services. Courtesy of the National Ocean Survey.

SLEEVE STRIPES AND SHOULDER MARKS
1/2" and 1/4" lace - - 1/4" spacing

Circles indicate positions of Corps Devices

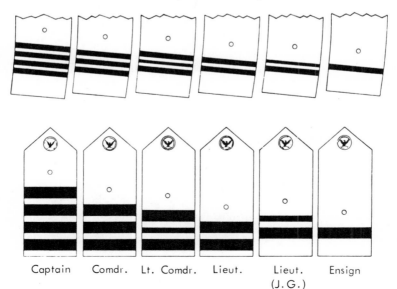

Captain      Comdr.      Lt. Comdr.      Lieut.      Lieut.      Ensign
(J.G.)

Officers up to and including the rank of lieutenant commander are addressed as Mr. _____. Titles are used in the higher ranks as Commander _____. An officer below the grade of captain may be in command of a vessel. When this is the case, he is addressed as Captain, regardless of his actual rank. Responsibilities and prerogatives for each rank are of necessity carefully specified. While these do not apply to civilian craft, some knowledge of them is generally useful.

Personal salutes are a mark of courtesy and respect to the uniform and what it represents, rather than to the individual who wears it. Upon meeting, the junior rank always initiates the salute, which will then be returned by the senior. Salutes are not rendered while uncovered, when not in uniform, or by civilian personnel.

Each commanding officer designates an area of his vessel as the *quarterdeck*. This area, usually near the stern of the vessel, where the national ensign is flown while in port, is used for formal assemblies of the crew and other special functions. The quarterdeck will include the area at the top of the gangway used for boarding.

An officer and his guests will use the starboard gangway if it is available and weather permits. All lower ranks use the port gangway. On reaching the top of the gangway or the quarterdeck, each officer and enlisted man will pause, face, and salute the national ensign. He will then turn, salute the waiting officer-of-the-deck, request permission to board, and when this is granted, will state his business. This ritual is reversed when leaving the ship, the final salute being made to the national ensign from the top of the gangway.

Order of precedence is sometimes confusing to civilians. Junior officers precede and seniors follow in transferring from a large ship to a small boat, but the seniors step ashore first. Seniors board a small boat from the shore last, but precede juniors when boarding a large vessel from a small boat.

When our national anthem, "The Star-Spangled Banner," is played, all uniformed men not in a formation shall come to attention and face the source of the music (unless the colors are being raised or lowered; then they shall face the colors). Men in uniform shall salute at the first note of the anthem and shall hold the salute until the last note. Men not in uniform shall remove any headdress at the first note and hold it just under the left shoulder until the last note. Men without headdress shall stand at attention with the right hand held just under the left shoulder.

## 4.04   The National Ensign

Flags (rectangular) and pennants (triangular or long, tapered shapes) have been used for many years for identification and for signaling from one vessel to another. These needs exist today in spite of radio transmitters, and all large vessels will carry the appropriate signals on board. Unfortunately some not-so-nautical boatmen have carried the use of signals to ridiculous lengths until they have become a travesty of the original use. Odd shapes, with little or no meaning, have no place on board. Their use should be discouraged.

Custom rather than law (except on the high seas) dictates the use of visible signals, and some variations are required by differences in boat construction. In general the recommendations made here conform to those of the North American Yacht Racing Union, as adapted from the codification of the New York Yacht Club.

The national ensign of the United States is the most important flag, ranking above all others, and as such is flown under somewhat stricter regulations. The national ensign is the familiar national flag with 13 horizontal stripes and 50 white stars on a blue field. This flag is correctly flown by all except documented vessels from 0800 hours to sunset. It is always hoisted flying with the hoisting halyard two-blocked. On Memorial Day it will be hoisted full and then lowered to half-mast until 1200, when it is hoisted full. On days of *national* mourning, it may be hoisted full and dropped to half-mast until sunset, or as directed.

The size of the national ensign flown should conform to the size of the boat. About one inch of fly for each foot of overall length is appropriate. The hoist will be two thirds of the fly.

The national ensign is properly flown only at anchor, when passing or saluting other vessels or shore establishments, or upon entering a harbor. It *must* be flown when entering foreign territorial waters, or a foreign port, or upon meeting a vessel in international waters. Its display under these conditions, while required, does not furnish acceptable proof of identity, which can only be established by documentary evidence.

The national ensign is displayed at:

(1) A stern or taffrail staff while at anchor. If the boom of a sailing vessel interferes with a staff amidships, the staff may be set slightly to starboard.

(2) The gaff of the aftermost mast of a powerboat under way. If there is no gaff, the display will be at the stern staff.

(3) The after peak of a gaff-rigged sailboat while under way.

(4) The leech of the aftermost sail on a Marconi-rigged sailboat under way. The display should be about two thirds of the distance from the clew to the head.

(5) The stern staff of a sailboat under power alone.

## 4.05   The Yacht Ensign

The United States yacht ensign has 13 horizontal stripes like the national ensign. The *canon* of the yacht ensign, however, consists of 13 white stars arranged in a circle around a fouled anchor, all on a blue field. This flag is authorized by law to be displayed *only by documented vessels*. It is, however, incorrectly flown by numbered vessels which should properly be flying the national ensign instead. The sizes suggested for the national ensign are appropriate for the yacht ensign also.

With one exception the yacht ensign is flown exactly like the national ensign. In international waters identity shall be established by hoisting the national rather than the yacht ensign. The yacht ensign may be flown in addition as a signal to identify a documented vessel.

## 4.06    The Burgee

The *burgee,* usually a triangular pennant instead of a flag, indicates membership in a yacht club or some similar organization. The design has been selected by the club and registered with Lloyds, which publishes lists of the registered designs for identification purposes. For a sailboat the burgee should have about one-half inch of fly for each foot of height of the highest mast truck above the waterline. On a powerboat the fly should be about one-half inch for each foot of overall length. The hoist should be about two thirds of the fly.

The burgee is displayed whenever the ensign is flown, and in addition may be flown separately between 0800 and sunset, at anchor or under way. The burgee is flown from:

(1) The bow staff of a mastless or a single-masted vessel equipped with a bow staff.
(2) At the truck of a single-masted vessel without a bow staff.
(3) The foremost truck of a vessel with two or more masts.

## 4.07    Private Signals

A boat owner may design a flag or pennant for his own use, to be flown only upon his own boat between 0800 and sunset. Private signals are frequently made in the form of swallowtails. In designing a private signal, preference should be given to simple shapes. Complicated designs and lettering should be avoided as they cannot be recognized at a distance.

If the owner is a flag officer in a yacht club or the United States Power Squadrons, his flag of rank shall fly in place of his private signal, day and night, as long as he holds the designated office.

A private signal is flown at:

(1) The bow staff of a mastless vessel in place of the burgee, while under way.
(2) The truck of a single-masted vessel with bow staff, at anchor or under way.
(3) The truck of a single-masted vessel without bow staff, in place of the burgee.
(4) The aftermost truck of a vessel with two masts.
(5) The main truck of a vessel with more than two masts.

## 4.08    Special Purpose Signals

A variety of flags are recognized for special purposes. Most of these are used only on large vessels and are mentioned here for purposes of recognition, rather than with the hope of promoting their use on small craft.

A rectangular red flag is hoisted during fueling. When this flag is flying, all nearby open flames should be extinguished.

A rectangular yellow flag is flown by a vessel awaiting or requesting clearance from quarantine.

The union jack, a flag with white stars on a blue field, is flown only from the jackstaff (not bow staff) of a vessel with two or more masts. It is flown between 0800 to sunset only, on Sundays and holidays only, and only while at anchor. The jack is little used except on naval vessels.

A rectangular blue flag is flown from the starboard spreader or yardarm, between 0800 and sunset only, when the owner is not on board.

A rectangular blue flag with a diagonal white stripe, flown from the starboard yardarm between 0800 and sunset, indicates that guests are in charge of the vessel.

A rectangular white flag may be displayed at the starboard spreader between 0800 and sunset while at anchor during the owner's meal hours.

A red pennant may be displayed at the port spreader between 0800 and sunset, while at anchor, during the crew's meal hours. In general, the port position is reserved for displays relating to activities of the crew.

## 4.09    International Code Signals

Communication to and from a vessel may be established by the use of the set of International Code flags. Each rectangular flag represents a letter of the alphabet; each pennant represents a number or has a special meaning.

A message may be painfully spelled out, letter by letter, but this is seldom necessary. Hydrographic Office publication H.O. 87, *International Code of Signals, Volume I, Visual and Sound*, contains more than 200 pages of words and phrases that are represented by the hoist of from one to four signal flags. Urgent messages are conveyed by a single flag; less critical phrases may require three or four. Thus, O means "man overboard," A over D means "must abandon my vessel," and N over C is "in distress, need prompt aid." If a club burgee is flown above the code flags, it indicates that the transmitter is using a special yacht code instead of the regular International Code.

A message is transmitted by putting together on a single signal halyard the flags needed to transmit the message. The entire string is then run up to the top of the hoist. When the message is understood, the receiving vessel will send the "answer" pennant to the top. When the message is complete, the transmitting vessel will send the "answer" pennant to the top.

A complete set of International Code Signals together with the code books needed to read them are expensive and bulky, and few small-boat skippers will carry them. Coast Guard and USN vessels will have them on board and will make use of them. The small-boat skipper may find an investment in a VHF radio more worthwhile.

On national holidays and at regattas the set of code flags is used to *dress ship*. The entire set, in no particular order except for a general mixing of flags and pennants, is hoisted from the bow to the foremost truck, thence aft to the trucks of any other masts, and then back to the deck at the taffrail. The ensigns, any private signal, and the club burgee are not hoisted in the display. A dressed ship should be at anchor, all dress hoists being lowered before getting under way.

## 4.10    The Ship's Log

Every commercial vessel, as well as those of the maritime services maintain logs of all events, whether the ship is at anchor or is under way. Recreational boatmen will do well to follow this practice. A countless number of details enter into the safe and effective operation of any boat. Human memories are notoriously faulty, and without a written record many pertinent facts will be forgotten. Many skippers find it convenient to keep two logs, the *sailing log* for all matters pertaining to movements of the vessel, and the *maintenance log* for items related to *upkeep*.

We have already seen the importance of knowing in detail the performance of one's vessel. These details can only be known by keeping an accurate sailing log with items such as rate of fuel consumption for various boat speeds, boat-speed to engine-speed relations, and checks on compass deviation. Documented information of this kind is required if a skipper is to calculate his future positions with any degree of confidence.

Log entries should be made as courses are plotted on the chart, the effects of current calculated, and the estimated arrival times (ETAs) are compared with the actual arrival times. Weather conditions should be noted at regular intervals or at any unusual event. Weather observations should include direction and velocity of the wind, barometric pressure, any notable changes in temperature, and the general condition of the sea.

On an extended cruise changes of watch and the time of lighting ship will be duly recorded. Records of food and water consumption will be of interest. Any unusual event should be recorded with the position and the time at which it occurred. A sailing log, in other words, should contain a concise but complete story of each cruise.

Similarly, a maintenance log should contain all items pertinent to the upkeep of the vessel. This log should list all stores that come on board, together with their location, so that valuable time is not lost in searching for them when they are urgently needed. Type-numbers on items that can fail, such as light bulbs, should be listed in the maintenance log.

Useful entries in the maintenance log include the amount of paint and varnish needed for certain jobs, the times at which various items were replaced, records of engine oil changes, addition of battery water, and so on. The maintenance log should contain a complete running account of jobs done and to be done.

Regulations of the Federal Communications Commission require that a log be kept of all radio communications to and from the ship. The log form specified in the regulations should be followed closely, for the communication log is subject to inspection by the licensing agency at any time.

## 4.11   Garbage and Sewage

The well-warranted national concern about air and water pollution has led to some drastic legislation governing the disposal of refuse from vessels while in territorial waters. The Federal Pollution Control Act authorizes the Administrator of the Environmental Protection Agency (EPA) to establish standards of performance for marine sanitation devices and systems. Under the law "*sewage* means human body wastes and the wastes from toilets and other receptacles intended to receive or retain body wastes" and "*discharge* includes, but is not limited to, any spilling, leaking, pumping, emitting, emptying or dumping" into the navigable waters of the United States. In general all state laws on this subject are preempted by the Federal statute.

The Coast Guard is charged with enforcing the very strict standards promulgated by the EPA. To that end, sewage treatment devices, where allowed at all, must comply with Coast Guard regulations. In all probability the EPA goal of ultimately eliminating all sewage discharge from small boats will prevail. It is essential that each boat owner and operator keep himself informed of the national and any local requirements that apply to the areas in which he operates.

Respect for the rights of others dictates certain procedures over and beyond those required by legislation. Past experience has shown that the most beautiful natural environment can be fouled by man in an incredibly short time. Many a boatman looks upon his own garbage as insignificant when tossed overboard in or near a harbor. When this act is repeated by the large numbers now using our crowded waterways, a trivial contamination becomes a disagreeable and dangerous mess. All trash and refuse from every small boat should be retained for proper disposal ashore.

When in port use the toilet facilities ashore. Be sure that the head installation on board conforms to all applicable regulations, and use it in accordance with those regulations. Only by the strictest control of all sources of pollution can our waterways be saved from destruction.

## 4.12    At Anchor

It is well known that sound travels long distances over water, but seemingly few boatmen remember this, particularly late in the evening. A snug, well-lighted cabin seems like an isolated little world, and it is easy to forget that other boats exist and may be anchored nearby. The party spirit can easily get out of hand to the point where sleep is impossible throughout a crowded anchorage. The crews of other boats may well have rugged sailing schedules ahead and can ill afford to lose all or part of a night's rest.

A curfew, explained to all on board before sailing, and strictly enforced, will go a long way toward eliminating late and noisy parties. Permit no exceptions to the stipulated curfew.

Sea-going record players, radios, and television receivers also are gross disturbers of the peace of a quiet anchorage. A curfew will help here also, but the best remedy, as in all phases of boating, is a liberal application of the golden rule. It is quite possible for the crew of one boat to enjoy any of these devices without disturbing others. Recreational boating is no longer the sport of a favored few who can cruise in isolated splendor far from all disturbing elements. Boating is now enjoyed by millions of people, each one of whom must accept the responsibilities along with the pleasures. Unless this is done, a magnificent sport will lose the very appeal that has made it so attractive to so many.

CHAPTER **5**

# Small-Boat Handling Under Power

## 5.01 Propellers

Methods of boat propulsion have fascinated inventive minds for many years; innumerable schemes have been devised in attempts to improve the performance of boats and engines. Some of these schemes have proved useful for particular applications, but the underwater propeller remains by far the most common form of powerboat propulsion.

When a propeller rotates in the direction designed to propel the boat forward, the water directly behind the propeller blades is thrust powerfully backward. The propeller and its shaft experience a force of reaction oppositely directed to the force exerted on the water. This force of reaction drives the boat forward. As the propeller forces water backward, more water moves in from the front of the blades to fill the void.

A propeller has two critical dimensions, diameter and pitch. Diameter is self-explanatory. Pitch is the amount of twist or spiral given to the propeller blades. A high-pitch blade is said to take a big bite on the water. A low-pitch wheel, on the other hand, moves the water back a smaller distance at each revolution.

Diameter and pitch must be properly matched to the weight and hull form of the boat and to the horsepower and speed characteristics of the engine. If, for example, a propeller is rotated at too high a speed, water cannot move in properly to fill the void left by that forced astern. Bubbles or *cavitation* may be produced at the forward faces of the blades. Some experimental designs operate in a state of cavitation, but in general this is to be avoided since it sharply reduces propeller efficiency. In addition, the sudden collapse of the bubbles, continually repeated, can lead to blade pitting and eventual destruction.

The classic example of cavitation occurred when the British Navy substituted a high-speed steam turbine for the old slow-speed reciprocating engine

69

in a destroyer. Ship performance, instead of being improved, was sharply reduced because of the intense cavitation. Reduction gears installed between turbine and propeller shaft eliminated cavitation and brought ship performance to that anticipated from the higher power of the steam turbine.

## 5.02    Propeller Handedness

Internal combustion engines may be designed to rotate in either direction; to match these two directions propellers are made with either a right-hand or a left-hand spiral. A propeller is *right-handed* if, when viewed from the *stern*, a *clockwise* rotation acts to drive the boat *forward*. Forward motion is obtained with a left-handed wheel when the shaft rotation is counterclockwise, viewed from the stern.

All automobile engines will require left-handed wheels if the engines are converted to marine use and installed in a conventional manner. Most single-screw boats equipped with an engine designed for marine use have a right-handed rotation. A twin-screw boat will usually have engines rotating in opposite directions, to balance out effects to be discussed later. Oppositely, rotating pairs are customarily installed so that the tops of the blades move outboard for forward thrust.

## 5.03    Rudder Action

Consider a single-screw vessel with a propeller of either handedness. When the propeller rotates, it forces a powerful stream of water backward past the rudder which for a straight course will be nearly central or amidships (Fig. 5-1A). In this position the water streams past the rudder without exerting any turning force on the vessel.

If now we make *left-rudder* (Fig. 5-1B), the stream of water will strike the forward face of the rudder and will be deflected off to the left. The rudder must exert a considerable force on the water to produce the deflection. The reaction to this deflecting force will be on the rudder, forcing it to the right. As the stern of the boat moves to the right, the boat will make a turn to the left. A *right-rudder* will of course produce a turn to the right.

It is important to note that there will be no rudder action unless water is streaming past it. A sailboat can be maneuvered only when she is moving relative to the water. A powerboat must be in motion, or at least the propeller must be revolving, if steering action is to be obtained. The minimum speed needed to make a vessel maneuverable is known as *steerageway*.

When a boat responds to either a left-rudder or right-rudder, she does not pivot about either bow or stern, but at some point in between, the exact point depending on the underwater design of the hull and the location of the rudder. A boat with a deep forefoot, relatively flat after-surfaces, and little deadwood

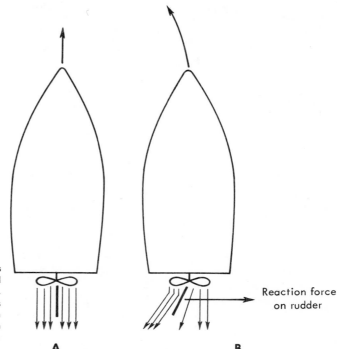

**FIGURE 5-1** (A) Water flows smoothly past a central rudder and the boat moves straight ahead. (B) With a left rudder water is deflected to the left, the reaction force on the rudder sets the stern to the right, and the boat makes a turn to port.

Reaction force on rudder

A                    B

will pivot well forward, with the stern swinging wide. Conversely, a boat running bow high with a considerable amount of deadwood will pivot farther aft, with the bow falling off sharply. *One must become thoroughly familiar with the pivoting characteristics of his boat to avoid scraping docks or other vessels when putting off.*

Since steering action depends on water flow past the rudder, the latter will be most effective when it is located where the water velocities are the highest. In a powerboat this will be directly behind the propeller. Thus a single-screw boat will have a single rudder directly behind the wheel, while a twin-screw boat will have two coupled rudders, each located behind the corresponding propeller.

## 5.04   Steering the Outboard Motor and Outboard Drive

The description of rudder action assumes an inboard engine with a rigid propeller shaft running out through a stuffing box to the propeller. In an outboard drive the propeller itself pivots about a vertical axis; there is no rudder in the ordinary sense. When the direction of the propeller thrust of an outboard drive is directed off the keel line, a very powerful turning force will be exerted on the stern. The unsymmetrical thrust will set the stern sharply either to the left or right as the case may be.

Because of the large side-thrust forces that can be directed at a large angle to the keel line, a boat with an outboard drive can make sharp turns that are impossible for a boat with a single-screw inboard engine. Operators of outboards sometimes forget this fact and expect evasive maneuvers that are impossible from an inboard-powered vessel.

## 5.05    Propeller Side Thrust

Consider now a vessel driven by a single-screw inboard engine. In addition to the main thrust that drives the boat forward, a propeller will generate a small but appreciable side thrust. In a right-handed wheel driving forward, this side thrust sets the stern to the right, causing the boat to tend to the left. A left-handed wheel driving forward will tend to swing the bow to starboard. Several explanations have been offered to account for this side thrust. We will accept its existence and note its direction without inquiring into its origin. It is important to remember that side thrust does not depend on the motion of water past the rudder. Side thrust is created by the revolving propeller, increasing as the propeller speed increases and reversing when the direction of propeller rotation is reversed.

In normal forward motion the turning tendency resulting from side thrust of a single screw is counteracted by the helmsman, who unconsciously applies a slight amount of rudder in the opposite direction. Side thrust must be consciously reckoned with whenever rudder effectiveness is reduced as in slow speed turns, backing, and in coming alongside.

With a single right-hand screw going forward the tendency to go to port is automatically compensated by a constant, slight right rudder. A turn to port can obviously be made more easily than one to starboard since in the one instance rudder thrust and side thrust add while in the other they oppose. A single-screw boat, with an engine of either handedness, will thus always favor a turn in one direction over the other. The amount of the difference will depend on the hull design and the characteristics of the propeller.

Differences in turning ability become more pronounced when backing. With a reversed rotation (Fig. 5-2A), water will be forced forward along the deadwood and keel. Water can easily fill the void behind the wheel without flowing close to the rudder surfaces. With a left rudder (Fig. 5-2B), some water may be deflected to produce a mild rudder action, but this will be much less than when the rudder is directly behind a solid stream of water from a forward driving screw. In backing, good steerage will not be obtained until considerable sternway has been obtained. When backing, propeller side thrust is as strong as when going forward but reversed in direction.

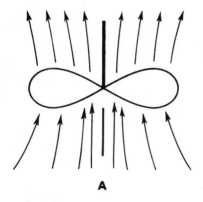 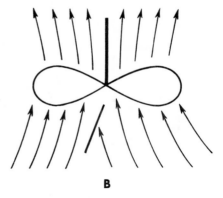

A                                          B

FIGURE 5-2   (A) Water flows symmetrically with a central rudder and a reversing propeller. (B) Only a little water is deflected with a reversing propeller and the steering action is much less than with forward drive.

In some boats the steering action of the rudder is so sharply reduced that they cannot turn in one direction when backing, no matter what the setting of the rudder. Thus the stern of a backing right-hand, single-screw boat can be readily set to port but may be completely unable to be swung to starboard. The exact behavior depends on the shape of the underwater hull and the location of the propeller. Sailing auxiliaries are notoriously poor backers, since they are usually low-powered, with the propellers poorly placed for effective action.

The response of a vessel to side thrust must be well understood before operations are conducted in close quarters. Figure 5-3 shows the difference between a neatly conducted maneuver and a lubberly affair. In Fig. 5-3A a boat with a single right-hand screw is making a correct turn in a narrow channel. The approach is made close to the left bank so as to execute a right turn (1). This turn will not be as sharp as a turn to the left because propeller side thrust acts to partially counteract rudder action. When backing down (2) side thrust sets the stern to port, helping the rudder to produce a tight turn. The gain in turning ability during phase (2) more than offsets any loss in (1). A forward right turn (3) completes the maneuver.

In the incorrect sequence (Fig. 5-3B), the forward left turn will be sharp as side thrust acts to assist rudder action. In backing, however (2), the best that can be achieved is a straight course as side thrust tends to counteract a weak rudder action. A second forward left (3) and a second reverse (4) may be required before the turn can be completed. If it is *known* that the turn can be completed without backing, a turn to the left is to be preferred; if this misses completion the situation of Fig. 5-3B will develop. All of the maneuvers will of course be reversed if the boat is equipped with a single left-hand screw.

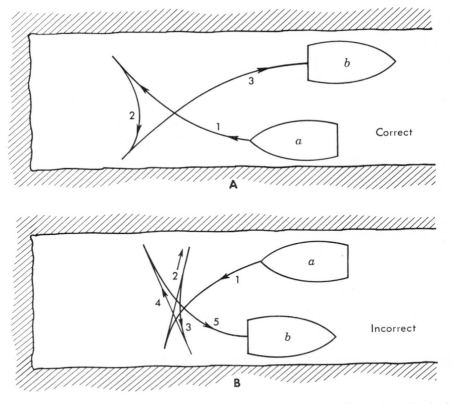

**FIGURE 5-3** (A) With a right-hand screw side thrust adds to the rudder action while backing. (B) In the incorrect sequence side thrust opposes rudder action while backing.

## 5.06 Propeller Slip

The novice skipper will soon discover that his boat is much less rigidly attached to the water than is his automobile to the road. Even when moving forward at a constant, sustained speed there is a certain amount of propeller *slippage*. This is the difference between the distance the boat actually moves forward with one revolution of the wheel and the theoretical distance advanced if the propeller is considered as a perfect screw. Slippage becomes even more important when a boat is just getting under way or is coming to a stop.

A boat dead in the water does not respond instantly to the first rotations of its propeller. The boat is heavy and so has a large inertia, which tends to resist any change in its state of motion. When the propeller first starts to turn, it slips excessively, pushing water astern with little forward motion of the boat. Side thrust, however, will be developed as soon as the propeller sets the water in motion.

When the clutch is engaged at low engine speed, some forward thrust will be developed together with a minimum of side thrust and a small rudder effectiveness. If, on the other hand, the propeller is spun rapidly for a few seconds, a large side thrust and strong rudder action will develop before the boat has a chance to move appreciably from the action of the forward thrust. This effect can be used sometimes to good advantage in "kicking in" the stern of a boat toward a dock without causing an appreciable forward motion.

Some skippers come alongside a dock or another vessel at a good speed, backing down hard to bring the boat to a standstill at the desired location. This maneuver does not always work as expected, because the hard backing may set the stern over from side thrust, leaving the boat dead in the water but at an undesirable angle. A better approach by far is to come in with barely enough way on to insure rudder effectiveness. A slow application of reverse will then bring the boat dead with little or no change in heading. If desired, a short burst of power can be used to set the stern over.

## 5.07   Twin-screw Maneuvering

All of the problems arising from propeller side thrust disappear in a twin-screw boat equipped with engines of opposite handedness. When both propellers are driving either forward or backward, the side thrusts will cancel so that there will be no tendency to turn either to the right or left.

When one screw drives forward, and the other astern (Fig. 5-4), a turning action with no forward or backward motion can be obtained. A twin-screw boat can literally turn in its own length, or by careful manipulation of clutches

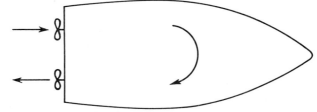

FIGURE 5-4  Using oppositely directed thrusts a twin-screw boat can turn with no forward progress.

and throttles can combine turning and longitudinal movements. As anchorages become more crowded, the high maneuverability of a twin-screw boat becomes more important.

## 5.08   Docking

Any waterfront habitué has witnessed small-boat dockings ranging from bow-on collisions and boathook approaches, where the boat is brought alongside by brute strength and shouting, to the veteran's precise, planned procedure. With knowledge of a boat's behavior and general wind and current conditions, there is little excuse for poor docking. Preplanning to utilize wind, current, and the boat's best performance to their fullest will assure a neat maneuver with no damage to boat, dock, tempers of the crew, and with little amusement to spectators.

In planning a docking maneuver, the effects of wind on the superstructure and current on the hull may be underestimated. Set due to wind and current may go unnoticed at cruising speed but may become an appreciable factor as the boat slows to approach a dock. In particular, the force of the wind on a high superstructure, such as a flying bridge, can seriously upset a docking situation if proper allowance has not been made.

Fenders are an essential in some docking situations and are most useful in any case. They should be made ready well in advance on the side the skipper plans to lay alongside the dock. Docking lines should be in readiness to take advantage of a situation that the helmsman can create, but that he may not be able to hold while lines are dredged out of remote lockers or are unfouled.

When there is no wind or current—an unusual situation—the bow is brought into the dock at a slight angle, Fig. 5-5. The good skipper will come in as slowly as possible, with just enough way on to maintain steerage as long

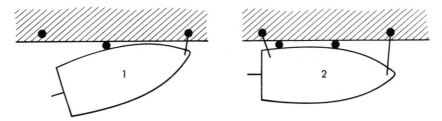

FIGURE 5-5    Docking with no wind or current.

as possible. A bow line can be passed and secured as the bow touches the dock. The stern will also be close aboard at this point so that a second line can be passed to secure the stern. Fenders should be placed where needed.

When the combined effect of wind and current is parallel to the dock (Fig. 5-6), the approach is again made at a slight angle, heading into the pre-

FIGURE 5-6    With a bow line made fast, current will bring in the stern for securing.

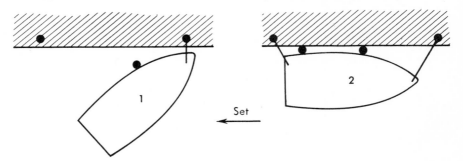

Set

vailing force. With no way on, and a bow line secured, this force will bring in the stern to a point where a line can be passed and secured.

When wind or current is setting toward the dock (Fig. 5-7), the boat is brought in nearly parallel to the dock, a few feet away. Wind and current will then bring her in against prerigged fenders. Experience will show whether bow or stern should be favored so as to come in exactly against the dock.

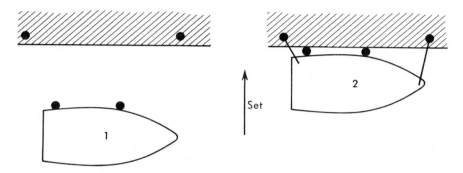

**FIGURE 5-7**  A stationary boat to windward will be brought into the dock by the current.

If the setting force is strong, the boat may come into the dock more rapidly than is desirable. In this case the boathook may be used to fend off and slow her down. When using a boathook *always* keep the pole *alongside* the body instead of against the abdomen or chest. Heavy use may break a pole, leaving a jagged end quite capable of inflicting a serious abdominal injury. Even the blunt end can produce a bruise or may force a crewman overboard before he can get clear.

In approaching the leeward side of a dock, the bow is brought in at an angle, and a bow spring line is rigged—Fig. 5-8 (2). Forward power, applied with the rudder turned away from the dock, will force the stern in until a

**FIGURE 5-8**  Forward power with right rudder and a spring line brings in the stern against the current.

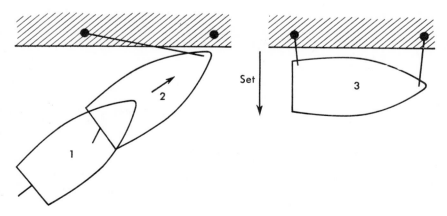

stern line can be passed and secured. Forward motion will be prevented by the spring line. Fenders must be tended during this maneuver, because the boat will bear rather heavily against the dock, and the point of contact will move aft as the stern comes in. The spring line will ordinarily be left in place, not removed as shown in Fig. 5-8 (3).

If the off-setting wind or current is not too great, the bow may be brought up to the dock and a bow line secured. A short burst of power with the rudder hard over may suffice to bring in the stern before an appreciable forward motion develops.

It is usually desirable to utilize propeller side thrust in backing into a narrow slip. Figure 5-9A shows the procedure with a single right-hand screw. The approach (1) is made with barely enough way to maintain steerage. Plan to bring the boat dead alongside (2). Backing will now set the stern to port and will help to bring her into the slip. Fenders should be at hand and tended. Excessive sternway can be checked by a stern line, which becomes a stern

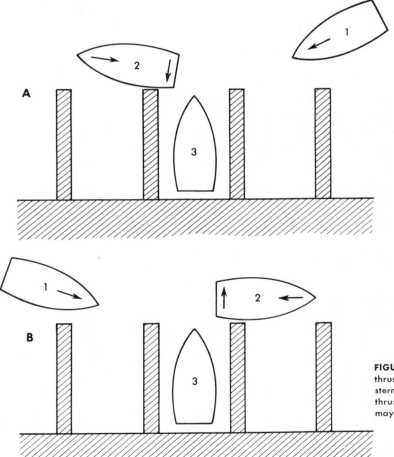

FIGURE 5-9 (A) Propeller side thrust aids in bringing the stern into the slip. (B) Side thrust from a right-hand screw may make the turn impossible.

spring line as it is payed out. In the incorrect approach (Fig. 5-9B), side thrust will act to keep the stern out of the slip. If wind and current are not too strong, she can be warped in without power by a stern line, which later becomes a stern spring line.

Picking up a mooring in a powerboat seldom presents a problem after the proper buoy has been identified. The approach is made into the wind or current, whichever prevails, to avoid being carried over the buoy. The proper approach direction can be determined by observing the set of neighboring vessels. During the approach to the buoy, way should be barely sufficient to maintain steerage, with a final drift estimated to put the bow dead at the buoy.

A sailboat will approach a mooring sailing close to the wind (Chapter 16), with the sails trimmed well in. Forward drive can be reduced by slackening the sheets and increased by trimming. When it is estimated that residual momentum will carry the boat to the mooring buoy, she is headed up into the wind. A little overshoot is to be preferred here to falling short, because wind pressure on the hull and rigging will slowly move the boat backwards.

Whenever a vessel with a stern tow slows or reverses, conditions at the stern must be carefully watched. For example, a small dinghy towed astern will not respond to reverse power applied to the main engine. During docking operations the small boat may drift up into the transom, producing scratches and gouges in the brightwork. As the small boat comes up, the towing line may sink and be sucked into the whirling propeller blades. A strong line caught in the propeller may bend the shaft or one or more of the blades or may jam between the propeller hub and a strut, stalling the engine. The danger of fouling is greatly reduced when the dinghy painter is made from one of the synthetic materials that float on the surface of the water. In any case the painter should be tended as the boat comes in to dock or to a mooring.

## 5.09   Leaving a Dock

In leaving a dock many skippers forget that a boat pivots about a point that is well forward of the stern. A sharp turn away may jam the stern into the dock, producing a bad scrape or more serious damage to planking or transom. If there is forward room, a gradual departure (Fig. 5-10) will work out the bow without scraping the stern. Once away from the dock the angle of turn may be increased.

More drastic measures are required when wind or current is setting the

**FIGURE 5-10**   A gradual turn away from a dock prevents scraping.

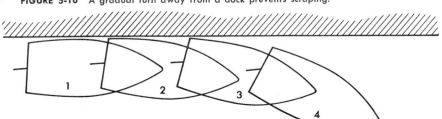

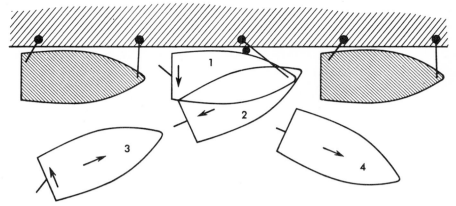

**FIGURE 5-11** Forward power with left rudder brings out the stern, pivoting on a bow spring line.

boat against the dock or when she is *dockbound* by other boats, Fig. 5-11. Under these conditions all lines except a bow spring are cast off. Going forward on the engine with the rudder angled toward the dock will set the stern away without forward progress. When stern clearance has been gained, the spring line is cast off, and the boat is backed straight out until turning room has been attained. Alternatively a stern spring line may be used with reverse power applied to bring out the bow. The boat can move forward as soon as the spring line is cast off. In either of these situations fenders must be tended during the first phase.

Whatever procedure is used to clear the dock, the departure should be slow, at a speed comparable to that used in the approach. A sudden application of power close to a dock can cause damage to other boats or to the dock itself, for which the offending skipper is financially liable. Speed should be built up gradually when there is no danger of producing damage from bow wave or wake.

## 5.10 Cycloidal Waves

A time comes to every boatman when his actions must be modified by the demands of weather, usually those associated with the short, steep waves of shallow water. In the deep waters of the open seas, wave motions take on a characteristic shape known as a *cycloid*, Fig. 5-12. Cycloidal waves have typically rounded *troughs* with gentle slopes leading up to somewhat sharper *crests*. These wave systems are called *swells* or *ground swells*.

**FIGURE 5-12** Long-wave-length cycloidal waves in deep water.

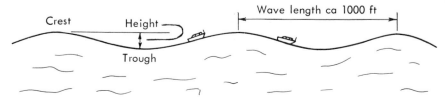

In deep water the distance between successive crests or troughs in a cycloidal wave system will range from several hundred to as much as two thousand feet. This distance is the *wave length* of the system. In a deep-water cycloid, the wave *height* or *amplitude,*—the vertical distance from trough to crest—may be many feet. A small boat will span only a small fraction of the wave length of a deep-water cycloid; and as a consequence will move smoothly up and down the waves without the bounce or chop experienced with the steeper waves of shallow water. A larger vessel, whose length more nearly approaches the wave length of the wave system, may experience a nasty chop, a much more disagreeable motion than the gradual rise and fall of the smaller vessel.

The free-water movements of the open ocean will be restricted when the cycloidal waves approach shallow water. The first effects will be noticed when the depth of the water is about one-half the wave length of the system. Interference between the bottom and the water will then slow the wave velocity and slightly increase the amplitude. The rounded troughs and tops of the cycloids will be replaced by sharpened peaks or *cusps,* Fig. 5-13. As shoaling

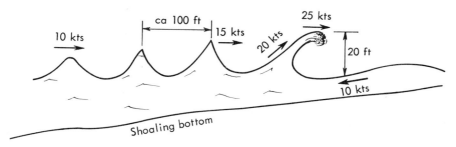

**FIGURE 5-13**  A shoaling bottom shortens the wave length and leads to the formation of breakers.

continues, the velocity at the base of the waves is further reduced by the off-shore rush of water from preceding waves. When the height exceeds about 1/7 of the wave length, the wave tops will curl forward and *break* over an almost vertical frontal wave surface.

Shallow-water breakers have a strong horizontal flow in addition to the vertical wave motion. The breaking crests move rapidly shoreward, while a strong return flow opposes the bases of the advancing waves.

In a short-wave-length system typical of shallow waters, a small boat may have a length that is an appreciable fraction of the wave length. The boat may extend nearly from crest to trough, creating a situation quite different from that existing in a long-wave-length cycloid. In steep waves the motion may be quite violent, with pitching and pounding.

In a very heavy, sustained blow, cycloidal waves with breaking crests may form in deep water off-shore. These seas must be considered dangerous to all small boats. A well-built, skillfully handled sailboat can cope with even these extreme conditions, although it is an unpleasant experience for the crew. The average power cruiser must, however, avoid seas of this nature or run a grave danger of serious damage or foundering. With present radio reporting of weather conditions, there is usually adequate warning of ocean storms of an intensity capable of producing ocean breakers.

## 5.11   Heavy Weather

The ability of any boat to stand up to the punishment from heavy seas depends on many factors in both design and construction. The importance of sound construction is obvious. A heavily framed and planked boat, well fastened, with all structural members sound will certainly be better able to withstand conditions inflicting heavy damage to a less seaworthy craft.

Design also plays an important role, both in the ability to survive in heavy seas and in the method of handling to insure survival. Some of the best surf boats have been designed for the Coast Guard and other life-saving services. Typically these surf boats have double-ended displacement hulls with round bilges, much like the classical whaleboat. In contrast, pleasure-boat designs have tended toward flat underwater sections with hard chines and broad transoms. This type of hull has been developed to obtain a planing action and the high speeds presently in demand. Because of their overwhelming numbers, discussion here will be confined to the latter hull type, exposed to the steep, choppy waves of relatively shallow inland waters. Operation in the rapidly shoaling waters of narrow inlets will be discussed later.

(a) *Running into a sea.*   As heavier seas build up in response to increasing winds, the bow of a vessel heading to weather will be driven into the waves instead of being lifted by them. Tremendous forces on hull, frames, equipment, and crew will be set up by this pounding which, if allowed to continue, may spring planking or break frames. Heavy objects, even the engine itself, may be torn loose to become battering rams capable of smashing through the hull if not promptly secured. The propeller may be alternately submerged and out of water with the engine alternately heavily loaded and racing wildly. Members of the crew may be flung violently against the boat, and they are in real danger of going overboard if not properly secured. Steps must obviously be taken to reduce these stresses.

Reducing speed is the most important weapon for combating the hazards of running into heavy seas. At slow speed the bow will have time to be lifted by the seas instead of having to batter its way through them. Spray will fly wildly from the bow, to be caught by the wind and driven against all exposed surfaces and persons topside. The going will be slow, bumpy, and wet, but tolerable and safe. If the seas are taken slightly off the bow instead of directly head on, the boat will both pitch and roll, which is usually a more comfortable motion than that which results when all of the wave energy goes into pitch alone.

Although heading into the seas is the safest course in moderately heavy going, constant vigilance is required of the helmsman. If the bow is lifted high on a wave while the stern is low, the exposed bow may be swung around by the wind while the protected stern stays fixed. Without prompt and vigorous action with the rudder and possibly power, the boat may fall off broadside to the seas, where she is vulnerable to filling or capsizing.

If the storm continues to increase, speed must be further reduced, sometimes to the point of making little or no headway. In this situation consideration must be given to *heaving-to*. Some hull forms may heave-to, or head into the seas without assistance and without power, but this is not apt to be the case with a small powerboat. A small amount of power will usually be required to maintain steerageway and some control of the boat's heading.

Some deep-water, all-weather sailors will stream a *sea anchor* or *drogue* (Fig. 5-14) from the bow to produce a drag, thus helping to keep the boat hove-to. Other equally competent skippers contend that a drogue is practically useless for this purpose. If a sea anchor is to be at all effective it—and the attached tow line—must be *large*. Some of the commercially available sea anchors fold for easy stowage but are far too small to be useful in a heavy sea.

If an adequate sea anchor is available, it should be streamed from the heaviest anchor rode, with the inboard end secured to a samson post or some other solid structure rather than to some fancy, fair-weather cleat. The very nature of a sea anchor makes its recovery by heaving in on the towing line almost impossible. A pull on the trip line will reverse the cone and permit easy recovery. The two lines may become fouled in which case recovery must be made by long, hard heaving on the main towing line.

FIGURE 5-14   A sea anchor or drogue.

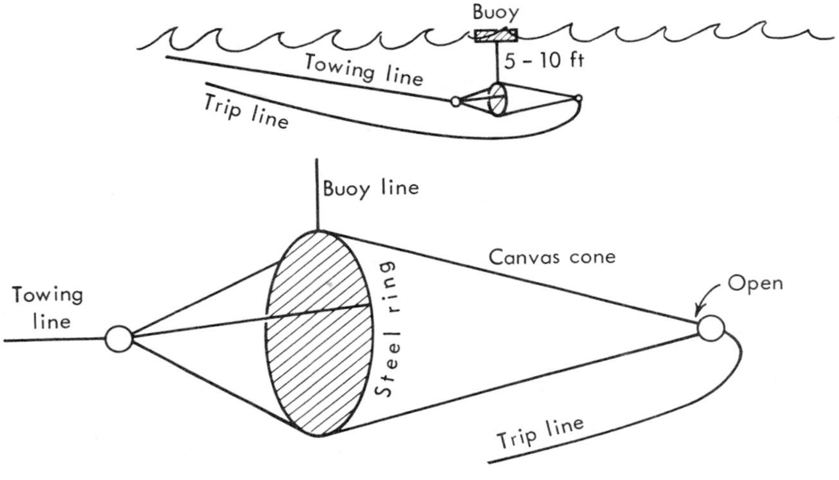

With the boat properly hove-to, the crew can devote its attention to maintaining buoyancy and preventing heavy objects from breaking loose. Bilges should be kept pumped since free water inside a hull rapidly degrades stability. Between pumpings, the entire crew may well ponder on the reasons why anyone goes to sea of his own free will.

(b) *Running with seas abeam.* In heavy seas, running in the troughs is to be avoided. In moderate weather one may run in a trough with the boat rolling uncomfortably but not dangerously. As the seas build up, the rolling may increase to put her on her *beam-ends* (Fig. 5-15), where all open compartments

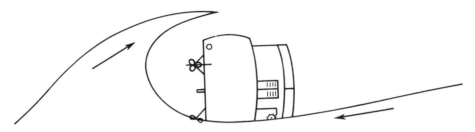

FIGURE 5-15 A power cruiser on her beam ends after broaching in the trough of a breaking wave.

will fill instantly. A good helmsman can anticipate some big seas while running in the trough and can meet them by bringing the bow up to take the wave on the forward quarter. When this procedure is required to avoid rolling over, it is better to change to a quartering course, which allows the seas to strike the vessel abaft the beam. Although the distance traveled will be greater, the total hazard will be reduced with the quartering courses.

(c) *Running before the seas.* This is probably the most dangerous aspect of heavy-weather operation. While running from the seas, the boat can be put in either of two dangerous situations:

(1) When running, the broad transom is exposed to the full force of the following seas. As they strike this large area they cause the boat to yaw wildly. If this yawing is not promptly and continuously controlled by vigorous rudder action, the boat will *broach:* be knocked broadside into a trough. Here she may be boarded and filled by the next sea, or rolled over on her beam-ends. A double-ender, with a tapered stern instead of a broad transom will show much less tendency to yaw and broach. In either type, the tendency to yaw can be reduced by suddenly cutting power as a following wave approaches the transom. The sudden slowing allows the wave to pass rapidly forward, giving it less time to exert forces on the stern.

It may be impossible to prevent broaching when on the downhill side of a cycloidal wave. In this position the bow will be deeply buried; the stern will be high, perhaps so high that both rudder and propeller are out of solid water. The boat is then completely out of control and at the mercy of the elements.

(2) If excessive speed is attained while running, it is quite possible to drive the bow under down the steep front face of a cycloidal wave. If the bow section has little or no flare and little overhang, its buoyancy will not increase rapidly with the depth submerged. As the bow moves rapidly down the steep wave front, it may go completely under, catching in the water while momentum carries the boat up and over in a movement known as *pitchpoling*. The disastrous effects of pitchpoling are too apparent to need comment. Alert helmsmanship, slow speed, and heavy stern drags are needed to reduce the danger of pitchpoling.

Heavy stern drags will reduce the tendency to yaw and to pitchpole. Heavy lines, perhaps with many simple overhand or figure-eight knots may be payed out astern. If a tender is along, it may be flooded and used as a drag. A floating tender, however, unless on a very long painter, may become a dangerous liability in heavy going. As the boat slows on striking a sea, the momentum of the tender can bring it up against the transom or actually aboard, with undesirable results. If the tender cannot be safely towed, it must be cut adrift.

## 5.12   Running Narrow Inlets

Many sheltered coves and rivers are connected to the sea by narrow inlets where the water may shoal rapidly. Shoaling is generally not gradual but is interrupted by bars or sand deposits that create an irregular bottom situation. As the deep-water cycloids approach the shallow inlet, they will change to steep waves with breaking crests. Because of the bars and the close proximity of the sides of the inlet, the transition will not be regular as is seen on a long, gradually shoaling beach. Instead, a confused, irregular wave pattern may exist in the inlet, the heaviest breakers indicating the presence of bars.

Although narrow inlets are run without incident hundreds of times every day, they call for the greatest skill in boat handling and an intimate knowledge of local conditions. Narrow inlets present all degrees of difficulty, ranging from that which is hazardous in all weather conditions to those which are readily passable except in severe storms.

The technique of running inlets cannot be learned from a book. Local knowledge and experience with a veteran are essential before one can safely assume responsibility for running one of the more difficult inlets. If caught outside in a storm, one may be faced with a hard choice. Running an inlet is tempting because only a few hundred yards of turbulent water may separate the open sea from the calm of a sheltered bay. Disaster can lurk in this short distance, however, and the alternative, even leading to heaving-to in open water, should be carefully weighed before the final decision is made.

Recommendations for a particular inlet, found on the chart and in the Coast Pilot, should be weighed in the light of the weather conditions existing at the time the decision must be made.

Sailboats and auxiliaries should at all times avoid inlets with breaking seas. These boats lack the maneuverability and propeller drive needed to successfully negotiate the broken water. Similarly, a powerboat unable to make 10-15 knots in smooth water should avoid breaking inlets, unless the hull has been specially designed for heavy surf.

In principle, inlet running is not difficult. One lies to outside the breakers to study the seas and pick a course that will avoid the most confused areas. In making the choice, remember that the breakers are actually larger than they appear from the sea.

An adequate sea anchor or drogue is made ready on the heaviest line available with the bitter end made fast to the most substantial stern fastening. A trip line will be needed for the drogue.

With the course determined, the boat is allowed to run onto the back surface of one of the smaller waves that occur occasionally mixed with the larger. As soon as forward motion is established, the drogue is streamed astern by the trip line. Nothing else must be towed astern. A tender is almost certain to board the powerboat over the transom or to foul the propeller with a slack line. A tender must be cut adrift before attempting a breaking inlet in bad weather.

The helmsman must now keep the boat on the back of the chosen wave as it races shoreward. If he feels the boat being pulled back by the return flow, he must apply power vigorously and promptly. To fall behind is to be caught and *pooped* by the following breaker, which will be close on the stern. If the boat surges forward and up toward the breaking crest, power must be taken off promptly and the drogue set. Too much forward progress will result in a pitchpole or a broach. In some cases power can be used advantageously with the drogue set. This has the advantage of providing the rudder with a powerful stream of water, which greatly increases the steering action. Under no circumstance should the propeller be reversed while running an inlet. This can only lead to loss of rudder action and almost certain broaching.

Eventually the wave crest will break just ahead of the boat which, with sufficient power, will be able to overcome the backward flow of water at the base of the wave. Calmer waters will soon be encountered, and the critical phase of inlet running is over.

It is possible to take a properly designed small boat through breaking surf to shore under oars alone. This should never be attempted in the dinghy type now so popular as yacht tenders. The Coast Guard surf-boat design is, however, well adapted for landing through heavy breakers. Because of the lack of large amounts of forward power, the technique described must be modified when under oars. In a rowed boat one must proceed slowly, exerting every effort to prevent the boat from being carried forward by the breaking seas. Safety lies in having the crests break and pass rapidly ahead of a nearly stationary boat.

Surf boats are frequently brought in stern first because in this position the greatest force on the oars can be exerted seaward. Between breakers the boat will be gently backed shoreward. When a breaker approaches, all oars will be pulled strongly seaward. Prompt action with rudder or steering sweep will avert a broach. This process will be repeated until calm water or the shore is gained. The boat will take on water and must be bailed, but skillful handling will avoid a broach, which will immediately overwhelm a small open boat of the rowing type.

## 5.13   Heavy Weather Procedures

A well-built, skillfully handled powerboat can weather a hard blow and high seas if there is no equipment failure. Reliable power must be available throughout a storm, maximum buoyancy must be maintained at all times, and all crewmen must be kept on board. All of these requirements are obvious, yet many boats leave port with a complete disregard for any one or all of them.

Marine service is hard on all kinds of equipment; constant vigilance is required to keep it in proper working order. Too many accident reports indicate disaster resulting from a missing or a faulty bilge pump, failing engine, and so on. Particular attention should be paid to the power plant and all of its accessories. Fuel tanks and lines must be kept clean. Heavy weather can stir up sediment and scale that, resting quietly on the tank bottom in calm weather, clog a carburetor jet just at the time when full power is most needed. Flying spray and sloshing bilge water may soak an ignition system and stop an engine at a critical moment. Fuel, thought to be adequate for the trip, may run out at an awkward moment. These, and many other failures, can be averted by regular inspections and preventive maintenance. In heavy weather a reliable power plant can mean the difference between life and death. Give it the attention it deserves.

Any boat in a sea will ship a lot of spray and may occasionally take on board quantities of solid water. A small cockpit can be filled without serious loss of buoyancy, and it will rapidly empty if fitted with large, crossed, self-bailing scuppers. The emptying process can be hastened by vigorous bucket action by members of the crew. Some water will inevitably trickle below, but this can be taken care of by an efficient bilge pump.

Every through-hull fitting should be provided with a sea cock to prevent a major leak in case of a hose or pipe failure with the working of the hull in heavy seas. Unfortunately a sea cock does not guarantee watertight integrity. Most sea cocks have conical barrels which may get jammed in the seat through excessive tightening or disuse. There is little time to free a stuck sea cock when a full stream of water is gushing out from a broken pipe. Sea cocks should be inspected regularly and kept in good working order. As a backup an assortment of wooden plugs should be readily available to stem a major flow of water until more permanent repairs can be made.

In a following sea with a stalled engine, it may be desirable to plug the exhaust pipes to prevent flooding the cylinders with seawater. If flooding occurs, the engine cannot be started without a major overhaul. Plugging exhaust pipes low down on a transom in a seaway is no picnic, but it can be done.

The numerous large windows on the modern power cruiser increases its vulnerability to flooding through broken panes. The impact of heavy seas is quite capable of breaking glass of ordinary thickness. Some protection is afforded by canvas dodgers covering the larger areas. Some cautious skippers carry plywood shields, which can be fastened over all windows not needed for running the ship.

Any hull or superstructure damage should be attended to promptly. Sprung planks can be stuffed with all sorts of material. Boards, gratings, and the like can be used for internal shoring against larger defects.

A man overboard in a heavy sea is a most serious matter even though he may be wearing flotation gear which will keep him from drowning immediately. Backing in a heavy sea is out of the question, and conditions may prevent the boat being turned around safely for an attempted rescue. To prevent this situation every man outside should wear a safety harness hooked to some substantial part of the vessel with a strong line. Double-snap hooks permit a second attachment before the release of the first. If adequate fastenings are not a part of the boat, they should be installed so that a man can reach any part of the vessel without unsnapping.

The foregoing sections may discourage some from acquiring and operating small powerboats. Such is not our intent. Although extreme danger rarely exists in the waters normally utilized by pleasure craft, it may occur, and an author would be negligent if he failed to point out the worst possibilities. One does not buy fire insurance because his house will almost certainly catch fire. No more does the small-boat skipper learn about heavy weather operations because he is almost certainly going to be overwhelmed. He will in all probability go through life needing neither the insurance nor the knowledge. Should disaster strike, his survival may well depend upon the thoroughness of his preparations.

CHAPTER **6**

# Deck Seamanship

## 6.01 Nautical Arts and Skills

Many nautical arts and skills must be learned by any boat owner desiring to maintain his vessel "ship shape and Bristol fashion" and intending to operate her in a safe and efficient manner. For many boatmen the acquisition of the knowledge and the ability to do the many tasks well is an important part of the fun of owning a boat. Others are satisfied to learn only the bare essentials, leaving as many items as possible to professionals. Some of the essentials involved in proper maintenance have been given elsewhere in this book and will not be repeated here.

Proficiency in deck seamanship must be acquired by anyone who is to be in command of a vessel under way. Simple considerations of safety require that the needed equipment be on board and in proper order. The skipper must be able, in time of need, to use this equipment to best advantage.

## 6.02 Rope

Rope has always been an indispensable part of boating. It was once used to hold parts of the boat together. Today, sailboats still require large amounts of rope, in a variety of sizes. The powerboat operator requires much less rope, but his need is no less acute.

Rope is *cordage*, made from a variety of materials, including wire, and obtainable in many sizes. The smaller sizes, known as *small stuff*, include thread, string, cord, yarn, and marlin, which is a tarred hemp of small diameter. All of the larger sizes come on board as rope but assume other names as they are put to work. Thus a rope may become an anchor *line* or *rode*, a *sheet*, or a *halyard*. In a few cases the word *rope* is retained, as in *bell rope* or *boltrope* (part of a sail).

Many types of natural fibers have been used in rope manufacture. Cotton, linen, sisal, and hemp are still used occasionally for special purposes, but *manila* is the most satisfactory natural fiber for most marine applications. Manila is made from the 10–15-foot-long fibers of the abaca plant, grown primarily, as the name indicates, in the Philippines.

Natural fibers are now being rapidly displaced by synthetics, notably nylon and Dacron, with polyethylene and polypropylene finding more limited use. Synthetics are stronger, smoother, and more pliable than any of the natural fibers. Prices for a given breaking strength are competitive with those for good manila, particularly when the greater durability of the synthetics is considered.

Stainless steel wire rope is rapidly displacing galvanized steel wire rope for most marine applications. The initial cost of stainless steel is high but is usually warranted since over many years there will be no appreciable loss of strength through corrosion. This affords a continued high factor of safety and greatly lengthens the time between replacements.

All *laid* or twisted rope is made by twisting the small fibers into *yarns,* several yarns into a *strand,* and either three or four strands into a rope. Most rope for marine use is three-strand and right-handed, meaning that the three strands spiral clockwise when viewed from the cut end. To prevent unlaying, fibers are twisted into yarns right-handed, yarns into strands left-handed, and strands into rope right-handed.

As normally produced, synthetic fibers are so soft and flexible that a rope readily becomes unlaid at a cut end in spite of the reverse twisting of the fibers. This tendency can be reduced by *stabilizing* (treating) the completed rope to give the fibers a permanent set. Wire rope is also often *preformed,* or given a permanent spiral twist, for the same reason.

Braided rope is more flexible and less subject to kinking than a simple laid rope. Braid is somewhat more expensive than laid rope but is frequently used on sailboats, particularly for the mainsheet.

## 6.03   Strength of Rope

Table 6-1 gives average breaking strengths of good quality ropes made from a variety of fibers.

Remember, however, that many factors besides the numbers given determine the allowable loading of any rope. Sharp bends over cleats or chocks, deterioration from age or abuse, and the presence of knots or splices are among the factors operating to reduce the loads that may safely be applied. The loads as given are ultimate, or breaking strengths. Normal working loads should not exceed one fifth of these values for manila and one quarter for the synthetics.

Note that the table gives rope sizes in both diameter and circumference. Both systems are in common use, requiring care to insure that the proper strength is being obtained.

As the table shows, nylon is the strongest material for a given size. Like the other synthetics nylon is quite resistant to most chemicals, and to the bacteria and molds that attack natural fibers. Nylon is resistant to abrasion, but it is somewhat weakened by exposure to the ultraviolet rays of strong sunlight. This weakening is of no concern in the larger sizes, since the ultraviolet cannot penetrate into the interior of the rope.

Nylon is characterized by a very high elasticity, stretching as much as 40 percent of its original length before breaking. This elasticity is an undesir-

**TABLE 6-1**

**Breaking Strength of Ropes**

| Size, In. | | | | Pounds | | |
| Diam. | Circ. | Manila | Nylon | Dacron | Poly-ethylene | Poly-propylene |
|---|---|---|---|---|---|---|
| ¼ | ¾ | 600 | 1850 | 1700 | 1150 | 1700 |
| ⅜ | 1⅛ | 1350 | 4000 | 3600 | 2400 | 3400 |
| ½ | 1½ | 2650 | 7100 | 6000 | 4000 | 5300 |
| ⅝ | 2 | 4400 | 10500 | 9000 | 6000 | 7600 |
| ¾ | 2¼ | 5400 | 14200 | 12000 | 9000 | 10000 |
| ⅞ | 2¾ | 7700 | 19000 | 16000 | 12000 | 13000 |
| 1 | 3 | 9000 | 24600 | 20000 | 15000 | 16500 |
| 1¼ | 3¾ | 13500 | 38000 | 24500 | 21000 | 22000 |
| 1½ | 4½ | 18500 | 55000 | 36000 | 29000 | 31000 |

able feature in some applications, as for halyards or sheets on sail boats. Nylon is unsurpassed for anchor or mooring lines where the great elasticity helps to absorb the shocks of heavy wave motions.

Any rope under great tension can be dangerous because if it parts, the loose ends may fly back with considerable force, seriously injuring personnel. In this particular respect, the great elasticity of nylon makes it somewhat more dangerous than manila. No one should stand in line with any rope under tension.

Dacron has nearly the breaking strength of nylon, but it is nowhere near as elastic. This makes Dacron the line of choice for sheets and halyards or any other application where stretch is undesirable. Dacron which has good resistance to abrasion and chemical attack, is little affected by sunlight. It is immune to attack by living organisms such as bacteria or marine borers.

Polyethylene is a slippery material somewhat lighter than water. Because it will float free of underwater propellers polyethylene is frequently used as a ski tow line or as a dinghy *painter*. Polypropylene is not as slippery as polyethylene, and it is sometimes used for a mooring line because of its elasticity, which is somewhat greater than manila.

Wet rope may have a breaking strength as much as 10 percent greater than the same rope when it is dry, but this fact should not be considered when procuring rope. Most rope also shortens when wet, sometimes as much as one inch per foot. A wet rope is capable of exerting great forces if it is stretched between nonyielding fastenings when dry. Fittings may be pulled out of masts by lines that have been left too tight when dry.

## 6.04    Permanent Moorings

In some areas the boat is best left at a permanent anchorage or *mooring*. Every part of a permanent mooring must be exceptionally strong and not subject to rapid deterioration from corrosion or attack by marine organisms. Some moorings are taken up when the boat is hauled for the winter, many are checked only every two or three years, and some stay down until some component fails.

The mushroom anchor (Fig. 6-1) is designed specifically for permanent moorings. The mushroom is not satisfactory on a rocky bottom, but its weight and shape cause it to sink into sand or mud. Four or five fathoms of heavy chain shackled to the mushroom serve the double purpose of keeping the

**FIGURE 6-1** A mushroom anchor used for a permanent mooring. A heavy bulb is sometimes put on the shank to increase holding power.

mooring line off the bottom and of making the pull on the anchor more nearly horizontal (Fig. 6-2). Large diameter nylon is the preferred connection between the chain and the boat. If manila must be used, it should be treated to resist attack by marine organisms.

The length or *scope* of the mooring line will depend on local conditions, such as the kind of bottom, anticipated extreme wind forces, and the amount of swing allowable in the anchorage. Whatever the conditions, an increased scope will increase the holding power of any anchor. Normally scope should not be less than five times the depth of water at high tide.

**FIGURE 6-2** Schematic diagram of a permanent mooring. The scope of 3D must be considered an absolute minimum.

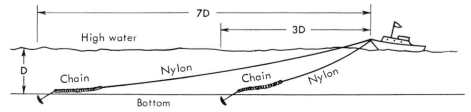

Table 6-2 gives suggested mushroom anchor weights and sizes of nylon lines suitable for permanent moorings.

Many permanent moorings are built around large blocks of concrete, old engine blocks, or other pieces of discarded iron, instead of a mushroom anchor. Many of these odd shapes hold by dead weight rather than by digging into the bottom, but they have the advantage of resisting pull about equally in all directions, while a mushroom anchor may have to reset itself after a strong reverse pull.

**TABLE 6-2**

**Mushroom Anchor Weights in Pounds**

| L.O.A. Feet | Boat Type | | | Nylon Diam. In. |
|---|---|---|---|---|
| | Power | Racing Sail | Cruising Sail | |
| 20-25 | 225 | 125 | 175 | ⅞ |
| 25-30 | 275 | 175 | 225 | 1 |
| 30-35 | 300 | 200 | 250 | 1⅛ |
| 35-40 | 350 | 300 | 350 | 1¼ |
| 40-45 | 450 | 400 | 450 | 1½ |

## 6.05   Mooring at a Dock

Strictly, a *dock* or *slip* is the water space between *piers* or *wharves* built for receiving and securing vessels. Through general usage, however, the terms have also come to refer to the structures to which boats are attached. These terms will be so used here, except in those cases where there may be some confusion.

A temporary tie-up, as for supplies, is readily made by any one of a number of hitches put around whatever cleats or bits are available on the wharf. Rubbing will be prevented by appropriately placed bumpers. A permanent mooring at a dock requires careful planning to permit free movement of the boat with the tides without contact between boat and wharf when the lines are slack.

Figure 6-3 shows the lines that can be used in tieing up alongside a pier. All of the lines shown will seldom be rigged because there is a considerable duplication of purpose. The lines actually used will depend primarily on the location of the bits and cleats on the dock.

Breast lines prevent sideways movement, spring lines limit fore and aft movement, while bow and stern lines may serve both purposes. Many skippers fail to appreciate the advantages of spring lines, particularly in localties where there are large tides. Spring lines can accommodate large tidal differences with relatively less slack than is needed in the shorter lines, and this reduces motion in the slip with less danger of taut lines at a very low tide.

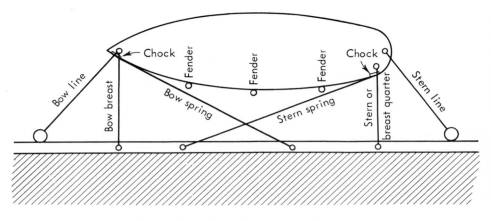

FIGURE 6-3   Lines that may be used in tieing up to a pier.

A common mooring arrangement consists of two bow lines, two quarter breast lines, and one springline (Fig. 6-4). When a regular slip is assigned, lines of proper length can be made up with eye splices and with chafing gear at the points of greatest wear. On leaving the slip the lines may be taken on board or left on the wharf.

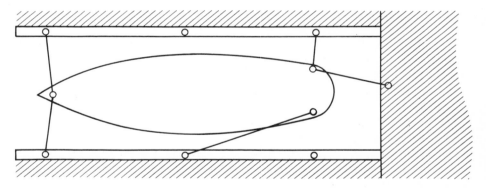

FIGURE 6-4   One arrangement for tieing up in a slip. In tidewater all lines must have sufficient slack to avoid becoming taut at tidal extremes.

## 6.06   Ground Tackle

As marinas with slips become more numerous, skippers tend to anchor only briefly to fish or swim. This has led to a neglect of *ground tackle*, which consists of anchor and anchor line, to the point where few boats have the equipment needed for anchoring in heavy weather.

A common mistake is to think that a mooring between piers is inherently safer in a storm than riding to an anchor. The wharf structure itself may be

94

more vulnerable to injury than the boat, mooring cleats may fail under the strain of a gale, and short mooring lines lack the shock-absorbing power of a long anchor line. The high tides associated with severe storms may tear boats from their moorings or allow them to ride up onto the pier. Failure of a single line will allow the boat to beat against the dock structure or to come down on top of a stake or pile. These are the reasons why many experienced boatmen will leave a slip to seek a protected anchorage with plenty of swinging room when strong winds and high tides are forecast.

Small boats usually operate in relatively shallow water close to land, thus increasing the need for adequate ground tackle and the ability to rig it quickly in time of need. In a moderate storm a boat can often head into the wind under reduced power, to take the seas on or near the bow, and a sailboat can heave-to. Under extreme conditions, however, anchoring may be the only safe way to ride out a storm. In a very strong wind the engine may lack power to provide steerage-way, or the sails of a sailboat may not be able to withstand the force of a gale. When there is a possibility of being driven ashore, anchoring may save the day.

Like other safety equipment, ground tackle should be carried well in excess of minimum requirements. There are several important points to consider in choosing ground tackle: the anchor itself, the attachment of anchor to the line, the kind and lengths of anchor line, the way the line is brought on board, the method of making the line fast, and the provision for securing the inboard or *bitter end* of the line. Ground tackle will be not stronger than its weakest link.

## 6.07   Anchors

Even though a yachtsman confines his cruising to a limited area, he will eventually be anchoring under a wide variety of conditions. A light anchor or *lunch hook* may suffice for a short period with a crew on board, but it would be hopelessly inadequate for an unattended boat over a period of days or weeks. A *general-purpose* anchor serving in all ordinary blows must be replaced by a *storm anchor* for extreme conditions.

Bottom conditions or *holding ground* will include soft mud, sticky mud, sand, eelgrass, kelp, gravel, rocks, and coral. There is no universal anchor best adapted for all of types of bottoms, and no small boat can carry the variety of anchors needed to cope most effectively with all conditions. Any anchors carried will represent a compromise best adapted to the bottom conditions most frequently encountered.

Figure 6-5 shows the principal parts of the traditional, old-fashioned or *kedge* anchor. The basic type is available in a number of modifications, each designed for maximum effectiveness in a particular type of bottom. A wide

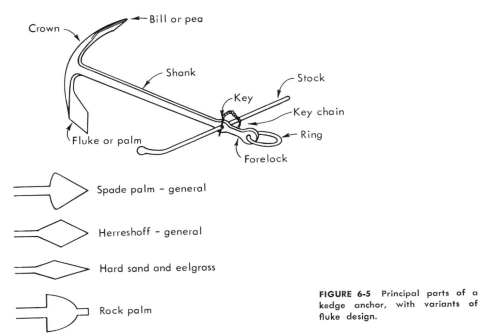

**FIGURE 6-5** Principal parts of a kedge anchor, with variants of fluke design.

fluke is obviously desirable in soft mud of poor holding power, but it may have difficulty in penetrating into a hard bottom. A sharp, narrow fluke will dig in through eelgrass, kelp, or gravel to bear on the solid ground beneath, but the small flukes will have little holding power in mud or ooze. The designs most usually carried are compromises between the extremes.

The kedge anchor is very effective on rocky bottoms, sometimes to the point where recovery is difficult or impossible. When a kedge is used among rocks, it is desirable to attach a buoyed *trip line* to the crown. A vertical pull on the trip line may dislodge an anchor that has resisted all attempts at recovery with the anchor line.

Any kedge anchor will set with one fluke exposed, and it is quite possible for wind and currents to swing the boat in such a way as to put one or more turns of the anchor *rode* around this fluke. When an anchor is thus *fouled*, a pull on the rode will tend to extract the buried fluke rather than to bury it deeper as is the case of a pull on a free rode.

The U.S. Navy uses a *stockless* anchor whose shank can be pulled up into a hawse-pipe, so that the flukes ride snugly against the ship's bow plates. The Navy type cannot foul because there are no exposed flukes to catch the rode. Navy anchors are relatively heavy for a given holding power and hence are not generally suitable for use on small boats.

The most popular anchors for small-boat use are known collectively as *patented* anchors, (Fig. 6-6). The *plow* (Fig. 6-6A) is a single-fluke anchor

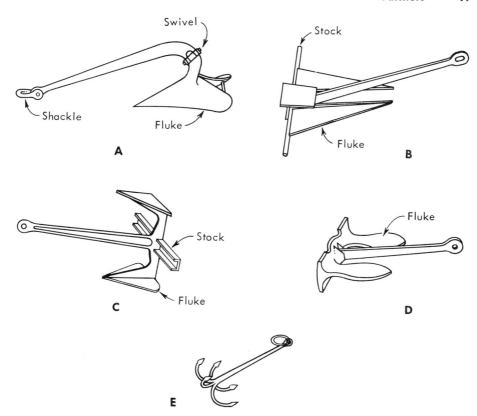

**FIGURE 6-6** Commonly used types of anchors: (A) plow, (B) Danforth, (C) Northhill, (D) Navy stockless, (E) grapnel. The latter is used only for anchoring small skiffs or for dragging for articles lost overboard.

that digs in well and deeply and will not foul. It is, however, a most miserable anchor to stow on board. Other patented anchors such as the Danforth (Fig. 6-6B) dig in well after the flukes are caught and tend to dig in more deeply as the pull increases. It is sometimes difficult to get these anchors to catch, particularly if the bottom is hard or covered with shells.

Preferably cruising boats should carry three anchors. One of these should be a heavy storm anchor, possibly a kedge weighing 1½–2 pounds per foot of length overall or an extra-heavy patented type. Although the storm anchor will seldom be used, it must be stowed where it is obtainable, probably in rough weather, without a major disarrangement. When stowed it should be securely lashed to prevent free motion in heavy going. A heavy anchor can cause serious hull damage if it can move freely in lumpy seas.

The regular anchor may be a smaller kedge or one of the patented anchors. Holding power-weight ratios vary considerably with design, so specific recommendations of the manufacturer should be consulted. Many skippers carry a light anchor of about one-half pound per foot loa or even less for temporary use while fishing or swimming. Handling and stowage problems are almost as great as with a regular anchor, with a considerable loss of holding power. If stowage space permits, the third anchor should be a second general-purpose anchor, rather than a lighter lunch hook.

Heavy anchors are useless unless there are available lines of adequate strength and length. One heavy anchor rode is not enough for a cruising boat. An anchor line may part or be rendered ineffective in any one of many ways. For example, if a hung anchor must be abandoned, a considerable length of line will also be lost. Anchor line is a most important part of the safety equipment carried on board. Stowage must be well away from batteries or other sources of corrosive vapors that may insidiously weaken the fibers.

An *anchor bend* or a *bowline* is commonly used to attach a fiber line to the anchor (Fig. 6-7). Over a protracted period serious chafing may occur, which is best prevented by the use of a metal-to-metal connection. An *eye splice* is made around a metal thimble which is then shackled to the anchor ring. The shackle pin should be wired in to prevent backing out. A similar shackle will be used to attach an anchor to a chain.

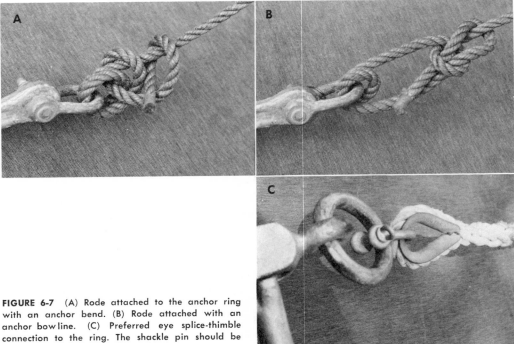

FIGURE 6-7   (A) Rode attached to the anchor ring with an anchor bend. (B) Rode attached with an anchor bowline. (C) Preferred eye splice-thimble connection to the ring. The shackle pin should be wired in for security.

## 6.08    Setting and Weighing Anchor

When preparing to anchor, the helmsman brings the boat's head up into the prevailing wind or current and removes all driving power. As the boat comes to a complete rest in the water, the anchor is put, *not thrown* over the side and lowered to the bottom. Anchor line is payed out as the boat falls away, assisted perhaps with some reverse power if the wind is light. The forward deck hand, holding the line, will feel the anchor scrape along the bottom until it suddenly sets and digs in. Line is then payed out until the desired scope is obtained, taking care to prevent any slack that might foul the propeller.

After the line has been secured, the boat will swing to a position determined by wind and current. Bearings should then be taken on prominent landmarks to establish an accurate position. When anchoring for overnight, be sure to pick objects that will be visible after dark. Any change in the bearings will indicate a dragging anchor.

Any anchor holds best when the pull on its shank is horizontal, or nearly so. Holding power is, therefore, increased as the scope of the line is increased. A scope of at least five times the depth of water at high tide is desirable for an overnight stay in the average anchorage. A scope of seven times the depth will increase the holding power and also the skipper's peace of mind.

A more nearly horizontal pull can be obtained by adding weight near the outboard end of the line. Two or three fathoms of heavy chain shackled directly to the anchor are useful and also serve to keep the soft fiber line off abrading bottom material. If a heavy blow comes, it may be undesirable to raise the anchor in order to rig a weight. Under these conditions a weight may be shackled around the anchor line and lowered to the desired position with a light auxiliary line.

Anchoring with a long scope requires a considerable amount of swinging room, because wind and currents may move the boat around a circle whose diameter is roughly twice the scope of the anchor rode. Two anchors properly placed may be used to hold a boat in a nearly fixed position with a sharply restricted swinging radius even though each scope is long for good holding power. To set two anchors, the approach is made into the prevailing current (Fig. 6-8 position 1), with all ground tackle ready for letting go two anchors from the bow. At position 2 one anchor (A) is let go, and line is payed out as the boat moves forward about twice the amount of scope desired to position 3. If power is required to reach 3, the helmsman and the forward deckhand must maintain utmost vigilance to insure that the anchor line to A is kept clear of the propeller. At 3 the first anchor is set by snubbing the line and surging ahead under moderate power. When A is set, B is dropped. The boat is now backed down to position 4, about midway between the anchors, with the deckhand paying out line to B and taking in line from A. Again care must be taken to avoid fouling the propeller. At position 4 the second anchor is set, the two lines

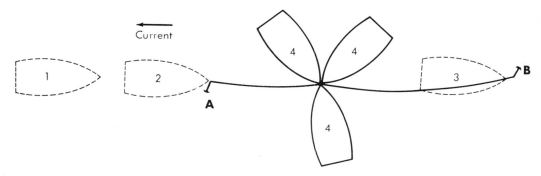

**FIGURE 6-8**   Mooring sequence in setting two anchors.

are adjusted to some slack and are then secured. The boat will now respond to wind and currents by swinging on a short radius around the midpoint of the two anchor lines.

An anchor is raised by bringing the bow of the boat directly over it so that the pull will be nearly vertical, taking care that there is no slack line as the boat moves forward. A good hard pull will usually suffice to break out the anchor, but occasionally extreme measures will be required. In some cases the anchor may be run out under power by running the boat around it in a large circle, thus subjecting the buried flukes to pulls from a number of directions. This maneuver may sometimes be used deliberately to foul a kedge anchor and thus aid in its removal. An anchor can sometimes be broken out by utilizing the buoyant properties of the boat. With all of the crew forward the line is brought in as taut as possible and cleated securely. When all of the crew go aft, the change in trim may exert a force considerably in excess of that obtainable on a direct pull. On a rising tide the same principle may be applied by snubbing the line taut and waiting patiently for the buoyant forces to break out the anchor. On rare occasions it may be necessary to abandon an anchor.

When two anchors have been used it is usually best to first retrieve the one to leeward. Thus if the current remained as shown in Fig. 6-8, rode B would be payed out and A taken in until the boat fell back to position 2. Anchor A would then be broken out and taken on board. When A is secured the boat is brought ahead to position 3, with the deckhand taking in rode B as fast as it is made available to him. At 3 anchor B is brought on board and secured, and the boat is put under way.

## 6.09   Deck Hardware

The strength and suitability of deck hardware should match that of the ground tackle. The anchor line will be led on board through a *chock*, and it will then be secured to a cleat, bitt, or samson post (Fig. 6-9). Chocks are

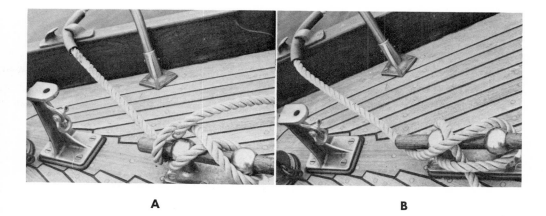

A                                                  B

**FIGURE 6-9** Deck hardware for handling anchor and mooring lines. Note the chafing gear at the chock. In the correct sequence (A), the line under tension goes on the cleat first. In the incorrect sequence (B), a strong tension may prevent the release of the line from the cleat.

made with smooth surfaces, but even so they are capable of seriously abrading and weakening a line under tension in a surprisingly short time. In a heavy blow *chafing gear* of canvas or other protective material should be wrapped around the line at points of wear. If severe conditions are sustained, it may be desirable to "change the nip" by adjusting the line so that the wear points are shifted. Sharp bends at chocks should be avoided at any time, particularly when the line is under heavy strain.

The anchor line should lead to the cleat at a level no higher than the base of the cleat. A single turn around the cleat, followed by a single half-hitch around the horn of the cleat, is usually sufficient to hold even the slippery synthetics. The free end of the line must be the last to go on the cleat. If the *working part*, which is the part under tension, is looped on last, it may be impossible to get sufficient slack to cast off the line.

A surprising amount of ground tackle is lost by allowing the *bitter end* of the line to go over the side. This may be prevented by permanently attaching this end of the line to one of the main strength members, as by an eyebolt into the keel.

## 6.10    Whipping

A landlubber will usually prevent a rope from unlaying at a cut end by tying a knot. This practice is unacceptable on board a vessel, not only because it is unsightly but because it prevents the rope from running through blocks. All rope ends in marine service should be *whipped* with a tight wrapping of small stuff. There are many variations of whipping, some quite fancy. The method shown in Fig. 6-10 is simple, reliable, and adequate for all ordinary applications.

Whipping is started with the rope held in the left hand, cut end to the

**FIGURE 6-10** Common method of whipping a rope end. After the loop has been pulled taut under the whipping, the ends are trimmed flush.

right. A loop of the whipping cord is placed along the rope, starting about three rope diameters from the end. Close turns are now wound on tightly for about two diameters. The final end is tucked through the initial loop and pulled part way under the whipping. Both loops are pulled tight and the free ends cut close.

The soft fibers of synthetic ropes will fray out down to the whipping to form an unsightly puff and bulge that will not feed easily into a block (Fig. 6-15, B and C). Fraying can be prevented by applying enough heat to the cut ends to lightly fuse the fine fibers together. In a sheltered spot the heat from a match will suffice to fuse the ends of lines up to about one-half inch in diameter. A hot soldering iron is more easily controlled and produces neater fusing than is usually achieved with an open flame.

## 6.11   Knots, Hitches, and Splices

To be useful a rope must be attached to something by some sort of a knot, hitch, or splice. A few basic definitions with reference to Fig. 6-11 will be needed before the general discussion.

> *Standing part:* the part of the rope under tension, leading up to the knot but not used in the tying.
> *Bight:* the half-loop formed when a rope is doubled back on itself.
> *Turn:* one complete turn or loop around some object, perhaps another part of the rope itself.
> *Round turn:* two turns or loops around an object.
> *Bend:* a knot uniting two ropes.
> *Hitch:* a knot securing a rope to some other type of object, as a pile or bollard.
> *Splice:* a union of two ropes, or of a rope with itself, made by interweaving strands.

On the long cruises made by the old windjammers, many of the seamen spent long hours working with rope, which led to the development of many varieties of knots and splices. Fortunately the practical sailor need learn only

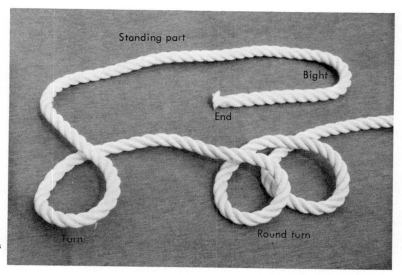

**FIGURE 6-11** Nautical terms for the parts of a rope.

a few of these unless he is interested in knots as a hobby. Far more important is to learn a few basic knots so well that they can be tied under all kinds of adverse conditions: in the dark, on a pitching deck, and with the rope presented in all orientations. The time may come when the safety of the vessel and crew may depend on the rapid tying of a proper knot or on releasing one that has been pulled tight by heavy tension. Any knot that becomes so hard that it must be pried apart with a marlinspike, or cut, is a dangerous and probably weak knot.

Any knot will weaken a rope to some extent because of the sharp bends required to form it. A knot will fail at some percentage of the breaking strength of the unknotted rope. This percentage is called the *efficiency* of the knot. Most knots, including the reef and the bowline, have efficiencies of about 50 percent. Splices, which do not have the sharp bends of a knot, may have efficiencies of 90–95 percent.

## 6.12    Stopper Knots

A stopper knot is used to prevent the end of a line from running through a block or a ring. The simplest stopper is the *overhand knot* (Fig. 6-12A), which is the first part of the usual square and bow knots. A turn is taken and the free end wrapped around the standing part. The knot is completed by pulling it tight.

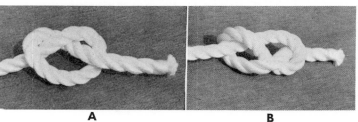

**FIGURE 6-12** Two common stopper knots: (A) simple overhand; (B) figure-of-eight.

**A**                    **B**

The *figure-of-eight knot* (Fig. 6-12B) makes a better stopper. It is a larger knot and is easier to open than the overhand after being jammed into a block. To tie a figure-of-eight take a turn, wrap the free end around the standing part, bring it through the loop, and pull it tight.

## 6.13    Square or Reef Knot

The square knot is commonly, but mistakenly, thought to be safe and foolproof, suitable for almost any application. In fact it must be recognized as a treacherous knot that has cost the lives of some who have trusted to it. In spite of its faults, the square knot has many uses on shipboard and must be learned. It will be used in all applications where a simple knot without extreme reliability is required to join either the two ends of a line or two lines of equal size. The square knot is used in tying in reefs, whence its alternate name. When reefing the knot is frequently tied as a *slipped hitch* (Fig. 6-13B) to permit a rapid release.

**A**                                                                    **B**

**FIGURE 6-13**   (A) Square knot formed but not pulled tight. Note that the two free ends come out on the same side of the knot. (B) A square knot tied as a slipped hitch by doubling back one of the free ends through the loop.

Figure 6-13A illustrates a correctly tied square knot. Each free end must come out of the loop alongside of its own standing part. If it does not, a *granny knot* (Fig. 6-14A) will result. The granny knot is completely unreliable and must never be used. Learn the square knot thoroughly so that you will never accidentally tie a granny.

One objection to the use of the square knot is the difficulty of untieing it after it has been under a heavy strain, particularly when wet. A more serious objection is its failure to hold under all circumstances, a trait most marked when the knot is used to join ropes of different diameters. A square knot may *upset* (Fig. 6-14B) to form two half-hitches around an almost straight rope. This configuration, which is most likely to form with two ropes of quite different diameters, has almost no holding power.

A                                    B

FIGURE 6-14  (A) A granny knot. (B) An upset square knot.

The tendency of a square knot to slip or upset can be greatly reduced by *seizing* each free end back to its own standing part by wrapping tightly with small stuff. When this is deemed necessary to insure reliability, it is probably preferable to use the more reliable *sheet bend* or *carrick bend*.

## 6.14   The Bowline

The *bowline*, sometimes spelled bowlin or bowling, is without doubt the sailor's most valuable knot. It has been called, with reason, the king of knots. The chief reason for this importance is the fact that a bowline will not slip. A simple bowline will make a loop that will not close. If the standing part is run through the loop formed by a bowline, a *running bowline* will be formed. This knot will not tighten down on the standing part.

A bowline can be untied even after it has been under tension and while wet. Any knot will present some difficulties under these conditions, but the bowline can be untied more readily than any other knot of comparable holding power.

Every sailor must learn to tie the bowline under the most adverse circumstances. Figure 6-15 illustrates three steps in forming a bowline. Hold the standing part of the rope in the left hand and make a small *overhand* loop.

FIGURE 6-15  Tieing sequence in forming a bowline. When completed as in (C), the knot is pulled tight to insure holding.

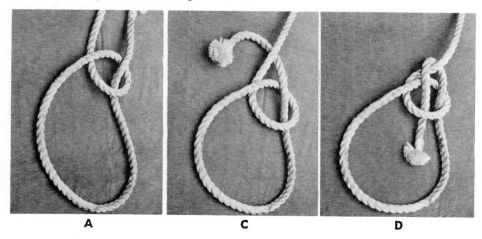

A                      C                      D

Pass the free end *up* through the loop (A) down and behind the standing part (B) and then down through the loop (C). The knot thus formed is pulled tight for holding. When the knot has been mastered under ideal conditions, extend your skill by learning to tie it in a variety of positions and with your eyes closed.

## 6.15    Bends

Many bends have been devised, but only two need be learned by the recreational boatman. The *carrick bend* (Fig. 6-16) is useful for joining ropes of different diameters, particularly if one of them is relatively large. It is a strong knot because there are no sharp bends in its construction. A carrick bend will not upset like a square knot, and it is much less likely to slip. If the ultimate in security is desired, the free ends of a carrick bend may be seized to their respective standing parts. The carrick bend can be tied by careful reference to Fig. 6-16, following exactly the sequence of over and under. It will seldom be needed, but when it is, the need may be acute. Practice should be continued until it can be tied without hesitation.

The *sheet bend* (Fig. 6-17) also can be used to join ropes of different sizes. A careful study of the illustration will show that the sheet bend is really a bowline tied with two pieces of rope instead of one. The sheet bend has the good holding power of the bowline, and it can be untied with relative ease. Some may find it advantageous to learn the sheet bend from the bowline instead of from the illustration.

## 6.16    Hitches

Two hitches will be needed by the boatman, the *clove hitch*, Fig. 6-18, and the *anchor bend* (Fig. 6-7A). Note that the latter is really a hitch and not a bend, as the name implies.

The clove hitch has a relatively high efficiency, because there are no sharp bends in its construction. It is useful for temporarily making fast to pilings or bollards. The clove hitch should not be used for extended or unattended service, for it may become loosened as the line slackens and pulls taut. The clove hitch will only take a strain perpendicular to the member around which it is tied. A strain along the member will cause the clove hitch to slide.

The anchor bend is used almost exclusively for attaching an anchor line to the anchor ring. It tightens under strain and so is hard or impossible to untie. A bowline may be used in place of the anchor bend. If either of these knots is used extensively, a careful check should be made of the amount of wear between the line and the anchor ring. With a tight hitch extensive wear may go undetected, allowing the line to part at some crucial moment.

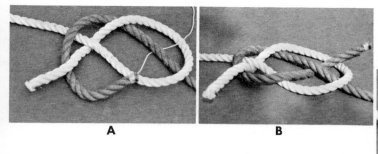

FIGURE 6-16 Tieing sequence to form a carrick bend. The small leader in (A) shows the future course of the free end.

FIGURE 6-17 Tieing sequence to form a sheet bend. A comparison with Fig. 6-15 will show the relation to the bowline.

FIGURE 6-18 A clove hitch formed and pulled tight for holding.

## 6.17    The Short Splice

Splices are the preferred method of joining rope ends permanently or for making permanent loops, as for mooring lines. Three splices should be learned: the short splice, the long splice, and the eye splice. The short splice, shown in Fig. 6-19, nearly doubles the rope diameter and so cannot be used on a line that must run through blocks. The short splice is the strongest splice and is somewhat easier to make than the long splice. Proficiency in either splice is, however, easily obtained.

(1) Place a temporary whipping about 12 diameters from the end of each rope. Put a temporary whipping on each strand and unlay the strands back to the first whippings. Mesh or *marry* the two ropes, alternating strands from each end.

(2) Remove the whipping from one of the ropes. Raise one strand of this rope with a *fid* or small *marlinspike*. Through this hole tuck a strand of the other rope, tucking *against* the lay (Fig. 6-19B). Choose that strand that will pass over one strand and then under the raised strand. Pull the tucked strand taut, and let out a little of the twist in the strand until it lays smooth.

(3) Pick up the second strand, pass it over, and tuck under the corresponding strands, as before. Repeat with the third strand to complete one full tuck, Fig. 6-19C.

(4) Repeat the process until four complete tucks have been made. One extra full tuck should be made when splicing the slippery synthetics.

(5) Remove the other whipping and proceed to tuck with the second set of free ends.

(6) Finish the splice by cutting the strand ends with about one inch protruding from the last tucks. Roll the splice underfoot on the deck to smooth the tucks, Fig. 6-19F.

A smoother splice can be made by tapering the strands after two complete tucks have been made. To taper a splice, cut away about one-third of each yarn before making the third tuck and about one half of the remaining yarns before the fourth tuck.

## 6.18    The Long Splice

The long splice must be used when the line must run through a block without jamming or binding.

(1) Put temporary whipping on each of the strands and unlay about 15 turns on each rope. Marry the two ropes as in the short splice, Fig. 6-20A.

(2) Choose one strand and unlay it back along the standing part, replacing it with the matching strand from the other rope, (A) and (D) Fig. 6-20B. Repeat, unlaying a strand from the second rope, (B) and (E). The remaining matching ends will be at the original position, (C) and (F).

(3) Tie an overhand knot in each pair, tieing with the lay.

(4) Tuck each free end four times as in a short splice, tapering to one half before the third and the fourth tucks, Fig. 6-20C.

(5) Cut off all strands after tucking.

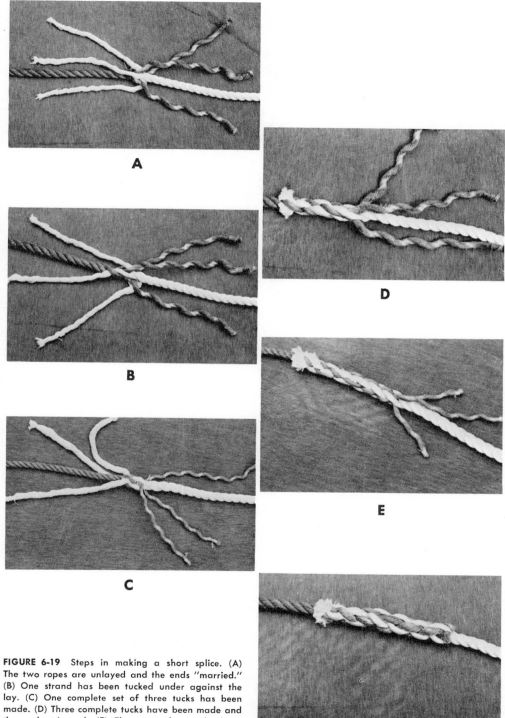

**FIGURE 6-19** Steps in making a short splice. (A) The two ropes are unlayed and the ends "married." (B) One strand has been tucked under against the lay. (C) One complete set of three tucks has been made. (D) Three complete tucks have been made and the ends trimmed. (E) Three complete tucks have been made with the second rope. (F) The completed splice has been trimmed and rolled.

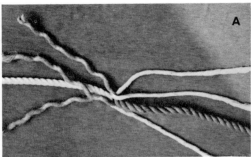
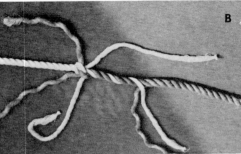
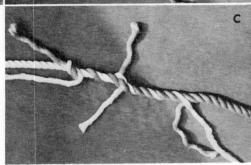

**FIGURE 6-20** Steps in making a long splice. (A) The strands are "married" as in a short splice. (B) One pair of strands has been tied at the original meeting point. One strand has been unlayed to the right with a strand from the left-hand rope following. (C) A strand has been unlayed to the left with a strand from the right-hand rope following and tied. In an actual long splice the unlays would be considerably longer.

## 6.19    The Eye Splice

This is the splice that is needed most often by the small-boat skipper. It is used to make a permanent loop in a mooring line to be dropped over a pile, cleat, or other fastening. A bowline may be used to form a loop that will not tighten around the pile, but such a knot will have an efficiency of about 50 percent, while an eye splice will retain about 90 percent of the strength of the unspliced rope.

The eye splice is made by tucking the unlayed strands under the strands of the standing part of the same rope. The preparation and the tucking are the same as for a short splice. The only critical point comes in the proper matching of the strands at the first tuck.

(1) Center the unlayed strands over the standing part at the point where the loop is to be closed, Fig. 6-21A.

(2) Make the first tuck with the center strand (B) tucking against the lay, Fig. 6-21B.

(3) Make the second tuck with the strand to the left of the first strand tucked, (A). The tuck is made under the strand just to the left of the one used for the first tuck, Fig. 6-21C.

(4) Carry the third unlayed strand (C) under (or behind) the standing part and tuck it under the remaining strand.

(5) The tucks are now repeated in succession as for a short splice, four full tucks for manila, at least five for synthetics. The eye splice may be tapered if desired.

**FIGURE 6-21** Steps in making an eye splice. (A) The strands have been unlayed and brought into position to form an eye of the desired size. (B) One strand has been tucked against the lay. (C) The second strand has been tucked against the lay. (D) The third strand has now been tucked. The tucking sequence is now repeated to obtain the desired strength.

## 6.20  Towing

Boats may suffer more damage in being pulled off from a grounding or while being towed than they would if left alone to be floated off at the next flood tide. In most cases a single deck fitting is not adequate to handle the strain of towing, which may well exceed the weight of the boat. A grounded vessel is more readily freed by a steady pull than by a sudden jerk, which will take out the slack with a rush, putting great strains on all equipment but accomplishing little.

Both towed and towing vessels should secure the tow line to more than one fitting unless one of great strength is available. The towed boat may make a bridle through both bow chocks, leading to both forward cleats, if available, or to some basic strength member. Similarly, the towing boat can rig a bridle through two after chocks for a line leading from some solid fastening. Sailboats may fasten the towing line to the foremast, close to the deck.

If all deck fittings are suspect, a bridle may be rigged around the entire boat, completing the loop with a bowline. Short lines attached to deck fittings will keep the bridle properly placed, out of the water.

The elasticity of nylon greatly reduces sudden strains on both boats from wave motions. Even with this advantage, it is desirable to use as long a tow line as possible, both to reduce stresses and to keep the tow from overriding the towing vessel should the latter slow or stop. In extreme cases extra springing action can be obtained by adding weight to the center of the line.

Occasionally taking a tow alongside is desirable. In this case the towing strain is taken by a diagonal line comparable to a spring line. This line will run from the bow cleat of the towing vessel to an after cleat on the tow. A breast line will hold the two bows together against judiciously placed fenders. Some line adjustments may be needed after the tow is under way.

## 6.21    Towing the Dinghy

Many small cruisers tow a dinghy astern instead of carrying it on deck or slung from davits. A dinghy is light and buoyant, short and wide, and has very little keel or skeg to keep it on a straight course. As a result a dinghy tows very poorly. Some wander from side to side, fetching up at the end of each excursion with a jerk on the tow line that sets the dinghy on a new tack. They also tend to race down the front face of waves, a maneuver that often puts them in the troughs, where they are likely to swamp. A swamped dinghy will certainly part its tow line or pull out its towing ring. An overtaking sea can easily throw a dinghy into the cockpit of the towing boat or heavily against her transom.

Every dinghy design tows differently, but most tow best from a ring placed low in the stem, near the waterline when the boat is at rest. This low point of attachment raises the bow so that the dinghy planes on her after portions. Some power boatmen try to tow their dinghies on the crest of the wave created by the propeller. It is difficult to keep a dinghy stable in this position, making a longer tow line usually preferable.

A dinghy can be made to tow straight with a constant drag on the tow line by a variety of methods:

(1) A drag, such as a long line, may be trailed from the stern of the dinghy.

(2) A bridle can be arranged at the end of the tow line. One end of the bridle will be attached to the bow, the other end back at the quarter, with the angle of pull adjusted so that the dinghy veers off with a slight angle of yaw.

(3) Heeling the dinghy with an unbalanced load will also cause her to veer off to one side.

Many varieties of dinghies are in use, and each has its own towing peculiarities. Experience will be needed to establish the most satisfactory towing arrangement for each particular design.

CHAPTER **7**

# Rules of the
# Nautical Road

## 7.01 Applicable Rules

Four sets of frequently conflicting pilot rules regulate waterborne traffic operating out of U.S. ports. These *Rules of the Road* are laws intended to prevent collisions between vessels. As outlined in Section 3.02, each set applies to specific bodies of water:

(1) *International Rules* apply to the high seas and connecting waters up to the boundary lines of the inland waters (Figs. 3-1, 3-2, 3-3).

(2) *Inland Rules and Regulations (Pilot Rules)* apply to all waters of the United States except those covered by Great Lakes and Western Rivers Rules.

(3) *Great Lakes Rules* apply to vessels of the United States operating upon the Great Lakes, their connections and tributaries as far East as Montreal, and to all vessels while on that part of these waters within the territory of the United States.

(4) *Western Rivers Rules* apply to vessels upon the waters of the Mississippi River and all of its tributaries and all of their tributaries from its source to the Huey P. Long Bridge, that part of the Atchafalaya River above its junction with the Plaquemine-Morgan City alternate waterway, and the Red River of the North.

The boundary lines between international and inland waters are long; at times a vessel may be uncertain as to her exact location and hence uncertain as to which set of rules applies. The Secretary of the Department of Transportation through the Coast Guard may relocate portions of the boundary, often bringing the dividing lines closer to shore. Offshore fishermen and others who may possibly cross into international waters should keep informed of any changes in the boundaries. All changes will be announced in Notices to Mariners (9.16).

## 7.02 Some Definitions

Several basic terms must be clearly defined before we can consider the rules designed to prevent collisions between vessels. Several different points of reference are mentioned in the rules. Everyone is familiar with *fore* and *aft,* referring to the front or bow and the back or stern, respectively. Bow and stern are connected with a *keel*, a heavy structure that defines the direction in which the boat is to move. Maximum length of the vessel from bow to stern is the *length overall*, or *loa. Load waterline length*, or *lwl*, is measured along a straight line at a point where the fully loaded vessel rides in the water.

The greatest width of a vessel is its *beam*. More important for present purposes, the measurement of beam defines a direction at right angles to the keel line, Fig. 7-1. Any object lying on an extension of the beam line is said to be *abeam*. An object ahead of this line is *forward of the beam;* anything behind is *abaft the beam*. There is a distinction between aft and abaft. The former term refers to a position near the stern of the vessel, the latter a direction with reference to any convenient object. Thus one could say "abaft the foremast" meaning a position well forward on the boat but directed toward the stern from the reference point.

**FIGURE 7-1** Some directions referred to a vessel. Note that the word *leeward* is pronounced "loo'ard," never as spelled.

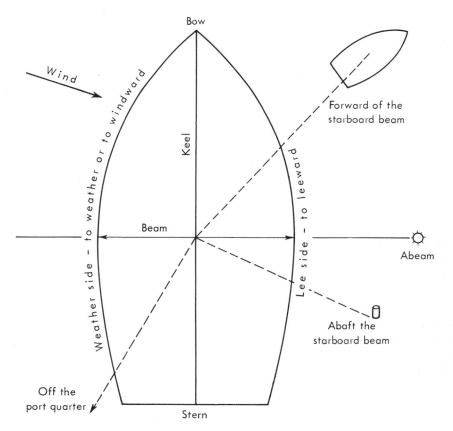

Port and *starboard* are common terms used to designate the regions to the left and right, respectively, of the keel line as one faces toward the bow of the boat. An object sighted "off the port bow" would be seen by looking slightly to the left of the keel line. "Off the port quarter" would be seen by facing aft and looking slightly to the right. The side of the vessel receiving the prevailing wind is the *weather* side. *To weather* defines the direction from which the wind blows. The sheltered side of the vessel is the *lee*.

Much use is made of angles in specifying directions to or from a vessel or with reference to the heading of the vessel itself. In olden times the unit of angular measurement was obtained by dividing a complete circle into 32 *points*. When this system was applied to the compass, it gave eight points between each of the *cardinal points* N, E, S, and W, Fig. 7-2. The old-time sailor was required to memorize the names and the proper sequence of the compass points. A recitation of the point sequence was known as *boxing the compass*.

**FIGURE 7-2**  Visual bearings are given in points referring to bow, beam, or quarter. Portside bearings follow the same scheme.

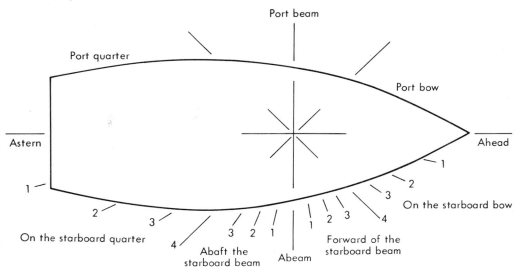

As more precise navigational instruments and methods were developed, greater angular precision was needed, and each point was subdivided into halves and quarters.

In most fields of science the *degree*, which is 1/360th of an entire circle, has proved to be the most useful angular unit. Like the point, the degree is a purely arbitrary unit; it has proved to be preferable mainly because of its more convenient size, and because 360 is evenly divisible by more numbers than is 32.

Preference for the degree has extended to marine activities, and it is now customary to use degrees instead of points for nearly all angular measurements. The point system may be encountered on the scale graduations of some older instruments and in some regulations, and so the conversion factors between the two systems must be kept in mind. Since a complete circle contains 360 degrees and also 32 points, 1 point is equivalent to 360/32 = 11.25 degrees, usually written as 11¼°. A quarter-point is then equivalent to 11.25/4 = 2.8125°. A right angle is 90° or 8 points; a reverse direction 180° or 16 points.

## 7.03    Relative Bearings

Collisions appear inevitable to most novices the first few times they take command of a boat in moderately crowded waters. Relative speeds and distances on the water are hard to estimate, so what seems like a sure collision course may become a clear crossing. Conversely, an apparently wide clearance may occasionally develop rapidly into a collision threat. Some criterion is obviously needed to permit an accurate estimate of collision risk.

International and Inland Rules have identical wordings on establishing the risk of collision:

International Rules Part C Steering and Sailing Rules

2. Risk of collision can, when circumstances permit, be ascertained by carefully watching the compass bearing of an approaching vessel. If the bearing does not change appreciably, such risk should be deemed to exist.

Bearings on approaching craft or on aids to navigation are almost always taken with a magnetic compass, to be described in detail in Chapter 11. As we shall see there, a marine compass may not always point exactly toward the *true*, or *geographical* North. For present purposes, however, we will assume a compass reading true directions. The graduated compass card will then always read 000° at North, 090° at East, 180° at South, and 270° at West, regardless of the direction in which the boat is heading.

In Fig. 7-3 a boat shown by the solid lines is proceeding on a course of 060°. The 060° line on the compass card will then lie along the keel line. An approaching vessel comes into view when we sight across the compass card in the direction of 155°. The vessel has therefore a *compass bearing* of 155°. The *relative bearing* referred to the course of the observing boat is 155 − 060 = 095°.

Now assume that the observing boat changes its course to 083°, as shown by the dotted lines. The compass card will remain fixed in space as the boat rotates until the keel lines up with the 083° graduation on the compass card. The approaching vessel will still be seen at 155° on the compass card and so has the same compass bearing as before. Because of the change in course, the relative bearing has changed to 155 − 083 = 072°.

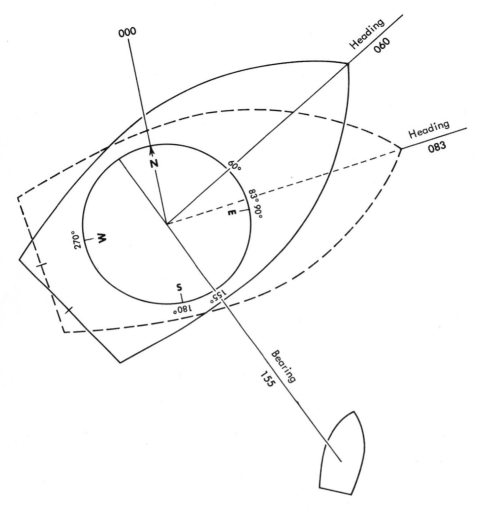

**FIGURE 7-3** Compass and relative bearings on a distant object. When the boat changes course the compass card does not rotate but remains in a fixed position relative to the earth. The relative bearing thus changes, but the compass bearing does not.

Now consider a boat at $A_1$ (Fig. 7-4A), sighting a second boat on a compass bearing of 155°. This bearing remains constant as observations are made at $A_2$, $A_3$, and $A_4$. It is evident that the boats are on a converging course and that a collision is inevitable unless one of the boats changes its course.

In Figure 7-4B the approaching boat is again sighted on a compass bearing of 155°, but this bearing continues to decrease as observations are made at $A_2$, $A_3$, and $A_4$. In this situation the courses tend to converge, but $B$ will cross the bow of $A$ without collision. In the reverse situation, Fig. 7-4C, the compass bearing continues to increase with time. Vessel $B$ will then cross safely under the stern of $A$.

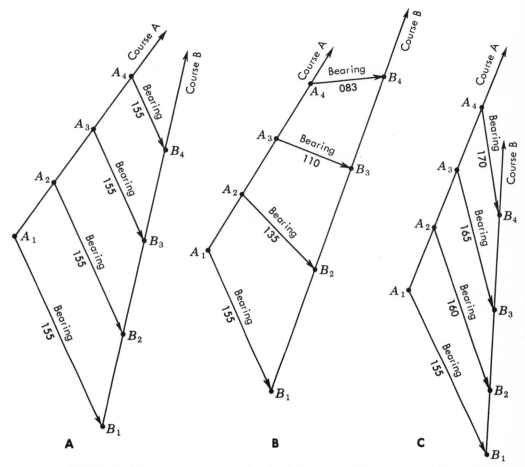

**FIGURE 7-4** (A) A constant compass bearing indicates a collision course. (B) The compass bearing draws forward and vessel B will pass ahead of A. (C) The compass bearing draws aft and vessel B will pass astern of A.

If vessel *B* had been sighted off the port side of *A*, an increasing bearing would have been associated with a bow crossing, and vice versa. The general rule is: If the bearing draws toward the bow of the observing vessel, the crossing will be ahead; if the bearing draws astern, the other vessel will cross astern.

Note that either boat might have altered her course during the sequence of observations without changing the general rule. A course change will change the *relative* bearing to the other boat, but it does not alter the compass bearing. If the latter remains constant, the possibility of collision exists.

## 7.04   Keep to the Right

In nearly every country automobile drivers have become accustomed to keeping to the right to avoid colliding with approaching vehicles. With some exceptions, the keep-to-the-right rule applies to boat operation as well. In a narrow channel every power-driven vessel when proceeding along the course of the channel shall, when is safe and practical, keep to the side of the fairway or midchannel which lies on the starboard side of the vessel. When two vessels are approaching head on, as in Fig. 7-5A, both rules agree that the preferred action is for one vessel, or both, to alter course to starboard in order to permit passing port side to port side. There is an exception to this rule when the two approaching vessels are operating in a river or in a narrow channel where a current may adversely affect the movement. Under these circumstances the vessel proceeding with the current shall have the right-of-way and shall determine in which direction passing is to be effected. Any signals required to establish on which side the vessels will pass shall be exchanged before they shall have arrived within one-half mile of each other.

Although the preferred action is the same under both rules, the associated whistle signals have quite different meanings. In international waters a vessel must signal every change of course and must change course after signaling, whenever another vessel is visible. When another vessel is visible, a change of course without signal or a signal without change of course is in violation.

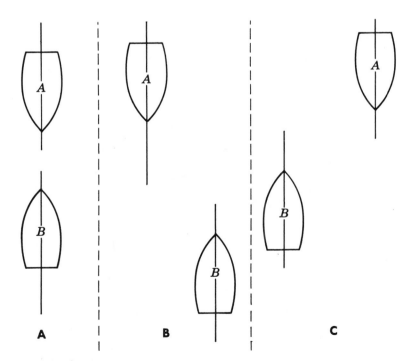

FIGURE 7-5   End-on meeting situations. The required actions are described in the text.

In international waters one short blast (about one second duration) means only, "I am changing my course to starboard." Two short blasts means only, "I am changing my course to port."

If the situation in Fig. 7-5A developed in international waters, one vessel, say A, would blow one short blast and would immediately alter her course to starboard. If this action removed all danger of collision, B would remain silent and would maintain her course and speed. If the master of B felt that the action taken by A was inadequate to avoid collision, he could so signify by five or more blasts on his whistle (the danger signal), requesting A to reexamine the situation. If collision seemed imminent, B would sound one short blast and immediately alter course to starboard.

In all inland waters whistle signals express intent rather than immediate action, and require an answer. Under these rules in situation 7-5A, vessel A will blow one short blast, meaning, "I intend to keep to the right so that we may pass port side to port side." Vessel B must make one of two responses. She may blow one short blast signifying, "I understand, agree, and will act accordingly." Alternatively, B may blow the danger signal of four or more blasts, meaning, "I do not understand your intent," or "I consider the action you signified unsafe." Vessel B must not, under any circumstance, blow a *cross signal*, which means answering one blast with two or vice versa. With the sounding of the danger signal, both vessels should slow or stop until the dangerous situation can be recognized and resolved.

Responsibility for initiating whistle signals is defined under Inland Rule 28(a):

> Except on the Great Lakes, when vessels are in sight of one another . . . whistle signals shall be sounded. . . .
> On the Great Lakes, whistle signals shall be sounded in all weathers by all vessels . . . before they approach within one-half mile of each other, whenever their course will bring them within that distance from each other.

In general, vessels meeting, "so as to involve risk of collision shall, in taking any course required or authorized by these [Inland] Rules, indicate that course by . . ." sound signals.

In narrow channels vessels shall keep to the right except when current adversely affects a vessel's movement. Then, in a meeting situation, the vessel moving with the current shall have the right of way. Either vessel may sound the appropriate signal to indicate on which side the vessels shall pass. The other vessel shall answer with the same signal, if she accepts the decision to so proceed. If she deems the signaled course dangerous, she shall sound the danger signal of four or more short blasts. When a danger signal is given or heard, each vessel shall immediately reduce speed to bare steerageway, reversing engines if necessary, until signals for safe passage are given, answered, and understood.

In the meeting situation of Fig. 7-5B, no action or signal would be required in international waters if, in the judgment of the masters, there was sufficient clearance between the vessels. If clearance is deemed inadequate, the preferred action would be one short blast by one of the vessels followed by a change of course to starboard. In all inland waters a single blast would be blown, and a reply of one blast would be required. In rivers and narrow channels the descending vessel's priority would govern, as described.

The rules recognize situations, as in Fig. 7-5C, in which passing port to port would probably increase rather than decrease the risk of collision. Here each vessel keeps the left and passes starboard to starboard, signaling or not, as required.

## 7.05    Audible Signals

The rules agree on the basic requirements for audible signals and on the equipment for producing them. Such signals shall be given by:

> power-driven vessels on the whistle;
> sailing vessels on the foghorn;
> towed vessels on the whistle or foghorn.

The word *whistle* means any device capable of producing the required audible blasts which are prescribed:

> "short blast" is of about one second's duration;
> "prolonged blast" is from four to six seconds' duration.

For certain types of vessels in certain areas the Coast Guard may require the use of an amber or a white light, visible for at least three miles around the entire horizon. Such a light shall be arranged to show in synchronism with, and for the duration of, any emitted sound signals. Any whistle signals prescribed by the rules may be synchronized with such a light.

Whenever a power-driven vessel nears a bend in a channel where an approaching vessel cannot be seen, she shall signal with one prolonged blast on the whistle when she shall have arrived within one-half mile of the bend. This signal shall be answered by a similar blast from any power-driven vessel approaching from the other side of the bend. Any such obscured bend shall always be rounded with extreme alertness and caution.

In addition to the one-blast and two-blast meeting, passing, and crossing signals, both rules agree in requiring an audible signal of three short blasts when engines are put in reverse. Inland Rules state: "Except on the Great Lakes, whenever a power-driven vessel's engines are going astern and in so doing may endanger another vessel, she shall so indicate by sounding three short blasts on her whistle."

Any vessel leaving a slip or other protected space and entering waters available to other craft shall sound a prolonged blast until the vessel is well clear and her action is apparent to any approaching vessel. This practice is strictly followed by ferryboats and other large craft. Small boat skippers will find it increasingly important to sound this signal as congestion on our waterways increases.

## 7.06    Danger Sector

> Inland and International Rule 19: When two power-driven vessels are crossing, so as to avoid risk of collision, the vessel which has the other on her own starboard side shall keep out of the way of the other.

This requirement establishes a *danger sector* covering the area from dead ahead, clockwise, to a line running two points abaft the starboard beam, Fig. 7-6. A vessel within the danger sector of another is *privileged;* the vessel in whose danger sector she moves is *burdened.*

In Fig. 7-6 *A* is the privileged vessel while *B* is burdened. Vessel *A* is required to hold her course and speed while *B* slows, stops, or otherwise maneuvers so as to pass under the stern of *A.*

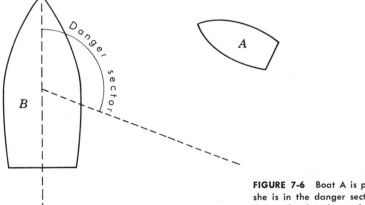

FIGURE 7-6   Boat A is privileged because she is in the danger sector of B, which is then a burdened vessel.

The same actions are required under Inland Rules, but whistle signals must accompany the action. *A* would sound one blast, indicating her intention to maintain course and speed. In the absence of danger, *B* would reply with one blast of agreement and would slow, stop, or direct her course to starboard so as to pass under the stern of *A.* Should *B* consider this maneuver to lead into danger, she should sound the danger signal, whereupon both vessels should slow or stop until the situation can be resolved.

There is an exception involving a vessel with tow descending a river and a second vessel crossing the river. Here the descending vessel has the right-of-way and signals her intention of maintaining course by three blasts on her whistle.

If for any reason privileged vessel *A* should desire to pass under the stern of the burdened vessel, she would blow two blasts, meaning, "I intend to alter my course to port." If *B* agrees, she will blow two blasts and will operate so as to permit *A* to carry out her intention. *B* may reply with the danger signal but not with a cross signal. Except in this situation, the burdened vessel shall operate so as to pass under the stern of the other.

As long as the privileged vessel has a priority on course, she has a very strict obligation to maintain this course at a constant speed. This requirement is an obvious necessity to avoid confusion. Any change of course or speed by the privileged vessel before all danger of collision has passed might alter the situation and place the burdened vessel in an impossible position.

If developments indicate that the efforts of the burdened vessel are not sufficient to avoid collision, the privileged vessel must then take action:

> Inland and International Rule 21: Where by any of these Rules one of two vessels is to keep out of the way, the other shall keep her course and speed. When, from any cause, the latter vessel finds herself so close that collision cannot be avoided by the action of the giving-way vessel alone, she also shall take such action as will best aid to avert collision.

A good deal of experience and judgment must be exercised in invoking Rule 21. Up to a given point the privileged vessel must maintain her course and speed, even though she seems to be going into increasing danger. Then her responsibility suddenly changes, and she is jointly responsible with the other vessel for taking whatever action is necessary to avoid collision.

## 7.07   Overtaking

Every vessel coming up on another from a direction more than two points abaft her beam is an overtaking vessel. As such she is burdened: "Rule 24. Notwithstanding anything contained in these rules every vessel, overtaking any other, shall keep out of the way of the overtaken vessel."

In international waters the usual rules of signaling and course change apply. Under Inland Rules an overtaking vessel desiring to pass to starboard will sound one blast, which in this case is a request for permission. An answer of one blast signifies that the permission is granted and that there are no hazards ahead which might make passing unwise. If, for any reason, the leading boat wants to deny the request, she must sound the danger signal. The overtaken vessel must not sound a cross signal of two blasts even though there is a good reason to prefer a passing on the side opposite to that requested.

If a passage to starboard is permitted, the overtaking vessel will pass into the danger sector of the overtaken vessel. Entry into this sector does not, however, make the overtaking vessel privileged; she is burdened until she has passed clear.

At night an approaching vessel can tell whether or not she is overtaking because each colored side light (Chapter 14) covers the sector from dead ahead to two points abaft the beam. If an approaching boat sees no colored lights, she is more than two points abaft the beam. By day the position cannot be established with certainty. In case of doubt, an approaching vessel should assume she is overtaking and keep out of the way.

## 7.08    Points of Sailing

A sailing vessel has special privileges under the Rules of the Road, and these privileges must be known to the powerboat operator as well as to the sailing skipper. In good weather at least, a powerboat operator has more freedom to choose a course than has the sailor. The latter must operate his boat with due regard to the direction and force of the wind, and some maneuvers may be dangerous if he is forced into them without adequate preparation.

A modern craft with *fore* and *aft* sails (as distinguished from the old *square-riggers*) can sail to within about 45 degrees of the wind direction. A vessel thus sailed (Fig. 7-7A) is said to be *close-hauled*. For the purposes of the rules governing sailing vessels, the *windward side* is defined as the side

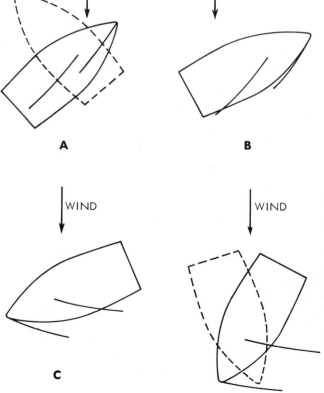

FIGURE 7-7 The points of sailing. A powerboat skipper can judge the status of a sailboat by observing the position of the main boom. (A) Close-hauled on the port tack. The dotted position shows about the least change of course possible when coming onto the starboard tack. (B) Close reach-port tack. (C) Broad reach-starboard tack. (D) Running on the starboard tack. The dotted position shows about the least change of course that will be made in gybing onto the port tack. A spinnaker may be hoisted here instead of the jib shown.

opposite to that on which the mainsail is carried, or on a square-rigger, the side opposite to that on which the largest sail is carried. Thus the boat shown in Fig. 7-7A has the mainsail slightly to the starboard side. The wind is on the port side, and the vessel is said to be on the *port tack*. If she attempts to head up much closer to the direction of the wind, she will lose all drive and must be headed off again if she is to keep moving. Any change of course to port must be at least 90 degrees, which would then put her close-hauled on the starboard tack, as shown dotted.

A vessel allowed to *fall-off*, so that its course makes an angle of about 60-70 degrees with the wind, is on a *close reach*, with the port tack illustrated in Fig. 7-7B. A vessel sails a *beam reach* when its course makes an angle of about 90 degrees with the wind. When the wind comes from slightly abaft the beam (over the starboard quarter shown), the boat sails a *broad reach*, Fig. 7-7C. When the wind is well aft the boat is *running* or *running free*, Fig. 7-7D. A sailboat is seldom operated with the wind coming directly over the stern because of the possibility of *gybing*, a maneuver that may endanger both boat and crew. In a gybe the main boom sweeps across the cockpit as the boat swings from one tack to the other, shown dotted in Fig 7-7D. In all but the lightest breeze, the boom may swing over with sufficient force to injure or kill anyone in its path or carry away rigging.

## 7.09    Sailboat Rules

When a sailboat is under power, she is governed by the same rules that apply to power boats. Under sail alone she operates under a special set of rules. International and Inland Rules concerning the rights of sailboats are identical in meeting, passing, and crossing situations.

(1) Except when overtaking, a sailboat is privileged over a power-driven vessel, but this privilege shall not give to the sailing vessel the right to hamper, in a narrow channel, the passage of a power-driven vessel which can navigate only in that channel.
When two sailing vessels are approaching one another so as to involve a risk of collision:
(2) When each has the wind on a different side, that vessel with the wind on the port side shall keep out of the way of the other.
(3) When both vessels have the wind on the same side, the vessel which is to windward shall keep out of the way of the leeward vessel.
(4) The windward side is defined, for these rules, as the side opposite to that on which the mainsail is carried. In a square-rigger windward is the side opposite to that on which the largest fore-and-aft sail is carried.

The intent of (1) is to prevent a sailboat from forcing a large, poorly maneuverable vessel to take evasive action when such action may put the larger vessel in jeopardy. At the same time the rule preserves the priority of sailboats

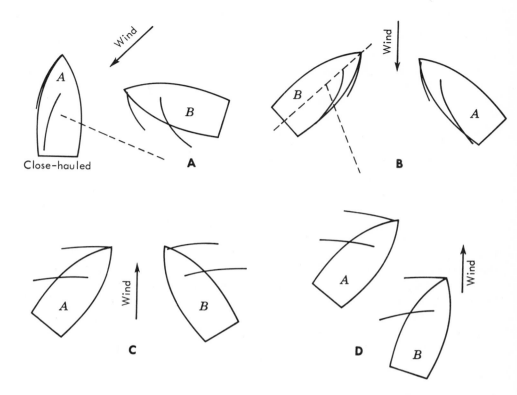

**FIGURE 7-8** Vessel A is privileged in each situation because: (A) In International waters she is to leeward of B. In Inland waters she is sailing closer to the wind than B. (B) In International waters she is on the starboard tack. In Inland waters she is on the starboard tack with equal points of sailing. (C) In International waters she is on the starboard tack. In Inland waters she is on the starboard tack with equal points of sailing. (D) In International waters she is to leeward of B. In Inland waters she is to leeward of B and on the same tack.

over those power-driven vessels that are capable of safely maneuvering in the waters in question. Fig. 7-8 illustrates the application of Rules 2, 3, and 4.

Sailing vessels do not sound passing or change of course signals in either Inland or International Waters. During periods of low visibility, as in fog, they are required to sound the prescribed recognition signals.

## 7.10   Low Visibility

In periods of low visibility the rules require: ". . . a moderate speed, having careful regard to the existing circumstances and conditions." One would expect such a loosely worded requirement to be the subject of much litigation and many court interpretations, and this is the case. These interpretations tend to define *moderate* as that speed at which a vessel can be stopped in one half of the distance of visibility. Even this specification is not easy to carry out in practice, for in dense fog this distance is hard to establish.

A second requirement states: "If a power-driven vessel hears a fog signal apparently originating forward of her beam, she shall, if circumstances permit, stop her engines and navigate with caution until the danger of collision is over."

The whistle signals prescribed for various passing and crossing situations are to be sounded only in periods of good visibility, when the other vessel is in sight. During fog, snow, or other atmospheric conditions which prevent direct vision, appropriate fog signals are to be sounded.

Rules for fog signals use the phrase *under way* in a technical sense which must be clearly understood. A vessel is under way unless she is anchored, made fast to the shore, or is aground. A vessel may be under way, but be stationary in the water. She is then *under way, but with no way on.* When in motion she is *under way, with way on.*

Power-driven vessels under way shall sound fog signals on the whistle or siren, sailboats on the fog horn.

*International* and *Inland Rules* except on the *Great Lakes:*

A power-driven vessel under way and making way shall sound one prolonged blast (from four to six seconds' duration) at intervals of not more than two minutes. A power-driven vessel under way, but with no way on, shall sound two prolonged blasts, with an interval of about one second between them, repeated at intervals of not more than two minutes.

A sailing vessel under way shall sound, at intervals of not more than one minute:

one blast while on the starboard tack
two blasts while on the port tack
three blasts when the wind is abaft the beam.

*Any* vessel less than 350 feet in length, at anchor, shall ring the bell rapidly for about five seconds at intervals of not more than one minute. On larger vessels the bell is to be located in the forepart and is to be supplemented by a stern gong of a tone not to be confused with a bell. This gong is to be sounded for about five seconds at intervals of not more than one minute. A vessel at anchor may, in addition, sound one short, one prolonged, and one short blast in succession to give her position to an approaching vessel.

Inland Rules provide certain exceptions for the Great Lakes. A power-driven vessel under way shall sound three distinct blasts at intervals of not more than one minute. A vessel at anchor shall ring a bell rapidly for three to five seconds at intervals of not more than one minute; in addition, vessels more than 350 feet in length shall give one short, one long, and one short blast at intervals of not more than three minutes.

## 7.11    General Requirements

A small-boat skipper may be confused by the complexities of the Rules of the Road. Some of the complications are being eliminated by a coordinated effort of all rule-making bodies. There is no choice but to conform to the present variable regulations. Courts have repeatedly held that the requirements represent only necessary minima and that circumstances may require even greater caution and precautions. For example, it may be necessary for a vessel anchored near a busy steamer lane to sound her fog bell much more often than the prescribed once a minute, and failure to do so may be in violation. Only the quantity of noise can be changed; to supplement or replace a prescribed sound by some other noisemaker is in violation even though the substitute may be more effective.

Great caution must be exercised in deducing the location of an unseen vessel from the apparent direction and intensity of its fog signal. Thick weather distorts sound waves so badly that little faith can be placed in the apparent direction of incoming signals. Even small noises aboard one's own boat can seriously interfere with the reception of faint fog signals from other vessels. Although not required, it is good practice to stop all engines and enforce quiet at intervals to listen for faint signals. Remember that the quiet period must last for at least one minute to insure covering the silent periods.

The novice should be warned that he cannot expect all ships to obey even the minimum requirements of the rules. Commercial shipping operates on tight schedules, and any disruption by laying to in a fog or slowing down as required may represent a substantial loss of revenue. Many masters take calculated risks and operate at normal or nearly normal speeds, with or without proper signals, in visibility that strictly calls for anchoring. It is a harrowing experience to be in a small boat in a period of low visiblty and hear the rumble of powerful engines close by as a ship passes unseen at nearly normal speed. At times like these there is no lack of enthusiasm on the part of the crew of a small boat for sounding their own fog signals.

The small-boat skipper must look upon periods of low visibility as periods of greatly increased danger. He should anticipate these periods as much as possible and attempt to get clear of heavily traveled steamer lanes before visibility is lost.

Many small-boat operators fail to appreciate the need for lookouts in both clear and dirty weather. All rules are explicit: "Rule 29. Nothing in these rules shall exonerate any vessel, or the owner or master or crew thereof, from the consequences of any neglect to carry lights or signals, or of any neglect to keep a proper lookout, or of the neglect of any precaution which may be required by the ordinary practice of seamen, or by the special circumstances of the case."

In fog at least one lookout—and preferably two—should be well forward, and if the size of the crew permits, one should be aft. Intense looking in a fog is very fatiguing and usually leads to nothing except at the last moment. These men are really listenouts rather than lookouts, and they should concentrate on sound signals rather than on visual signs. Even though the crew may be small, lookouts should be assigned a minimum of other duties and should be relieved frequently to avoid undue fatigue.

The rules regarding rights of way with respect to deep-draft vessels should be honored by all small-boat skippers in all waters. Insisting on a right-of-way is frequently unwise, particularly in a situation involving a small boat and a large or unwieldy craft. A small, highly maneuverable power cruiser or a sailboat would be ill-advised to insist on any privileges he might have over, say, a tug with barges in tow. Forcing such a tug to take evasive action might well increase rather than decrease the danger of collision.

# CHAPTER 8

# Accident Prevention

## 8.01 Command Responsibility

Although recreational boating is exactly what the name implies, responsibilities as well as pleasures are associated with it. To many, the responsibilities are a real part of the pleasures, and meeting them forms, in large measure, the character of the seasoned skipper. Others accept the responsibilities as necessary to realize boating's recreational possibilities. A very few fail to assume command responsibilities, and by so doing, contribute unnecessarily to the number of maritime accidents.

The small-boat owner cannot escape responsibility for the safety of all lives aboard his own craft, and for those on other vessels who might be endangered by unwise actions on his part. Command afloat has two distinct requirements: (1) the vessel shall, in all respects, be seaworthy for the type of waters in which she is to be operated; and (2) she shall be operated so as to insure the greatest safety to all concerned.

A goodly portion of the first requirement can be purchased. Sound advice and expert workmanship are available and can be sought out and paid for. Even here, however, the owner must be able to recognize the quality of the services rendered.

Few small-boat owners are in a position, even if they so desired, to hire professional captains. When a vessel leaves her mooring, she is in the sole charge of her skipper. His subsequent actions will depend in a large measure on how well he has prepared himself to assume command.

Many expert boatmen develop the necessary competence through a lifetime of personal experience with boats and through contacts with other experts. In our present busy times, home study, preferably supplemented by classroom instruction, becomes the only practical method for acquiring the necessary knowledge in a reasonable time. Classroom instruction is available in most boating centers. The classes conducted by the United States Coast Guard Auxiliary or by the United States Power Squadrons are excellent.

The required study is seldom a chore although some mental effort is needed. Any effort spent on a boating education will be repaid many times over in an increased appreciation of maritime operations and a confidence in one's ability to solve problems as they arise.

## 8.02 Accident Reporting

In spite of strong efforts by safety-conscious organizations a regrettable number of maritime accidents occur each year. The Motorboat Act of 1940, as amended; the Federal Boating Act of 1958; and the implementing regulations require a prompt written report of certain types of accidents. According to federal regulations a report is required if the accident results in:

a. Loss of life.
b. Personal injury that incapacitates any person for more than 24 hours. This provision is construed to be impairment such that the individual cannot perform normal functions or usual occupations during the specified time.
c. Property damage in excess of $100.

The written report must be submitted within 48 hours of any accident resulting in death. Reports on other types of reportable accidents must be filed within five days after the event. Accident reports are to be filed with the numbering authorities of the state in which the involved boat was numbered, or with the Coast Guard in those areas where it maintains numbering jurisdiction.

A good many states require an accident report under their own regulations, which in every case will be at least as strict as those required by the federal government. Thus may states require a written report on *every* accident involving personal injury; others require reports whenever property damage exceeds $50 or even $25. Each skipper and owner must familiarize himself with the regulations applicable to his vessel.

The Coast Guard makes detailed studies of all accident reports to find probable causes and to define areas needing greater preventive efforts. Past studies have served to expose certain accident patterns that seem to be repeated year after year.

## 8.03 Accident Patterns

At least half of all maritime accidents are attributable to "operator error," and another 20 percent are caused by "other persons." The skipper must also bear some responsibility for this latter group, because he should be at all times in control of his crew and passengers. In contrast to human error, less than 10 percent of the reported accidents are caused by adverse conditions of wind and sea or from a failure of the hull or propulsion machinery.

Open motorboats of classes A and 1 contribute most heavily to the accident statistics, but these are also the most numerous classes, so the risk per boat is not quite as great as it first appears to be. Irresponsible operation is implicated because a high percentage of all fatalities results from persons in the water, either from a capsize or from falling overboard. *Most of these victims were not wearing the lifesaving devices that were available on the vessel, and in too many cases, no such devices were on board, even though they are required by law.*

Common sense as well as Coast Guard regulations require some sort of approved flotation gear for every person on board. This gear must be readily available at all times, not stowed away in the most inaccessible part of the vessel. When someone goes overboard, seconds—not minutes—may make the difference between life and death. When guests first come on board, show them where the flotation gear is located and instruct the uninitiated how to use it.

Collisions make up a large proportion of accidents when all types, fatal and nonfatal are considered. Carelessness rather than inexperience seems to be the rule, because a larger proportion of seasoned skippers, rather than novices, are involved in collisions.

The most common cause of a collision is an inadequate lookout. Also, carelessness rather than adverse weather seems to be the important factor, for collision frequency does not increase in periods of low visibility, as in fog, even though greater care must then be taken to avoid them.

Fires, explosions, and other mishaps make small contributions to the overall accident pattern. There is an old adage "if it can happen, it eventually will," but continued vigilance may make "eventually" a very long time indeed.

## 8.04  Loading and Trim

Seagoing vessels carry a *plimsoll mark* on the hull to show the allowed limits of cargo loading for the various waters in which they operate. Plimsoll lines are carefully located so as to insure reserve buoyancy adequate to cope with any anticipated winds and seas.

There is nothing like a plimsoll line that applies to pleasure craft, which may be loaded to any extent allowed by the master. Overloading is one of the most common causes of small-boat disasters. Too large a static load is bad enough, but an excessive number of passengers is doubly dangerous. Passengers not only reduce the freeboard, but their movements may seriously upset the trim of the boat to the point of capsize.

Most "man overboard" situations arise from overloading or from concentrating the cargo or human load too high above the center of buoyancy, Sec. 1.10, or from operating with too large a load that can shift its position with the trim of the boat. Bilges must be kept pumped because any water there will always flow to the low side of the hull, adding to an already upset equilibrium. Passengers must be prevented from crowding to one side of a small boat, thus inviting a capsize. Even large steamers have capsized and sunk, with a large loss of life when a number of passengers crowded to one rail.

Sudden changes in fore-and-aft trim can also lead to dangerous situations. One too-common type of accident occurs in small outboards in which bilge water has been allowed to accumulate. As the operator moves aft, perhaps to start the engine, his weight trims the boat down by the stern. The bilge water immediately runs aft, depressing the stern still further until water pours in over the transom notch, with prompt flooding.

In another type of outboard accident a single operator *stands* near the stern as he starts the engine. When the engine suddenly catches the rapid acceleration catapults the operator over the transom and into the water. Without flotation gear his last sight may be that of his boat rapidly moving away from him.

It is not possible to give a loading formula that will apply under all combinations of weather, sea, and load distribution, but several guides have been proposed for use under normal conditions. One proposal is

$$\text{maximum load} = 7.5 \times L \times B \times D \text{ pounds} \qquad 8\text{-}1$$

$$\text{maximum number number of passengers} = \frac{L \times B}{15} \qquad 8\text{-}2$$

where $L$ = overall length, $B$ = maximum beam, and $D$ = least distance from the bottom of the boat to the point where water can enter the hull. All dimensions are to be taken in feet.

### ILLUSTRATIVE EXAMPLE

Calculate the allowable loading for a hull 15′ long, 6′7″ beam, and 18″ least depth.

From 8-1   Load = $7.5 \times 15 \times 6.58 \times 1.5 = 1,100$ pounds

From 8-2   Passengers = $\dfrac{15 \times 6.58}{15} = 6$

Any combined loading should not exceed the allowed weight.

## 8.05   Fueling

Gasoline is the most commonly used fuel for pleasure-boat engines, because of the large amount of energy released from a relatively small quantity and because its volatile components form explosive mixtures with air even at low temperatures. These same properties, together with the fact that the volatile vapors are heavier than air, make gasoline a dangerous substance, one to be handled with greatest care.

Nothing can be taken for granted with gasoline; a tank that was tight last year may spring a leak today. A tight connection in the fuel line may loosen at any time; vibration may fatigue and crack a hard-drawn copper fuel line. These are only a few of the hazards that must be guarded against.

In considering the steps involved in safe fueling, let us assume a properly installed fuel system. The fill-pipe will be outside the cockpit coaming so that the heavy vapors will escape overboard instead of down into the bilges. The fill-pipe will extend nearly to the bottom of the tank to prevent splashing and to present a liquid rather than a vapor surface. Internal tank baffles will prevent excessive sloshing about as the boat pitches and rolls in a sea. The tank vent will be terminated outboard and will be fitted with a fine gauze flame arrestor. The tank itself will be securely fastened to heavy structural members (Fig. 8-1).

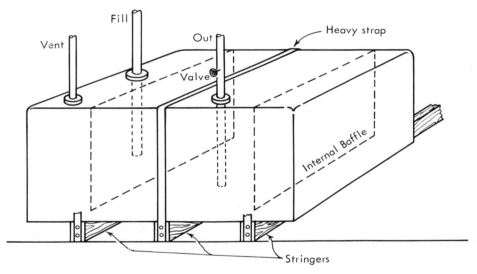

**FIGURE 8-1**   Schematic plan of fuel tank installation.

Fuel take-off will be installed at the top of the tank, where a leak can be more readily controlled than at the bottom. The introduction of air at the top of the fuel take-off will break the liquid continuity and will stop the flow to the carburetor, a useful adjunct to the regular shut-off valve. In our hypothetical installation the fuel line will have been installed with due regard for vibration, an effective filter will be in the line, and an approved and clean flame arrestor will be on the carburetor. Fire extinguishers will be on board in known and available locations, and others will be on the fueling dock.

With all this equipment in good order, we may consider the essential steps for a safe fueling:

(1) Although the stay at the fuel dock may be short, tie up securely. There is no time in the middle of a fueling operation to adjust lines or to haul in a boat slipping away from the dock with a fueling hose stuck in its fill-pipe.

(2) Put all passengers off the boat and onto the dock.

(3) Shut off all electrical devices, no matter how inconvenient this may be. A master switch that will kill the entire system insures a complete shutdown.

(4) Extinguish all open flames, cigarettes, cigars, and pipes in the near vicinity of the fuel delivery.

(5) Close all ports, doors, and hatches.

(6) Remove filler cap and keep it and the wrench in a safe place. A cap dropped overboard serves no useful purpose.

(7) Keep metal to metal contact between the filler pipe and the hose nozzle or the delivery cans. Sparks between nozzle and tank can be produced from frictional electricity generated by the flowing liquid. Some fueling stations use a special grounding wire to insure spark suppression.

(8) Know the amount of fuel required and avoid overfilling. Spillage afloat is much more serious than spillage in a filling station ashore.

(9) When fueling is complete, cap the tank and wipe up any spillage.

(10) Open up all ports and hatches. Start the bilge ventilating fan if one is available.

(11) Inspect the tank compartment and smell the bilges. The extra fuel may just possibly have opened up a leak not present with a lighter load.

(12) When completely satisfied that no hazard exists, start the engine and re-embark the passengers.

This fueling schedule may seem unnecessarily complicated, but in fact it is quite practical; no step can be omitted without increasing the hazard of this operation. Most dockmasters and skippers are safety conscious, but nevertheless fires and explosions from improper handling of fuel take an unnecessary toll of lives and property.

Fewer precautions are required when transferring diesel fuel. The high temperature required for ignition together with the low content of volatile components make this fuel relatively safe. It is not, however, absolutely safe and must be treated with respect. By definition all fuels are burnable and can be ignited by one means or another. On one occasion sawdust was thrown into a deep bilge to absorb spilled diesel fuel, but the soggy mess was not promptly removed. Sometime later it was ignited by a dropped match, and a stubborn and damaging fire was started. Common sense and good housekeeping will insure safe diesel fueling without all of the elaborate precautions required for handling gasoline.

## 8.06   Galley Safety

The traditional galley stove was a coal burner, and these are by no means extinct on larger vessels. Coal, coke, or wood have none of the hazards associated with the use of liquid fuels, but the space required for the stoves and the storage of the solid fuels limit their use on small craft. A solid-fuel stove becomes generally heated so that some sort of nonflammable insulation must be provided to protect surrounding woodwork. Smoke pipe temperatures become so high that a water collar or *deck iron* must be provided to protect the deck.

The principal products of solid-fuel combustion are solid ash and carbon dioxide. The use of coke reduces the nuisance of handling ashes. When solid fuels are burned for long periods of time, as for cabin heating, care must be taken to insure adequate ventilation so that the concentration of carbon dioxide does not rise to a dangerous level. Water vapor is one of the products formed in the burning of liquid petroleum fuels or alcohol. The water vapor thus produced will condense on the colder surfaces to produce a warm but moist cabin.

Alcohol is undoubtedly the fuel of choice for the pleasure-craft galley. Alcohol has a high fuel value, ignites readily, and burns with a clean flame. Alcohol stoves may flare up, valves may stick, and tanks may leak, as with any other liquid fuel. Alcohol, however, is distinguished from petroleum-based fuels by its ability to mix with water in all proportions. Large quantities of water thrown on an alcohol fire will diffuse and mix with the alcohol to produce an unburnable mixture. Similar treatment of a gasoline fire will only spread the blaze as the burning gasoline rises to the surface and spreads in a thin film in all directions.

Like petroleum, alcohol vapors are heavier than air and hence will seek out the lower portions of the bilge. However, the much smaller quantities involved permit fueling the galley stove without all of the elaborate precautions needed when fueling the engines. In transferring alcohol, all open flames should be extinguished and care taken to avoid spills. Fuel containers should be closed as soon as possible, and any spillage promptly wiped up. Common-sense precautions will serve for handling alcohol. No smoking, of course.

Solid fuels based on alcohol are quite satisfactory for marine use. Solid fuels do not require the open burning of liquid fuel during burner warm-up and hence are relatively free from flare-up. The rate of combustion is built into solid fuel at manufacture, and hence it lacks some of the control possible with liquids. Solid-alcohol fuels are rather expensive if much cooking is done.

A number of petroleum gases liquefy under only moderate pressure, permitting the storage of a considerable amount of fuel in a relatively small tank or cylinder. When pressure is released by opening a valve, the liquid escapes as a gas which may be consumed in a burner designed for its use. This type of fuel is known as liquid petroleum gas or *LPG*. Except for electricity LPG is probably the most convenient fuel for the marine galley, but it cannot be recommended from the standpoint of safety. All LPG gases are heavier than air and so any that esape inside the vessel will settle in the bilge, like gasoline vapor. LPG has little odor itself, but highly odorous tracers are added so that it can be detected before explosive concentrations are reached. LPG vapors will actuate the electrical devices designed for the detection of gasoline vapors in the bilge. In spite of the availability of these detection methods, LPG must be considered a relatively unsafe galley fuel.

Leaks may develop at valves, at tubing connections, or from cracks in tubing opened up by vibration. An unattended stove burner may be blown out by a sudden breeze, and the unburned gas that follows will immediately seek the lowest part of the vessel. LPG tanks and regulators must be secured in positions where escaping gas cannot reach the bilge, machinery spaces, living accommodations, or any enclosed areas.

Only LPG gases known to be odorized should be allowed on board. Changing a depleted cylinder should only be done by experienced personnel in accordance with the following schedule:

(1) Close the empty cylinder valve and burn out the gas in the supply lines to the burners.

(2) When each burner goes out, shut it off at once.

(3) Disconnect the empty cylinder, leaving all valves closed.

(4) Connect the full cylinder and open the delivery valve.

(5) Light all burners at once and burn them until certain that no air is trapped in the lines to later interrupt the flow of flammable gas.

(6) Shut off the burners and test the system for leaks with soapsuds applied to all joints. *Never look for leaks with an open flame.*

Considerable thought must be given to galley equipment, whatever the fuel. The stove itself must be secured against shifting in heavy seas. Gimbals are desirable to maintain a horizontal burner surface, but the stove as a whole must be weighted well below the pivot points to insure stability and it must be rigidly mounted. Flare-ups with liquid fuels must be kept in mind when locating flammable objects such as curtains over or near stove burners. Fuel lines from separate tanks must be rigidly fastened, yet they may require some flexibility to prevent cracking from vibration fatigue. Galley fire extinguishers must be handily located so that they will be accessible even in the presence of a flaming stove or fuel tank.

Do not compromise on the quality of galley equipment. Check the safety features of a stove before purchasing, and be sure that the installation is in accord with the best safety practices.* Can pressure be released quickly and with certainty from a pressure-fed fuel system? Does a gravity-fed fuel system have a positive shutoff that can be operated even in the presence of a severe stove flare-up? Are the cups for warm-up fuel large enough to contain the required amount of liquid without danger of a spill in a seaway? Will reserve fuel be stored in a safe place and in safe containers? These are only examples of the questions that must be answered in choosing and installing galley equipment.

---

* *Fire Protection Standard for Motor Craft.* National Fire Protection Association, 60 Batterymarch St., Boston, Mass.

## 8.07    Fire-fighting Equipment

The fire-fighting equipment legally required for recreational boating has already been described. Unfortunately, many boat owners look on these requirements as maxima rather than as minima, giving no thought to the fact that fire extinguishers are on board for the sole purpose of saving lives and property.

Too often fire-fighting equipment is tossed into the most inaccessible locker to deteriorate from attack by moisture along with life preservers and other essential gear. Serious thought must be given to the location of each extinguisher. Accessibility is paramount, for a small, readily extinguishable blaze can expand rapidly into an uncontrollable conflagration. Consider the possible location of fires, and place extinguishers so that they will be handy but will not be cut off by the flames. Mount all extinguishers securely so that they will not break loose in a seaway.

Most extinguishers approved for marine use contain gas under pressure. Remember that any pressure vessel can leak, in spite of careful design and construction. Check each pressure extinguisher that is not equipped with a reliable gauge at least twice a season by weighing. Cylinders even only slightly discharged should be refilled at the earliest opportunity. Factory-loaded refills are available for some types. Carbon dioxide cylinders should be serviced only by authorized dealers equipped to handle them properly.

When laying up for the winter, remove the extinguishers and store them at home in a dry place. Inspect pressure cylinders for deep rusting. Repaint as needed to halt further attack. Before installing in the spring, refresh your memory as to the method of operation.

## 8.08    Safety Under Way

When under way the small-boat skipper has multiple responsibilities. First of all, he must see to the safety of all on board his own craft. He must cause his vessel to be so operated as to insure maximum safety, and he must enforce discipline on board so that foolhardy behavior on the part of one individual does not put all in jeopardy. When necessary the skipper must not hesitate to use the authority which is his and his alone. Split authority, or none at all, can only lead to chaos in a tight situation.

The skipper must operate his vessel with due regard for the rules of the nautical road and for the rights of others. In practice this is not enough. A liberal application of the golden rule and the use of common sense by all boat operators would improve existing conditions immensely. In many situations it is most unwise to insist on the rights that are conferred by a strict interpretation of the rules. Remember that a privileged vessel has a responsibility to maintain course and speed, unless it will shortly lead her into peril. A sudden maneuver by a privileged vessel may leave her still privileged, yet she may be solely responsible for the ensuing collision.

In crowded waterways each skipper must operate at speeds consistent with existing conditions. Running at too high a speed across the face of a crowded marina or in confined waters may not immediately violate the law, but it is not likely to win friends among the other boatmen. Crew members whose duties have been interrupted or ruined by the wake of a speeding boat are apt to remember the offender and repay him manyfold if opportunity presents.

Each boat operator must remember that he is legally responsible for any damage caused by his wake. Suits are seldom brought on these grounds, but more may well be forthcoming. The violations are many, and the law is explicit on this point.

In establishing safety regulations for the crew of his own vessel, the skipper must take into consideration existing and anticipated conditions. It would be ridiculous, for example, to impose conditions suitable for a stormy night during a short cruise on a calm afternoon. To do so will only break down the entire safety program.

Probably the greatest hazard facing the small-boat skipper is the loss of a man overboard. Powerful lights and other items of modern survival equipment have somewhat reduced the hazards, but in spite of all these, a man overboard at any time—and particularly at night—is a most serious situation.

No matter what the weather, every person topside at night should wear a safety belt and some sort of approved flotation gear. The skipper's judgment must govern the ordering out of flotation gear and safety belts when bad weather comes during daylight hours. When in doubt the skipper should err on the side of caution. One does not become a tough old sea dog by going without proper lifesaving equipment when conditions indicate its use.

When a safety belt is worn (Fig. 8-2), it should be hooked to or around some integral part of the boat *at all times*. Progress from one point to another is made by successively hooking and unhooking the two lines, until the desired working area is reached. Even below-deck areas are not absolutely safe in heavy weather. In a harrowing experience during the 1960 Newport-Bermuda

**FIGURE 8-2** A safety belt with two hooks.

race, a man with an unhooked safety belt was projected overboard while standing well down in the companionway.

The return, location, and rescue operations, particularly at night, may well take several hours, much too long for even a powerful swimmer in good condition to stay afloat without help from flotation gear. A tossed life ring is not a complete answer to the problem, for the man may be partially disabled and unable to make use of the ring even if he reaches it. If he is wearing properly designed equipment when he goes over, he will be supported face upward even though he may have been knocked unconscious by a gybing boom.

A powerboat helmsman must always remember that a whirling propeller is a lethal weapon, capable of inflicting fatal injury to any human coming in contact with it. There is a powerful suction ahead of a large wheel, quite capable of drawing at least a portion of a swimmer into the blades. *The utmost care must be taken when under way in an area where there may be swimmers.* A floating head is a small object, easily missed by a casual lookout.

## 8.09  Man Overboard

When a man goes overboard, either night or day, there is no time to plan a course of action. The first steps must be automatic reflex actions which can only be the result of careful preplanning and practice. The helmsman must be sufficiently alert at all times to become aware of the accident as soon as the man starts to leave the boat. The first steps must be taken in far less time than it takes to tell them:

(1) If there are other persons on board, the helmsman must immediately sound the alarm "man overboard." All available help will be needed to effect a rescue.

(2) Injury from propellers is avoided by swinging the stern sharply away from the man in the water, or by disengaging the clutches until he is clear of the stern.

(3) A life ring or a horseshoe life preserver is thrown near to but not on top of the man. Either of these devices can cause injury with a direct hit. If no life preserver is immediately available, throw any floating gear with a high visibility to aid in returning to the scene of the accident.

(4) If available, one crew member should be assigned the *sole* job of keeping track of the victim. If any sea is running, one can easily lose sight of a head or even a brilliantly colored life preserver.

With the preliminary steps taken, immediate preparations are made to return and rescue the victim. Let us first consider recovery with a powerboat. Under no circumstance should the return be attempted by reversing engines and backing down. Instead, with the boat in position 2, Fig. 8-3, a tight turn is made in the direction of the boat's better performance, 3. During phase 4 the boat stands away to insure adequate maneuvering room later on. Turn 5

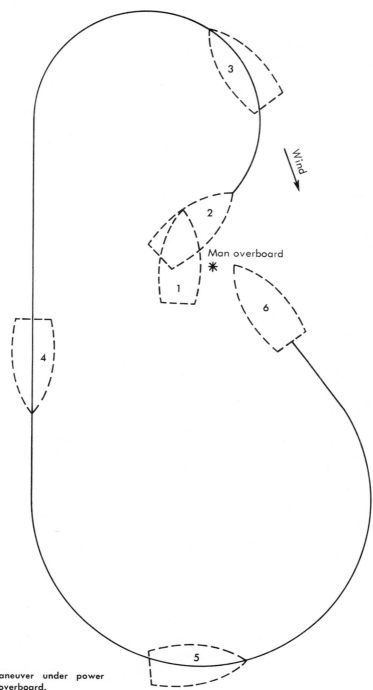

Wind

Man overboard

FIGURE 8-3 A maneuver under power to pick up a man overboard.

141

can then be made somewhat less than the tightest possible so that the final approach, 6, can be an almost straight course, with minor adjustments in either direction. Without some maneuvering room, wind and current may set the boat so that it is impossible to return to the scene on the first pass. Plan to make the pickup with the boat headed nearly into the wind or current, as in docking. Come in slightly to windward rather than to leeward. This will provide some shelter and will also insure that the boat is not blown out of reach at the critical moment, which will almost certainly require another full circle and a second try.

If crew numbers permit, all preparations for boarding will have been made during the return swing. A boathook and boarding ladder should be available. If the latter is lacking, a makeshift should be contrived, for the victim should be brought back on board as gently as possible, lest some injury be aggravated.

If a dinghy was being towed at the time of the accident, it may provide the most rapid means of rescue. The powerboat will then be brought dead in the water rather than being swung back to the scene. A dinghy already in the water may be of assistance in reboarding in any case, even if it is not used for the return. It is doubtful that time should be taken to launch a dinghy being carried on board. A dinghy should not be used unless sea conditions are satisfactory, and even then all crew members in it should wear life jackets.

By the time the boat is brought alongside, lines should be ready with bowlines tied, to be used as footholds. An injured person may have to be secured by lines through the crotch and under the armpits prior to being hauled on board. In a seaway a spare life preserver may be rigged to spare the victim some severe banging against the hull, but this must be a secondary consideration to the main effort to get the man back on board as soon as possible.

Recovery under sail is much more difficult. If the boat is an auxiliary, the engine should be started at once, and the rescue made with power available to aid in maneuvering. If there is enough crew on board, the sails can be dropped as soon as the engine is started and the boat is headed into the wind.

Without power, and sailing with the wind forward of the beam, the boat must be gybed to return to the scene. The gybe must be carried out with even more care than usual, for any mishap will only compound an already serious situation. With the gybe properly executed the boat can be sailed back to the man and rounded up into the wind for the pickup.

When sailing before the wind at the time of the accident, probably the best plan is to come up into the wind until it is about abeam. After sailing away a few boat lengths the skipper can come about and return on a reach, heading up into the wind for the actual recovery.

Under the best conditions the recovery of a person overboard is an exacting business, requiring an intimate knowledge of boat performance, complete cooperation from all crew members, and a thorough understanding of the basic maneuvers. When optional rescue methods are available, the skipper must make an almost instantaneous choice and must assume full command of the entire operation. When a man is overboard, there is no time for the discussions and confusion that accompany split authority.

A man overboard must be considered a most serious situation under any circumstance, even if he is wearing flotation gear at the time of the accident. In broad daylight it is quite possible for the search vessel to pass close to the victim without seeing or hearing him. Locating a swimmer at night is out of the question unless he has reached a lighted buoy thrown over at the time of the accident.

Automatic radio transmitters are available, designed to be thrown over at the time of the accident for the purpose of providing a homing signal. The desirability of using these devices is open to question. Once in the water and in operation they will transmit continuously for some time on the distress frequency. This uncontrolled transmission may effectively deny the use of the channel for other distress calls. In any case, using one of these units constitutes operating an unlicensed transmitter.

The dangers inherent in a man overboard are compounded in cold water. Men have been rescued after an immersion of more than 30 hours in warm water, but it appears that a body temperature compatible with life can be maintained for only a few hours at a water temperature of 50-55° F. As water temperatures drop below this range, survival times decrease rapidly, probably to only a few minutes at 40° F.

Even warm waters may present a prompt and serious threat to a man overboard. Sharks and other predatory fish tend to frequent the warmer waters and may hesitate only a few minutes before attacking. Repellants are available but will diffuse away and become ineffective with time.

The lowly jellyfish or sea nettle may be dangerous to man because of the enormous numbers present in some of our navigable waters. Some individuals react violently to only a single encounter with one of the creatures, and even the least sensitive can expect a severe reaction if he repeatedly comes in contact with them.

Practice sessions for a man overboard should be held regularly, with each member of the crew taking the leading role in turn. Someday it may be the skipper himself who is overboard! Toss over some expendable item of a size comparable to a human head and time the recovery with one member of the crew inactive. You will be impressed with the improvement resulting from only a few sessions.

A fall overboard can lead to disaster even when it occurs at anchor in a quiet harbor. Cases are on record of drownings following exhausting attempts to reboard an anchored vessel that presented the solitary swimmer only a smooth hull surface and a slender anchor line. Always keep a boarding ladder rigged when you are at anchor with people on board.

## 8.10   Groundings

Groundings account for only a small percentage of marine accidents, but they result in a disproportionate amount of property damage. Groundings vary tremendously, from the gentle touching on a soft bottom by a vessel slowly coming in to some poorly charted cove to a hard drive onto a rocky bottom in a heavy sea.

When one is operating in tidewaters, groundings should be risked, if some risk seems necessary, only on a flooding, but not on a full flood tide. If grounded in tidewater, a determination should be made *at once* as to whether the tide is on the make or on the ebb. If the latter, prompt action will be needed if the vessel is to be gotten off before she becomes more firmly set. On a flooding tide a bit of watchful waiting, with a few precautions to prevent a more solid grounding, will usually suffice to refloat with only pride and a time schedule upset.

The common impulse on grounding is to reverse all engines full power. This may indeed be the proper procedure, for a backing force will be exerted on the hull, and in addition the stream of water thrust toward the bow by the propellers may wash away some of the mud or sand holding her fast. Before applying reverse power, however, a check should be made to determine that the propellers are themselves free of the bottom. If not, severe damage to the wheels or shafts may result, preventing future use in getting free. When reversing in shoal water, engine temperature and cooling water flow should be watched carefully. Sand or mud may be pulled into the strainer, plugging it and causing overheating and engine damage.

Frequently one can float free from an easy grounding by changing the trim of the vessel. Bringing all hands aft and moving ballast may lighten the bow sufficiently to refloat. A deep-keel sailboat can sometimes be freed by heeling her over on a bilge. This can be done by getting the crew outboard on the boom, which has been swung athwartship. If a dinghy is available, a kedge anchor may be planted inshore and a line run to the main halyard. A strain on the halyard will exert a powerful heeling moment which may roll her sufficiently to lift the keel off the bottom.

Sometimes wave motions may be used to advantage in freeing a stranded vessel. As each wave passes, a lightly grounded boat may become buoyant enough to be freed in a series of movements either by its own power plant or by a strain taken on a kedge anchor. In calm waters a passing vessel may be willing to make a few extra passes to create an effective wave action.

In general boatmen are a sympathetic lot, and you may expect offers of assistance when your plight becomes known. Any offer of a tow must be accepted with caution. If you have been aground for some time with an ebb tide, you are probably firmly set. In this case increased buoyancy is the only safe and effective remedy. A powerful tow in this case may do more harm to the hull than the actual grounding, unless sea conditions are apt to break her up before she can be refloated.

If you accept a tow, rig the tow line around some strong part of the vessel. The average cleat or bitt is apt to be quite inadequate to take the strain of a heavy towing pull. A samson post, a through bolted cleat, or the butt of a mast will be adequate.

A steady pull is more effective than a series of sharp jerks although a change in the direction of pull may be advantageous. Keep all crew members out of line with the towing cable. Should such a stressed line part, severe personnel injury may result from whiplash of the broken ends.

Both crews must look lively when the stuck vessel comes free. If the towing vessel stops suddenly, she may be overrun by her tow, or the towing line may slacken and foul her propeller. One man on the towing boat should devote full time to tending the towing line to prevent fouling.

If the grounding occurred in a fairly heavy sea with the tide flooding, it may be necessary to prevent her from being driven harder onto the shoal as the tide rises. If a small boat is available and can be launched, a kedge anchor should be taken into deeper water. In some cases a good strain on this line may bring her off. If not, it will prevent the rising tide from working her forward and grounding her harder, finally deserting her at the height of the flood. If a small boat is not available, a kedge may be thrown as far off the stern as possible, but it will probably be too close to be effective.

When aground in heavy surf, a kedge anchor is essential to prevent broaching. Most waves have a component along the beach as well as one directly ashore, and the alongside force will tend to swing the vessel parallel to the line of breakers. It may be impossible to plant a kedge effectively in heavy surf from a small boat. The vessel is then at the mercy of the seas until she broaches and fills, is broken up, or is rescued by outside help.

In any grounding do not let pride prevent a call for help if help is needed. A wait for a rising tide in calm water is an annoyance but little more. A hard grounding with deteriorating weather may be quite another matter, and a prompt call for help may be the sensible course of action.

## 8.11   Distress Signals

The time may come to even the well-prepared and competent yachtsman when he requires help from other vessels or from the shore. Distress signals are prescribed by International Rules, Inland Rules, and the Pilot Rules. The latter two are essentially abridged versions of the International Rules, which have been carried over by custom into all waters.

No ship in distress should refrain from sounding a distress call because she lacks the proper equipment to follow regulations. The basic idea is to attract attention by whatever means are available.

Distress signals are recommended in International Rule 31.

(a) A gun or other explosive fired at intervals of about one minute.

(b) A continuous sounding of any type of fog signal.

(c) Rockets or shells throwing red stars, fired one at a time at short intervals.

(d) A signal transmitted by radiotelegraphy consisting of the group · · · − − − · · · which forms the letters SOS in the International Morse Code.

(e) The spoken word "MAYDAY" transmitted by radiotelephony.

(f) Flying the International Code signals for the letters NC with the N uppermost, Fig. 8-4.

(g) Flying a signal consisting of a square flag with a ball either over or under it, Fig. 8-4.

(h) Open flames on the vessel as from a burning tar barrel or an oil barrel.

(i) A rocket parachute flare showing a red light.

(j) A smoke signal giving off a volume of orange-colored smoke.

(k) Slowly and repeatedly raising and lowering outstretched arms.

In addition to prescribing the signals, Rule 31 explicitly forbids their display for any except the intended purpose. Rule 31 also forbids the use of any signal that might be reasonably confused with those prescribed.

Some of the signals listed in Rule 31 are of dubious value to small boats. Few indeed are apt to have a tar barrel on board for emergency purposes, and should this be the case it would appear inadvisable to ignite it in time of trouble.

On small boats a distress signal recommended by the Coast Guard is made by slowly and repeatedly raising and lowering the outstretched arms to the sides. The inverted national ensign, Fig. 8-4, is also an accepted distress signal, but its meaning is not always recognized.

A variety of flares and other signaling devices are available from marine suppliers. Modern packaging methods will keep out moisture and presumably will maintain the devices in good condition. However, since they are relatively cheap, and when needed are needed desperately, it seems wise to replace them after no more than two seasons. Dispose of old flares properly. Do not attempt

**FIGURE 8-4** Visible signals indicating a vessel in distress. The relative positions of the square flag and the black ball may be reversed.

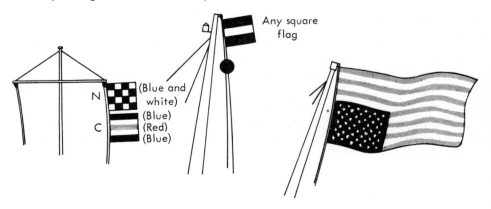

to fire them while under way, for if they function properly, they may be seen and interpreted as a true distress signal.

Every skipper should be aware of the distress signals emitted by disabled submarines and aircraft. A disabled submarine will fire a parachute flare high in the air, producing a slowly descending red light visible for many miles. This signal may be very confusing to a surface craft in the vicinity, for if the submarine is on the bottom, there will be no apparent source of the signals. A disabled aircraft will fire red flares from a Very pistol.

A small-boat operator is not likely to see either of these two distress signals for their use is fortunately very rare. Should either signal be encountered, every effort should be made to get help at once for the need is apt to be acute.

With the growing interest in skin and scuba diving, the recreational boatman may frequently see a vessel flying a red flag with a diagonal white stripe, Fig. 8-5. This flag is *not* a distress signal but indicates that the vessel is attending

**FIGURE 8-5** A red flag with a white diagonal slash indicates a vessel attending divers. Stand clear!

one or more skin divers. Assistance is not being requested, and all vessels not involved in the diving operations should keep clear, approaching not closer than several hundred yards. The entry of a spectator vessel into the diving area can only increase the hazard to the men below.

## 8.12    Seasickness

Seasickness, or more generally, motion sickness, is primarily the result of an overstimulation or an unusual sensitivity of a person's balance mechanism. Balance is normally maintained after the brain receives and evaluates the information supplied from three sensory systems. The semicircular canals in the inner ear perceive the forces of gravity and accelerations; sensory nerves in muscles and tendons perceive the weight of the head, arms, and legs; and the eyes perceive spatial relationships with objects in the environment. Motion sickness occurs in many people when there is some confusion in the interpretation of the meanings in the three sets of stimuli.

Some people are so sensitive to motion that they can become seasick while watching waves from a pier. Others are very resistant although probably excessive motion somewhat reduces normal feelings of well-being in the most hardy. Fatigue, fear, cooking odors, and other secondary factors may add to the basic causes of seasickness through psychic stimulation. Some medical conditions may also contribute to an unusual sensitivity. The recent use of alcohol will nearly always increase sensitivity to motion sickness. Children tend to be less susceptible than adults, probably because of a smaller psychic component.

Symptoms vary in severity from a mild feeling of uneasiness to tightness in the throat, fatigue, excessive salivation, yawning, queasiness, loss of appetite, headache, dizziness, and nausea, and on to violent vomiting, prolonged retching, and prostration, with all the elements of shock, clammy and cold sweating, stupor, and collapse.

The majority of sufferers experience these symptoms to only a mild degree. Most people become adjusted to the motion after one to three days unless there is a prolonged spell of extremely violent seas.

All medicines used for the prevention and cure of motion sickness reduce the sensitivity of the nervous system. Some of the older depressant drugs such as bromides, barbiturates, and narcotics are beneficial but frequently render the victim helplessly lethargic. A seasick but functional crew is to be preferred to one drugged into uselessness.

Some of the newer antinauseant drugs are more selective in their action. These drugs depress parts of the nervous system selectively, leaving the intelligence centers relatively untouched. However, most antinauseants, being akin to tranquilizers, can severely depress the psyche, sometimes producing an indifference to danger. The short-term use of these drugs, particularly when taken before seasickness starts, is not dangerous, but their action is cumulative. After two or three days of heavy dosing, a person or a whole crew may be reduced to a state of indifference in which proper decisions are difficult or impossible.

When rough weather is expected, anticipate seasickness by administering a moderate dose of an antinauseant drug before going on board. Keep busy, and think of things other than the condition of the stomach. If at all possible stay above decks where the horizon will be visible, so that the ship's motion can be seen as well as felt throughout the body. Fight fatigue with rest, rather than with stay-awake pills, coffee, or other stimulants. Alcoholic beverages are particularly bad; their initial action is stimulating, and their aromatic nature contributes to unsettling the stomach.

## 8.13    Resuscitation

A submerged person's breathing may stop after he has inhaled a surprisingly small amount of water. Irritation of the delicate membranes of the
respiratory passages may cause a spasmodic attempt at coughing with short
gasps, or a spastic paralysis comparable to having the "breath knocked out."
Respiratory reflexes regulating breathing as well as consciousness are lost from
lack of oxygen in the brain. This occurs in one minute, or less, after effective
breathing stops, but death may not occur for many more minutes. The significance of these facts is that a rescuer should *never* speculate as to whether
resuscitation will or will not be effective, and he should not delay artificial
respiration because of some preconceived idea of the amount of water to be
drained from the chest. Artificial respiration should be started *at once*.

Victims of smoke or the inhalation of noxious fumes, head and chest injuries, or heart attacks often require artificial respiration. The technique is the
same for all persons not breathing. Mouth-to-mouth breathing has proved to be
the best way to get an adequate amount of air into the victim's lungs. All
methods using pressure on the chest and manipulation of arms have been discarded. The following procedure is recommended:

(1)  Place the victim on his back. Kneel at the side of his head. If there is water
in his lungs or if the victim is in shock, try to place him on a slope with his
head lower than his body but do not delay resuscitation for this purpose.

(2)  Air passages must be open. Turn the victim's head to one side and wipe
out the mouth and back of the throat with a finger. When available, use a
handkerchief or other cloth over the end of an index finger.

(3)  Now turn the victim's face up with his head tilted backward and his chin
elevated.

(4)  Grasp and elevate the lower jaw with one hand by placing the thumb in
the mouth over the teeth and fingers under the angle of the jaw.

(5) Pinch the nostrils closed with the other hand.

(6)  Now with your lips surrounding the victim's mouth and over your thumb,
blow to expand the victim's lungs. Watch to see his chest expand.

(7)  Remove your mouth from the victim's mouth, allowing him to exhale.

(8)  Repeat the cycle every 3 seconds or 20 times per minute.

If the chest does not expand, check the throat again for obstructions. The
base of the tongue will not interfere with the air passage if the head is fully
extended and the tongue is held with the thumb. It may be necessary to elevate
the shoulders.

An *airway* is a plastic or metal device to be inserted into the mouth and
throat to help maintain an unobstructed air passage. A *resuscitation tube* is a
long airway with a flange to make an airtight seal around the mouth. To insert
an airway or resuscitation tube, the head is extended and the jaw elevated as
before. The airway is made to follow a curved course over the tongue until it

reaches the throat. The flange of a resuscitation tube is pressed down against the lips. The nose is pinched closed, and air is blown into the tube to expand the lungs. Much better aeration of the lungs is possible with the resuscitation tube. A wise boatman will provide himself with one.

Fortunately, the heart can beat for many minutes after breathing stops. All is not necessarily lost even if the heart also stops, for sometimes its function can be restored with external heart "massage" or cardiac resuscitation. Two persons will usually be needed, one to provide mouth-to-mouth breathing, the other to resuscitate the heart. The latter is attempted by applying short jabs of pressure on the lower third of the breast bone. About once a second a pressure pulse lasting about one-half second is applied with the two hands, one on top of the other, with the heel of the lower placed on the breast bone. While astride the victim's legs, with elbows straight, the weight of the shoulders is used to apply short bursts of pressure. A heavy, strong man must exercise judgment to avoid fracturing the breast plate or the ribs, particularly if the victim is small. Each pressure application squeezes a small amount of blood out of the heart, thus providing some circulating blood. Except for the brain, the tissue most vulnerable to lack of circulating blood is the heart itself. A successful resuscitation effort may prevent irreversible damage to each of these tissues.

## 8.14    Sunburn

Sunburn is caused by a portion of the ultraviolet light radiated from the sun. Ultraviolet light intensities may be very high on the water, even on an overcast day, because the light reflected from the water will add to that received directly from the sun. The rays responsible for sunburn can penetrate only a very short distance through the human skin, but if there are no absorbing pigments in the skin, these rays can cause injury to the cells beneath. This injury may range from a slight reddening of the skin, or erythema, with subsequent development of pigmentation, to the destruction of large numbers of cells. Cellular death is accompanied by the production of toxic substances, and if large areas of the body are involved, the amount of these substances may be sufficient to produce a high fever and injury to the kidneys and other vital organs.

Sensitivity to sunburn is highly individualistic, fair-skinned persons being most vulnerable. In spite of previous experiences many persons each year underestimate the intensity of the ultraviolet rays and receive severe burns. On a small boat extreme care must be taken to avoid undue exposures, for sunburn can easily become too serious for treatment without the services of a physician.

The best practice is to avoid sunburn by restricting exposures until a protective tan has been developed. The natural skin pigments may be supplemented by the application of ultraviolet absorbing lotions and creams.

The victim of a severe sunburn should be carefully nursed to help maintain his vital functions, such as kidney output. He should be bathed in cool water to keep his temperature down and to reduce the swelling and pain. His intake of food and liquids should not burden the digestive system. Oversedation with drugs or alcohol must be avoided. A patient afloat requiring this type of care should be placed in a doctor's hands as soon as possible.

A severe overexposure to ultraviolet light may produce an acute inflammation of the eye or conjunctivitis. This will be first observed as a "sandy" feeling, followed by severe pain. Exposure to light should, of course, be reduced as much as possible as soon as the symptoms are recognized. The pain may be almost uncontrollable for perhaps 24 hours, but it will then subside, apparently leaving no residual injury. If other areas are extensively sunburned, the eye injury will be a complicating factor emphasizing the need for medical aid.

Blisters resulting from sunburn, or from any other burn, should not be punctured even if they coalesce to form large water pouches. The skin should be left intact until the new layer has formed, to reduce the chance of infection. Lotions and creams should not be used if there is a chance of injuring severely burned skin.

## 8.15   Shock

Shock is a collapse of the circulatory system characterized by a fall in blood pressure, a rapid and thready pulse, pallor, cold sweats, weakness, profound thirst, mental confusion, unconsciousness, and ultimately death. If the victim is apprehensive, excited, and agitated, his state of shock may not be apparent until he loses consciousness.

Nearly all injuries produce some degree of shock. Some people are more prone to shock than others. Since it often progresses in severity, it should be recognized early and treated immediately. The degree of injury does not always foretell the extent of the shock to follow.

Shock should be anticipated in all injured persons. The most important rule is to stop bleeding if it exists. However, a tourniquet is a dangerous application. Its use should be confined to lacerations of very large vessels in extremities. It should never be used when local pressure above and below an injury can control the bleeding. Always try local pressure and do not give up easily. After controlling the bleeding for 10 or 15 minutes by finger pressure, try a moderately tight bandage over a pad of gauze or cloth. Stitches to close a wound and control bleeding should be undertaken by inexperienced persons only if victim's survival is at stake.

Blood and plasma transfusions are specific treatments for shock. Any severely injured person should be gotten to a medical facility as quickly as possible, primarily so that shock can be adequately combated. En route, the victim should be at rest and kept warm if there is a tendency to shiver. *Never give a depressing drug or alcohol* unless directed to do so by a competent physician who is well informed about the case in question. Alcohol in particular will increase rather than decrease the severity of shock.

The victim of severe burns should sip a solution of soda and salt in water (1 teaspoonful of baking soda and ½ teaspoon of table salt in a quart of water). This will restore fluids lost in the swelling blisters and through the skin. An accident victim without burns can sip salt water (1 teaspoon of salt to a quart of water). *Never* allow anyone, sick or well, under any circumstances, *to drink seawater as a substitute for freshwater* or one of the solutions mentioned above.

## 8.16   Food Poisoning

*Food poisoning* (ptomaine poisoning and gastroenteritis) is one of the most probable and devastating medical emergencies to befall the small-boat man. It can be caused by:

(1)  Putrefaction (spoilage without bacterial contamination);

(2)  Chemical contamination (as insect repellents, preservatives, or any of the toxic chemicals now available);

(3)  Poisonous foods (as certain mushrooms, some tropical fish);

(4)  Bacterial growths (toxic products of bacteria which in themselves are not harmful to man);

(5)  Bacteria capable of producing disease in man.

The first three of these food poisoning sources can be controlled fairly readily by good practices in housekeeping and in the control of dangerous substances that may be on board. Bacterial contamination is difficult to prevent and is almost impossible for the layman to detect. Even heavily infected food may appear, smell, and taste normal. If there is any reason to doubt the quality of food, it should be discarded without tasting, for in some cases even a minute quantity can prove fatal. *Any food which is unnaturally soft or mushy or which shows evidence of gas formation should be rejected.* Any canned foods showing swelling of the container, or displaying unusual internal pressure upon opening, should be discarded immediately.

Symptoms of food poisoning may vary from mild and transient to severe and prolonged, and in some cases death may ensue. The outstanding symptoms are diarrhea, nausea, vomiting, gripping abdominal pain, prostration, and unconsciousness. These primary symptoms may be accompanied by fatigue, headache, dizziness, and visual disturbances. An initial chill may be followed by a slight rise in temperature.

Bacteria and bacterial toxins (including the deadly botulinus toxin found in some spoiled canned food) are destroyed by heat. Boiling for 20 minutes or more will make almost any infected food safe. Cooking is the ultimate solution to the problem of food poisoning. It may seem ridiculous to boil a piece of

Bologna sausage or some other apparently well-preserved food, but that is what should be done if there is any doubt as to the quality, and an adequate supply of food of known quality is not available.

The proper treatment of severe cases of food poisoning requires the administration of drugs, such as paragoric, obtainable only upon prescription. Any skipper planning an extended cruise during which medical help may be lacking should consult his personal physician to obtain detailed advice and medical supplies for treating food poisoning.

## 8.17    Alcohol on Board

Some of the preventable marine accidents are caused by ignorance, some by carelessness, and some by a deliberate disregard of safety rules, either written or implied. Among the latter must be classed those caused by the excessive use of alcohol by one or more of the persons on board.

Statistics do not reveal the exact number of marine accidents resulting from alcohol abuse, but the number is substantial. These accidents are strictly preventable by the skipper, who by example and authority can control the use of alcohol on board his vessel.

To a small number of persons a boat is a release or a refuge where the ordinary limits of conduct may be relaxed, perhaps to a dangerous degree. From the standpoint of safety, there is a sharp distinction between a boat under way and one tied to a dock or at anchor. In the one case, all mental facilities are needed to operate the vessel properly, avoid collisions, and keep track of the existing and expected condition of wind and sea.

In the other case, safe in harbor, with the boat secure, restrictions may be relaxed somewhat. Even here the possibility of a serious accident exists, and the skipper must be sure that drinking does not get out of control. Some captains have an iron-clad rule against sailing the day after a big party. This is a laudable safety measure provided a day of idleness does not lead to another party, and so on.

Safety afloat has been most ably expressed by Lane: *

> . . . in the final analysis, a vessel is no safer than the human beings who operate her. She will seldom meet with shipwreck, grounding, stranding, or dismasting unless she has been placed in such danger by ignorance, or stupidity, or carelessness, or drunkenness by the hand at her controls.

## 8.18    Trailer Safety

Many small boats now travel more miles on land, trailerborne, than they do on the water. One must be acutely conscious of the extra responsibility involved in towing a heavy trailer, boat, and engine at present highway speeds.

* Carl D. Lane, *The Boatman's Manual*, Rev. ed. (New York: W. W. Norton and Co.), 1951, p. 535.

A trailer must be chosen with almost as much care as the boat itself. Above all the trailer must be strong, fully capable of carrying the weight of boat, engine, and equipment. The trailer must be well suited to the boat, providing support to the hull at the proper places. In particular the hull must be supported at the transom which will be carrying the weight of a large engine.

Tiedowns must be substantial, well placed, and tightened so that the boat and trailer form almost a single unit. All equipment inside the boat must be secured before starting out. Shifting pieces of gear can cause damage to the boat and can also produce a dangerous sway to the trailer.

Safety lies in keeping the trailer and car together while traveling. The trailer hitch should never go on the bumper of a car, no matter how strong the bumper appears. Weld, bolt, or rivet the hitch to the frame of the car or to some auxiliary extension which in turn is securely attached to the frame.

Car brakes are called on for extra service when trailering. A reduced life must be expected and replacements installed before failure occurs. Always drive with a greater safety factor than is needed for the car alone. Even a small boat and trailer may seriously interfere with the driver's rear vision. The specially designed mirrors, one mounted on each of the forward fenders will be useful for observing the behavior of the trailer and the overtaking traffic.

Particular attention must be paid to the trailer wheels and tires. The small trailer wheels revolve at two to four times the speed of the car wheels. Demands on the wheel bearings are severe even under the best of conditions, and the usual environment of a trailer wheel is far from ideal. Unloading with the wheels immersed means that water may penetrate into the bearings, even though they have been solidly packed with grease. This probability will be increased if the wheels are very hot when they are immersed in cold water. Corrosion and rapid bearing wear follow promptly, particularly if the immersion was in salt water. Rapid tire wear to the point of early destruction follows hard upon the bearing failure. Constant vigilance while driving, coupled with frequent inspections and repacking after immersion appear to be the best procedures for combating rapid bearing deterioration.

Even with wheel bearings in perfect condition the tire pressures must be kept at the recommended values, which are much higher than those customarily used on passenger cars. The high pressures reduce flexing and heating and thus reduce the danger of premature failure and blowout.

Know the laws governing trailering in all of the states in which you plan to tow your boat. These laws are for the protection of you and others using the highways. Look on these laws as minimum requirements, and add other precautions of your own.

CHAPTER **9**

# Aids to
# Navigation

## 9.01 History

From the earliest days sailors have recognized the need for markers to aid them in making safe and accurate passages. The first known aid to navigation, a lighthouse built about 200 B.C. in the harbor of Alexandria, Egypt, was one of the seven wonders of the ancient world. So well was this structure built that it endured until destroyed by an earthquake in 1301 A.D.

The first Congress of the United States recognized the importance of navigational aids by making them the subject of the ninth law enacted (August 7, 1789). Twelve lighthouses already established by the colonies, including the first, Boston Harbor Light (September 14, 1716), were ceded to the Federal Government.

From this modest beginning the system of aids to navigation has increased until there are now more than 44,000 in the U.S. alone. This vast network of aids marking our coasts and navigable streams is established, maintained, and operated by the U.S. Coast Guard. Each aid is chosen to have specific characteristics best suited to its function and its location.

In addition to manned and unmanned lighthouses there are lightships, a wide variety of floating buoys, light stations, daybeacons and unlighted markers which may be erected either on shore or in shallow water. Many of the light sources and audible signals from these aids are radio-controlled. Modern technology is making its impact in this area, particularly in the case of lightships, which are being replaced by enormous automated buoys. Several lightships have been replaced by permanent structures resting on foundations driven into the ocean floor.

Aids containing lights and radio transmitters operated from nuclear power sources have been deployed experimentally. Efforts are being made to standardize types and reduce the variety of aids while still providing the required information to the sailor. A uniform buoyage system has been approved for waters under state and private control.

155

Publications describing the aids and the dangers to be avoided are important adjuncts to the markers themselves. The most complete list of navigational aids is found in the *Light List* issued annually by the Coast Guard. This publication contains a list of lights, fog signals, buoys, daybeacons, lightships, radio beacons, and loran stations. Five volumes cover the navigable waters of the United States:

Vol. I.   Atlantic Coast—St. Croix, Me., to Little River, S.C.
Vol. II.  Atlantic and Gulf Coasts—Little River, S.C., to Rio Grande River, Texas. Includes Puerto Rico, Virgin Islands, Guantánamo Bay, and Navassa Island
Vol. III. Pacific Coast and Islands
Vol. IV.  Great Lakes
Vol. V.   Mississippi River System

Light lists and other publications, such as charts and tide and current tables, are aids to navigation as important as the devices erected in or near the navigable waters. Charts are of special importance and will be discussed separately in Chapter 10.

## 9.02   The Buoyage System

Buoys and all actual navigational aids are so placed as to mark dangers or obstructions and to indicate channels in which vessels may be safely operated. Because of the many types of dangers, it is desirable that each buoy shall convey as much information as possible without involving a marking system too complicated to be readily recognized.

Buoys must be recognizable in conditions of poor visibility, such as fog, rain, or darkness. Markings must be distinctive so that positive identification can be made under adverse conditions. All devices such as shape, color, and distinguishing marks are used to avoid confusion.

United States buoys are deployed according to the *lateral* system under which a buoy—by its shape, color, number (odd or even), and light characteristics—indicates to the navigator the need to direct his course laterally, either to the right or left of the buoy, so as to operate safely. The U.S. system prescribes distinguishing characteristics for the right or left sides of a channel as seen aboard a vessel proceeding from the open sea toward the head of navigation, a port or harbor.

The simple lateral system cannot be applied universally, for many passages are not made directly from the open sea to a harbor. To cover such cases the following arbitrary choices were made. Proceeding from seaward means, in situations which are not obvious:

A southerly direction along the Atlantic Coast.
A northerly and westerly direction along the Gulf of Mexico.

A northerly direction along the Pacific Coast.
A northerly and westerly direction on the Great Lakes.
An upstream direction on the Mississippi and Ohio Rivers and their tributaries.

The Coast Guard has established a uniform system of buoyage applicable to all the waters under its jurisdiction—that is, coastal waters, lakes, and rivers navigable to the sea. Waters wholly within one state and not navigable to the sea are the responsibility of the individual states. Many states have adopted uniform marking systems based on the lateral system of the Coast Guard, with perhaps some special aids used for particular situations.

The steps being taken to insure uniformity throughout the United States are an encouraging note. With the advent of high-speed boat trailers, a boat may be used in waters hundreds of miles apart within a period of only a few days. Safe operation would be almost impossible without a uniform system of marking navigational aids.

## 9.03   Color, Number, Shape

The buoyage system adopted by the Coast Guard is based on the rule: *Proceeding from seaward toward harbor, red buoys shall be kept on the right side of the vessel, black buoys on the left.* All other combinations can be deduced from the basic rule. As an aid to memory one may think of the three Rs: *R*ed to the *R*ight *R*eturning (to harbor). Note that to avoid confusion these directions have been given as left and right instead of port and starboard.

To aid in identification red buoys are given even numbers, black buoys odd. An attempt is made to start the numbering sequence at the seaward end of a channel, with numbers increasing as the vessel proceeds toward the harbor. Numbers are kept in approximate correspondence by omitting some numbers if one side of the channel requires more markers than the other. It is not always possible to maintain the proper numerical sequence; all buoy markings must be carefully checked on a chart or against the light list.

Several distinct shapes are used as a further aid in buoy identification, Figs. 9-1, 2, 3, and 4. A black buoy may be a *can,* or one of the *skeleton* structures carrying a light or an audible signaling device. A red buoy may be a *nun* or a *skeleton.*

A can buoy is a watertight steel cylinder with parallel sides with heavy lugs projecting from the top for lifting. A nun buoy is also made of steel with a cylindrical submerged portion and a typical conical shape above the waterline. Skeleton structures are made of steel frames rising above a buoyant steel cylinder, which houses the necessary mechanisms for activating the signaling devices.

Nun and can buoys are used in a variety of sizes, primarily depending on the weight of mooring chain each must support. Size is not determined by a buoy's relative navigational importance. The Coast Guard's classification of the three most popular sizes is given below.

| Class | Height above the water | |
|---|---|---|
| | Nun | Can |
| First | 11'5" | 9'10" |
| Second | 7'11" | 6'10" |
| Third | 4'5" | 3'5" |

New buoys are being provided with increased capabilities for reflecting visible light and radar signals. Highly reflecting markings assist buoy identification with comparatively feeble lights. Radar reflecting surfaces have been added to the upper portions of buoys, without destroying the characteristic profile.

Alongside each of the buoy shapes, shown in Fig. 9-1, is the corresponding symbol used on charts issued in the United States. The diamond-shaped symbol is positioned on the chart so as to produce the least interference with other markings. The dot is placed at the location of the sinker holding the buoy in place and so represents the most probable or average position of the buoy.

Sinker and anchor chain are calculated to be heavy enough to hold the buoy in position in any blow. This is usually the case, but occasionally a buoy may break loose or drag its sinker a considerable distance. In any case the anchor chain must have a length or *scope* several times the depth of water in which the buoy is anchored. This permits the buoy to change its position somewhat with changes in wind and current. These swings are not large enough to interfere with the primary use of the buoy as a warning device. *Floating aids should not, however, be used as markers when accurate bearings are desired,* for here small changes in position may introduce large errors in angle. Shore-based landmarks should be used for this purpose.

Floating aids should not be passed close aboard, for they are subject to the vagaries of wind and current, and a sudden yaw may bring the heavy buoy down against the hull of a closely passing vessel. Remember that each buoy has a long submerged portion, which may, in a strong current, project upstream at a rather shallow angle. Risk of collision occurs when a deep keel boat passes close aboard on the upstream side.

Close approaches to fixed navigational aids should also be avoided, for many of these are protected from ice and heavy seas by large deposits of heavy stones or *riprap*. A sporting approach to one of these structures can easily lead to serious underwater damage at some distance from the visible structure.

Care must be taken when using audible or electronic aids in heavy weather. It is quite possible to home so accurately on a lighthouse or lightship as to be in actual collision with the aid.

In the event of collision with, or damage to any navigational aid, the person in charge of the colliding vessel must report the event to the nearest

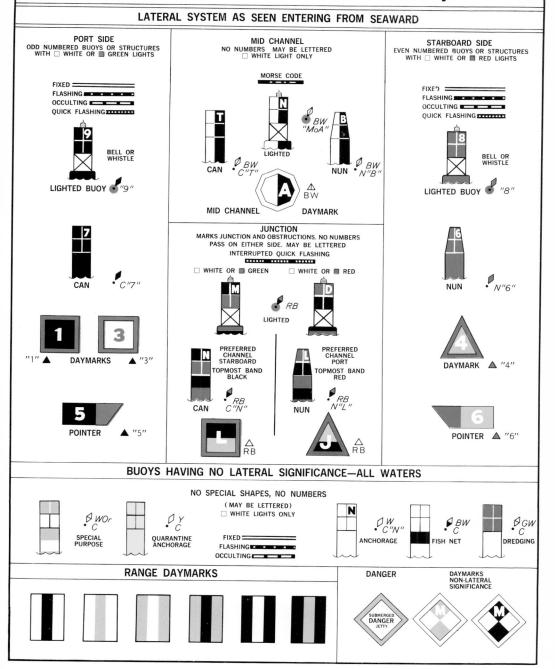

**FIGURE 9-1** Aids to navigation. Courtesy of U.S. Coast Guard.

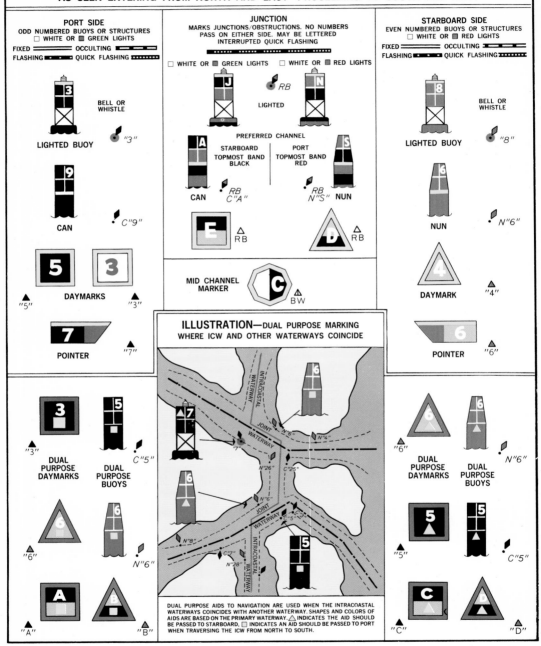

FIGURE 9-2   Aids to navigation. Courtesy of U.S. Coast Guard.

# AIDS TO NAVIGATION ON WESTERN RIVERS

## AS SEEN PROCEEDING IN THE DIRECTION (DESCENDING) OF RIVER FLOW

| LEFT SIDE | JUNCTION | RIGHT SIDE |
|---|---|---|

### LEFT SIDE

☐ WHITE OR ■ RED LIGHTS
GROUP FLASHING (2)

**LIGHTED BUOY**

**NUN**

**PASSING DAYMARK**

**CROSSING DAYMARK**

123.5

**MILE BOARD**

### JUNCTION

MARKS JUNCTIONS AND OBSTRUCTIONS
PASS ON EITHER SIDE
INTERRUPTED QUICK FLASHING

☐ WHITE OR      ☐ WHITE OR
■ RED LIGHTS     ■ GREEN LIGHTS

    LIGHTED   

NUN          CAN

**PREFERRED CHANNEL TO THE RIGHT**
TOPMOST BAND RED
WHITE OR RED LIGHT

**PREFERRED CHANNEL TO THE LEFT**
TOPMOST BAND BLACK
WHITE OR GREEN LIGHT

### RIGHT SIDE

☐ WHITE OR ■ GREEN LIGHTS
FLASHING

**LIGHTED BUOY**

**CAN**

**PASSING DAYMARK**

**CROSSING DAYMARK**

176.9

**MILE BOARD**

## BUOYS HAVING NO LATERAL SIGNIFICANCE—ALL WATERS

NO SPECIAL SHAPES, NO NUMBERS
(MAY BE LETTERING)
☐ WHITE LIGHTS ONLY

FIXED
FLASHING
OCCULTING

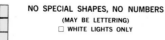   

| SPECIAL PURPOSE | QUARANTINE ANCHORAGE | | ANCHORAGE | FISH NET | DREDGING |

**FIGURE 9-3** Aids to navigation. Courtesy of U.S. Coast Guard.

# UNIFORM STATE WATERWAY MARKING SYSTEM

## USED BY STATES IN STATE WATERS AND SOME NAVIGABLE WATERS

### REGULATORY MARKERS (Information)

SWIM          AREA

**BOATS KEEP OUT**

EXPLANATION MAY BE PLACED OUTSIDE
THE CROSSED DIAMOND SHAPE, SUCH AS
DAM, RAPIDS, SWIM AREA, ETC.

ROCK

**DANGER**

THE NATURE OF DANGER MAY BE IN-
DICATED INSIDE THE DIAMOND SHAPE,
SUCH AS ROCK, WRECK, SHOAL, DAM, ETC.

**5**
MPH

**CONTROLLED AREA**

TYPE OF CONTROL IS INDICATED IN
THE CIRCLE, SUCH AS 5 MPH, NO
ANCHORING, ETC.

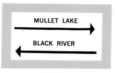

MULLET LAKE

BLACK RIVER

**INFORMATION**

FOR DISPLAYING INFORMATION SUCH
AS DIRECTIONS, DISTANCES, LOCATIONS, ETC.

DAM

BUOY USED TO DISPLAY
REGULATORY MARKERS

### AIDS TO NAVIGATION

(ALL MAY SHOW WHITE REFLECTOR OR LIGHT)

**RED-STRIPED
WHITE BUOY**

INDICATES THAT BOAT
SHOULD NOT PASS BETWEEN
BUOY AND NEAREST SHORE

**MOORING
BUOY**

WHITE WITH BLUE BAND

**7**

**BLACK-TOPPED
WHITE BUOY**

BOAT SHOULD PASS TO
NORTH OR EAST
OF BUOY

**2**

**RED-TOPPED
WHITE BUOY**

BOAT SHOULD PASS TO
SOUTH OR WEST
OF BUOY

**CARDINAL SYSTEM**

(MAY SHOW GREEN REFLECTOR OR LIGHT)          (MAY SHOW RED REFLECTOR OR LIGHT)

**3**

**RED AND BLACK CAN BUOYS**

ARE USUALLY FOUND IN PAIRS
VESSELS SHOULD PASS BETWEEN
THESE BUOYS

**4**

LEFT SIDE —————————— (LOOKING UPSTREAM) —————————— RIGHT SIDE

**FIGURE 9-4** State marking systems. Courtesy of U.S. Coast Guard.

Officer in Charge, Marine Inspection, U.S. Coast Guard. Vessels must not tie up to any aid, and no person shall deface, obscure, or tamper in any way with any aid.

Conversely buoys cannot be placed in the navigable waters of the United States by private citizens or organizations without specific permission of the Coast Guard. This requirement assures that any buoy approved will serve a useful purpose and will conform as closely as possible with the master system. Aids thus authorized are classified as *privately maintained* on charts and in the light list. The Coast Guard jurisdiction does not extend to waters wholly within one state or to streams that have not been declared navigable.

## 9.04  Complications

The simple colored buoy marks an obstruction and directs avoidance either to the right or left depending on the color and the direction in which the vessel is proceeding. Navigational hazards are too complex to be completely handled by the simple two-color system, and so color variations have been introduced.

One complication arises at the junction of two channels where there is a choice of routes, or a point at which there is an obstruction near the center of an otherwise clear channel. Such a point will be marked by a buoy with black and red horizontal bands, Figs. 9-1, 2, and 3, the color of the top band showing the preferred channel. The can, having an upper black band as shown, indicates that a vessel may pass well clear on either side but that the preferred course is to starboard (the buoy to be kept on the left side) for a vessel entering harbor. A *junction* or *middleground* buoy will usually have a shape associated with the color of the top band; black for cans, red for nuns. Lighted junction buoys have the typical skeleton structure with color banding. Junction buoys may be lettered but are unnumbered. The coloring of the chart symbol does not identify the color of the top band, which must be inferred from other chart information.

A *midchannel* buoy, Fig. 9-1, has vertical black and white stripes. It may be a nun or can, either of which is denoted on charts by the divided diamond. A midchannel buoy may be passed close aboard on either side with no preference. Midchannel buoys may be lettered but not numbered.

Figure 9-5 shows a group of buoys with no lateral significance, directing attention neither to the right nor to the left. These buoys will now be found as cans, never as nuns. Solid yellow denotes an area where ships from foreign ports must await medical clearance before entering port. Solid white buoys mark approved anchorage areas. White buoys banded with black show areas where fishnets may be set. A green upper band denotes a dredging area. Orange-banded buoys are used for a variety of unusual situations.

## 9.05    Whistle, Gong, Bell, and Horn

Simple cans and nuns usually have some reflecting material attached so that they may be more readily picked up by a searchlight or radar at night. Except for this, there is no aid to help in locating them in conditions of low visibility. Buoys placed at important locations where identification is essential may be lighted at night or may emit audible signals.

A bell buoy has a large, centrally located bell around which are four heavy clappers, swinging freely as the buoy pitches. Except in the calmest sea, a bell buoy will emit a single characteristic tone at irregular intervals as the swells swing the clappers against the bell.

By contrast, a gong has three or four gongs, each with a different tone and an individual clapper. As in the bell, the gong clappers are actuated by the motion of the buoy in the water. A gong buoy emits three or four tones at irregular intervals and in a random sequence as the pitching actuates the clappers in random order.

A whistle buoy is actuated by air compressed inside the buoy as it rises and falls with the waves. The noise is a low-pitched whistle somewhat comparable to the note produced by blowing gently across the mouth of a large bottle. Whistle buoys require a different motion than bells or gongs for efficient operation, and so they are usually placed where there is a rather continuous groundswell.

In some inside locations mechanical means are used to actuate a horn or a bell at regular intervals, using power sources located inside the buoy itself. Renewing these sources at regular intervals is just one of the many services required to keep the buoyage system in operation. It is not surprising that an occasional failure occurs, a possibility that the mariner must always keep in mind.

## 9.06    Buoy Lighting Conventions

Buoys placed at locations of more than ordinary importance are lighted, and they may or may not be equipped with audible signaling devices. Lighting schemes are necessarily complex, for at night the light must convey all of the information contained by day in color, shape, and number.

Each light, be it a buoy or any other lighted aid, has a *character*, or a particular scheme of emission by which it can be identified. Character is obtained through the use of various colors and emission patterns. The emission patterns (Fig. 9-5) are made up of variations in the following basic types:

*Fixed*, abbreviated *F*, is a continuous, steady light showing no change in color or intensity.

*Fixed and flashing, F Fl*, is a fixed light varied at regular intervals by a flash of greater brilliance of the same color.

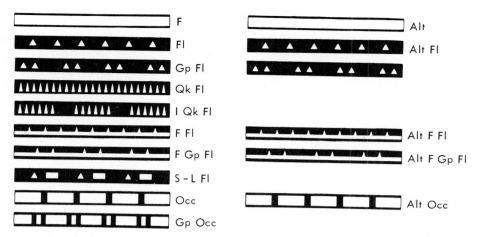

**FIGURE 9-5** Emission patterns of lighted buoys. From CG-158, *List of Lights,* U.S. Coast Guard.

*Fixed and group flashing, F. Gp Fl,* is a fixed light varied at regular intervals by groups of two or more flashes of greater brilliance of the same color.

*Flashing, Fl,* is a single light flash with no change in color, repeated at regular intervals, with not more than 30 flashes per minute. The duration of each flash will always be less than the intervening dark time.

*Group flashing, Gp Fl,* is a closely spaced group of two or more flashes, repeated at regular intervals.

*Group flashing* (_____), *Gp Fl* (___), *composite group flashing,* is a group flashing light in which the flashes are emitted in alternate groups of different numbers. The numbers are shown in the bracket. Thus a light emitting a single flash alternating with three flashes will be designated by *Gp Fl* (1 3).

*Morse code, Mo* (    ), is a group flashing light in which flashes of different duration are grouped so as to produce a character or characters in the Morse code. The characters formed will be shown in the brackets. Thus a light flashing the group "dot, dash" would be shown on a chart or in the Light List as Mo (A), Fig. 9-1. A list of Morse code characters will be found in Appendix VI.

*Quick flashing, Qk Fl,* is a light flash with no change in color, repeated at least 60 times per minute.

*Interrupted quick flashing, I Qk Fl,* shows a series of flashes of a single color at the quick flashing rate for a period of about four seconds. This will be followed by a dark period of about four seconds.

*Equal interval, E Int,* is a light with exactly equal periods of light and darkness.

*Occulting, Occ,* is a light totally eclipsed at regular intervals, with the duration of the light always equal to or greater than the duration of the darkness.

*Group occulting, Gp Occ,* is a light of a single color subjected to groups of two or more eclipses repeated at regular intervals.

*Alternating, Alt,* is a continuous light which alternates between two colors, with very little change in intensity between the colors.

*Alternating flashing, Alt Fl,* is a single flash repeated at regular intervals, with two colors alternating, with not more than 30 flashes per minute. The duration of each flash will always be less than the intervening dark time.

*Alternating fixed and flashing, Alt F Fl,* is a fixed light of one color, varied at regular intervals by a flash of a different color.

*Alternating fixed and group flashing, Alt F Gp Fl,* is a fixed light of one color, varied at regular intervals by groups of two or more flashes of a different color.

*Alternating occulting, Alt Occ,* is a light totally eclipsed at regular intervals, with each light duration equal to or greater than the duration of the dark periods, with alternate flashes of different colors.

Although many combinations of the basic types can be formed, it is obviously not possible to give each light a distinctive character. Many lights have similar characters, differing only in the time required to complete one *period* of emission. The period of a light, as shown on charts and in light lists, is the time required to complete one emission cycle. It is not necessarily the time between successive emissions. If considerable skill is not attained in mentally counting seconds, it may be necessary to carry a stopwatch in order to identify positively the periods of closely spaced lights.

Some lighting characteristics are to be associated with a definite type of buoy. These associations are shown in Table 9-1. *Particular attention should be paid to quick flashing lights.* These are used at important points where extra caution is required. Except for this, there is no significance in the periods of flashing lights.

**TABLE 9-1**

**Color and Lighting Assignments**

| Buoy | Light Color | Light Character |
|------|-------------|-----------------|
| Black | White or Green | F, Fl, Qk Fl, Occ |
| Red | White or Red | F, Fl, Qk Fl, Occ |
| Junction | White, Red, or Green | 1 Qk Fl |
| Midchannel | White only | Mo |
| Miscellaneous | White only | F, Fl, Occ |

## 9.07   Candlepower and Range

Range of visibility is a most important characteristic of any lighted aid. On the one hand, it is desirable to pick up and identify each light at the greatest possible distance in order to get the earliest possible position check. On the other hand, there is probably no more fatiguing duty on shipboard than that of the lookout searching the darkness for an expected light far ahead of the time it can be seen.

The range of visibility of any light depends on many factors. If we assume for the moment a normal human observer and a perfectly clear atmosphere, range will depend primarily on the strength or *candlepower* of the source, its color, its height above the water, and the observer's height above the water.

Dependence on candlepower is obvious and needs no detailed comment. Color is an important factor, depending in a complicated way on atmospheric conditions and the nature of the light source. The normal human eye is most sensitive to green light, but green is more readily scattered and lost from a beam than light of longer wave length, such as red. Any small particles in the air such as dust or water droplets can serve to scatter and diffuse a beam. Light sources such as incandescent electric lights or gas burners emit more of their energy as red light than as green or even shorter wave lengths. Thus, for a given power input, less energy will be radiated as green light than as red. At extreme recognition distances it is easy to confuse a green and a white light, while red is a more distinctive color.

Light rays travel in straight lines, or nearly so, and thus the ultimate range of any light, no matter how high its candlepower, is limited by the curvature of the earth. Range can only be increased by increasing the height of the light, of the observer, or both.

Figure 9-6 shows the situation, greatly exaggerated for the purpose of illustration. A navigational aid at $L$ has a light $H$ feet above sea level emitting light uniformly in all directions. An observer at $A$ will see the light regardless of his own height above the water. An observer at sea level cannot directly see the light beyond $B$, no matter how intense the source. Beyond this point the light rays are intercepted by the earth before they can reach the observer's eye. A ray emitted in direction $C$ will miss the surface of the earth completely. If, however, the observer is at a height $h$ feet above sea level, he will be able to see the light from position $D$.

The relations developed in Fig. 9-6 were based on the assumption that the light rays traveled in exact, straight lines. In fact the rays are bent slightly toward the earth by atmospheric *refraction*, to give ranges about 8 percent greater than would be calculated from geometrical considerations alone. Bright lights are often reflected from clouds and dust particles in the air creating a *loom* that can be seen from points beyond visual range. Under normal atmospheric conditions, range $R$ in nautical miles and height $H$ in feet are related by:

$$R = 1.14 \sqrt{H}$$

**FIGURE 9-6**   Range limitations of a light due to the curvature of the earth.

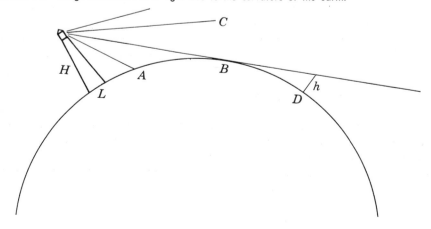

The same type of relation applies to the height of the observer, $h$, so the total range is given by:

$$R = 1.14\sqrt{H} + 1.14\sqrt{h}$$

The maximum possible range can thus be readily calculated, or values may be taken from Table 9-2.

**TABLE 9-2**

**Visible Range-Height Relations**

| Height Feet | Range Nautical Miles | Height Feet | Range Nautical Miles |
|---|---|---|---|
| 5 | 2.6 | 90 | 10.8 |
| 10 | 3.6 | 100 | 11.4 |
| 15 | 4.4 | 120 | 12.5 |
| 20 | 5.1 | 140 | 13.5 |
| 25 | 5.7 | 160 | 14.5 |
| 30 | 6.3 | 180 | 15.4 |
| 40 | 7.2 | 200 | 16.2 |
| 50 | 8.1 | 250 | 18.1 |
| 60 | 8.9 | 300 | 19.8 |
| 70 | 9.6 | 350 | 21.4 |
| 80 | 10.2 | 400 | 22.9 |

ILLUSTRATIVE EXAMPLE

Calculate the limit of visibility of Gay Head Light, 170 feet above sea level, as seen by an observer 15 feet above the water.

From Table 9-2:

By interpolation Range for 170 feet    15.0 miles
Range for   15 feet    4.4

Total range   19.4 miles

The range of this light given in the light list is 19 miles for an observing height of 15 feet. It appears that in this case range is thus limited by height, not candlepower.

Most lights emit rays equally in all directions around the horizon, but a few are arranged to exhibit a *sector* of a secondary color or to have a dark sector where there is no emission. Such a light is fully described in the light list. The angles given in the list, measured clockwise from the north as usual, are those at which the light is seen by an approaching vessel. Each angle from light to vessel will be the *reversed*, or so-called *reciprocal bearing*, Fig. 9-7.

## 9.08    Optical Bearing Beacon

The optical bearing beacon is composed of two standard lanterns coupled in their flashing characteristic to provide the observer with means of determining his true bearing *from the beacon* without the use of a compass. One lantern consists of a rotating optic which emits a pencil beam every 60 degrees. The

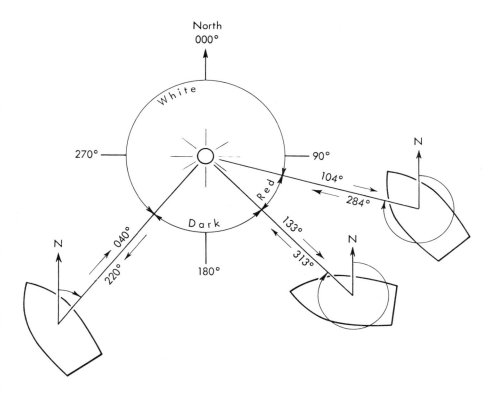

**FIGURE 9-7** Lighted and dark sectors of a lighthouse. Bearings to and from approaching vessels are shown.

six beams rotate in a clockwise direction at a rate of one revolution per minute, and the light will therefore be seen to flash once every 10 seconds. Five of the six beams will be either red or green, the sixth white. Consider the white beam to be the key beam from this lantern.

The other lantern is omnidirectional and contains a xenon flash tube for a light source. A xenon flash tube light is very crisp and distinct and possesses a slightly bluish hue.

When the white flash of the rotating beacon passes through true North bearing, the xenon flash tube will flash. This will occur once a minute. To obtain a true bearing from the beacon, measure the time in seconds from the flash of the xenon flash tube until the flash of white beam of the rotating beacon. By multiplying the time in seconds by six, a true bearing from the beacon is obtained. The time may be measured by stopwatch, wristwatch, or even quite accurately by counting "a thousand one," and so on. An accuracy of one-half second will provide a bearing accurate to three degrees. The useful range is about 10 miles in very clear weather.

Approximate positions may be determined with the use of two beacons in a given area. By noting the time delay from each beacon, two bearings can be obtained and plotted on a chart to obtain an estimated position. A conventional bearing on another object can easily fulfill the third line requirement for completing the fix.

## 9.09    Lighthouses and Lightships

Lighthouses and lightships display signals of the same types as those described for buoys. The larger structures, particularly land-based lighthouses, are free from the power limitations imposed on small floating buoys. More powerful light sources and louder audible signals are usual from the larger aids. Many lighthouses are tended by *resident personnel,* but, with the new electronic controls available, more and more are shifting to automatic or remotely controlled, unattended operation.

Each lighthouse is an individual structure constructed to fit its specific location. Lighthouses are frequently located on an isolated rock where the tower may cover the entire hazard. The individuality is carried over to the color of the exterior paint; many lighthouses have a unique color pattern to aid in visual recognition, Fig. 9-8.

FIGURE 9-8 Charleston, S.C., Light Station has a distinctive red and white tower 163 feet high. The 28 million candlepower light is the most powerful in the Western Hemisphere. Official U.S. Coast Guard photograph.

Lightships moored to heavy anchors with a long scope of chain have been used for many years. Lightships swing on a long radius and should never be passed close aboard. Neither should a vessel home directly on their radio signals in periods of low visibility.

FIGURE 9-9 The first lightship to be replaced by a deep-water offshore structure, at anchor in harbor. Official Coast Guard photograph.

Lightships were built to a common basic pattern with enough variations to provide some visual recognition in addition to the visual signals displayed. Each lightship has the name of its station prominently displayed on its hull, Fig. 9-9. A few relief ships are available for general duty when the regular ship is in port for repairs.

Lightships were originally assigned to stations where the depth of water prevented the construction of a lighthouse. The development of the Texas Tower technique by the oil industry has permitted the construction of bottom-based structures in deep water. Fig. 9-10 shows the first of these offshore struc-

FIGURE 9-10 The deep-water structure that replaced the Buzzards lightship. Official Coast Guard photograph.

tures, commissioned by the Coast Guard in November 1961. The lantern is installed at the base of the skeleton tower structure carrying radio antennas.

Successful experiments with enormous ocean buoys spell the doom of most, if not all, lightships. The Coast Guard considers these buoys adequate replacements for lightships, since they contain weather reporting equipment and light and sound signals. These fully automated aids have spared many Coast Guardsmen very lonely duty.

Several types of high-powered audible signals are utilized by lighthouses, lightships, and the offshore stations. A *diaphone* produces sound by the motion of a slotted piston actuated by compressed air. If two tones are emitted, the higher pitch will be sounded first. *Diaphragm* sources utilize a metal diaphragm actuated by compressed air or electricity. Horns of different pitch may be combined to produce a chimelike note. *Reed* horns produce sound by the motion of a vibrating reed actuated by compressed air. *Sirens* may be operated by air or electricity.

When a fog signal is emitted in groups which form a character or characters in the Morse code, it will be designated on charts and in the Light List as *Horn Mo* (   ), *Dia Mo* (   ), and so on. The letter equivalent of the Morse characters will be given in the brackets. When a fog signal emits signals in alternating groups of different numbers, it is designated as *Horn* (   ), *Siren* (   ), and so on, with the numerical sequence given in the brackets. Detailed characteristics of each fog signal will be found in the Light List.

## 9.10   Daymarks

As the name indicates, daymarks are without either lights or audible signals, being intended for daylight use only. In general these aids are located to mark minor hazards in areas where the water is shallow enough to permit the erection of a fixed structure at small expense. Daymarks may also be constructed along the shoreline and may sometimes be paired to form a range, 11.11.

Daymarks originally varied considerably in design, but they are now as standardized as buoys. For craft entering from seaward, daymarks on the port side are square, exhibiting odd numbers on either a white or a black background edged with green. On the starboard, triangular markers show even numbers on a red or orange field. Daymarks establishing a range are rectangular, with simple geometric patterns displayed in white, black, or orange. On the Western rivers, crossing and passing areas are indicated by daymarks.

## 9.11   Aids on the Intracoastal Waterway

Except for the quarantine buoy, a yellow color indicates a navigational aid on the Intracoastal Waterway. On the Waterway, any can, nun, or lighted buoy will thus bear a yellow band near the top. Black odd-numbered cans will be left to port by anyone traversing the Waterway *from* North and East *to* South and West, while red even-numbered nuns will be left to starboard. Lettered, banded junction buoys have the usual significance. Vertically striped mid-channel buoys are not used on the Waterway.

Where the Intracoastal Waterway coincides with another type of navigable water, the standard buoy types for the latter are used. The top yellow band is omitted, and each can or nun is marked with either a yellow square or a yellow triangle. Vessels traversing the Waterway must treat the square as a black can and the triangle as a red nun, no matter what type of buoy is bearing the mark. Daymarks or range markers on the Waterway follow the regular Inland conventions, but each is edged or top-banded with yellow.

## 9.12    Western Rivers and State and Private Waters

All conventional buoy shapes and colors are used on Western rivers, while only can buoys in a variety of colors are prescribed for state controlled and private waters. Unlighted buoys on Western rivers are distinguished by a yellow band around their upper edges. On state and private waters, day markers take on characteristics of signs directing traffic, marking dangers, and showing speed limits, Fig. 9-4.

## 9.13    The Light List

The Coast Guard's *List of Lights* (see Fig. 9-11) provides more detailed information about navigational aids than can be printed on a chart, but it complements rather than replaces the chart. Safe navigation requires a knowledge of the surroundings as well as the characteristics of the aid itself. It is not enough to rely implicitly on the rule of the 3 Rs and its variations.

The following abbreviations are used in the light list:

| | | | |
|---|---|---|---|
| bl | blast | (M) | Mississippi River |
| cp | candlepower | | type buoy |
| cl | class | RBN | radiobeacon |
| ec | eclipse | R | red |
| ev | every | (R) | unlighted buoy with |
| FS | fog signal | | radar reflector |
| G | green | s | seconds |
| gp | group | si | silent |
| KHz | kiloHertz | (s) | special buoy |
| lt | light | W | white |

## 9.14    Tide Tables

All of the navigational aids described have been designed to establish a position and thus help the mariner avoid collision with some hazard. Less frequently, but no less urgently needed, is detailed information on the state

| (1) No. | (2) Name / Characteristic | (3) Location — Lat. N., Long. W. | (4) Luminous Range Intensity | (5) Geographic Range | (6) Structure — Ht. above ground / Ht. above water | (7) Remarks / Year |
|---|---|---|---|---|---|---|
| 215 | PETIT MANAN LIGHT ........... F. Fl. W., $120^s(2^s$fl). Resident Personnel. | On east point of island. 44 22.1 67 51.9 | 16F 60,000 25Fl. W. 2,500,000 | 17 | Gray granite tower ......... 119 / 123 | HORN, diaphragm; 1 blast ev $30^s$ ($3^s$bl). Bell; 1 stroke ev $20^s$, if horn is disabled. 1817–1855 |
| 6 320 J176 | HALFWAY ROCK LIGHT ........... Alt. F. W., R., and Fl. R. $90^s$(F. W., $59^s$, F. R., $14^s$, R. fl., $3^s$(high intensity). F. R., $14^s$). Resident Personnel. | On rock, midway between Cape Small Point and Cape Elizabeth. 43 39.4 70 02.2 | 19W 190,000 14R 18,000 22 Fl. R. 800,000 | 14 | White granite tower attached to dwelling. 77 / 76 | RADIOBEACON: Antenna 30 feet 160° from light tower. Distance finding station. (See p. XX for explanation.) HORN, diaphragm; gp of 2 blasts ev $60^y$($3^s$bl-$3^s$si-$3^s$bl-$51^s$si). 1871 |
| 525 | James Longstreet Lighted Buoy WRJL. I. Qk. Fl. G. | In 13 feet, marks Naval aircraft. bombing target. 41 49.7 70 03.1 | ......... | ..... | Black and red horizontal bands. | Replaced by can buoy from Nov. 15 to Apr. 15. |
| 546 | Handkerchief Lighted Whistle Buoy H. Mo. (A) W. | In 48 feet 41 28.8 70 04.5 | ........ 140 | ..... | Black and white vertical stripes. | Replaced by can when endangered by ice. |
| 796 | WARWICK LIGHT ........... Occ. G., $5^s(3^s$lt). Resident Personnel. | On north side of entrance to Greenwich Bay. 41 ... | 11 3,000 | 13 | White conical tower ......... 51 | HORN, diaphragm; 1 blast ev $15^s(2^s$bl). 1827–1932 |
| 900 | Watch Hill Light ........... Alt. Occ. W. and Gp. Fl. R., $15^s$ $10.0^s$Wlt., $1.1^s$ec. $0.3^s$Rfl., $2.2^s$ec. $0.3^s$Rfl., $1.1^s$ec. 2 flashes | On point, north side of east entrance to Fishers Island Sound. 41 18.2 71 51.5 | 14W 25,000 16R 20,000 | 13 | Square, gray granite tower attached to white building. 45 / 61 | HORN, diaphragm; 1 blast ev $30^s$($3^s$bl). Storm warning signals displayed during daytime. 1807 |
| 1078 | PISTOL POINT RANGE FRONT LIGHT 82. Qk. Fl. W. | On shore ......... 41 36.7 72 36.8 | ......... 300 | ..... | White diamond daymark with black center, on red skeleton tower, small white house, on red posts. 25 | 1892–1960 |
| 1079 | PISTOL POINT RANGE REAR LIGHT 82. E. Int., $4^s$ | 115 yards 127° from front light. | ......... 500 | ..... | White square daymark with black center on red skeleton tower, small white house on red posts. | Visible on range line only. 1892–1960 |

FIGURE 9-11  Sample extract of light list. From *List of Lights*, U.S. Coast Guard.

| (1) No. | (2) Name / Characteristic | (3) Location Lat. N. / Long. W. | (4) Luminous Range Intensity | (5) Geographic Range | (6) Structure Ht. above ground | Ht. above water | (7) Remarks | Year |
|---|---|---|---|---|---|---|---|---|
| 2747 | Thomas Point Shoal Light / Fl. W., 2 R. sectors, 5ˢ (1ˢfl) / Resident Personnel. | In 7 feet ...... / 38 53.9  76 26.2 | 12W / 6,000 / 9R / 1,300 | 12 | White hexagonal tower on brown piles. | 43 | Red from 011° to 051½° and 096½° to 202°. / See p. XXI for Special Radio Direction Finder Calibration Service. / HORN diaphragm; 1 blast ev 15ˢ(2ˢbl). Standby fog signal if main fog signal is disabled. 1 blast ev 15ˢ (2ˢbl). | 1875 |
| | **SOLOMONS ISLAND** | | | | | | | |
| 3458 | SOLOMONS ISLAND WHARF LIGHT F. G. | On end of wharf ...... | | ..... | Post ...... | 14 | Private aid. | 1940 |
| | Solomons Island Approach Daybeacon 2. | In 19 feet ...... | | ..... | Red triangular daymark on pile . | 12 | Red reflector. | |
| 3459 | SOLOMONS ISLAND APPROACH LIGHT 3. / Fl. W., 4ˢ | In 5 feet ...... | | ..... | Black square daymark on pile .. | 16 | Green reflector. | 1924–1944 |
| | Swash Channel Eastern Entrance Buoy. | In 18 feet ...... / 38 19.2  76 26.0 | | ..... | Black and red horizontal bands; can. | | White reflector. | |
| | Swash Buoy 1 ...... | In 14 feet ...... | | ..... | Black can ...... | | White reflector. | |
| | Swash Buoy 3 ...... | In 12 feet ...... | | ..... | Black can ...... | | White reflector. | |
| | Solomons Island Approach Buoy 4 | In 11 feet ...... | | ..... | Red nun ...... | | Red reflector. | |
| 3460 | SOLOMONS ISLAND HARBOR JUNCTION LIGHT. / 1. Qk. Fl. W. | In 8 feet ...... / 38 19.3  76 27.2 | | ..... | Red and black rectangular daymark on pyramidal top, upper half red on pile. | 14 | Red over green reflector. | 1949–1964 |
| 3460.50 | MILL CREEK LIGHT 2 / Fl. R., 4ˢ | In 10 feet ...... | | ..... | Red triangular daymark on pile . | 15 | Red reflector. | 1966 |
| 3460.60 | MILL CREEK LIGHT 3 / Fl. G., 2.5ˢ | In 9 feet ...... | | ..... | Black square daymark on pile .. | 15 | Green reflector. | 1966 |
| 3460.70 | MILL CREEK LIGHT 5 / Fl. W., 4ˢ | In 7 feet ...... | 170 | ..... | Black square daymark on pile .. | 15 | Green reflector. | 1966 |
| 3460.80 | LUSBY POINT JUNCTION LIGHT / 1. Qk. Fl. W. | In 9 feet ...... | 170 | ..... | Black and red rectangular daymark on pile. | 15 | Green over red reflector. | 1966 |
| 3461 | BACK CREEK LIGHT 2 / Fl. R., 4ˢ | In 6 feet ...... | | ..... | Red triangular daymark on pile . | 14 | Red reflector. | 1942 |
| | Back Creek Buoy 4 ...... | In 7 feet ...... | | ..... | Red nun ...... | | Red reflector. | |
| 3462 | BACK CREEK LIGHT 5 / Fl. W., 4ˢ | In 4 feet ...... | | ..... | Black square daymark on pile .. | 14 | Green reflector. | 1942–1943 |

of the tides and the currents resulting from them. As a routine matter no one should operate a vessel in water so shallow that a high tide is required to avoid grounding. Occasionally, however, a successful passage may require an exact knowledge of a tidal situation. If a grounding has occurred, a knowledge of whether the tide is at ebb or flood is vital.

Tides, or the *vertical* rise and fall of large bodies of water, result from the powerful gravitational attraction of the moon and the sun. Being much closer, the moon is by far the more powerful influence. The effect of the sun appears as a small distortion superimposed on the main movement.

One tidal cycle is the time required for the moon to make one circuit around the earth. This time is about fifty minutes longer than our solar day, so we have slightly less than one tidal cycle, consisting of two highs and two lows, in each 24 hours.

At new and full moon the tidal forces of moon and sun are in the same direction, to produce larger-than-average or *spring* tides. At first and last quarter the two forces oppose, producing smaller or *neap* tides. Other variations are known but are small.

The mechanisms producing tidal action have been known well enough for more than a century to permit predictions of tidal motions in both time and amount. These predictions are issued annually as *Tide Tables* by the National Ocean Survey. The two volumes of most interest to the small-boat operator are:

(a)  *East Coast of North and South America, including Greenland*
(b)  *West Coast of North and South America, including the Hawaiian islands*

The Tide Tables tabulate times and magnitudes of high and low water for a series of reference stations. Auxiliary tables permit the estimation of tides at about 2000 secondary stations, using the tabulated values for the nearest reference station. Detailed directions for making the calculations are given in the Tide Tables.

As the excerpts show, tidal ranges vary tremendously from one location to another. All tabulations in the Tide Tables are average values, since long-range predictions can take no account of weather disturbances, which may temporarily change tides drastically. A hard blow may aid or resist, accelerate or delay a tide from its normal expectancy.

## 9.15  Tidal Current Tables

There is some confusion between the meanings of *tide* and *current*. The former refers to the *vertical* motion of large bodies of water under the gravitational attraction of sun and moon. Current is the *horizontal* flow of water as bays and basins fill and empty in response to the varying heights of the sea. In open waters wind also contributes to the horizontal movements of surface waters. It is current and not tide that sets the mariner off course, or adds or subtracts from the normal speed of his boat.

Excerpts from the *1973 East Coast Tide Tables:*

## TIMES AND HEIGHTS OF HIGH AND LOW WATERS

| EASTPORT, MAINE, 1973 JULY | | | | | | SANDY HOOK, N.J., 1973 JULY | | | | | | KEY WEST, FLA.,1973 JULY | | | | | |
|---|---|---|---|---|---|---|---|---|---|---|---|---|---|---|---|---|---|
| Day | Time | Ht. | Day | h. m. | ft. | Day | Time | Ht. | Day | Time | Ht. | Day | Time | Ht. | Day | Time | Ht. |
| | h. m. | ft. | | | | | h. m. | ft. | | h. m. | ft. | | h. m. | ft. | | h. m. | ft. |
| Su 1 | 0502 | -2.9 | M 16 | 0522 | 0.0 | Su 1 | 0216 | -0.9 | M 16 | 0219 | 0.0 | Su 1 | 0315 | 0.1 | M 16 | 0329 | 0.3 |
| | 1108 | 19.6 | | 1122 | 17.1 | | 0813 | 5.1 | | 0811 | 4.3 | | 0948 | 2.1 | | 0955 | 1.7 |
| | 1722 | -1.6 | | 1736 | 1.0 | | 1419 | -0.5 | | 1421 | 0.5 | | 1703 | -0.7 | | 1656 | -0.3 |
| | 2327 | 21.2 | | 2334 | 18.3 | | 2029 | 6.2 | | 2023 | 5.2 | | 2311 | 0.9 | | 2305 | 0.9 |
| M 2 | 0555 | -3.0 | Tu 17 | 0600 | -0.1 | M 2 | 0306 | -1.0 | Tu 17 | 0255 | 0.0 | M 2 | 0410 | 0.1 | Tu 17 | 0409 | 0.2 |
| | 1200 | 19.8 | | 1159 | 17.4 | | 0906 | 5.1 | | 0849 | 4.3 | | 1042 | 1.9 | | 1030 | 1.6 |
| | 1816 | -1.7 | | 1815 | 0.8 | | 1512 | -0.5 | | 1458 | 0.5 | | 1743 | -0.6 | | 1723 | -0.3 |
| | | | | | | | 2121 | 5.9 | | 2059 | 5.1 | | 2353 | 1.0 | | 2335 | 1.0 |
| Tu 3 | 0020 | 21.0 | W 18 | 0011 | 18.3 | Tu 3 | 0353 | -0.9 | W 18 | 0330 | 0.0 | Tu 3 | 0507 | 0.0 | W 18 | 0450 | 0.2 |
| | 0648 | -2.9 | | 0638 | -0.2 | | 0959 | 5.1 | | 0927 | 4.4 | | 1131 | 1.8 | | 1107 | 1.5 |
| | 1253 | 19.7 | | 1236 | 17.6 | | 1603 | -0.3 | | 1534 | 0.5 | | 1824 | -0.4 | | 1752 | -0.2 |
| | 1909 | -1.5 | | 1853 | 0.7 | | 2212 | 5.6 | | 2138 | 4.9 | | | | | | |
| W 4 | 0113 | 20.4 | Th 19 | 0050 | 18.3 | W 4 | 0442 | -0.7 | Th 19 | 0403 | 0.1 | W 4 | 0034 | 1.1 | Th 19 | 0001 | 1.1 |
| | 0738 | -2.3 | | 0716 | -0.1 | | 1055 | 5.1 | | 1006 | 4.5 | | 0611 | 0.0 | | 0535 | 0.2 |
| | 1345 | 19.5 | | 1315 | 17.8 | | 1657 | 0.0 | | 1612 | 0.6 | | 1227 | 1.5 | | 1148 | 1.4 |
| | 2001 | -1.1 | | 1934 | 0.7 | | 2304 | 5.2 | | 2215 | 4.7 | | 1902 | -0.2 | | 1820 | -0.1 |
| Th 5 | 0207 | 19.6 | F 20 | 0129 | 18.1 | Th 5 | 0527 | -0.4 | F 20 | 0438 | 0.1 | Th 5 | 0117 | 1.2 | F 20 | 0030 | 1.2 |
| | 0830 | -1.6 | | 0754 | 0.1 | | 1146 | 5.0 | | 1045 | 4.6 | | 0715 | 0.0 | | 0624 | 0.1 |
| | 1436 | 19.0 | | 1355 | 18.0 | | 1749 | 0.3 | | 1653 | 0.7 | | 1322 | 1.3 | | 1236 | 1.3 |
| | 2056 | -0.5 | | 2017 | 0.7 | | 2357 | 4.8 | | 2300 | 4.6 | | 1941 | -0.1 | | 1848 | 0.0 |
| F 6 | 0301 | 18.5 | Sa 21 | 0214 | 17.8 | F 6 | 0618 | -0.1 | Sa 21 | 0511 | 0.2 | F 6 | 0202 | 1.3 | Sa 21 | 0105 | 1.3 |
| | 0922 | -0.6 | | 0835 | 0.4 | | 1237 | 4.9 | | 1132 | 4.7 | | 0824 | 0.0 | | 0724 | 0.1 |
| | 1531 | 18.4 | | 1438 | 18.0 | | 1850 | 0.5 | | 1743 | 0.8 | | 1425 | 1.0 | | 1328 | 1.1 |
| | 2150 | 0.1 | | 2103 | 0.7 | | | | | 2347 | 4.4 | | 2016 | 0.1 | | 1917 | 0.2 |
| Sa 7 | 0354 | 17.5 | Su 22 | 0301 | 17.4 | Sa 7 | 0047 | 4.4 | Su 22 | 0556 | 0.3 | Sa 7 | 0248 | 1.4 | Su 22 | 0148 | 1.4 |
| | 1013 | 0.3 | | 0924 | 0.7 | | 0712 | 0.2 | | 1221 | 4.8 | | 0940 | 0.0 | | 0833 | 0.0 |
| | 1625 | 17.8 | | 1527 | 18.0 | | 1328 | 4.8 | | 1848 | 0.8 | | 1539 | 0.8 | | 1434 | 0.9 |
| | 2247 | 0.7 | | 2152 | 0.7 | | 1951 | 0.7 | | | | | 2052 | 0.2 | | 1952 | 0.3 |
| Su 8 | 0454 | 16.6 | M 23 | 0354 | 17.1 | Su 8 | 0138 | 4.1 | M 23 | 0043 | 4.2 | Su 8 | 0342 | 1.4 | M 23 | 0239 | 1.5 |
| | 1109 | 1.2 | | 1015 | 1.0 | | 0805 | 0.4 | | 0653 | 0.3 | | 1100 | 0.0 | | 0957 | -0.1 |
| | 1721 | 17.3 | | 1622 | 18.0 | | 1420 | 4.8 | | 1320 | 4.9 | | 1704 | 0.7 | | 1559 | 0.7 |
| | 2345 | 1.2 | | 2249 | 0.7 | | 2050 | 0.7 | | 2001 | 0.8 | | 2141 | 0.3 | | 2035 | 0.4 |

Meridian 75° W. 0000 is midnight. 1200 is noon.
Heights are reckoned from the datum of soundings on charts of the locality which is mean low water.

In most inshore locations tidal currents *flood* as the tide rises to fill low lying areas and *ebb* as these areas empty. The moment at which the direction of flow reverses is *slack water.* Offshore the currents are more apt to change direction continuously, producing a *rotary current* with no time of slack water.

Two volumes of tidal current predictions for United States waters are now issued annually by the National Ocean Survey: *Tidal Current Tables, Atlantic Coast of North America, including Puerto Rico,* and *Tidal Current Tables, Pacific Coast of North America.* The East coast predictions are made for 20 reference stations. Auxiliary tables permit current estimates at about 1,000 secondary locations, using the values tabulated for the nearest reference station.

Excerpts from the 1973 *Tidal Current Tables* for the Atlantic Coast of the United States:

**HELL GATE (off Mill Rock), EAST RIVER, N.Y., 1973**
F—flood, direction 050° true
E—ebb, direction 230° true

JULY

| Day | Slack Water Time | Maximum Current time | Vel. |
|---|---|---|---|
| | h. m. | h. m. | kn. |
| Su 1 | | 0049 | 5.1E |
| | 0421 | 0717 | 3.8F |
| | 1019 | 1312 | 5.0E |
| | 1638 | 1940 | 3.9F |
| | 2246 | | |
| M 2 | | 0144 | 5.1F |
| | 0515 | 0812 | 3.8F |
| | 1113 | 1407 | 5.0F |
| | 1734 | 2036 | 3.9F |
| | 2340 | | |
| Tu 3 | | 0238 | 5.0E |
| | 0609 | 0905 | 3.7F |
| | 1207 | 1503 | 4.9E |
| | 1830 | 2129 | 3.7F |
| W 4 | 0035 | 0332 | 4.9E |
| | 0702 | 0958 | 3.6F |
| | 1301 | 1555 | 4.8E |
| | 1926 | 2226 | 3.6F |
| Th 5 | 0129 | 0427 | 4.7E |
| | 0756 | 1054 | 3.4F |
| | 1355 | 1653 | 4.6E |
| | 2023 | 2325 | 3.4F |
| F 6 | 0224 | 0521 | 4.5E |
| | 0851 | 1151 | 3.3F |
| | 1449 | 1750 | 4.4E |
| | 2121 | | |
| Sa 7 | | 0023 | 3.2F |
| | 0319 | 0617 | 4.3E |
| | 0946 | 1250 | 3.1F |
| | 1544 | 1849 | 4.3E |
| | 2218 | | |

**CHARLESTON HARBOR (off Ft. Sumter), S.C., 1973**
F—flood, direction 335° true
E—ebb, direction 120° true

MAY

| Day | Slack Water Time | Maximum Current time | Vel. |
|---|---|---|---|
| | h. m. | h. m. | kn. |
| Tu 1 | 0111 | 0342 | 2.3F |
| | 0659 | 1004 | 2.8E |
| | 1319 | 1604 | 2.8F |
| | 1930 | 2236 | 3.1E |
| W 2 | 0200 | 0433 | 2.4F |
| | 0745 | 1050 | 2.9E |
| | 1404 | 1653 | 3.0F |
| | 2019 | 2324 | 3.2E |
| Th 3 | 0250 | 0521 | 2.5F |
| | 0832 | 1137 | 3.0E |
| | 1450 | 1742 | 3.1F |
| | 2108 | | |
| F 4 | | 0015 | 3.3E |
| | 0341 | 0610 | 2.5F |
| | 0921 | 1225 | 3.0E |
| | 1539 | 1831 | 3.1F |
| | 2159 | | |
| Sa 5 | | 0104 | 3.2E |
| | 0433 | 0703 | 2.4F |
| | 1012 | 1318 | 2.9E |
| | 1631 | 1923 | 3.0F |
| | 2253 | | |
| Su 6 | | 0200 | 3.1E |
| | 0528 | 0754 | 2.2F |
| | 1108 | 1413 | 2.7E |
| | 1728 | 2018 | 2.8F |
| | 2350 | | |
| M 7 | | 0255 | 2.9E |
| | 0627 | 0851 | 2.0F |
| | 1209 | 1511 | 2.5F |
| | 1829 | 2117 | 2.5F |

**Cape Romain, 5 miles SE. of Lat. 32°57' N., long. 79°17' W.**

Hours after maximum flood at Charleston Harbor, see page 82

| Time | Direction (true) | Velocity |
|---|---|---|
| | Degrees | Knots |
| 0 | 6 | 0.2 |
| 1 | 38 | 0.2 |
| 2 | 55 | 0.3 |
| 3 | 67 | 0.3 |
| 4 | 93 | 0.3 |
| 5 | 114 | 0.3 |
| 6 | 167 | 0.2 |
| 7 | 212 | 0.2 |
| 8 | 242 | 0.3 |
| 9 | 244 | 0.4 |
| 10 | 262 | 0.3 |
| 11 | 292 | 0.3 |

Time meridian 75°W.    0000 is midnight.    1200 is noon.

The tabulated material is supplemented by detailed information on particular areas.

The Gulf Stream is a current of non-tidal origin that has a profound effect on the weather patterns and on offshore navigation on the eastern coast of the United States. The Gulf Stream enters the narrow channel between the Florida Keys and Cuba. It then flows northward and eastward roughly along the 100 fathom depth line to Cape Hatteras where it swings more easterly up to the Grand Banks off Newfoundland, across the Atlantic to the northern coasts of Europe. Gulf Stream currents vary, but an average value for a Florida-Bahamas crossing is 2½ knots with a northerly set.

As is evident from the excerpt, page 174, the effect of a current can be appreciable. There is a difference of about nine knots between flood and ebb at Hell Gate, a difference well worth taking advantage of by properly timing a proposed passage.

A study of the tables will show little relation between the times of maximum current and the tides causing them. This is because the currents depend on many details of the shoreline, such as the volume that must flow through a restricted opening and the entering flow of rivers. Note that the directions of ebb and flow need not be exactly 180° apart. As with tides, current predictions may be temporarily upset by weather conditions.

## 9.16    *United States Coast Pilot*

Modern charts supply an enormous amount of information in highly compressed form, with the details of each navigational aid given in the light list. More information still is needed if vessels are to venture safely and expeditiously into unfamiliar waters. This information is supplied by the *United States Coast Pilot* series prepared at intervals by the National Ocean Survey and kept up to date between editions by supplements.

Nine volumes of the *Coast Pilot* cover the seacoast of the United States from Eastport, Maine, to Washington State, including Hawaii and Alaska. Written in narrative form, the *Coast Pilot* supplies many miscellaneous bits of information needed for course planning and effective navigation. There is little duplication of information supplied by other publications. Important lights or other navigational aids may thus be mentioned in the *Coast Pilot,* but the characteristic details of operation will not be found.

An example of the supplementary nature of chart and *Coast Pilot* can be found on Chart 550, Chesapeake Bay, Eastern Bay and South River. The chart shows a bridge with the following notation: "Bascule Bridge. Hor. Cl. 75 ft. Vert. Cl. 16 ft." This does not convey sufficient information to plan a passage upstream. From the *Coast Pilot No. 3,* 1961:

> 203.310 Severn River, Md.; bridge (highway) near Annapolis, Md. (a) The leaves of the draw shall be promptly raised to their full height so as to provide full horizontal clearance through the bridge at any time during the day or night

for all vessels desiring to pass through it whose masts are 15 feet or more in height or for any vessels whose hulls, deckhouses, or cargo are of such height that they will not pass under the bridge when it is closed.

(b) Vessels have the right of way over vehicles or persons using the bridge.

(c) A vessel approaching the bridge shall signal by three blasts of a whistle or horn. The signal shall be answered by three blasts of a whistle or horn that can be heard three-fourths of a mile from the bridge, and the draw shall be opened forthwith. In case, however, of accidents to the machinery or other contingency involving unavoidable delay in opening the draw, the signal shall be answered by one blast of a whistle or horn.

In addition to providing information directly bearing on navigation, the *Coast Pilot* lists facilities for anchoring, repairs, and stores. Some assessment is made of the safety of various anchorages during strong gales and hurricanes. Even items not related to navigation but of general tourist interest will be found in the *Coast Pilot*.

## 9.17   Notices to Mariners

In any large district changes are constantly being made in the location and characteristics of navigational aids. Channel improvements in some areas and new obstructions such as wrecks, new highway bridges, and silt deposits in other areas must be marked by relocated or new aids. Storms and ice sometimes dislocate or damage buoys and day beacons.

News of changes in aids to navigation and other matters concerning navigation is published by the Coast Guard in *Notices to Mariners*. Upon request local notices, issued as often as daily, are available to the private boatman from his nearest Coast Guard District Office (see Appendix II). Charts, Light Lists, Coast Pilots, and lists of radio aids should be kept up to date by noting the changes in the notices.

### EXERCISES

See Section 10.12 regarding the use of chart 1210 Tr on which these exercises are based.

**9-1.**   Since the 1963 edition of chart 1210 Tr, the light emission characteristics of midchannel buoys have been changed to Mo (    ). On chart 1210 Tr there are four BW buoys whose coding has been changed to Mo (A). Locate these buoys and correct your copy of the chart accordingly. How has this change altered the basic nature of the light emissions? See Appendix VI.

**9-2.**   You are entering Buzzards Bay from the Southwest in a period of low visibility and a calm sea. What characteristics will be useful to you in identifying buoys "2B," "4," and "6," before their numbers are visible?

**9-3.**   What is the emission characteristic of the light on the SW tip of Cuttyhunk Island?

**9-4.**   There are three red lights governing the approaches to Newport Harbor: Castle Hill, Fort Adams, and Rose Island. What are the distinguishing characteristics of these three lights?

**9-5.** On the way from Old Harbor, Block Island, to the Sakonnet River you pass close aboard buoys W or "A" and W or "B". What is the nature of the light emissions from W or "A"? What is the significance of these buoys?

**9-6.** How can you distinguish between buoys BW(A) and BW(SR) located off the mouth of the Sakonnet River?

**9-7.** As you proceed up Buzzards Bay toward the entrance to the Cape Cod Canal, you pass between buoys R"8" and BW. Identify buoy BW.

**9-8.** You next pickup buoy RB. What is the purpose of this buoy? What action do you take on approaching it?

**9-9.** Is the limit of visibility of Point Judith light limited by the curvature of the earth or by its candlepower to an observer 15 feet above the water?

**9-10.** Using the Tide Table excerpt, page 173, when does the lowest water level occur at Sandy Hook on 3 July 1973?

**9-11.** Using the Current Table excerpt, page 174, what is the most favorable time to proceed upstream through Hell Gate, N. Y., on 2 July 1973?

## ANSWERS

**9-1.** The basic emission characteristic is unchanged because the Morse symbol for (A) is • —, which is comparable to the previous S-L emission.

**9-2.** "2B" at least 50 red flashes per minute.

"4" one red flash every four seconds, no sound in calm.

"6" one red flash every four seconds, no sound in calm.

**9-3.** Two white flashes closely grouped every 10 seconds.

**9-4.** Castle Hill—red light interrupted (occulted) once every four seconds.

Fort Adams—one red flash every five seconds.

Rose Island—steady red light.

**9-5.** W or "A"—one white flash every four seconds. These are buoys marking a range where submarine torpedos are test fired. When in use the range will usually have a surface patrol in addition to the buoys.

**9-6.** BW(A)—lower portion black, top white, one white flash every three seconds.

BW(SR)—vertical black and white stripes, white light Mo(A).

**9-7.** BW—black and white vertical stripes, unlighted.

**9-8.** RB is an obstruction buoy marking a small shoal. A deep draft boat should keep well clear on either side.

**9-9.** Range limit from curvature 13.6 miles, curvature limited.

**9-10.** The water level was estimated to be 0.9 feet below the mean low water datum at 0353 Eastern Standard Time.

**9-11.** Maximum flood was predicted for 2036 Eastern Standard Time, 3.9 kts.

# CHAPTER 10

# Charts and Maps

## 10.01   Charts and Maps

Any representation of a portion of the earth's surface on a plane surface is a map or chart. The former term is reserved for those representations emphasizing land areas, with boundaries, roads, and general geographical features. Charts depict the information necessary for planning and carrying out safe passages in navigable waters. Emphasis is placed on items such as depths of water, obstructions to passage, and aids to navigation, but prominent features of adjacent land areas are included. Maps are usually used for informational purposes. Charts also have carefully prepared working surfaces on which course lines, bearing lines, and other information pertinent to a passage can be plotted. To preserve the integrity of this working surface, charts should be handled with care. Whenever possible, charts should be rolled rather than creased or folded to facilitate accurate plotting.

Charts have been used since ancient times, although there are vast differences between the amount of detail presented then and now. Early chart-makers, dealing only with limited areas, did not realize the difficulties of transferring details from a spherical surface to a plane. As more of the sea areas became known, the problem of *projection* became evident. Some projection methods were in use in B.C., but modern chart projection really started in 1569 when Gerhard Kremer published a chart constructed on the *Mercator* projection. This is the form of chart used in almost all navigation today.

Early chartmakers were seriously handicapped by a lack of methods of reproduction. Charts were drawn by hand on parchment with many embellishments but with a complete lack of uniformity. Charts were then used for reference purposes; they were much too valuable to use in laying out courses. Even in the nineteenth century charts were expensive. They were reused many times with previous course plottings carefully erased between voyages.

The modern chart, available for two dollars or less, is an amazing production. An enormous amount of information is presented on a single chart in an abbreviated form that is simple yet hard to mistake. Thousands of depth measurements and other details are required for a chart of even a limited area. Methods of reproduction have been developed to reduce distortion of the paper during preparation. This is an important point since modern methods of navigation require measurements to be made on the chart itself.

One may say that no aid to navigation is absolutely indispensable, for safe passages were made before any aids were available. However, of the aids that we now think of as indispensable, the chart is probably the most important. With it one can venture into unknown waters with a considerable degree of confidence; without it one must proceed with the utmost caution and with little assurance of a successful passage.

Various agencies of the federal government produce and sell thousands of different charts for marine and for air navigation. Fortunately only a small number of the many types now available need concern the small-boat operator.

Charts prepared and issued by the National Ocean Survey of the National Oceanic and Atmospheric Administration (NOAA), of the Department of Commerce, will be used almost exclusively in inland and nearby coastal waters. Charts of the high seas, foreign waters, and charts for use with loran or other special navigational aids are issued by the Oceanographic Office, U.S. Navy. The U.S. Army Corps of Engineers produces charts covering the Great Lakes and various other lakes, rivers, and canals within the borders of the United States.

Charts may be obtained by mail order or by over-the-counter purchase from a variety of distribution centers. Mail order sales are conducted from the following addresses:

*Inland and nearby coastal waters:*
   National Ocean Survey, Distribution Division, Riverdale, Maryland 20840
*Offshore and foreign waters:*
   Naval Oceanographic Distribution Center, 5801 Tabor Avenue, Philadelphia, Pa. 19120
*Great Lakes and connecting waters including the N.Y. State barge canal, Lake Champlain, St. Lawrence River, and the Minnesota-Ontario border lakes:*
   U.S. Army Engineer District, Lake Survey, 630 Federal Building, Detroit, Michigan 48226
*Great Lakes and Canadian coastal waters:*
   Chart Distribution Office, Canadian Hydrographic Service, Surveys and Mapping Building, 615 Booth Street, Ottawa, Ontario, Canada
*Lower Mississippi River, Gulf of Mexico to Ohio River, and other rivers:*
   U.S. Army Engineer Division, P.O. Box 80, Vicksburg, Mississippi 39181
*Middle and Upper Mississippi River and Illinois Waterway to Lake Michigan:*
   U.S. Army Engineer Division, 536 South Clark Street, Chicago, Illinois 60605
*Missouri River:*
   U.S. Army Engineer Division, P.O. Box 103, Downtown Station, Omaha, Nebraska 68101
*Ohio River:*
   U.S. Army Engineer Division, P.O. Box 1159, Cincinnati, Ohio 45201

## 10.02    Earth Coordinates

The earth is an oblate spheroid, or a sphere slightly flattened at the poles. The equatorial diameter is 6,888 miles, the polar diameter 6,865 miles. The difference of 23 miles is sufficient to require attention in making charts and in many of the calculations involved in navigation over long distances. For the moment we will neglect these refinements, considering the earth to be a perfect sphere.

Any plane surface passing through the center of a sphere will intersect the surface of the sphere in a *great circle*. Any plane passing through the poles and the center will intersect the surface of the sphere in a particular great circle called a *meridian*. The *equator* is an example of a great circle that does not include the poles.

Measurements made along the equator from one particular reference meridian determine the *longitude* (*Lo*) of the meridian passing through the point *to* which the measurement is made. International agreement has designated the meridian through Greenwich, England, as the zero point of all longitude measurements. There are 360 degrees of angle around the equator. Longitude is measured in degrees, minutes, and seconds of arc up to 180° W and 180° E, Fig. 10-1.

**FIGURE 10-1**    Meridians of longitude and parallels of latitude serve as coordinates to locate any point on the surface of the earth.

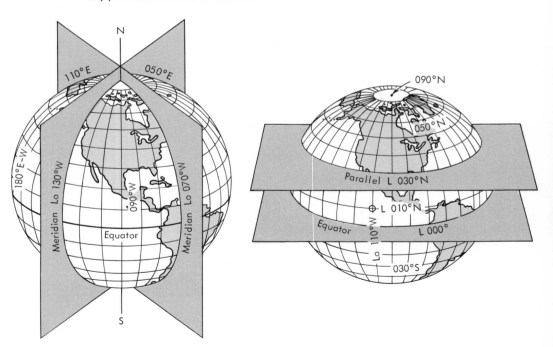

A plane passed through the sphere parallel to the equator but above or below it will not pass through the center of the sphere. It will then form a *small circle* at its intersection with the surface. As the plane approaches either of the poles the radius of the small circles will decrease drastically. These small circles are *parallels of latitude*. There will be 180 degrees of angle measured along a meridian from pole to pole. Latitude ($L$) is the angle measured along a meridian from the equator to the parallel in question; values range from 0° to 90° N and 0° to 90° S. Latitude and longitude are *coordinates* which serve to locate any point on the earth's surface.

The distance measured along the equator between two meridians one degree apart is 60.12 nautical miles. One minute of arc along the equator is then 1.002 nautical miles. Since the two meridians converge and meet at the poles, one minute of arc will represent less than the equatorial value at any latitude away from the equator.

One minute of arc of latitude, measured along a meridian, is 0.995 nautical miles at the equator and 1.005 nautical miles at the poles. Except for very small corrections each minute of latitude will represent a distance of one nautical mile at any latitude.

## 10.03   Sphere, Plane, and Projection

In transferring features from a sphere to a plane some plan of *projection* must be used which will preserve as many desirable characteristics as possible. Among the desirable characteristics of a projection we may list:

(1)  Physical features such as coastlines or land masses should project into their true shape for ready recognition.

(2)  Angles should project without changing values. Any projection satisfying this requirement is *conformal*.

(3)  Areas should project in correct relative proportions.

(4)  The projection should have a constant scale value for ease in making distance measurements.

(5)  Great circles should project as straight lines.

(6)  Rhumb lines should project as straight lines.

All of these six requirements cannot be satisfied simultaneously. For example, it is not possible for both great circles and rhumb lines to be straight in the same projection. There is no universally best projection; each has characteristics best suited for a particular use. In large-scale charts covering small areas, there is little difference between the various projections.

The *rhumb line* (pronounced *rum*) of requirement (6) is a line customarily used by pilots and navigators in plotting and sailing all but the longest ocean voyages. A rhumb line course is almost always somewhat longer than a great circle course between the same two places, but in rhumb line sailing a single course direction will take the vessel from the point of departure to its destina-

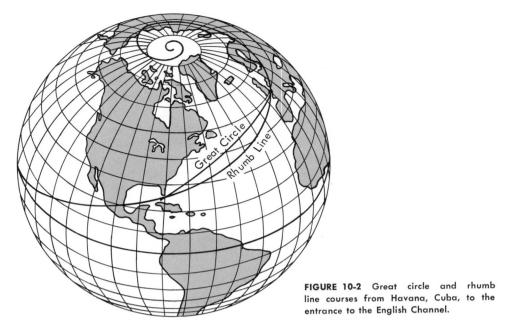

**FIGURE 10-2** Great circle and rhumb line courses from Havana, Cuba, to the entrance to the English Channel.

tion, 10.07. This simplification arises from the fact that a rhumb line makes the same angle with every meridian that it crosses. On the sphere a rhumb line spirals inward toward the poles to form a curve known as a loxodrome, Fig. 10-2.

## 10.04 Mercator Projection

Most marine charts are constructed on a Mercator projection. It is frequently stated that a Mercator projection is made by surrounding the sphere with a cylinder and projecting the sphere onto the cylinder, which is then unrolled to form a flat chart. This construction is not, however, a Mercator projection.

Consider (Fig. 10-3A) a portion of the earth's surface contained between two meridians to be peeled off from the sphere and projected onto a plane. The peel is shown with parallels of latitude and with two squares of equal area. If great circles (including meridians) are to project as straight lines, the upper portion of the peel must be expanded by a factor which increases with increasing latitude, in order to convert the converging meridians to parallel straight lines. This process of expansion cannot be carried out clear to the poles, since it is impossible to multiply a zero distance by any number known to obtain the required constant width.

The result of expanding the parallels of latitude is shown in Fig. 10-3B. Since the amount of expansion increased with latitude, the squares are now distorted. Neither angle nor shape has been preserved. To restore the angles it is now necessary to expand the vertical scale by stretching each meridian. At each parallel of latitude the factor for meridian stretching must be the same as that used at the same point for expanding the parallel of latitude. The meridian stretching completes the procedures needed to construct a Mercator projection, Fig. 10-3C.

The increased meridian stretching at high latitudes can be seen by comparing the distances between the parallels of latitude in the original peel with those in the final Mercator projection. Neither of the squares projects as a square, for the sides are no longer straight lines, even though each angle is still 90°. The increased expansion near the poles is shown by the relative sizes of the two squares, which were equal before projection.

Now we may consider how well the Mercator projection fulfills our six requirements:

(1) No area projects exactly into its correct shape, but the amount of distortion over the area covered by most charts is acceptable. An area as large as a continent is badly distorted.

(2) Angles are projected exactly.

(3) The Mercator construction expands areas by an amount which increases with latitude.

(4) The scale value is sufficiently constant for a chart covering a small area but changes drastically over an area as large as a whole ocean (sailing charts).

(5) Meridians and the equator are the only great circles that project as straight lines. Meridians appear as vertical lines with parallels of latitude horizontal.

(6) Rhumb lines are straight on a Mercator projection.

**FIGURE 10-3** Steps in the conversion of a sector of a sphere to a Mercator projection. (A) Projection of the sector onto a plane surface. (B) Expansion to make the meridians parallel. (C) Expansion to restore angles.

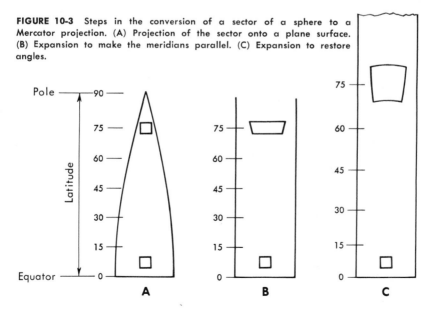

Although they are by far the most common, Mercator charts are not used exclusively in marine navigation. For example, they cannot be used in the polar regions, because of the great distortion at high latitudes. *Polar transverse Mercator* charts, made by starting the typical Mercator peel from a meridian instead of from the equator, are useful for navigation in high latitudes. A variety of other projections are also available for use in the polar regions, but they are of limited usefulness to the small-boat sailor.

## 10.05   Conic Projections

In the Lambert projection a cone is imagined intersecting the earth at two parallels of latitude (Fig. 10-4). These two *standard parallels* are chosen to be those where the least distortion is desired. Features on the earth are projected onto the cone by lines running out from the center of the sphere. The cone is then cut and unrolled to form a plane chart.

Angles are preserved in a Lambert construction, which also preserves relative areas far better than the Mercator. Great circles are so nearly straight lines on a Lambert projection that they may usually be plotted as such. Radio direction finder (RDF) bearings may also be plotted directly without the corrections frequently needed with Mercator charts.

Maps are frequently made by *polyconic* projection onto a series of cones, each tangent to the sphere. The cones are subsequently unrolled as in the Lambert projection. Angles are not preserved in polyconic projection, and so it is not used for ocean navigation. Survey charts of the Great Lakes and other inland waters are, however, based on polyconic projections.

## 10.06   Gnomonic Projection

This, probably the oldest of all projections, is made onto a plane surface tangent to the earth's surface at the point desired as the center of the chart. Each point on the earth's surface is projected along a straight line from the center of the sphere until it hits the plane.

Areas and angles are badly distorted except near the point of tangency. Distances cannot be easily scaled on a gnomonic chart. The one important feature of this projection is the fact that all great circles project as straight lines. Because of this feature, charts constructed on gnomonic projection are commonly known as *great circle charts*.

Great circle charts are used primarily in navigation for preplotting long-distance, great circle courses. From the straight-line great circle plot a series of points can be transferred to a Mercator chart to form the curved representation typical of great circles in this projection. Great circle charts may also be used for plotting radio bearings obtained from distant transmitters, but tabular corrections are to be preferred.

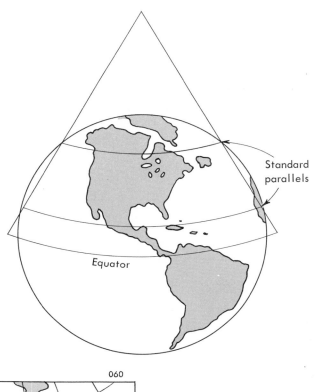

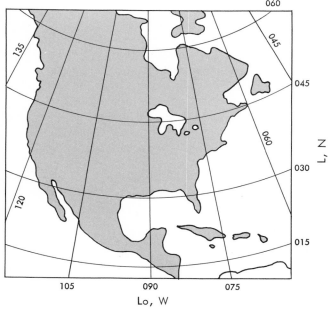

**FIGURE 10-4** Development of the Lambert projection.

185

## 10.07    Great Circles and Rhumb Lines

The shortest distance between any two points on a sphere will be a portion of the great circle passing through the points. If all factors, such as wind and current, were identical, it would always be advantageous to sail on a great circle course. Even on a long voyage the difference in distance between a great circle and a rhumb line course may not be very great; perhaps 20 miles out of 5,000. To those accustomed only to automobile driving this may seem like an insignificant difference. To a ship, an essentially constant speed device, 20 miles saved may mean a gain of more than one hour, which might make the difference between a favorable or unfavorable current, or a gain of position in berthing or unloading.

On a great circle course the ship will in fact always be headed directly toward its destination although it does not appear to do so on a Mercator chart (Figs. 10-2 and 10-5). The course sailed will not be constant, for a great circle does not cut all meridians at a constant angle. Meridians themselves and the equator are exceptions to this since they are both great circles and rhumb lines. With these exceptions any great circle course will be sailed as a series of rhumb lines, the number depending on how closely the navigator wishes to approximate the great circle course. A rhumb line, on the other hand, is a constant course from departure to destination, yet the ship never heads exactly toward the latter until the very last moment.

Few small-boat skippers will be concerned with laying out great circle courses and converting them to a program of rhumb line sailings. They may, however, wish to correct observations made with some types of radio direction finding equipment before making a plot on a Mercator chart.

Under normal atmospheric conditions signals from a distant radio transmitter travel along great circles rather than along rhumb lines. These signals

**FIGURE 10-5**  Rhumb line and great circle courses, Hawaii to Yokohama, on a Mercator projection.

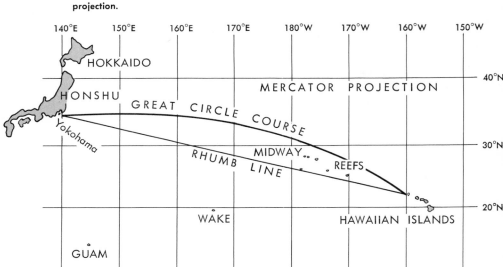

will, therefore, arrive at a vessel from a different direction than would be expected from a plot of the rhumb line. For example, we see from Fig. 10-5 that a vessel departing from the Hawaiian Islands would have to apply a substantial correction to the direction of any radio signals received from a Yokohama transmitter. The correction to be applied depends on the latitude and the longitude of both the transmitter and the receiving vessel. Great circle-rhumb line corrections can be important at long distances from the transmitter, but may be neglected by nearby vessels.

## 10.08    Chart Types and Scales

Eight types of charts, utilizing a wide range of plotting scales, cover the Great Lakes, the coastal waters of the United States, and adjoining oceans. (1) *Pilot charts* are used for planning long-distance voyages rather than for detailed navigation. Three pilot charts are published each month by the Oceanographic Office: (a) "The North Atlantic Ocean," (b) "Greenland and the Barents Sea," and (c) "The North Pacific Ocean." Some coastal details are included on these charts, but the emphasis is on oceanographic and meteorological data.

Pilot charts depict, for the month issued, average values obtained from past experience for prevailing winds with the expectations for gales, calms, fog, ocean currents, air and water temperatures, limits of field ice, and icebergs. The location of ocean weather vessels and the recommended tracks of regular steamer routes are shown, Fig. 10-6.

Using data from the pilot chart one can plan a course to take the greatest advantage of winds and currents, avoiding or paralleling steamer lanes as desired, and can estimate the chance of gales or other unpleasant weather.

(2) *Sailing charts* are *small-scale* charts covering large areas of the ocean. They are used for planning and navigating offshore passages to distant ports, for plotting positions at sea, and for making approaches to the coast from the open ocean. Modern sailing charts (Fig. 10-7) show networks of the hyperbolic position lines of the loran system, 13.15. These lines permit a rapid and accurate determination of a ship's position from a pair of loran readings.

Sailing charts are usually constructed on a scale of 1:600,000, 1:1,200,000, or even smaller. With these scaling factors, details of the shoreline and land topography are necessarily missing. Inshore soundings, usually within the 60 foot line, are omitted. Only principal lights and offshore buoys are charted.

(3) *General charts* are plotted to scales of from 1:100,000 to 1:600,000. They are used primarily for coastwise navigation outside of reefs and shoals, but in waters where positions can be determined from landmarks, lights, buoys, and depth soundings. This series shows many more aids to navigation and much more coastal detail than can be shown on sailing charts. Fig. 13-4 is an example of a general chart.

(4) *Coast charts* are plotted to scales of 1:50,000 or 1:100,000. These charts

# PILOT CHART OF THE NORTH ATLANTIC OCEAN

N.A.—AUGUST 1963

(THIS CHART SHOULD NOT BE USED FOR NAVIGATIONAL PURPOSES)

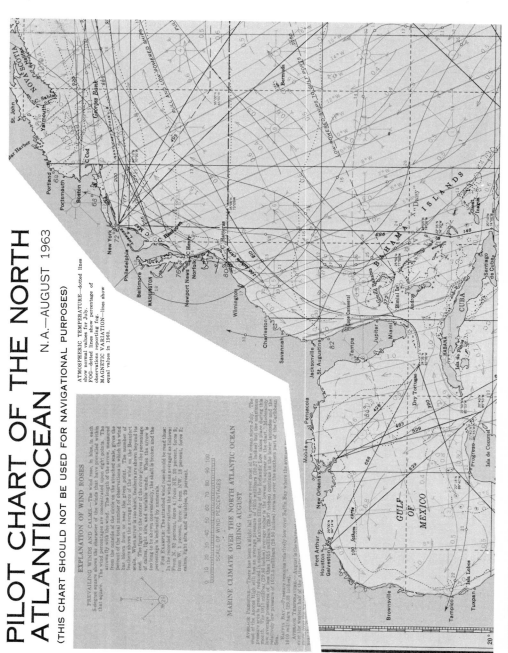

**FIGURE 10-6** Portions of the pilot chart for the North Atlantic Ocean for May 1971. There is a wealth of information given, much of it beyond the scope of this text. From "H.O. 1400" published by the Hydrographic Office, USN.

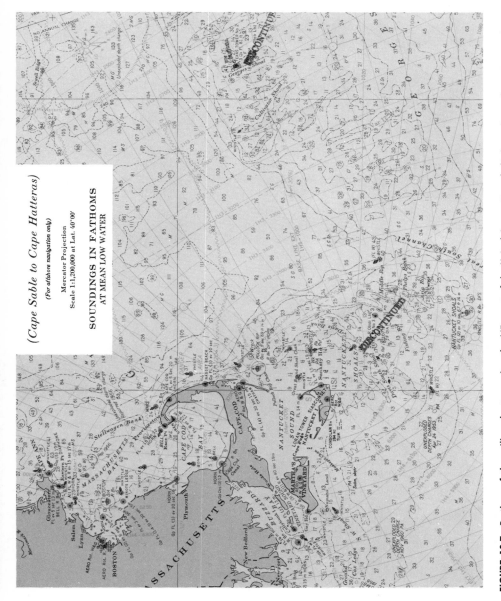

**FIGURE 10-7** Portions of the sailing chart covering the NE coast of the United States. Hyperbolic loran lines of position can be seen. From "Chart No. 1000" issued by the National Ocean Survey.

have sufficient detail to assist navigation into bays and sounds, inside of out-lying reefs and shoals. Charts in this series necessarily cover a smaller area than do the general charts. Figure 11-11 shows a portion of a coast chart.

(5) *Harbor charts,* scaled 1:50,000 or even larger, show sufficient detail to permit navigation into harbors or other restricted areas. All pertinent details of land and water are included, Fig. 12-2.

(6) The National Ocean Survey has recognized the needs of small-boat pilots by issuing *Small Craft Charts* arranged to cover areas of intense boating ac-tivity. The special format of these charts makes for easy use on small chart tables or, folded, on the pilot's lap. Basic chart scales in this series are usually 1:40,000, although some harbor inserts are scaled to only 1:10,000. The great popularity of the small craft series has led to a rapid increase in the number made available, and more are to be anticipated. Charts in this series are designated by the letters "SC" followed by the chart identification number.

(7) The Intracoastal Waterway, running from Manasquan Inlet, N.J., to Brownsville, Texas, with interconnections, is covered by a special series of SC charts. Each chart in this series is supplemented by descriptive material listing controlling depths of water, bridge clearances and hours of operation, and other pertinent information.

(8) Charts prepared by the U.S. Army Corps of Engineers for use on the Great Lakes are based on polyconic projections rather than on the Mercator. Because of the small span of latitude covered by each chart, the convergence of the meridians is scarcely noticeable. Traffic on the lakes is so heavy that specific sailing courses are recommended and are plotted on the charts. Distances on the Great Lakes charts are given in statute rather than in nautical miles, and scales are given in feet, yards, meters, and statute miles. Note, however, that the latitude scales along the vertical edges of these charts will give distances in nautical miles, with one mile per minute of latitude, as on a Mercator chart, Fig. 10-10.

Many states now issue charts covering the navigable waters within their boundaries. Many of these issues are based on NOS charts or surveys, some-times modified by additions or deletions. One common addition is the insertion of recommended course lines for some of the more popular passages.

## 10.09    Chart Symbols and Abbreviations

A series of International Hydrographic Conferences has attempted, among other things, to standardize the symbols used on the charts of every nation. They have been partially successful in this, and most of the symbols on charts produced in the United States conform to the international recommendations.

The list of symbols is so large that a 25-page booklet, "Chart No. 1, Nautical Chart Symbols and Abbreviations," is published by the National Ocean Survey. The complexity of the symbols requires their classification into 21 lettered sections. A few examples are shown in Fig. 10-8.

## A. The Coastline

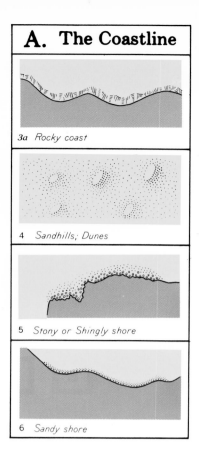

3a   Rocky coast

4   Sandhills; Dunes

5   Stony or Shingly shore

6   Sandy shore

## S. Quality of the Bottom

| | | |
|---|---|---|
| †1 | Grd | Ground |
| 2 | S | Sand |
| 3 | M | Mud; Muddy |
| 4 | Oz | Ooze |
| 5 | Ml | Marl |
| 6 | Cl | Clay |
| 7 | G | Gravel |
| 8 | Sn | Shingle |
| 9 | P | Pebbles |
| 10 | St | Stones |
| 11 | Rk; rky | Rock; Rocky |
| 11a | Blds | Boulders |
| 12 | Ck | Chalk |
| 12a | Ca | Calcareous |
| 13 | Qz | Quartz |
| †13a | Sch | Schist |
| 14 | Co | Coral |
| (Sa) | Co Hd | Coral head |

## K. ( ! new optional symbol)   Lights

| | | | |
|---|---|---|---|
| †1 | | ☆ | Position of light |
| 5 | Bn | Bn | Light beacon |
| 6 | | | Light vessel; Lightship |

## O.   Dangers

| | |
|---|---|
| 5 Rk<br>5 Shoal sounding on isolated rock (replaces symbol) | 11<br>Wreck showing any portion of hull or superstructure (above sounding datum) |
| 2¼Rk  2¼Wk  2¼Obstr<br>6a Sunken danger with depth cleared by wire drag (in feet or fathoms) | Masts<br>12 Wreck with only masts visible (above sounding datum) |

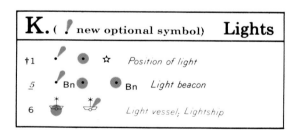

**FIGURE 10-8**  Typical symbols from "Chart No. 1," National Ocean Survey.

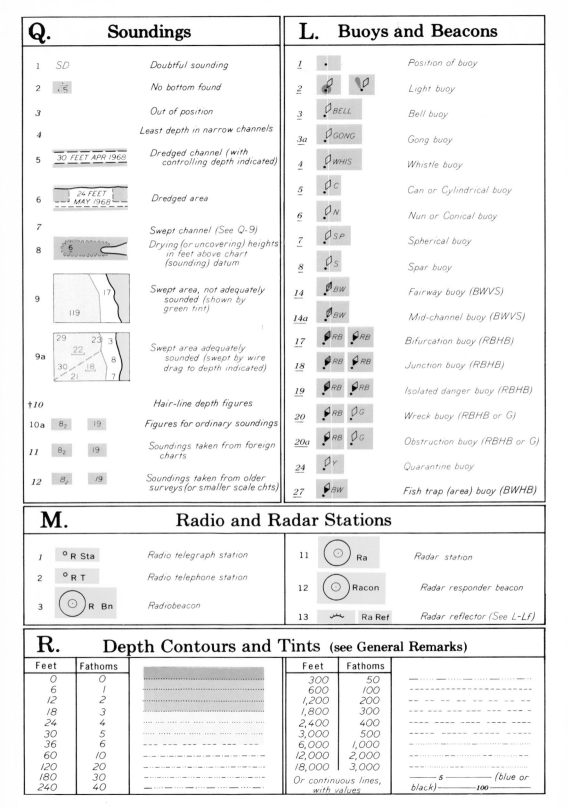

**FIGURE 10-8** Typical symbols from "Chart No. 1," National Ocean Survey.

Chart construction is expensive and time-consuming, so it is obviously necessary to use one basic survey as long as it is applicable, adding new features between printings and making corrections by hand as important changes occur during the life of one edition.

National Ocean Survey charts are frequently reprinted and are current at the printing date. Any changes that occur between the date of printing and the date of use must be obtained from Notices to Mariners and added to the chart by hand. The date of printing and the revision status is given in the lower left margin. For example:

CAUTION

16th Ed., May 27/72          This chart has been corrected from the Notice to
**1210**                     Mariners published weekly by the U.S. Naval Ocean-
                             ographic Office and the Local Notice to Mariners
                             issued periodically by each U.S. Coast Guard district
                             to the print date shown in the lower left hand corner.

Charts in the SC series are issued annually, each edition canceling the previous issues. The issue date is found in the lower left corner of each chart page. Corrections are not made to SC charts after the issue date.

The title of a chart conveys important information beyond designating the area to which it applies. For example on "Chart No. 1000" (a sailing chart), the title reads:

ATLANTIC COAST—CAPE SABLE TO CAPE HATTERAS
(For offshore navigation only)—Mercator projection
Scale 1:1,200,000 at Lat 40°00′
Soundings in fathoms at mean low water

"Harbor Chart No. 566" has the title:

CHESAPEAKE BAY—SEVERN AND MAGOTHY RIVERS
Mercator projection Scale 1:25,000 at Lat 39°01′
Soundings in feet at mean low water

Some coastal states issue material covering local areas in which small-area reproductions of NOS charts are used. It must be kept in mind that some of these reproductions may not be current when purchased. The same applies to charts comparable to road maps that are issued by some commercial companies. Drastic changes in aids are seldom made, but in some cases the use of obsolete charts can lead to piloting errors.

In each of these examples the *sounding datum* or reference line was *mean low water*. This is the usual datum since it presents the average least favorable condition. Certain charts present an even more unfavorable situation by using *lower low water*, a datum somewhat below mean low.

Shorelines are usually shown for mean high tides. Heights such as bridge clearances are usually calculated above *mean high water* to present an unfavorable average, but not an extreme situation. Remember that at extreme low or high tides neither soundings nor vertical clearances may represent existing conditions.

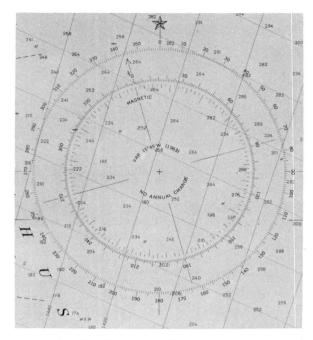

**FIGURE 10-9** Typical compass rose used on charts published by the NOS.

## 10.10 Compass Rose

A most important feature of every chart is the *compass rose*, Fig. 10-9. The standard rose consists of two graduated circles, the outer presenting *true* or *geographical* directions measured from north as the zero point. The inner circle indicates *magnetic* directions measured clockwise, taking as the zero point the direction in which the north end of a perfect compass points when it is located at the position of the compass rose. All modern charts have roses graduated in degrees, replacing the older markings in points.

There would be no need for two sets of graduations if the North Magnetic Pole of the earth coincided with the North Geographical Pole of the earth. Unfortunately the two poles do not coincide, and furthermore the North Magnetic Pole moves about in an only partially predictable manner. The angle, both in amount and direction, by which the magnetic scale is rotated from the true scale is known as *variation*. Much more will be said about variation in Chapter 11.

## 10.11 Distance Measurements

An important part of either inshore piloting or offshore navigation involves the measurement of distances on the chart or the laying off of distances on it. These measurements must always be made with the utmost accuracy and sometimes with considerable rapidity; a thorough understanding of the principles involved is essential.

In 10.02 we pointed out that the length of one nautical mile was chosen to

Chart 1210 Tr    193

be equal to the distance associated with a change of one minute of arc of latitude measured anywhere along a meridian of longitude. The expansions involved in converting from a spherical peel to a Mercator projection distort both the arcs of latitude and the features on the earth, and at any latitude the distortion of every distance will be by the same factor. On a Mercator projection, then, *the latitude scale,* laid off along the meridians at the sides of the chart, can be used to measure distances at or near the same latitude. In making these measurements each minute of arc of latitude will represent one nautical mile.

The latitude scale is not uniform because of the increased expansions as one leaves the equator and proceeds toward the poles, Fig. 10-10. Because of this changing scaling factor, all distance measurements should be made on that portion of the latitude scale directly, or nearly opposite (west or east of) the distance being measured. The differences in scaling factors are not great on a large-scale plot, such as a coast or a harbor chart, but all navigators should develop the habit of making all distance measurements correctly to avoid errors when working on small-scale charts.

Note carefully that the longitude scales, laid off along parallels of latitude at the top and bottom of each chart, cannot be used for distance measurements. These scales, shown displaced in Fig. 10-10 for easy comparison, have no simple or constant scaling factor between minutes of arc and distance.

## 10.12   Chart 1210 Tr

One chart in the National Ocean Survey's Coast Series is of such great importance to the student pilot that it warrants special attention. Several years ago chart No. 1210 covering the Atlantic Coast from Martha's Vineyard to Block Island and including Buzzards Bay and Narragansett Bay was selected as a training aid. The regular 1210 chart is kept up to date in the usual way and carries all of the corrections up to the date of publication. Chart 1210 Tr was once current, but corrections are no longer applied to it. It is as useful as a fully corrected chart for training purposes but should not be used for navigation. To emphasize its obsolescence, 1210 Tr is marked:

CAUTION<br>This chart is not intended for use in navigation

Since no corrections are made on 1210 Tr, it can be printed in large quantities on a paper stock that lacks some of the superior qualities of that used in the regular issues. As a consequence the training chart can be obtained for a fraction of the cost of a regular chart ($0.25 at the time this was written), from any of the regular distribution centers for NOS charts.

Exercises included in this text assume that the student has a copy of 1210 Tr available.

Latitude

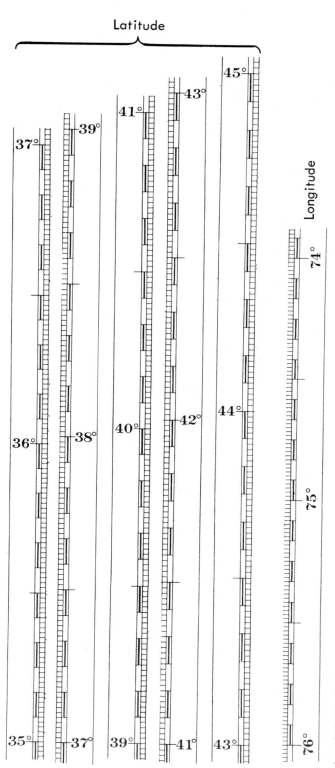

FIGURE 10-10 Scales from a Mercator pilot chart. The latitude scales show the increasing expansion as the latitude increases. The longitude scale is quite different from any portion of the latitude scale and must never be used for distance measurements.

194

## 10.13     Chart Reading

Every skipper must rely on charts when he operates his boat in waters with which he is not thoroughly familiar. As boat speeds increase, the need for accurate and rapid chart reading becomes more important. Situations will arise when there will be no time to consult at length with the List of Symbols to determine the meaning of some chart marking.

Proficiency in chart-reading can be achieved only by detailed study of the charts themselves, with reference to the List of Symbols for each unfamiliar item. Charts are cheap, so a small investment will provide many hours of profitable and enjoyable study. The word enjoyable is used deliberately; the wealth of information on any chart provides a real challenge to the serious boatman, who will derive real satisfaction in meeting the challenge.

Charts should always be used when under way, even when sailing on familiar waters. It is good practice to keep a close check on the boat's position at all times, for occasionally when least expected, this knowledge may be of great value in averting serious trouble.

### EXERCISES

**10-1.**   What is the distance from lighted black buoy "1" at the entrance to Buzzards Bay to the: (a) obstruction buoy at Elisha Ledge, (b) lighted black buoy "3A," (c) red buoy "2 S & P," (d) Gay Head Light?
**10-2.**   Identify all of the aids to navigation found within a three-mile radius of midchannel buoy "BB."
**10-3.**   You are at lighted red buoy "11" in the entrance channel to New Bedford harbor. Identify the aids to navigation observed in the following true bearings: (a) 140°, (b) 185°, (c) 201°, (d) 216°, (e) 318°.
**10-4.**   What are the magnetic bearings of the aids specified in 10-3?
**10-5.**   You are at obstruction buoy "VS" near Buzzards lighted offshore aid. What is the magnetic bearing and the distance to: (a) lighted black buoy "29," (b) Gay Head light, (c) lighted red buoy "2B"?
**10-6.**   You are at whistle buoy "2" off Point Judith on board a power cruiser drawing 3' 8" bound for upper Narragansett Bay by way of the West Passage. A logical course would be on a rhumb line to Whale Rock light and then a rhumb line course to black can "IPB" near the highway bridge at Plum Beach: (a) Draw the rhumb lines and examine them for obstructions that might be hazardous to your passage. (b) What is the course direction (both M and T) and distance to Whale Rock light? (c) What is the course and distance to "IPB" from Whale Rock?
**10-7.**   Butler Flats light and a 34' high structure showing an occulting light from a range into New Bedford harbor. (a) What are the true and magnetic bearings of the range on entering the harbor? (b) What are the true and magnetic bearings of the range on leaving the harbor? (c) What is the distance between the two range markers?

### ANSWERS

**10-1.**   (a) 5.5 miles, (b) 4.8 miles, (c) 3.2 miles, (d) 10.3 miles.
**10-2.**   Lighted obstruction buoy at Lone Rock, lighted red buoy "6," black can "7" at Great Ledge, black can "9" at Phinney Rock, black gong "3" at

Negro Ledge, black can "1," black can "3A," lighted red "4," red "4A" at Mosher Ledge, red "2A" at West Ledge.

**10-3.**   140°—daybeacon off Sconticut Point, red nun "2A."

           185°—red nun "6A" at Decatur Rock.

           201°—lighted red "4" on the Sandspit.

           216°—red nun "4LR" at Lone Rock.

           318°—spire in the city of New Bedford.

**10-4.**   155°, 200°, 216°, 231°, 333°.

**10-5.**   (a) 112°M 6.4 miles, (b) 118°M 7.8 miles, (c) 024°M 4.5 miles.

**10-6.**   (a) No hazards on either course; (b) 021°T 036°M 7.1 miles; (c) 009°T 024°M 4.6 miles.

**10-7.**   (a) 155°T 170°M; (b) 335°T 350°M; (c) 1.5 miles.

CHAPTER **11**

# The Mariner's Compass

## 11.01   The Need

Sooner or later every boatman will meet a situation in which he can no longer pilot his craft within the sight of familiar landmarks and aids to navigation. Darkness, low visibility due to fog or other causes, and sparsely located aids are the most common conditions requiring the use of instruments.

Three bits of information are required if a boat is to be piloted successfully under conditions of low visibility:

(1) An initial location. This can be determined in a variety of ways to be described in Chapter 12.

(2) The speed of the boat over the bottom. Speed with respect to the water can be obtained from a previous calibration of engine speeds or from log readings. Speed over the bottom can then be estimated if there is any information available on tidal currents and winds.

(3) The direction in which the boat is moving. This direction is usually determined with some form of *compass*, a name derived from the Latin *compassus*, meaning equal divisions.

Any device that will determine directions on the earth's surface, independent of visual aids, can be used as a compass. Several such instruments are available, but the only one practically useful on small boats is the magnetic or mariner's compass. The origin of the mariner's compass is lost in antiquity. There is some reason to think that is was known to the Chinese long before the Christian era, but this is not certain. The magnetic compass was certainly known in Europe and used for navigation in the 12th century. Columbus used a magnetic compass on his voyages to the New World and was familiar with at least one of the conversions required by a magnetic instrument.

The earliest magnetic compass consisted of a chunk of the iron-bearing ore *magnetite*. When suspended so that it was free to rotate, one end of the chunk would point roughly toward the North Star or Polaris, sometimes called the *lodestar*. Because of this tendency these magnetic ores were known as *lodestones*.

The orienting component in a modern compass is made of hardened steel or of some alloy capable of being strongly magnetized, and of retaining this magnetism. These metals can be made *permanent magnets* by exposing them to a strong magnetic field produced by sending a strong electric current through a coil of wire.

## 11.02   The Earth's Magnetic Field

A lodestone or a permanent magnet orients itself because the earth is a huge, although weak magnet. The earth has two *magnetic poles,* located near but not exactly at the corresponding geographical poles.

Every magnet is surrounded by what we call a *magnetic field,* which is to say, a region in which one magnet will exert a force on a second. A small exploratory magnet can be used to map out the field produced by a large magnet. At every point in the field the tiny magnet will align itself along what we call a magnetic line of force, Fig. 11-1. The lines of force in a magnetic field can be visualized by scattering fine iron filings around a magnet. Each tiny particle will align itself in the direction of the field at that particular place.

**FIGURE 11-1**   A small test magnet used to find the directions of the magnetic lines of force that surround the earth. Courtesy of NOS.

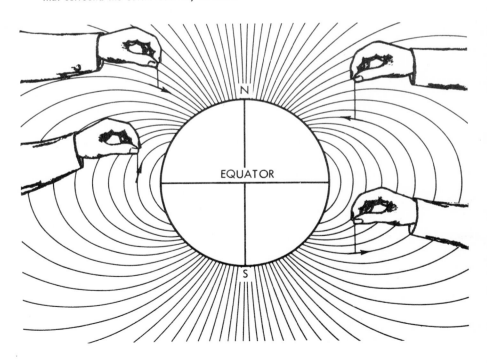

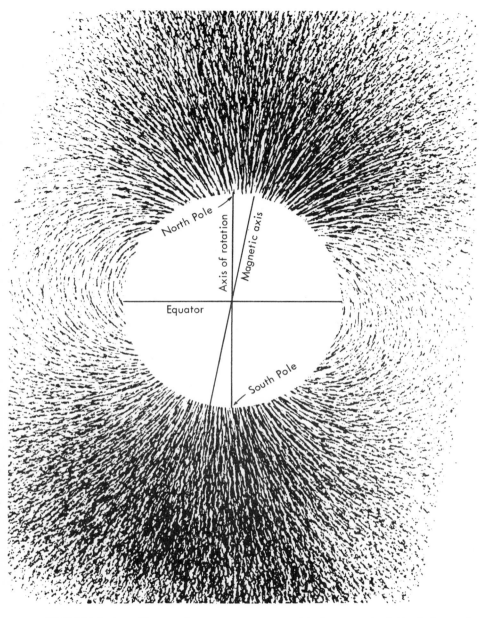

The labels within the figure read: North Pole, Axis of rotation, Magnetic axis, Equator, South Pole.

**FIGURE 11-2** Iron filings and a strong magnet model the magnetic field of the earth. Courtesy of National Geographic Society and the National Ocean Survey. Copyright **NGS**.

The lines of force associated with the earth's field appear to flow out of the North Magnetic Pole, into the space around the earth, finally returning through the South Magnetic Pole, Fig. 11-2. Any secondary magnet will distort the normal flow of the lines of force due to the earth's field to produce a locally disturbed field, Fig. 11-3. Since the small test magnet responds to the

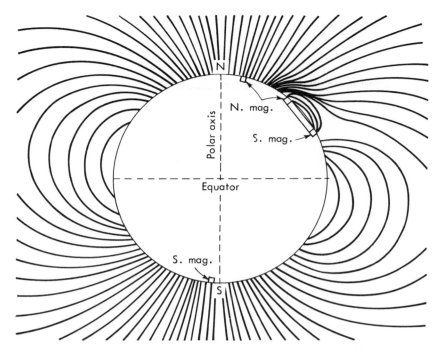

**FIGURE 11-3** Any secondary source of magnetism will locally distort the earth's field. The disturbing magnet shown is relatively much larger than any that actually exist.

combined effect of whatever fields act upon it, we would expect magnetic directions near such a disturbance to deviate from the directions that would be observed in a nearby undisturbed space. In a few areas, usually near land, the earth's field is locally distorted, presumably because of nearby iron deposits. One of these areas of magnetic disturbance is shown on the chart, Fig. 11-13. A more common source of disturbance is magnetism arising within the boat itself.

## 11.03   The Mariner's Compass

Small, hand-held compasses used on land usually consist of a magnetized needle pivoted on a jewel bearing so that it is free to swing over a graduated *compass card*. The marked end of the needle will point to the earth's North Magnetic Pole. When the compass body is rotated until the north marking on the card coincides with the north end of the needle, the card graduations will show angular directions from magnetic north, measured in a clockwise direction.

In the true mariner's compass several strong magnets are attached *to* the compass card so that card and magnets rotate as a unit about a central jewel bearing. If we temporarily disregard local disturbances, to be discussed later, the magnets will line up with the earth's magnetic field, with one end pointing to the North Magetic Pole. The compass card graduations will then show angular directions around the entire horizon, measured clockwise from magnetic north.

Some compasses originally designed for military use have been adapted for marine service. These may have the magnetic needle and card mounted independently, as in the simple land compass. The use of these adapted instruments will be readily understood from a knowledge of the standard marine-compass construction.

The main body of a marine compass, which will be rigidly attached to the boat, has a vertical index mark called the *lubber line* or the *lubber's line*. When the compass is installed, it must be very carefully set so that a line through the central pivot and the lubber line will be parallel to the keel of the boat. In a properly mounted mariner's compass we have the following relations: The zero of the compass card will (neglecting local distortions) always point to magnetic north while the lubber line will rotate with the boat as the latter changes its direction of movement or *heading*. The intersection of the lubber line with the graduations on the compass card will give the magnetic direction in which the boat is heading.

## 11.04   Compass Construction

Although the basic principle on which the compass operates is simple, a vast number of development and design refinements are built into a modern instrument. Above all, a marine compass must be dependable and capable of functioning under all of the roll, pitch, and yaw experienced in rough weather. Rarely nowadays can a compass be blamed for a navigational error. When a compass reading fails to coincide with a "feeling" for the correct course, the wise navigator trusts the compass.

The magnetic forces orienting the compass card are small, hence the greatest care must be taken in the design and construction of the central bearing. This bearing usually consists of a hardened-alloy pointed pin, resting on a jewel. Friction at the pivot can be minimized by reducing the weight resting on it. This is done by filling the entire compass bowl with a liquid which will buoy up the moving system and thus reduce pivot pressure.

The liquid filling also serves the most important function of *damping* any oscillations of card and needle. In an undamped system with very low friction, any disturbance such as a sudden boat movement will cause the moving magnets to swing wildly to either side of the magnetic pole to which they are trying to point. Undamped oscillations will eventually die out, but in a marine installation other disturbances will almost certainly appear before the effects of the first have disappeared. Reasonable readings can scarcely be obtained on a shipboard with an undamped compass. A moving system immersed in a damping fluid will return to its equilibrium position in a single movement, without overswinging. The damping fluid eliminates the oscillations but has no effect on the equilibrium position of the moving system.

Light-viscosity petroleum products and alcohol-water mixtures are the most commonly used damping liquids. Since these liquids are exposed to the intense rays of the summer sun, they will absorb large amounts of ultraviolet light, and they may become discolored as a result. When this occurs, the compass should be returned to the manufacturer for refilling. Damping fluid must completely fill the compass bowl without even the smallest air bubble. To take care of the differential expansion of bowl and fluid with changes in temperature an expansion diaphragm or bellows is built into the bottom of the bowl.

A well-designed pivot bearing will permit the card to rotate freely when the compass is a few degrees off level, but a simple pivot system cannot accommodate the large angles of heel that may be attained, for example, by a sailboat hard on the wind.

In the spherical compass (Figs. 11-4 and 11-5), the glass or plastic top of the compass is accurately ground to form a portion of a sphere. The entire compass, including card, pivot, and lubber line, may then be *internally gimbaled,* or mounted so that the card will always remain horizontal, with the pivot vertical, as the vessel rolls and pitches. Gimbals are customarily constructed to take care of heeling angles up to 90°, where the boat would be filling and sinking. Gimbals for fore and aft pitch are usually restricted to 40-50 degrees, which is an adequate range.

With proper design the damping fluid in an internally gimbaled compass will prevent overshooting on heel and pitch as well as on card rotation. An important feature of the spherical compass is the card magnification obtained by the lens action of the fluid. Reading is facilitated, because the magnification makes the card appear considerably larger than its actual size.

The *flat-bowled* compass (Fig. 11-6), does not lend itself to internal gimbaling. A good flat compass is reliable up to several degrees of roll or pitch and can be readily fitted with external gimbals to extend this range. Usually external gimbals are needed only to take care of heel. There is no fluid magnification in a flat compass, the card appearing natural size.

The compass is customarily removed from a boat when laying up for the winter. There is little danger that the damping fluid will freeze even in extreme temperatures, but there is no need to subject a precision instrument to the rigors of a winter out-of-doors. Compasses not internally gimbaled are preferably stored upside down to remove all pressure from the pivot during periods of disuse.

A single lubber line is satisfactory if the compass is mounted directly in front of the helmsman, who will then view it along the same line of sight as the bow of the boat. In some boats, particularly in sailing craft, it is more convenient to mount the compass alongside the helmsman, a position which may make the forward lubber line unreadable. To provide for this contingency

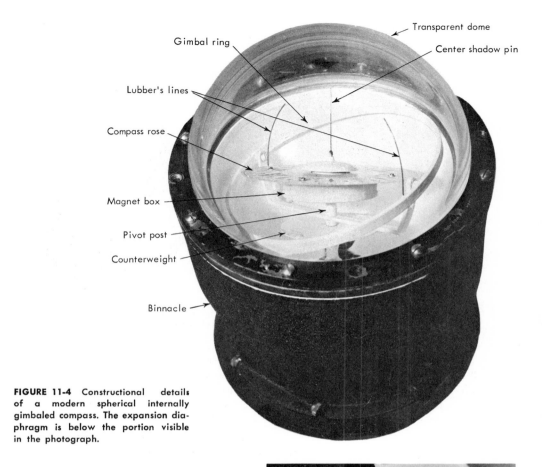

Transparent dome

Gimbal ring

Center shadow pin

Lubber's lines

Compass rose

Magnet box

Pivot post

Counterweight

Binnacle

**FIGURE 11-4** Constructional details of a modern spherical internally gimbaled compass. The expansion diaphragm is below the portion visible in the photograph.

**FIGURE 11-5** Spherical compass and binnacle mounted near the rudder post in a sailboat. The shadow pin can be seen in the top photograph, the four lubber lines in the lower view.

**FIGURE 11-6** A flat-top marine compass, externally gimbaled and equipped with a bearing circle. The mirror shown near the front sighting vane is used for star sights and not for terrestrial observations. Courtesy of Weems System of Navigation.

some marine compasses are fitted with four lubber lines instead of one, Fig. 11-5. The three additional lines are carefully set by the manufacturer at 90, 180, and 270 degrees from the forward lubber line. The helmsman must keep in mind at all times which lubber line he is using and make the proper allowance for it.

The compass shown in Fig. 11-5 has a pin projecting vertically upward from the pivot. This is the *shadow pin,* so-called because its shadow will be projected onto the compass card when the sun shines on the spherical dome. The use of the shadow pin will be explained later.

## 11.05   Compass Cards

In past times directions at sea were universally given in terms of points, and compass cards were graduated accordingly. In this system the card is first marked with the four *cardinal points N, E, S,* and *W,* spaced 90° apart. Midway between these are the four *intercardinal* points *NE, SE, SW,* and *NW.* At the midpoint of each 45-degree interval thus formed, there is a point characterized by a triple designation, as *NNE, ENE,* and so on. The resulting 22½ degree spans are halved by points denoted by "x" or "by," such as *NxE,* read "North by East," and so on.

The divisions described lead to the 32 basic points of the compass, each point being equal to 11¼ degrees. Each of these points is further subdivided into *quarter points.* All old-time pilots and navigators had to acquire the ability to *box the compass,* or to name each of the points and quarter points in order around the card. Even more difficult was the requirement to name pairs of

**FIGURE 11-7** A compass card marked in degrees and points. Compare with the card shown in Fig. 11-5, which has only cardinal and intercardinal points.

points opposite each other across the card. Today it is usually considered sufficient to know the four cardinal and the four intercardinal points.

There has been an increasing use of compass cards divided into 360 degrees, starting with zero at the north and proceeding clockwise around the card. The simplicity of the degree system and its universal use on charts is making the point system obsolete. Many compass cards have dual markings, Fig. 11-7. Other cards omit the point markings altogether.

The simplicity of the degree markings is particularly evident in calculating *reverse* or *reciprocal* bearings, a procedure required very frequently in piloting. In the degree system a reverse bearing is obtained by simply adding or subtracting 180° as required. Thus 047° + 180° = 227° and 319° − 180° = 139° are two examples of reciprocal bearings. This is to be compared to, say, NNEx½E which has SSWx½W as its reciprocal bearing.

For small-boat operation cards graduated in 5-degree intervals are usually adequate. It is rarely possible to hold a small boat to better than 3-4 degrees to either side of a prescribed course, so finer graduations are of little use, and they may even interfere with readings under adverse lighting conditions.

## 11.06  Compass Card Displacement

When the north index, or zero, of the compass card does not point to the true or geographical north, the compass is said to have an error. This is an unfortunate use of the word, for in a well-made marine compass the needle will faithfully align itself with the local magnetic lines of force, whatever their direction. If the field lines do not coincide with the geographical meridians, it is not a fault or error of the instrument, which can have no knowledge of geographical directions. Obviously the *displacement* of the compass card from true north is not an instrumental *error* in the usual sense, and we will not use the term.

If the zero index of the card is displaced, all directions indicated by it will be displaced by the same amount. Conversely, if a conversion can be applied to bring the indicated north reading to the true north, that same conversion applied to any other reading on the card will convert it to a true geographical reading.

On shipboard there are two sources of compass card displacement, *variation* and *deviation*. Variation arises because at most locations on the surface of the earth the direction of the earth's magnetic field, given by the local magnetic meridians, does not coincide with the true north-south meridians of longitude, Fig. 11-8. Deviation results from the very local distortion of the earth's field by magnetizable materials on the boat itself.

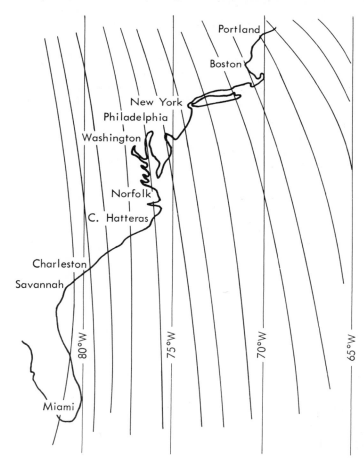

**FIGURE 11-8** Geographic and magnetic meridians along the East Coast of the United States. The two sets of meridians are parallel over a small area near Lo 080°W. Here variation will be zero.

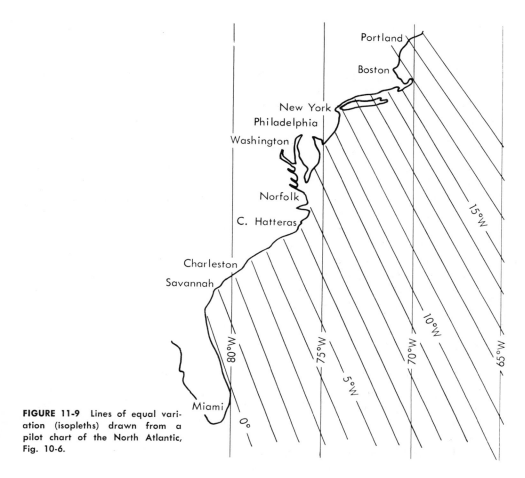

**FIGURE 11-9** Lines of equal variation (isopleths) drawn from a pilot chart of the North Atlantic, Fig. 10-6.

## 11.07 Variation

The magnetic poles of the earth are large, slowly moving areas located well within the Arctic and Antarctic circles but still several hundred miles from the geographical poles. Since the magnetic meridians converge toward the *magnetic* poles, there will be few places on the earth where a compass will read true values.

Variation is an *angle* having a definite value for every point on the earth, equal to the number of degrees measured *from geographical north to magnetic north*. Variation at any point is equal to the number of degrees between the geographical and magnetic meridians at that point.

The direction of variation is as important as its magnitude. When the magnetic meridian points west of the northbound geographical meridian, variation is west. A compass with no other displacement will then have its card rotated to the west of the geographical scale. A reverse situation leads to an easterly variation, where an otherwise undisplaced compass will have a card rotated to the east of true north.

Values of variation have been obtained from careful magnetic measurements made over practically all land and sea areas of the globe. Charts published by the NOS carry double compass roses, Fig. 10-9. The outer scale is based on a zero at true or geographical north. Directions taken from the inner scale are *magnetic*. The two scales are offset by the amount of variation existing at that point on the chart date, the value being given near the center of the rose. To keep the charts current the annual change in variation is also given. Annual changes are usually small compared to the steering errors on a small boat, but they may accumulate over a number of years to an appreciable value.

When a chart covers a large area, as a sailing chart, it is not feasible to reproduce enough compass roses to show the changes in variation. Instead, these charts display lines of equal variation, Figs. 10-6 and 11-9.

Although variation may change with time, its value at a given time and place is a constant, independent of the heading of the boat. If a compass reading is corrected for variation, the same conversion factor will apply to all readings of that compass at that place.

## 11.08    Deviation

Some metals, notably iron and steel, become magnetized when they are placed in a magnetic field. Soft iron may lose this *induced* magnetism as soon as it is removed from the field, but hard steels and some alloys may retain it for many years. Some stainless steels show no magnetic properties even though they have a high iron content.

In general any iron-containing object brought near the compass will become magnetized from the needle, and the resulting forces may change the compass reading by as much as 20-30 degrees. Errors much smaller than this are very serious in an instrument used for navigation. An iron-containing object as small as a beer can, placed close to the compass, will seriously affect the reading. Massive iron objects on board, such as the engine or an iron keel, may have become magnetized during manufacture to a degree capable of affecting compass readings from a distance of several feet. An electric current flowing in a loop of wire also produces a magnetic field capable of disturbing a magnetic compass.

Chrome plating, used freely on marine hardware, is frequently laid down over a layer of nickel plate. Nickel is one of the metals capable of being appreciably magnetized. Because of this any chrome near the compass, as in its mount or *binnacle*, must be investigated to determine its effect on the compass. Nickel on a fixed part of the binnacle will have only a constant effect, but this may increase the deviation to undesirably large values. Nickel plating on a movable binnacle hood may produce a deviation which changes with hood position. This change may amount to 8-10 degrees, which is unacceptable.

All of the magnetic sources on board add together to produce a local field, independent of the earth's field. This local field will combine with the field of the earth to produce a local distortion. The compass will respond to the combined, disturbed field rather than to the field of the earth alone, for the compass magnet has no way of distinguishing the separate fields in which it finds itself.

Deviation is the angle by which a compass card is offset from the *magnetic meridian* by the local field. Direction of deviation is as important as the amount. When the compass zero points west of the magnetic meridian, deviation is west, and vice versa.

The amount and direction of deviation will vary with the ship's heading since the local fields will turn with the boat, while the direction of the earth's field remains constant. When the boat is so headed that the local magnetic field lines up exactly with the magnetic meridian, there will thus be zero deviation, for the disturbing field will simply add to or subtract from the earth's field without changing its direction. At other headings the local effect will change the direction of the combined fields, and there will be corresponding values of deviation, Fig. 11-10.

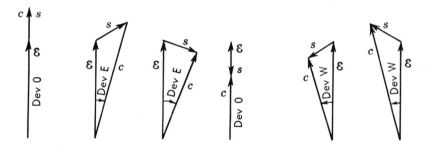

**FIGURE 11-10** Any magnetic field S, originating on the ship, will combine with the earth's field ε. The resulting deviation may be zero, East, or West.

Considerable thought should be given to the location of a ship's compass. The preferred position is that where deviation will be a minimum and most nearly constant. The ideal location can seldom be realized, because the compass must be located close to the helmsman, who in turn is usually located close to the engine and other sources of magnetic disturbance.

Deviation will seldom be zero, and since it can be allowed for, it is of more practical importance to insure that magnetic conditions at the compass location are as constant as possible. *Care must be taken at all times to insure that magnetizable objects are not moved to or from locations where they may affect the compass.* Deviation must be measured both with and without various electrical circuits being energized. The wires leading to the compass light are highly suspect because of their proximity to the compass needle. The magnetic effect of an electric circuit can be minimized by keeping the supply and the return wires close together. Any circuits close to the compass should be either parallel paired wires or preferably twisted pairs.

Although deviation can be determined and allowed for it is desirable that the conversion angles be small. With the complex metal and electrical installations on modern craft, deviation angles may be much larger than one likes. This is particularly true on large, steel-hulled vessels which may actually become magnetized from working the steel in the earth's magnetic field.

Large deviation angles can be greatly reduced or eliminated by placing small compensating magnets near the compass, carefully positioning them so as to annul as much as possible the fields originating on board. A compass so treated is said to be *compensated.*

The complete compensation of a magnetic compass on board a large steel vessel involves the placement of several sets of magnets and masses of soft iron in which magnetic poles are induced. With this elaborate treatment, satisfactory compensation can be achieved for all headings and for all angles of pitch and roll. A complete compass compensation should only be undertaken by an expert, with considerable experience and auxiliary equipment.

Fortunately, the usual small-boat compass seldom needs the full compensation treatment. For these it is usually sufficient to make the main compensation adjustments, which will reduce some of the deviation conversions to zero and make the others conveniently small. A nautical chart is the only equipment needed to carry out this degree of compensation. A simple compensation procedure is described in Appendix V.

### 11.09    Direction of Compass Displacements

Variation and deviation make any compass reading two steps removed from reading true geographical directions, and one step removed from reading directions in terms of the magnetic meridians. Either of the two displacements may be either east or west, and conversions must be applied with care to properly change one system of readings to another. There are four possible combinations.

Consider the situation shown in Fig. 11-11A. In the location where the boat is operating, the magnetic meridian points 007° west of the geographical meridian, so variation is 007° W. Let us assume that with the boat heading as shown, the local magnetism on board deflects the compass card 010° to the west of the magnetic meridian. Deviation is then 010° W.

The lubber line coincides with 044° on the compass card so the ship's course is 044° *psc* (per ship's compass) or more simply 044° *C*. Since the compass zero is 010° west of the magnetic meridian, the ship's course must be 044 − 010 or 034°*M*. Since the magnetic meridian is 007° west of the true meridian, we have 034 − 007 = 027° *T* as the ship's course referred to the geographical or true scale of angles.

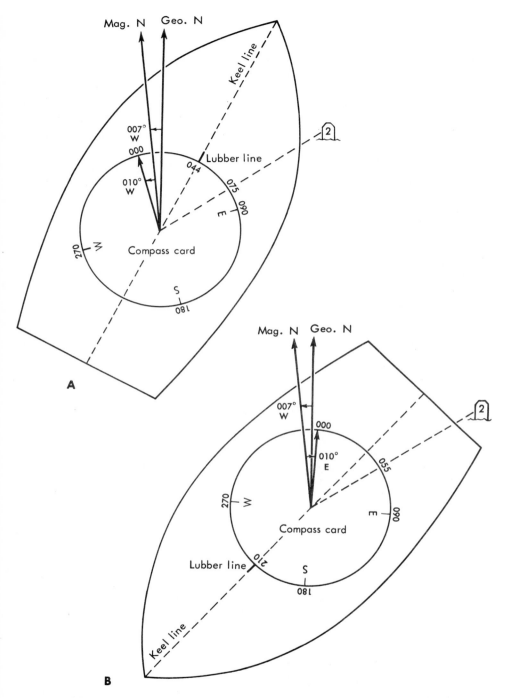

**FIGURE 11-11** Angular relations between the *T, M,* and *C* scales when a change of course changes the deviation.

The relationships just developed apply to all angular readings and not just to the ship's heading. Again referring to Fig. 11-11A, we see that a buoy is sighted across the compass card at 075°. The buoy has then a bearing of 075° C. As before 075 — 010 = 065° M and 065 — 007 = 058° T. The direction 058° T can be plotted on a chart, measuring from the geographical north, or 065° can be plotted from the magnetic north displayed on the inner compass rose of the chart. The original reading of 075° C has no meaning on the chart.

The vessel now changes its course to 210° C, and let us assume that the compass deviation is now 010° E, placing the compass zero to the east of the magnetic zero, Fig. 11-11B. The course is now 210 + 010 = 220° M. Variation is 007° W as before so the course is 220 — 007 = 213° T.

We can now calculate the expected compass bearing on the previously sighted buoy, assuming that the vessel has not changed its position appreciably after the change in course. From the previous calculation we know that the buoy bears 058° T or 065° M. Since the compass zero is now 010° east of the magnetic zero, the bearing will be 065 — 010 = 055° C. If we sight across the card at 055°, the buoy should be sighted.

Other combinations of variation and deviation can be worked out from the examples given. A conversion from a compass reading to a true direction can be made by combining the two conversion factors in proper fashion and then applying this single value. Unless considerable proficiency in these manipulations is attained, it is suggested that all conversions be made in two steps. Of the utmost importance is that all conversions be made without error in either amount or direction. Remember the proper sequence:

$$\text{TRUE} \pm \text{VARIATION} = \text{MAGNETIC} \pm \text{DEVIATION} = \text{COMPASS}$$
$$\text{COMPASS} \mp \text{DEVIATION} = \text{MAGNETIC} \mp \text{VARIATION} = \text{TRUE}$$

Easterly errors are sometimes referred to as *clockwise* because a clockwise rotation amounts to turning the scale to the east. Westerly errors will then be *counterclockwise*. A safer method is to keep in mind the basic relations between the five quantities along with a clear mental picture of the directions of the shifts associated with *east* and *west*.

## 11.10    Compass Conversions

Practical piloting requires the frequent conversion of angles from true to compass and from compass to true. For example, an aid to navigation may be sighted and a bearing taken on it. The bearing angle is necessarily taken in the compass system of angles. These angles must be converted to the magnetic or to the true system before the bearing can be plotted on the chart as a line of position. Conversely, a navigator will determine from the chart a true course that must be made good in order to attain the next objective. The true course must be converted to the compass system of angles for the helmsman because his only piloting instrument, the compass, does not read either true or magnetic directions.

The term *correcting* is sometimes used in connection with making conversions from compass to magnetic and from magnetic to true. *Uncorrecting* is applied to conversions in the direction true-magnetic-compass. This is an unfortunate usage, for each of the systems of angle measurement is as correct as either of the others. Each has a separate meaning and can be converted rather than corrected to the others.

A number of schemes have been contrived to assist the memory in properly applying the conversion factors. A better method is to keep firmly in mind the direction of the displacements associated with the terms East and West. With these directions established no trouble will be experienced in applying the conversion factors with the proper sign.

## 11.11    Determining Deviation

As we have seen, a compass will not provide values of courses and bearings suitable for plotting unless the deviation of the instrument is known. Unfortunately deviation, unlike variation, cannot be expressed as a single number. Depending as it does on the ship's heading, deviation must be determined for a number of headings and the results put in the form of a table or graph for easy use.

The first step in obtaining a deviation table is to stow permanently all objects capable of changing the deviation. When using the deviation table, all of these objects must be in the position they occupied when the deviations were being determined.

In principle deviation is easily measured. One need only compare some accurately known direction with that same direction as measured by the compass. This comparision is then repeated for a number of boat headings, usually about every 15 degrees, for a total of about 24 readings.

*Swinging ship* is the method most available to the average small-boat navigator. In this method the boat is put on a series of headings while compass bearings are taken on some accurately known direction. A ship may be swung at her moorings by warping her around a pile, or she may be run repeatedly across a *range* on a series of headings. The latter scheme is probably the more useful.

A range is a direction determined by two accurately located, fixed objects such as landmarks on shore or lighthouses and fixed beacons. Floating aids such as buoys are not suitable for determining a range because they can change their positions with changes in tidal currents. To obtain the required precision the boat should operate at least one mile from the range-determining structures.

A flat-top compass can be equipped with a *bearing circle* or *azimuth circle*, Fig. 11-6, to facilitate the taking of bearings. A bearing circle consists of a circular frame which fits over the compass body and rotates around it. The circle carries two sight vanes with a narrow slit and a line index which can be set upon a distant object. The angle is then read off the compass card under the index line. A bearing circle cannot be used conveniently with a spherical compass. In this case it will be necessary to use an auxiliary sighting instrument or *pelorus*. We will neglect this complication for the moment and consider a boat equipped with a flat-top compass and a bearing circle.

## 11.12   Swinging Ship

As an example consider swinging ship in the waters just NNE of the entrance to Marblehead Harbor, Fig. 11-12. The light on Hospital Point and a spire define a range bearing 276° *T* as seen from the water. The compass rose shows variation to be 015° W, which makes the range bearing 291° *M*.

Fig. 11-13A shows the situation on board as the ship crosses the range line on a heading of 030° *C*. This heading is determined from the fact that the lubber line coincides with 030° on the compass card. As the helmsman strives to maintain this course, an observer keeps the bearing circle trained on one of the objects defining the range line. At the instant the ship crosses the range line the two objects will be seen in line, and the bearing is then read off the compass card. In the example cited the reading was 281° *C*. The ship is now put across the range line on another heading, as in Fig. 11-13B, where the lubber line shows a course of 225° *C* and the range bears 303° *C*.

As the ship was put across the range on a series of headings, the data shown in Table 11-1 were obtained. If there had been zero deviation on all

**TABLE 11-1**

**Data for Deviation Calculations**

| Heading | Bearing | Deviation | Heading | Bearing | Deviation |
|---|---|---|---|---|---|
| 000 C | 286 C | 005 E | 180 C | 296 C | 005 W |
| 015 | 284 | 007 E | 195 | 299 | 008 W |
| 030 | 281 | 010 E | 210 | 301 | 010 W |
| 045 | 279 | 012 E | 225 | 303 | 012 W |
| 060 | 278 | 013 E | 240 | 304 | 013 W |
| 075 | 278 | 013 E | 255 | 303 | 012 W |
| 090 | 279 | 012 E | 270 | 302 | 011 W |
| 105 | 281 | 010 E | 285 | 301 | 010 W |
| 120 | 283 | 008 E | 300 | 299 | 008 W |
| 135 | 287 | 004 E | 315 | 296 | 005 W |
| 150 | 290 | 001 E | 330 | 293 | 002 W |
| 165 | 293 | 002 W | 345 | 290 | 001 E |

headings, each bearing measured would have been 291° *C*. Each difference between this value and that actually observed will then be the deviation for that particular heading. As an example consider the bearing of 281° *C* obtained when the boat was heading 030° *C*. The deviation is 291 − 281 = 010°, and

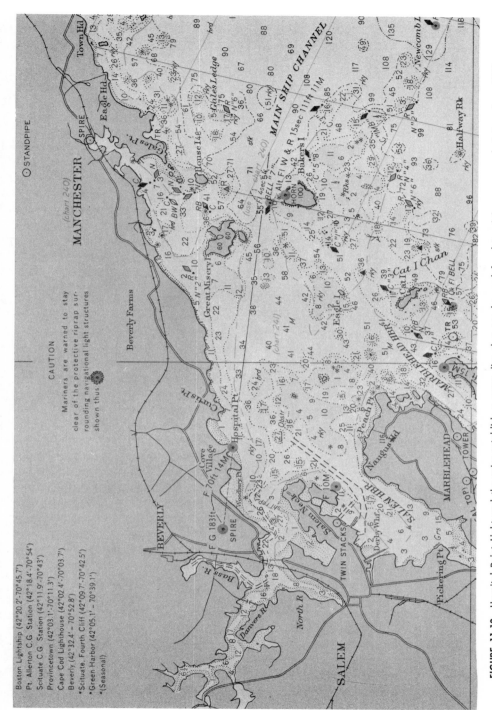

**FIGURE 11-12** Hospital Point Light and the spire establish a range line that can be used for determining compass deviation. From NOS chart No. 1207.

215

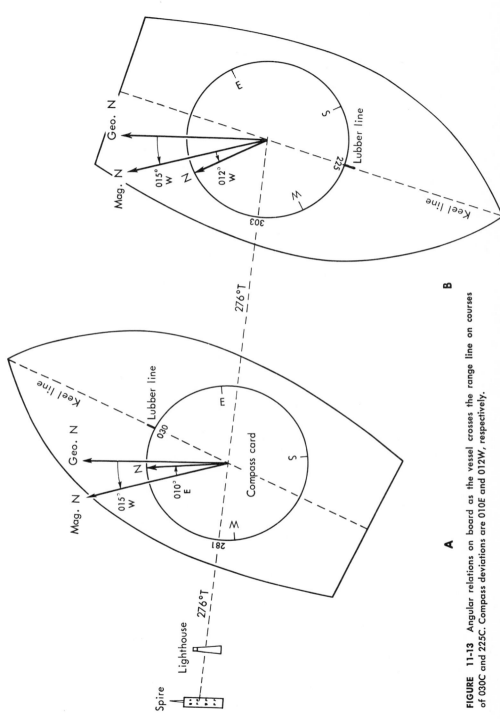

**FIGURE** 11-13 Angular relations on board as the vessel crosses the range line on courses of 030C and 225C. Compass deviations are 010E and 012W, respectively.

it only remains to fix the name. Since the compass reading is *less* than the magnetic bearing, the zero of the compass scale must have been 010° to the east of the zero of the magnetic scale. The deviation on this heading is, therefore, 010° *E*.

## 11.13   Deviation with the Pelorus

The use of a pelorus introduces only a slight complication into the determination of deviation. A pelorus, named apparently after a pilot employed by Hannibal in 200 B.C., consists of a graduated circle, much like the compass card but without magnets. The pelorus card is free to rotate so that the observer may set the zero of the scale to any desired position. A lubber line is marked on the fixed portion of the pelorus, as on the compass. A movable sight vane and index rotate above the graduated circle (Figs. 11-14 and 12-4).

FIGURE 11-14 Flat-top compass converted to a pelorus and mounted on the companionway slide.

To obtain data for calculating deviations, the helmsman concentrates on holding the ship on a steady predetermined compass course as before. The observer will set the pelorus circle so that its zero coincides with the lubber line. The pelorus scale will then give bearings referred to the heading of the boat.

As before, the observer will sight on one of the two objects determining the range and will read the pelorus scale when the two come in line. From this relative bearing and the compass reading, the compass bearing of the range is readily calculated, and the deviation is then determined as before. Table 11-2 shows data obtained with a pelorus and compass corresponding to the previous data obtained with compass and bearing circle.

Consider again the situation on a heading of 030° *C*. The range now bears 251° clockwise from the ship's heading, and since this heading is 030° *C*, the bearing of the range is 251 + 030 = 281° *C*. This agrees, as it should, with the bearing obtained directly with the compass. With the range bearing established, calculations of deviation proceed as before.

**TABLE 11-2**

Deviation Data by Pelorus and Compass

| Heading | Relative Bearing | Compass Bearing | Deviation |
|---|---|---|---|
| 000 C | 286 | 286 | 005 E |
| 015 | 269 | 284 | 007 E |
| 030 | 251 | 281 | 010 E |
| 045 | 234 | 279 | 012 E |
| 060 | 218 | 278 | 013 E |
| 075 | 203 | 278 | 013 E |
| 090 | 189 | 279 | 012 E |

## 11.14   Deviation Tables and Graphs

The deviations calculated and displayed in Table 11-1 answer only one half of the problems regularly encountered in piloting. With the information in Table 11-1 one can quickly calculate a course in terms of the magnetic and true scales, given the course by compass. If, for example, the course is 120° C, a deviation of 008° E is read from the Table, and the course calculated as 120 + 008 = 128° M. A simple interpolation will permit a similar calculation for courses between the measured points. A course of 125° C, thus falls at ⅓ of the interval between 120° and 135°. In this 15° interval the deviation changes from 008° E to 004° E, or a change of 004° downward going from 120° to 135°. The deviation change for a 005° change will then be 004/3 = 1⅓, which is rounded off to 001° by dropping the fraction. At 125° C, then, the deviation will be 008 — 001 = 007° E.

The same result may be obtained by plotting the calculated deviation values in terms of the corresponding compass courses, Fig. 11-15. A deviation curve can then be *faired in* between the plotted points and used to determine deviation at any desired course. The curve of Fig. 11-15 thus shows the deviation at 125° C to be 007° E as before.

The reverse problem cannot be solved with the deviation data of Table 11-1. Suppose a navigator chooses a course of 120° M and must give a proper course to the helmsman. Table 11-1 is of no help as it stands because there is no entry for a course of 120° M. The entry for 120° C will not do, for this corresponds to a course of 128° M, as we have seen.

We can, however, use the data of Table 11-1 to calculate a magnetic heading for each of the compass headings listed. This calculation leads to the values given in Table 11-3.

There are now enough data to plot a curve of deviation against *magnetic* headings (Fig 11-16), comparable to the curve previously plotted in terms of compass headings. In the new plot the points will not fall on exact 15-degree intervals, but this is of no consequence because there are enough points to permit fairing in a representative curve. In fact, the original data will seldom be obtained at regular 15-degree intervals as shown in Table 11-1. With our new

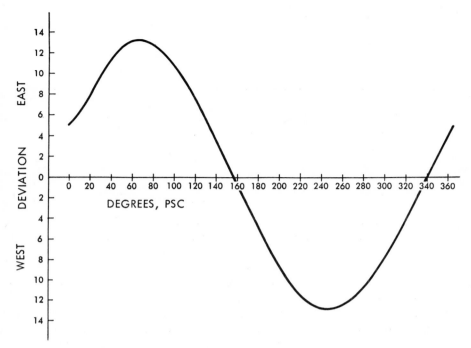

**FIGURE 11-15** A plot of deviation against compass courses.

**FIGURE 11-16** A plot of deviation against magnetic courses.

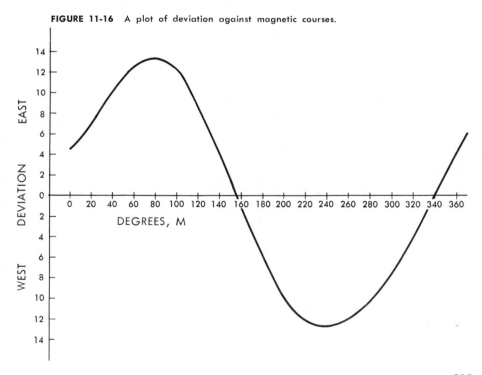

219

**TABLE 11-3**

**Headings and Deviations**

| Heading | Deviation | Heading | Heading | Deviation | Heading |
|---------|-----------|---------|---------|-----------|---------|
| 000 C | 005 E | 005 M | 180 C | 005 W | 175 M |
| 015 | 007 E | 022 | 195 | 008 W | 187 |
| 030 | 010 E | 040 | 210 | 010 W | 200 |
| 045 | 012 E | 057 | 225 | 012 W | 213 |
| 060 | 013 E | 073 | 240 | 013 W | 227 |
| 075 | 013 E | 088 | 255 | 012 W | 243 |
| 090 | 012 E | 102 | 270 | 011 W | 259 |
| 105 | 010 E | 115 | 285 | 010 W | 275 |
| 120 | 008 E | 128 | 300 | 008 W | 292 |
| 135 | 004 E | 139 | 315 | 005 W | 310 |
| 150 | 001 E | 151 | 330 | 002 W | 328 |
| 165 | 002 W | 163 | 345 | 001 E | 346 |

curve we can proceed with the conversion of magnetic to compass headings. From the curve we see that the deviation for a magnetic heading of 120° is 009° E. The helmsman will then be given a course of 111° C.

Deviation data may be plotted in a variety of ways to suit individual preferences. The use of two curves, as described here, is cumbersome and can lead to error by conversion from the wrong chart. In the Napier plot (Fig. 11-17), a single curve suffices for conversion in either direction. The numerical values along the vertical scale apply to both the solid-line magnetic scale and the dotted-line compass scale. Note that distances between the intersections of the oblique scales represent 15 degrees as on the vertical scale. Calculated deviation values are laid off along the dotted compass scales since the measurements were made in terms of compass bearings. A smooth curve is faired in between the plotted points.

As an example of the use of the Napier diagram, consider again the compass course to be steered so as to make a magnetic course of 120°. The Napier plot is entered at point A, corresponding to 120 M, and is followed along the magnetic line until the deviation curve is reached at B. Point B is then projected parallel to the compass lines until it intersects the vertical line at C. Point C then gives the course as 111 C as before. Here, as in the previous examples, all fractional values have been rounded off to the nearest whole number. The ordinary equipment found on a small boat is incapable of fractional degree accuracy, and this accuracy is not needed in small-boat piloting.

A blank Napier diagram will be found inside the front cover of this book. This diagram may be used for the exercises of this chapter or for a vessel's actual deviation curve.

## 11.15   Deviation by Shadow Pin

When a compass is equipped with a shadow pin as in Fig. 11-5, deviations can be obtained from the bearings of the shadow cast by the sun as the boat is

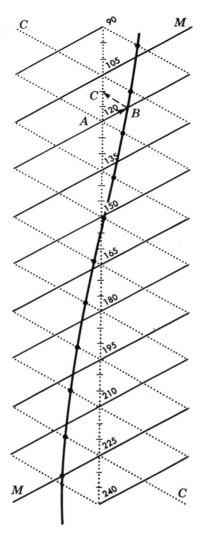

WEST      EAST

**FIGURE 11-17** Deviations plotted on a Napier diagram permit compass-magnetic conversions in either direction.

put on a series of headings. The observed bearings are compared with values calculated from the sun's position, which in turn must be computed from data given in the *Nautical Almanac*. These calculations require a knowledge of nautical astronomy beyond that possessed by most small-boat skippers. The details of the use of the shadow pin and the sun compass are described in advanced texts.

No special knowledge is required to establish the presence or absence of deviation in a compass equipped with a shadow pin. In the unlikely event that the shadow remains on a constant angle on the compass card as the ship is swung through a complete circle, the compass will have a zero deviation on all headings.

221

Whatever his preferred method, the pilot should maintain up-to-date deviation data on his compass. *Any gross change in the iron on board or in the electric circuits calls for a recheck of the deviation table.*

## PROBLEMS

**11-1.** Fill in the missing values in the following table.

|   | Compass | Deviation | Magnetic | Variation | True |
|---|---------|-----------|----------|-----------|------|
| a | 183 |       | 187 | 006E |     |
| b |     | 004W  |     | 005W | 213 |
| c |     | 005E  | 087 |      | 075 |
| d | 358 | 006E  |     | 006E |     |
| e |     | 008W  |     | 012E | 115 |
| f | 228 |       | 221 |      | 217 |
| g |     | 002E  |     | 008W | 006 |
| h | 019 |       | 027 | 009W |     |
| i | 057 | 003W  |     |      | 047 |
| j | 264 |       | 269 | 003W |     |

**11-2.** The vessel whose deviation data were given in Secs. 11.12–11.14 is proceeding on a course of 100C when it sights an overtaking vessel at a bearing of 230C. What is the magnetic bearing of the overtaking vessel? The first vessel maintains course and 20 minutes later observes the overtaking vessel at 228C. What do you infer as to the risk of collision?

**11-3.** The first vessel in Prob. 11-2 changes course to 140C and 15 minutes later observes the second vessel at 225C. What is the magnetic bearing of the second vessel? What do you now infer about the risk of collision?

**11-4.** Assume a variation of 009W and calculate the true course of the vessel in Probs. 11-2 and in 11-3 after the course change.

**11-5.** The pilot of the vessel in Prob. 11-2,, sailing in an area where the variation is 007W, finds that he must make a course of 305T if he is to clear a shoal. What compass course will he give the helmsman?

**11-6.** A vessel is swung across a range line bearing 136T in a harbor where the variation is 6°45' W. From the observations given in part below, calculate the compass deviations and make a deviation plot in terms of compass headings.

Course C    000 015 030 045 060 075 090 105 120 135 — — — — — — —
Bearing C   146 148 151 150 148 147 145 143 141 140 — — — — — — —

**11-7.** Using the deviation data from 11-6, make a plot of deviations in terms of magnetic headings.

**11-8.** The vessel referred to in 11-6 and 11-7 is proceeding on a course of 085C when a buoy is sited on a bearing of 030C. What is the true bearing of this buoy? What is the bearing of the boat from the buoy? While still on a course of 085C an overtaking vessel is observed at 215C. What is the magnetic bearing of this vessel?

**11-9.** The vessel of 11-8 changes course to 020C and now observes the overtaking vessel at 230C. What do you infer about the risk of collision? At the moment of the course change, what was the compass bearing of the buoy?

**11-10.** A vessel equipped with a spherical compass and a pelorus swings ship, making use of a range formed by Beavertail light and the Brenton Reef off-shore light structure (chart 1210 Tr). A portion of the observations are:

| Course C | 000 | 015 | 030 | 045 | 060 | 075 | 090 | 105 | 120 |
|----------|-----|-----|-----|-----|-----|-----|-----|-----|-----|
| Rel. Bearing | 344 | 331 | 319 | 307 | 295 | 283 | 271 | 259 | 246 |

| Course C | 135 | 150 | 165 | 180 | 195 | 210 |
|----------|-----|-----|-----|-----|-----|-----|
| Rel. Bearing | 232 | 218 | 203 | 187 | 171 | 154 |

Calculate the corresponding deviations in terms of compass readings and magnetic headings.

**11-11.**  What is the true course of a vessel with the deviation schedule of 11-10 when on a course of 055C? On this course what is the true bearing of a light that bears 010C?

## ANSWERS

**11-1.**

|   | C | D | M | V | T |
|---|-----|------|-----|------|-----|
| a | 183 | 004E | 187 | 006E | 193 |
| b | 222 | 004W | 218 | 005W | 213 |
| c | 082 | 005E | 087 | 012W | 075 |
| d | 358 | 006E | 004 | 006E | 010 |
| e | 111 | 008W | 103 | 012E | 115 |
| f | 228 | 007W | 221 | 004W | 217 |
| g | 012 | 002E | 014 | 008W | 006 |
| h | 019 | 008E | 027 | 009W | 018 |
| i | 057 | 003W | 054 | 007W | 047 |
| j | 264 | 005E | 269 | 003W | 263 |

**11-2.**  Bearing 219M. The change in bearing is too small to permit a firm decision.

**11-3.**  Bearing 222M. The vessel will pass astern.

**11-4.**  Course in 11-2 102T. Course in 11-3 134T.

**11-5.**  325C.

**11-6.**

| Course C | 000 | 015 | 030 | 045 | 060 | 075 | 090 | 105 | 120 | 135 |
|----------|-----|-----|-----|-----|-----|-----|-----|-----|-----|-----|
| Dev. | | 003W | 005W | 008W | 007W | 005W | 004W | 002W | 000 | 002E | 003E |

**11-7.**

| Course M | 357 | 010 | 022 | 038 | 055 | 071 | 088 | 105 | 120 | 135 |
|----------|-----|-----|-----|-----|-----|-----|-----|-----|-----|-----|
| Dev. | | 003W | 005W | 008W | 007W | 005W | 004W | 002W | 000 | 002E | 003E |

**11-8.**  Buoy bears 020T. Bearing of boat from buoy 200T. Overtaking vessel bears 212 M.

**11-9.**  Vessel now bears 223M; will pass astern. Buoy bears 030C.

**11-10.**  Variation 015W. Range line bears 341T, 356M.

| Course C | 000 | 015 | 030 | 045 | 060 | 075 | 090 | 105 | 120 | 135 |
|----------|-----|-----|-----|-----|-----|-----|-----|-----|-----|-----|
| Dev. | | 012E | 010E | 007E | 004E | 001E | 002W | 005W | 008W | 010W | 011W |
| Course M | 012 | 027 | 037 | 049 | 061 | 073 | 085 | 097 | 110 | 124 |

| Course C | 180 | 195 | 210 |
|----------|-----|-----|-----|
| Dev. | | 011W | 010W | 008W |
| Course M | 169 | 185 | 202 |

**11-11.**  Course 042T. Bearing 357T.

# CHAPTER 12

# Small-Boat Piloting

## 12.01   Art and Science

*Navigation* is that combination of art and science used to establish a boat's position, and with this knowledge, to determine the course to be steered and the distance to be run to the next objective. *Piloting* is that part of navigation concerned with the conduct of a boat along coasts and through narrow channels and shoal waters. In determining position, observations are made on objects of known position, which may range from nearby aids to navigation to chosen celestial bodies. More or less complicated calculations then serve to determine the position of the observer.

Piloting usually calls for more precise determinations of position than are needed for navigation in the open ocean. At sea an uncertainty of five miles or so is a small fraction of the distance to the nearest obstruction and so is usually of little consequence. In *pilot waters*, on the other hand, a position error of five miles will almost certainly be unacceptable. In some cases an error of only 100 yards can put a boat in jeopardy. Periods of low visibility can very quickly increase the problems of the small-boat pilot, who relies to a large extent on landmarks and visible aids to navigation, and is in general only a few miles away from natural hazards or waterborne traffic.

Either piloting or offshore navigation involves three related functions: making observations on objects of known position, putting these observations in a form suitable for plotting on a chart, and determining from the plotted position the course direction and the time required to attain the next objective. The latter function must be performed with a combination of science, art, and experience, keeping in mind the main purpose of the passage. In many cases a simple rhumb line course will be most advantageous. A navigator in the Newport-Bermuda race will choose a course which he hopes will give him the least unfavorable currents when he crosses the Gulf Stream. An East River pilot will attempt to time his arrival at Hell Gate so that he will have an aiding rather than an opposing current. Any skipper under way in periods of reduced visibility must depend on instrument readings and calculations if he is to know his position with respect to navigational hazards. The science of piloting is readily acquired; only experience can add the art.

## 12.02   Speed, Time, and Distance

The problem most frequently encountered in piloting involves the relations between speed, time, and distance. These relations are used so frequently that many mechanical aids have been developed for obtaining answers rapidly. Computational aids should not be used, if at all, until the direct, arithmetical methods of solution have been mastered. When this competence has been developed, many problems can be solved by mental arithmetic, without recourse to mechanical aids, while attending to other duties. In night piloting, for example, the improved vision of dark-adapted eyes may be most important. Whenever a pilot or helmsman turns on a light to read his computer, he will destroy his dark-adaptation for several minutes, during which time he will have a reduced acuity for recognizing objects in the darkness.

We are concerned with relations between speed, time, and the distance of a *run* or *passage* from one reference position to another, or to a position where course or speed are to be changed. Every computation will refer to a run made at constant speed. When speed is changed, the position at the time of the change must be established, and a new speed, time, and distance calculation made.

The basic relations between the three quantities are extremely simple. Thus:

$$\text{DISTANCE} = \text{SPEED} \times \text{TIME}$$

or
$$D = S \times T \tag{12-1}$$

This relationship may also be written as:

$$S = \frac{D}{T} \tag{12-2}$$

$$T = \frac{D}{S} \tag{12-3}$$

If two of the three quantities are known, the third can be found by a single multiplication or division. The only complication arises from the units in which the quantities are measured.

*Distance* is always measured in *nautical miles* and must always be used as such in the computations. Except in unusual circumstances, distances will be given only to the nearest one-tenth of a mile.

*Speed* is always measured in *nautical miles per hour,* or *knots,* and must always be use as such in the computations. Except in unusual circumstances speed will be given only to the nearest one-tenth of a knot.

*Time* is measured in *hours, minutes,* and perhaps *seconds.* Time may be used in the computations in either of two different ways:

(1) With the distance given in nautical miles time may be expressed in hours after converting all minutes to decimal parts of an hour.

(2) Time may be expressed in minutes if the distance in nautical miles is multiplied by 60. This is equivalent to replacing $D$ by $60D$ in all three of the equations.

Either of the two methods may be used, at the convenience of the navigator. In general, time will be given only to the nearest minute, or to the nearest one-hundredth of an hour.

### ILLUSTRATIVE EXAMPLES

(a) A boat maintains a constant speed of 15.5 knots for 2 hours and 22 minutes. How far does she travel in this time?

Since there are 60 minutes in one hour, 22 minutes are equivalent to $22/60 = 0.366$ hours, and so the total elapsed time is 2.366 hours. Using relation (12-1):

$$D = 15.5 \times 2.366 = 36.67 \text{ or } 36.7 \text{ miles}$$

For the second method of computation $T = 2 \times 60 + 22$ or 142 minutes. Then:

$$60D = 15.5 \times 142 \qquad D = \frac{15.5 \times 142}{60} = 36.7 \text{ miles}$$

(b) A run of 24.6 miles was made in 1 hour and 47 minutes. What speed was maintained?

Converting as before, 47 minutes $= 47/60 = 0.783$ hours, the total time of the run is 1.783 hours. From (12-2):

$$S = \frac{24.6}{1.783} = 13.9 \text{ knots}$$

Using the second method in which $T = 60 + 47 = 107$ minutes:

$$S = \frac{24.6 \times 60}{107} = 13.9 \text{ knots}$$

Both of the speed answers have been rounded off to the nearest one-tenth knot.

(c) What time is required to make a passage of 34.6 miles at a constant speed of 16 knots?

Relation (12-3) can be used directly:

$$T = \frac{34.6}{16} = 2.163 \text{ hours}$$

which may be rounded off to 2.16 hours. Since watches do not read in decimal parts of an hour, it is customary to convert this answer to hours and minutes. Then:

0.16 hours $= 0.16 \times 60 = 9.6$ minutes, and again
0.6 minutes $= 0.6 \times 60 = 36$ seconds

The last part of the answer is meaningless because of inaccuracies in determining speed, so the final answer will be:

$$T = 2 \text{ hours, 10 minutes}$$

By the second method $T = \dfrac{34.6 \times 60}{16} = 130 \text{ minutes} = 2 \text{ hours, 10 min.}$

Problems such as those involving S, T, and D can be easily solved by the use of logarithms, wherein addition replaces multiplication, and subtraction division. The logarithmic scale on the front inner cover of this book can be used without any knowledge of logarithms themselves. Only a pair of dividers is required to solve any of the three types of S T D problems.

## 12.03   Speed-measuring Instruments

Obviously, successful piloting requires an accurate knowledge of boat speeds. Long ago, at least once in every watch, a *chip log* was dropped in the water astern. The chip was a thin, kite-shaped piece of wood weighted to make it float in an upright position and thus catch in the water. As the chip fell away astern, it unrolled a light *log line* from a free-running reel. The log line was marked with knots tied at precisely determined intervals. The number of knots crossing the taffrail in a fixed time would then give the speed of the vessel in nautical miles per hour or *knots*. After each measurement the chip was reeled in for future use. The chip log is now obsolete for routine measurements of speed, but present-day instruments for measuring either speed or distance traveled are known as *logs* or as *patent logs*.

Some of the more popular designs of logs are shown in Fig. 12-1. The *pitot tube* type of instrument operates from the difference in pressures in two small tubes, one with an open end directed into the flow of water, and one whose open end is parallel to the direction of water flow. The pressure difference is transmitted to the speed indicator, which is characterized by a crowded scale at low speeds and an open scale at higher speeds.

The *taffrail log* makes use of the spin of a carefully designed and constructed rotor which is towed astern, well behind the turbulence created by the vessel's passage. Water flowing past the propeller-like blades of the rotor causes it to spin, and this spin is transmitted through the rotation of the braided towing line to a recorder mounted on the taffrail. From the known characteristics of the rotor, the recorder dial can be graduated to read directly in nautical miles traveled. Speed is determined by computation from a knowledge of the distance traveled in a measured time. The taffrail log, though rather heavy and bulky, is still in use as it is particularly useful in measuring distances run on a long passage.

A taffrail log rotor is *streamed* or payed out very simply with the vessel under way, because the rotor will be almost stationary in the water until all of the line is payed out and the inboard end is connected to the recorder.

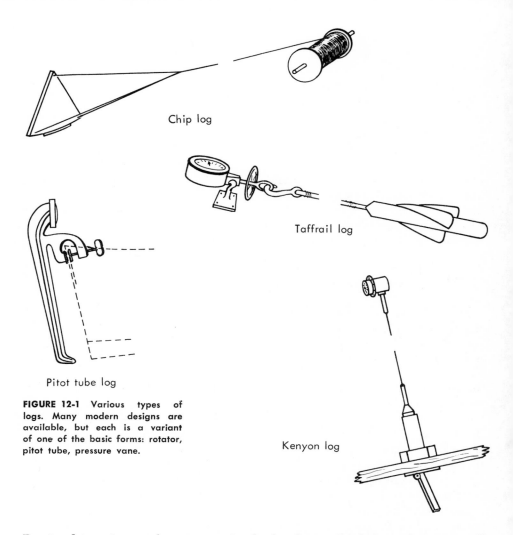

Chip log

Taffrail log

Pitot tube log

**FIGURE 12-1** Various types of logs. Many modern designs are available, but each is a variant of one of the basic forms: rotator, pitot tube, pressure vane.

Kenyon log

Retrieval is quite another matter. As the log line is hauled in, the rotor will continue to spin; since this rotation cannot be taken care of at the hauling end, the after deck will soon be covered with a mess of tightly kinked line. Retrieval is easily accomplished by unhooking the inboard end of the line from the recorder and paying out this end of the line astern as the rotor is hauled in. When the rotor is in hand the entire log line will be streaming astern. This line can then be brought on board without difficulty, since there is no longer any tendency to rotate, and all of the previous twist in the line will have been taken out.

Modern electronic developments have led to methods for recording the rotations of small spinners located close to the center of the hull, where the water flow will be relatively free of turbulence and only slightly affected by pitch and heel. The rotor may contain a small magnet so that the spin can be recorded without any direct mechanical or electrical connection. This magnet will usually be located deep in the water, well away from the compass, but its effect on compass deviation should be investigated.

Another common method of measuring speed through the water makes use of the force exerted on a small vane protruding out from the hull in a turbulent-free position. The force exerted on the vane by the moving water can be converted to indications of speed by a variety of mechanical or electrical arrangements.

The response of either small rotor or vane systems is such that open, uncrowded speed scales are possible at slow speeds. This is a feature of particular importance to the sailing skipper. Although these systems respond primarily to speed they may be arranged to record the total distance traveled during some desired time.

A variation of the old chip-log method is sometimes useful at low speeds when the crowded scale of a patent log may make accurate speed determinations impossible. An expendable object capable of floating for a short time, as a can with a slow leak, is thrown into the water ahead of the vessel, and the time required to pass it from stem to stern is determined with a stopwatch. Knowing the length of the vessel, one can readily calculate the speed.

ILLUSTRATIVE EXAMPLE

Determine the speed of a sailboat 35 feet loa, which required 14.8 seconds to pass a floating object.

At a speed of 1 knot a ship will cover a distance of one nautical mile in one hour, which is a distance of 6,076 feet in 3,600 seconds. Then at 1 knot the ship will travel a distance of $6,076/3,600 = 1.69$ feet in one second. At 1 knot the 35-foot length of our boat will require $35/1.69 = 20.7$ seconds to pass a stationary object. In the example given the speed is then $20.7/14.8 = 1.4$ knots.

Some logs indicate speed only, some only distance, some both. Whatever the design, logs lack the accuracy of the automobile speedometer because of the lack of rigid connection between the boat and the water. Any of the logs practically available can only measure the movement of the boat relative to the water in which it is operating. Since piloting requires a knowledge of movement with respect to the earth itself, or movement *over the bottom*, additional information on current flows will be needed.

## 12.04  Speed Curves

Logs are commonly used on sailboats and on some powerboats whose owners like to have a direct speed indication at all times. The majority of powerboat operators, however, make use of the indicated speed of the main engine, using the driving propeller as the *transducer* or converter of boat speed to engine speed. The latter is determined by a tachometer, a device that can be readily installed on almost any engine not already so equipped.

The relationship between engine speed (rpm) and boat speeds depends on many factors including the shape of the hull, condition of the underwater surfaces, amount of loading, and both fore-and-aft and lateral trim. Therefore, a table of values or a graph known as a speed curve, must be prepared relating engine speeds to boat speeds. Remember, however, that *a speed curve will only apply to the boat when it is kept in a constant condition.* Should the bottom become heavily infested with barnacles, for example, one could not use a speed curve that had been prepared just after the bottom had been cleaned and repainted.

Speed trials may be run on one of the measured-mile courses laid out by the Coast Guard specifically for this purpose, or on any straight run of a mile or more between charted markers. A suitable engine speed is selected, and the boat is then put on her proper course with the first marker well ahead, to insure a steady speed by the time the first marker comes abeam. Throughout the timed run between the two markers, the helmsman must make every effort to keep the boat on her proper course. Runs must be made in pairs, in opposite directions, to eliminate the effects of wind and current. Each pair of runs must be made in quick succession to avoid changes in wind and current.

From the measured times and the known distance of the run the speed can be calculated from relation (12-2). The two speeds calculated from each pair of runs are averaged to obtain the speed in still water. Note that it is not proper to average the two times in a pair of runs and then use this time in a single-speed calculation.

## ILLUSTRATIVE EXAMPLE

A twin-screw 27-foot cabin cruiser runs a series of speed trials over the measured mile in Miami Harbor, Fig. 12-2. Paired runs are made on courses of 116° T and 296° T with the following results:

| Engine RPM | 116° course | 296° course | Knots | Average |
|---|---|---|---|---|
| 800 | 12:05 | | 4.96 | |
| | | 13:35 | 4.47 | 4.7 |
| 1000 | 10:00 | | 6.00 | |
| | | 11:00 | 5.45 | 5.7 |
| 1250 | 08:25 | | 7.13 | |
| | | 09:28 | 6.34 | 6.7 |
| 1500 | 07:00 | | 8.57 | |
| | | 08:25 | 7.13 | 7.9 |
| 1750 | 06:30 | | 9.23 | |
| | | 07:15 | 8.28 | 8.8 |
| 2000 | 04:46 | | 12.59 | |
| | | 05:37 | 10.68 | 11.6 |
| 2250 | 03:44 | | 16.07 | |
| | | 04:10 | 14.40 | 15.2 |
| 2500 | 03:15 | | 18.46 | |
| | | 03:25 | 17.56 | 18.0 |

(Time: Minutes and Seconds)

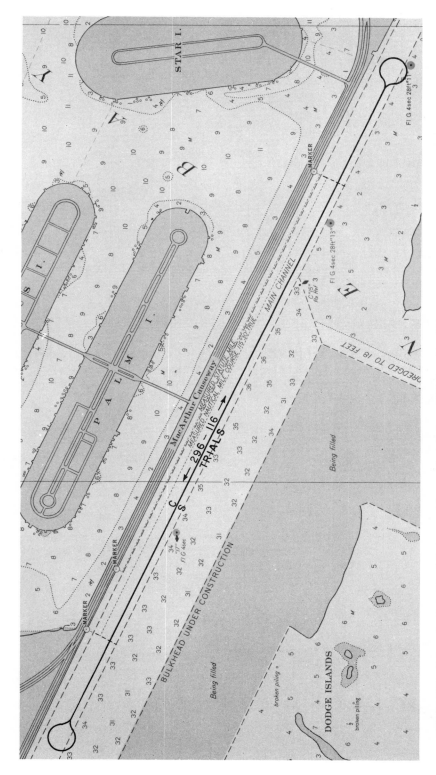

**FIGURE 12-2** Measured mile in Miami Harbor used for speed trials. From NOS chart No. 547.

Consider the pair of runs made at 2000 rpm:

At 116°     $S = \dfrac{1 \times 60}{4.77} = 12.59$ knots

At 296°     $S = \dfrac{1 \times 60}{5.62} = 10.68$ knots

Average speed in still water:  $\dfrac{12.59 + 10.68}{2} = 11.7$ knots

If we have incorrectly used the average time of $\dfrac{4.77 + 5.62}{2} = 5.20$ minutes, we

would have calculated a speed of 11.5 knots.

A complete speed curve is obtained by making a graph of average speeds plotted against rpm. Fig. 12-3 shows the speed curve for the data used in the illustrative example.

## 12.05   Position Finding By Cross Bearings

During an extended passage a pilot or navigator will make frequent position determinations. These determinations are needed to insure that the vessel will clear all navigational hazards and to provide an estimated time of arrival at destination, known as an *ETA*.

**FIGURE 12-3** Speed curve plotted from the data given in the illustrative example.

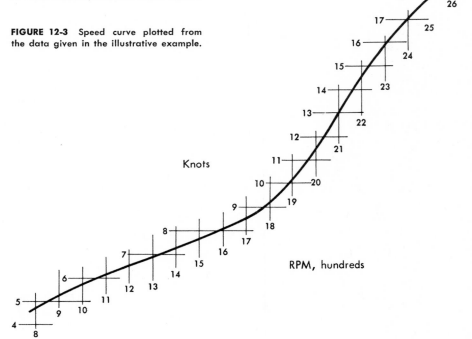

Knots

RPM, hundreds

**FIGURE 12-4** The three basic instruments of piloting: compass, lead line, and pelorus. The latter is gimbaled and weighted to keep the scale horizontal. Courtesy of Weems System of Navigation.

In making these position determinations the pilot will make use of the three basic instruments shown in Fig. 12-4: compass, pelorus, and lead line. The simplest method of position determination is to pass a fixed aid to navigation close aboard so that the position of aid and vessel can be considered identical at the moment of passage. More generally in pilot waters aids will be visible but not close aboard, and position will be found by the method of *crossed bearings*.

Consider a vessel operating in Buzzards Bay, with both Gay Head and Cuttyhunk lighthouses visible to the pilot, Fig. 12-5. At a given moment the pilot determines, either by compass or pelorus readings, that Gay Head lies due East of the vessel, which is to say that the light has a bearing of 090T *from the vessel*. At the same time Cuttyhunk light is found to bear 350T from the vessel. Each of these observations serves to establish a *line of position* (LOP), but neither line can be plotted on the chart because the vessel's position is unknown.

The reverse or *reciprocal* bearing on Gay Head is 090 + 180 = 270°T, and this line of position, from lighthouse to vessel, can be plotted since the position of the light is known exactly. Similarly the reciprocal of the Cuttyhunk bearing, 350 − 180 = 170°T, can be plotted as an LOP from light to vessel. The vessel must lie on each of these LOPs and so is at their intersection. A position established by two nearly simultaneous observations is known as a *fix*, and is so labeled on the chart together with the time of the observation, Fig. 12-5.

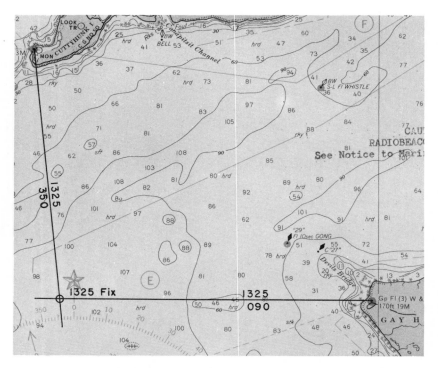

**FIGURE 12-5** Cross bearings on two aids to navigation intersect to give a fix.

Bearings on distant aids will be obtained in a variety of ways. Visual observations are made with a compass or a compass-pelorus combination. Use of the radio direction finder (RDF) is described in Sec. 13.05. Note that at ordinary boat speeds, the vessel's movement between the times of taking the two observations will be insignificant.

## 12.06 Relative Bearings

When the zero of the pelorus card is set on the lubber line, all angles will be measured from the boat's heading, to give *relative bearings*. These must be converted for plotting from a knowledge of either the magnetic or true heading. In practice the observations of pilot and helmsman must be closely coordinated. At the instant a sight is made, the pilot will cry "mark," and the helmsman will observe the compass heading of the boat, Fig. 12-6A. With variation and deviation known, both course and relative bearing are readily converted to their respective "true" values. The conversion steps are:

(1) Apply deviation to the compass course to obtain a magnetic course or heading. *Use deviation for the ship's heading, not that for the bearing.* Apply variation to obtain the true course.

(2) Add the relative bearing to the true course to obtain the true bearing. If the sum exceeds 360°, subtract 360 from it.

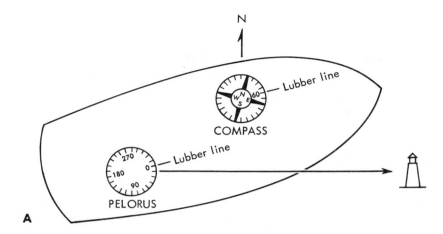

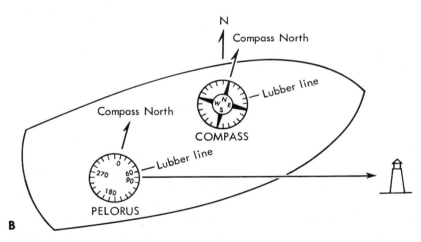

FIGURE 12-6   (A) Relative bearing with the pelorus zero set on the lubber line. (B) Compass bearings with the pelorus zero set on the compass zero.

## ILLUSTRATIVE EXAMPLE

A boat whose compass deviation is given by the data in Table 11-1 is on a compass course of 315° in Buzzards Bay where the variation is 014° W. At 1325 hours the pilot obtains relative bearings of 154° on Gay Head Light and 054° on Cuttyhunk Light.

From the table the deviation on a course of 315° C is 005° W. Then

Ship's course = 315C − 005 = 310M − 014= 296° T

True bearing of Gay Head = 296 + 154 = 450 − 360 = 090°. A similar calculation gives the true bearing of Cuttyhunk Light as 350°.

A true bearing may be calculated by first adding the compass reading and the relative bearing to obtain a compass bearing. This is then converted to a true bearing by applying deviation and variation. In using this method great care must be taken to use the deviation corresponding to the course.

ILLUSTRATIVE EXAMPLE

From the data in the previous example:

Bearing on Gay Head          $315 + 154 = 469 - 360 = 109°C$
Bearing on Cuttyhunk Light   $315 + 054 = 369 - 360 = 009°C$

Deviation on course 315°C is 005°W. Variation is 014°W.

Bearing on Gay Head          $109C - 005 = 104M - 014 = 090°T$
Bearing on
Cuttyhunk Light   $009C - 005 = 004M - 014 = 010 + 360 = 350°T$

The bearings thus calculated are directions *from* the boat *to* the objects sighted. These bearing lines are lines of position because the boat lies on each one of them, but they cannot be plotted on the chart since the position of the vessel is unknown. Each *reverse* or *reciprocal* bearing, in this case $090T + 180 = 270°T$ and $350T + 180 = 530 - 360 = 170°T$, is a bearing *from* the known position of the object sighted *to* the vessel. Each of these lines of position can be drawn on the chart, and the vessel must lie at the intersection, Fig. 12-5.

## 12.07    Compass, Magnetic, and True Bearings

With a good helmsman compass bearings can be obtained directly from a pelorus reading. The course being steered is set on the pelorus card opposite the lubber line, Fig. 12-6B. This synchronizes the pelorus card with the compass card as long as the ship's heading does not change. The helmsman concentrates on maintaining the course that has been set. When he is exactly on course, he will cry "mark," and the pilot will then read the angle of his sight on a distant object. Bearings thus taken will be in terms of the readings of the ship's compass and may be converted to magnetic and true bearings in the usual way.

Magnetic bearings may be taken directly with a hand-held sighting compass, Fig. 12-7. This device consists of a small magnetic compass and a sighting vane so arranged that the distant object is seen superimposed on the compass-card graduations. The sighting compass is used at eye level and at a position considerably farther removed from magnetic influences arising within the ship than is the case for the usual compass mount. The sighting compass is assumed to have zero deviation in all directions, an assumption that is probably justified, at least on wooden and fiberglass vessels.

Bearings may also be taken with a flat-top compass and a sighting ring if the compass is mounted so that sights can be taken in all directions. Bearings so taken are subject to the deviation corrections of that particular compass.

**FIGURE 12-7** Hand-held bearing compass showing a reflected scale reading aligned with the sighting index. Courtesy of Weems System of Navigation.

## 12.08   Distance to Visible Objects

Position can be determined by means other than the use of cross bearings. For example, position could be established from a single line of position with a measurement of the distance from the object sighted. Unfortunately there is no generally useful distance-measuring instrument available to the small-boat operator. Naval vessels use range finders for various purposes, but these instruments must be large if a reasonable accuracy is to be attained. Radar may be used in some cases, but this is a rare installation on board small recreational boats, and it lacks the desired accuracy.

Distance finding from synchronized radio beacons is described in Sec. 13.06. This provides a most useful bit of information in thick weather, but it cannot be considered sufficiently accurate for routine piloting even if it were operative at all times.

Some distance determinations can be made by combining a succession of bearings with a knowledge of the boat's forward progress. The trigonometric relations involved are given in Appendix IV.

## 12.09   Position by Soundings

*Soundings* or measurements of water depth are of great importance when operating in pilot waters. Repeated soundings provide direct information most important in the avoidance of grounding. If there are sudden, well-charted changes in depth, a series of soundings may serve to establish, at least roughly, a line of position.

In thick weather the pilot's information about his position may be almost limited to soundings. If the contour of the bottom is sufficiently variable, it may be possible to establish an approximate position from a series of soundings. The procedure is:

(1) Soundings are taken at regular, timed intervals while the boat is proceeding on a known and constant course at a constant known speed. The most suitable interval will depend on circumstances. About ⅛ mile is probably a good average value.

(2) A course line is drawn on a sheet of transparent paper along with some reference lines needed to insure proper alignment when the sheet is placed over the chart.

(3) The results of the soundings are plotted along the course line at the proper intervals as determined from the speed and the elapsed times.

(4) The transparent paper is moved over the chart, always keeping the course line in proper orientation, until there is a reasonable match between the soundings and the charted depths. An exact match is not to be expected because of tidal differences. A reasonably close match, with corresponding *changes* in depth, will provide an almost certain position location.

Electronic depth-finders provide almost continuous soundings. When these are not available, a *lead line* is used. Originally the lead line was marked at each fathom with an odd assortment of leather, cotton, and wool, intended to facilitate identification in the dark. Modern lead lines tend to be marked in feet with colored tags.

The leadsman, standing well forward, casts the lead and a length of free line well ahead of the boat, which must be proceeding slowly. He brings the surplus line in smartly as the boat runs up to the lead. When the line is vertical, he reads the depth at the surface of the water and brings the lead up over the side.

The time required to cast and retrieve the lead limits the depths at which it is practically useful. Electric fathometers for small craft are usually effective to perhaps 200-300 feet. Vessels operating beyond these depths are said to be *off-soundings*.

## 12.10   Plotting Courses and Bearings

Repeated references have been made to the laying out of courses and bearings on charts; it is now time to consider the proper methods of making these plots. Good plotting habits should be developed from the start. Although the methods may vary, the final result should be in a standard form instantly understandable by anyone who might have the next watch.

Most navigational charts are too large to be spread out full size on small boats. Usually only a small portion is needed at one time so they may be used partly unrolled on a small chart table. Lap boards are available and are quite satisfactory in crowded quarters.

In addition to the chart table, the pilot will need several medium soft pencils, eraser, scratch pad, dividers, drafting compass, and some sort of plotting instrument. The last item can be chosen from a number of satisfactory designs including parallel rules, rolling rule, one-arm protractor, and the ordinary draftsman's protractor and triangles, Fig. 12-8.

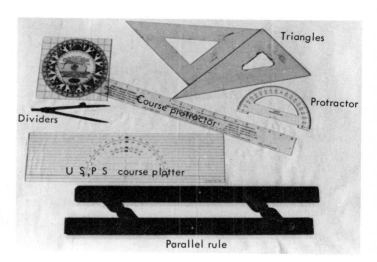

**FIGURE 12-8** Various types of course-plotting instruments. Individual preference will determine the one used.

Two basic problems are involved in plotting courses and bearings. The first involves either laying down on the chart a line in a given direction or the determination of the direction of a line already on the chart. The second problem requires the determination of distances between two points on the chart or the inverse: the laying off of a given distance along a course line.

Several guides are available for the angular measurements. Each compass rose gives both true and local magnetic directions around the entire 360 degrees. From the nature of the Mercator projection all meridians run true north-south, and all parallels of latitude are true east-west. How these standard direction lines will be used depends on the type of plotting device.

The USPS course plotter consists of a series of lines drawn parallel to the long edges of the instrument and a protractor scale. In finding the direction of a plotted line, the plotter is placed with one of the parallel lines on top of the course line. The plotter is then moved along the course line until the center of the protractor scale intersects a meridian. The course direction is then read at the intersection of the meridian and the protractor scale.

In drawing a bearing line from a reference point as, say, a lighthouse, a long edge of the plotter is held against a pencil or divider point placed at the

240    Small-Boat Piloting

chart symbol. The plotter is then slid and swung until the center of the protractor scale and the desired angle coincide with the nearest meridian. The bearing line can then be drawn along the edge of the plotter.

Detailed instructions for the use of the various plotting devices cannot be given here; they will be furnished with each instrument when it is purchased. Each instrument, by one means or another, transfers a direction either to or from a reference standard. When the transfer is made by a repeated "walking" process, as with parallel rules, there is a good chance of slippage, particularly if the plotting is being done in a lumpy sea. Only experience will lead to the choice of the instrument with greatest accuracy best suited to the individual.

Distant measurements are made easy by the fact that each minute of angle of latitude, which is measured along the meridians, is equal to one nautical mile. Thus the vertical latitude scales along the sides of every chart may be used directly to measure distances. From the nature of the Mercator projection the latitude scale will not be uniform, so a given distance on the chart must be compared with the latitude scale directly opposite. On a large-scale harbor chart, the scale difference between different latitudes will be negligible, but one should get in the habit of transferring distances directly across in every case. Note that the latitude scale gives distances on the chart at the same latitude, regardless of the direction in which the chart distances are taken. There are no circumstances under which the longitude scales at the top and the bottom of a chart can be used for distance measurement.

## 12.11    Position Fix

When a pilot has *accurately* established the ship's position, by whatever means, he has a *fix*. The term "accurately" is somewhat flexible, meaning essentially an error that is small compared to the distance to the nearest hazard to navigation. A fix obtained by passing an aid to navigation close aboard may have an error of only a few feet. A fix obtained from the intersection of two lines of position will have a greater uncertainty because there will be some observational error associated with each of the measurements. Other things being equal, the least error will occur when the two lines of position cross at about 90°, or make a *good cut*. There is no critical angle below which a fix is unacceptable, but errors increase rapidly at angles of less than 45° and greater than 135°, Fig. 12-9.

In plotting, a fix is considered to be an exact representation of position. It is marked on the chart by a small circle drawn around the established point ⊙, and labelled *Fix* Sec. 12.15.

## 12.12    Dead Reckoning

With a fix established the pilot can draw a *course line* or *dead-reckoning track* along which he desires the boat to move. The dead-reckoning track will be drawn through the fix in the desired direction of motion, with no account

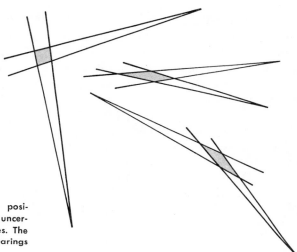

FIGURE 12-9 Uncertainties in the position of a fix for a five degree uncertainty in each of the bearing angles. The least uncertainty occurs when the bearings are at right angles.

taken of the effects of wind and current. From a speed curve or from log readings, the pilot can estimate his time of arrival (*ETA*), at any point along the course line where perhaps he must change course or where he can confirm his position by another fix.

A position along the dead-reckoning track obtained from a previous fix by a simple calculation of speed and time is known as a *dead-reckoning position* or a *DR*. A *DR* is identified on a chart by a point and circle ⊙ and labeled *DR*. A *DR* is the least accurate determination of position, for it takes no account of steering errors, errors in speed estimation, or of the effects of wind and current. *DR*'s and *ETA*'s are of great importance, however, when piloting in confined waters. A comparison of a dead-reckoning point with a concurrent fix will permit an estimate of the combined effect of all of the errors entering into the *DR*. This estimation will be useful in planning the next course to be run.

During periods of low visibility or on a long run out of sight of navigational aids, dead reckoning may provide the only information as to the vessel's position. All elements going into dead reckoning should be rigorously controlled. Careful steering, knowing performance of boat and engine, and accurate, up-to-date chart work must be maintained when operating beyond familiar landmarks.

## 12.13   Estimated Position

An improvement in a dead-reckoning position resulting from additional information (but insufficient for a fix) establishes an *estimated position* (*EP*). An *EP* may be only slightly more reliable than a *DR*, or it may be only slightly less reliable than a fix. The exact situation depends on the precision of the additional information and the dependability of the dead reckoning. For example, little improvement in knowledge of position will result when the effect of a weak current is applied to a carefully run *DR* course. On the other hand, if soundings reveal the instant the boat crosses a sharply defined depth contour marked on the chart, the reliability of the position estimate may be considerably improved.

Consider a vessel (Fig. 12-10) approaching from the east on a course of 270° *T* at a speed of 12 knots. At 0800 a bearing is obtained on B-W whistle buoy "H". The line of position obtained from this bearing cuts the course line at *A*, somewhat behind the 0800 *DR*. No other aid is visible to permit obtaining a fix by cross bearings. An *EP* is obtained by drawing a line through the 0800 *DR* perpendicular to the 0800 line of position. The *EP*, at the intersection of the perpendicular and the line of position, is marked with a small square and labeled *EP*.

Although an *EP* should represent a more probable location of the vessel, this is not necessarily so, and in fact an *EP* may occasionally be worse than a *DR*. Because of this possibility, a course line is never extended from an estimated position. As shown in Fig. 12-10, the course line is continued from the 0800 *DR* rather than from the *EP*.

Every opportunity should be taken to obtain even a single line of position. In addition to its use in converting a *DR* to an *EP*, a line of position may be *advanced* for future use with a second line of position, *LOP*.

## 12.14   Running Fix

Frequently so much time elapses between two observations that account must be taken of the movement of the boat during the interval. Two observations spaced in time may be used to obtain a *running fix* or *R Fix*, which, for short time intervals, may establish a position nearly as well as a fix obtained from essentially simultaneous observations.

To obtain a running fix the first line of position is advanced parallel to itself along the *DR* course by a distance equal to that traveled between the two observations. The intersection of this advanced *LOP* with the second *LOP* will give the running fix. An *LOP* can be advanced even though the course was changed between the two observations. The accuracy of a running fix depends primarily on the accuracy with which the ship's advance is known.

In Fig. 12-10, the ship continued on 270° *T* until 0810 when the course was changed to 319° *T*. At 0850 Black Whistling Buoy "1" was sighted bearing 305° *T*. No other aid was visible at this time so the 0800 *LOP* was advanced to obtain a running fix. Between 0800 and 0810 the ship advanced 2 miles along 270° *T*. This distance is laid off along the *DR* track from point *A* where the 0800 *LOP* intersects to give point *B*. A line through *B* bearing 232° *T* is the 0800-0810 advanced *LOP*. This line cuts the new course line at *C*. From 0810

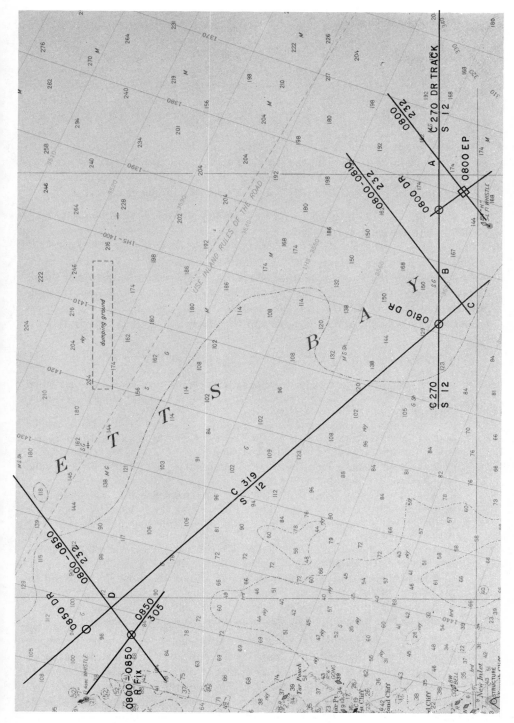

**FIGURE 12-10** A typical course plot showing a running fix advanced from a *DR* rather than from an *EP*.

243

to 0850 the ship travels 8 miles, so this distance is laid off from $C$ along the new DR track to give point $D$. A line through $D$ bearing 232° $T$ will be the 0800-0850 advanced *LOP*. The intersection of this advanced *LOP* with the 0850 *LOP* obtained from buoy "1" will give the running fix, plotted and marked in the figure.

The amount by which a line of position may be safely advanced depends on the accuracy with which the ship's course and speed are known and on the reliability required of the running fix. In pilot waters an advance of 1-2 miles may be maximal, but at sea an advance of 75 miles is common.

## 12.15    Labels and Symbols

Strict conformity to convention is required in identifying lines and points put on a chart if they are to be understood by all who may need to use them. Every line and point should be completely labeled as soon as it is plotted. Some essential bit of information can be quickly forgotten if it is not promptly recorded. Put only the required labels on the chart. Any others may only confuse.

The following conventions apply, as illustrated in Fig. 12-11:

a. A course line is identified by the letter $C$ with the true course in three figures above the line. The letter $S$ and the speed in knots are placed below the line directly under the course label.

b. A bearing line is identified by the time of observation in four figures above the line, and the true direction of the bearing *from the vessel* in three figures below the line and directly under the time.

c. A range is identified by the time of observation in four figures above the line. Nothing is placed below the line.

d. A dead reckoning point is identified on the course line by a small circle. It is labeled with the time in four figures followed by the letters *DR*. The labels should be written at an angle to the course line to avoid any possible confusion with other data.

e. An estimated position is identified by a small square drawn around the point. It is labeled with the time in four figures and the letters *EP*.

f. A fix is identified by a small circle drawn around the point. It is labeled by the time in four figures and the letters *Fix*.

g. A running fix is identified by a small circle drawn around the point. It is labeled by the two times in four figures and the letters *R Fix*.

*Neat chart work is of the greatest importance.* Every chart is already heavily populated with symbols of many kinds, and additional letters and numbers will only increase the chance of confusion. Every effort should be made to avoid errors in calculations and in the application of the results to the chart. An occasional error is inevitable and must be erased. Erasures should be made carefully but thoroughly to eliminate all chances of mistaking a partially removed line or symbol.

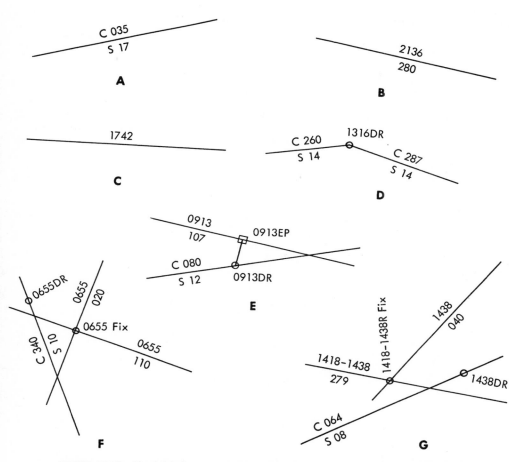

**FIGURE 12-11** Chart labeling conventions: (A) course line, (B) bearing or *LOP*, (C) range line, (D) dead-reckoning point, (E) estimated position, (F) fix obtained by any means, in this case by cross bearings, (G) running fix.

## 12.16 Current

When under way, the movement of a boat relative to the land is the sum of her movement relative to the water and the movement of the water relative to the land. The sum is not a simple addition of two numbers representing speeds, because the two movements will not be, in general, in the same direction. A boat heading directly across a river in which there is a current will reach the opposite bank downstream from her starting point. If she returns on a course straight across the river, she will be carried still further downstream, rather than being returned to her original starting point. A direct passage across can only be made by heading the bow somewhat upstream.

River currents are highly variable, changing with time and with the location in the stream. Current information for the major navigable rivers can be obtained from the regional offices of the Army Corps of Engineers. This information must be supplemented by careful observation of river currents and their behavior at sharp bends and at shoals.

Current patterns in tidewaters differ sharply from river currents. In tidewater the current ebbs and floods, making one complete cycle in about 12 hours and 45 minutes. When the current reverses its direction, there will be short periods of still water known as *slack before flood* and *slack before ebb*.

**FIGURE 12-12** Current is responsible for the difference between the 1450 DR and the 1450 Fix.

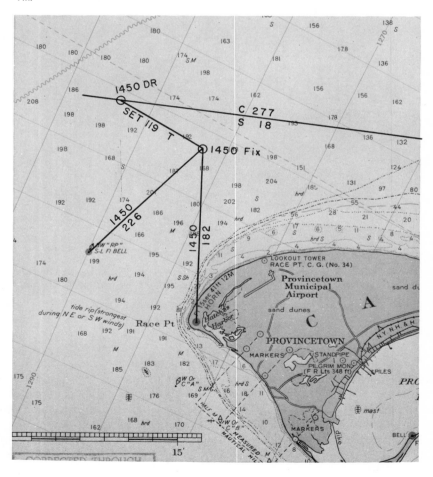

Most ocean currents are slow and may flow in circular patterns rather than in a linear to-and-fro movement. In constrictions, particularly those connecting large bodies of water, tidal currents may rise to 8 knots or more. Small-boat operators must reckon seriously with current flows well below these extreme values.

A navigator will attribute a discrepancy between a *DR* position and a *Fix* to current. In fact the discrepancy is probably a combination of the effects of current, wind, steering error, and uncertainty in the speed curve. If the navigator has good reason to believe that the discrepancy is really due to current, he may apply a current correction to a *DR* position to obtain an *estimated position with current*. Past experience can only be applied to future dead reckonings over that period when there is no appreciable change in the tidal currents.

Two factors enter into calculations involving the effects of current. *Set* is the direction in which the current flows, measured either in compass, magnetic, or true angles. *Drift* is the velocity of the current in knots. Fig. 12-12 shows a large-scale plot of the effect of current. In a run of 1450-1320 = 0130 or 1.5 hours, current set the boat from the 1450 *DR* to the 1450 *FIX*. Measurement shows this distance to be 1.5 miles in the direction of 119° T. Set is then 119° T, drift is 1.5/1.5 = 1.0 knots.

## 12.17   Model Cruise

The power cruiser *Manikin* makes a daylight coastal passage from Springfield to the Black River entrance. Her navigator's work is illustrated in the accompanying plot (Fig. 12-13) and navigator's log. The local magnetic variation is 005° W, and excerpts from the deviation table are given in Table 12-1. The speed curve is given in Fig. 12-3.

**TABLE 12-1**

**Deviation Table**

| Heading P.S.C. | Deviation | Heading Magnetic |
|---|---|---|
| 060° | 013° E | 73° |
| 075° | 013° E | 88° |
| 090° | 012° E | 102° |
| 105° | 010° E | 115° |
| 180° | 005° W | 175° |
| 195° | 008° W | 187° |
| 210° | 010° W | 200° |
| 225° | 012° W | 213° |
| 255° | 012° W | 243° |
| 270° | 011° W | 259° |
| 315° | 005° W | 310° |
| 330° | 002° W | 328° |

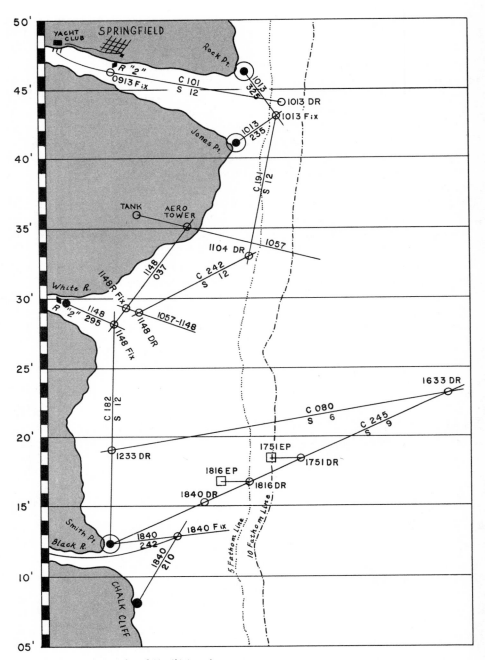

**FIGURE 12-13** A plot of *Manikin's* cruise.

## MANIKIN'S LOG

### Cruise from Springfield to Black River

| Time | Symbol | Notations |
|------|--------|-----------|
| 0843 | — | Cast off lines from Yacht Club Pier, Springfield. Motored out of river.<br>Wind N.E., 15 mph; visibility 10 M |

| 0913 | Fix | Took departure—R"2" close abeam to port.<br>Initial course: |

|  |  | Compass | 095° | Engine R.P.M., 2040 |
|  |  | Deviation | 011° E | Speed 12 Kt |
|  |  | Magnetic | 106° |  |
|  |  | Variation | 005° W |  |
|  |  | True | 101° |  |

Run for 1 h 00 m

$$\text{Distance} = \frac{12 \text{ Kt} \times 60 \text{ m}}{60} = 12.0 \text{ M}$$

| 1013 | *DR* | Plotted |
| 1013 | Fix | Cross bearings: |

|  |  |  | Rock Pt.<br>Lt. bears: |  | Jones Pt.<br>Lt. bears: |
|--|--|--|--|--|--|
|  |  | Compass | 319° |  | 229° |
|  |  | Deviation for |  |  |  |
|  |  | Heading | 011° E |  | 011° E |
|  |  | Magnetic | 330° |  | 240° |
|  |  | Variation | 005° W |  | 005° W |
|  |  | True | 325° |  | 235° |
|  |  | From Lt. | (−180°) 145° | (−180°) | 055° |

Second Course:

|  |  | Compass | 205° | Engine R.P.M., 2040 |
|  |  | Deviation | 009° W | Speed 12 Kt |
|  |  | Magnetic | 196° |  |
|  |  | Variation | 005° W |  |
|  |  | True | 191° |  |

| 1056-45 | Range | Crossed Range Line, Plotted |

Run from 1013 Fix to change of course at 1103-45 DR − 50 m 45 s

$$\text{Distance} = \frac{12 \text{ Kt} \times 50.75 \text{ m}}{60} = 10.2 \text{ M}$$

| Time | Symbol | Notations |
|------|--------|-----------|

1103-45    *DR*    Plotted
Third Course:

| | | |
|---|---|---|
| Compass | 259° | Engine R.P.M., 2040 |
| Deviation | 012° W | Speed 12 Kt |
| Magnetic | 247° | |
| Variation | 005° W | |
| True | 242° | |

Run from 1104 *DR*—43 m 50 sec to 1147-35 *DR*/

$$\text{Distance} = \frac{12 \text{ Kt} \times 43.8 \text{ m}}{60} = 8.76 \text{ M}$$

1147-35    *DR*    Plotted

1147-35    Running    Crossed Advanced 1057 Range Line and Bearing on Aero
           Fix        Tower:

| | | |
|---|---|---|
| Compass | | 054° |
| Deviation for | | |
| Heading | | 012° W |
| Magnetic | | 042° |
| Variation | | 005° W |
| True | | 037° |
| From Tower | (+180°) | 217° |

1147-35    Fix    Cross bearings:

| | | Aero Tower bears: | R"2" White River bears: |
|---|---|---|---|
| Compass | | As above | 312° |
| Deviation for | | | |
| Heading | | | 012° W |
| Magnetic | | | 300° |
| Variation | | | 005° W |
| True | | | 295° |
| From Lt. | | (−180°) | 115° |

*Note:* "Current" set boat to the southwest,
*Note:* Difference between Running Fix and Fix because of current's effect after range crossed at 1057.
*Note:* Weather threatening. Wind increased to 22 mph. Storm approaching from N.E. Plotted course line to Black River entrance and determined distance and course to steer from plot:

| Time | Symbol | Notations |
|------|--------|-----------|

Fourth Course:

| | |
|---|---|
| True | 182° |
| Variation | 005° W |
| Magnetic | 187° |
| Deviation | 010° W |
| Compass | 197° |

Engine R.P.M., 2040
Speed 12 Kt

Distance     15.8 M

$$\text{Minutes} = \frac{60 \times 15.8 \text{ M}}{12 \text{ Kt}} = 79.0 \text{ m} = 1 \text{ h } 19 \text{ m } 00 \text{ sec}$$

Estimated Time of Arrival Black River Entrance: 1148 + 1 h 19 m 00 sec = 1307

*Note:* By 1233 weather deteriorated. Heavy rain, wind 35 mph, rough sea. Visibility zero. Lee shore off starboard bow. Must change course for boat's safety.

Run from 1148 Fix to 1233 DR = 45 m

$$\text{Distance} = \frac{12 \text{ Kt} \times 45 \text{ m}}{60} = 9 \text{ M}$$

**1233     *DR***     Plotted—New course to take seas on port bow and head offshore at half speed;

Fifth Course:

| | |
|---|---|
| Compass | 072° |
| Deviation | 013° E |
| Magnetic | 085° |
| Variation | 005° W |
| True | 080° |

Engine R.P.M., 1060
Speed 6 Kt

*Note:* By 1633 weather and seas moderated. N.E. wind now 19 mph. Continuous rain, visibility 500 yards.

Run from 1233 *DR* to 1633 DR = 4 h 00 m

$$\text{Distance} = \frac{6 \text{ Kt} \times 240 \text{ m}}{60} = 24.0 \text{ M}$$

**1633     *DR***     Plotted

*Note:* Plotted course line from 1633 *DR* to Black River entrance and determined the course, distance and ETA at ¾ speed.

| Time | Symbol | Notations |
|------|--------|-----------|

Sixth Course:
True            245°              Engine R.P.M., 1780
Variation       005° W            Speed 9 Kt
Magnetic        250°
Deviation       012° W
Compass         262°

Distance        26.25 M

$$\text{Times in Minutes} = \frac{60 \times 26.25 \text{ M}}{9 \text{ Kt}} = 2\text{ h }54\text{ m }58\text{ sec}$$

E.T.A. $1633 + 2\text{ h }55\text{m} = 1928$

*Note:* To estimate position more accurately, soundings taken continuously.

**1751**

Crossed 10-fathom line.
Run from 1633 *DR*, 1 h 18 m

$$\text{Distance run} = \frac{9 \text{ Kt} \times 78 \text{ m}}{60} = 11.74 \text{ M}$$

**1751     *DR***     Plotted

**1751     *EP***     Located by a line drawn perpendicular to the 10-fathom line and intersecting the 1751 *DR*

**1816**               Crossed 5-fathom line.

Run from 1751 *DR* to 1816 *DR* = 25 m

$$\text{Distance} = \frac{9 \text{ Kt} \times 25 \text{ m}}{60} = 3.75 \text{ M}$$

**1816     *DR***     Plotted

**1816     *EP***     Located by a line drawn perpendicular to the 5-fathom line and intersecting the 1816 *DR*. Course and speed unchanged.

| Time | Symbol | Notations |
|------|--------|-----------|
| 1840 | | Smith Point and Chalk Cliff Lights identified. |

Run from 1816 *DR* to 1840 *DR* = 24 m

$$\text{Distance} = \frac{9 \text{ Kt} \times 24 \text{ m}}{60} = 3.6 \text{ M}$$

| Time | Symbol | Notations |
|------|--------|-----------|
| 1840 | *DR* | Plotted |
| 1840 | Fix | Cross bearings: |

|  | Smith Point Lt. | Chalk Cliff Lt. |
|--|----------------|-----------------|
| Compass | 279° | 227° |
| Deviation for | | |
| Heading | 012° W | 012° W |
| Magnetic | 267° | 215° |
| Variation | 005° W | 005° W |
| True | 262° | 210° |
| Plot | 082° | 030° |

*Note:* "Current" has set *Manikin* several miles to the southwest.

Final course into river under direct vision. Speed variable.

| 1947 | | Passage completed. |

## EXERCISES

**12-1.** You have been running in a dense fog for one hour and 27 minutes with the engine slowed to give a speed of 3.2 knots. How far have you progressed during this run?

**12-2.** You are under way at 1018 for a 1200 rendezvous with a friend at Sand Cove, 24.7 miles distant. What speed must you maintain to make the agreed meeting? If Fig. 12-3 is the speed curve for your boat, what engine speed will be required to attain the desired speed?

**12-3.** At 1053 on the run specified in 12-2, a malfunction forces you to reduce the engine speed to 1000 rpm. How far had you gone at the time of the engine trouble? What will be your speed at the lower rpm? What is your new ETA?

**12-4.** On an almost windless day a sailboat 28' loa was moving at a speed that was too low to produce a reading on the log. Some small holes were punched in a beer can to insure eventual sinking, and this was tossed out ahead of the boat. What was the relative speed of the boat past the can if 55 seconds were required to pass the can from stem to stern?

**12-5.** A boat is making use of two aids to navigation charted 1.6 miles apart for determining a speed curve. At 1800 rpm the two running times in the opposite directions were 11:18 and 12:48 minutes. What is the boat speed in still water?

**12-6.** You left midchannel buoy "SR" at the mouth of the Sakonnet River at 0835 on a course of 223°T bound for The Harbor, Block Island. At 0900 you observe Point Judith Light on a bearing of 294C and Brenton Reef offshore aid at 353C. The deviation data for the compass are given in Table 11-3. Determine your 0900 position. What is the speed made good?

**12-7.** From the 0900 Fix in 12-6 you plot a course of 221T to fetch bell buoy "1" at The Harbor, Block Island. Previous speed is maintained and at 1930 Point Judith Light is observed on a bearing of 012C. Brenton Reef aid is now obscured in haze so the 0900 Point Judith LOP is advanced to obtain a Running Fix. Locate your 0930 position. What is your ETA at bell buoy "1"? Why did you not advance the 0900 LOP on the Brenton Reef aid?

**12-8.** Proceeding from Long Island Sound to New Bedford, you have whistle buoy "2" off Point Judith close abeam at 1120. You may lay a course of 074T and set the engine speed to make 12 knots. Your compass deviation data are given in Table 11-3. At 1200 Brenton Reef aid is observed at a relative bearing of 238, and the abandoned lighthouse on Sakonnet Point is on a relative bearing of 330. Plot the 1200 position and compare it with the 1200 DR. What is the speed made good?

**12-9.** At 1230, after continuing with the same course and speed as in 12-8, the Brenton Reef aid is no longer visible, and the Buzzards aid has become obscured by a fog rapidly moving in from the East. To determine your position before you are totally obscured you observe the abandoned lighthouse on a relative bearing of 268. Use this and the advanced 1200 sight on the Brenton Reef aid to establish a 1230 Running Fix. What is your 1230 position? What course do you set to make Whistle Buoy "1" just North of Buzzards, and what is your ETA at this buoy?

## ANSWERS

**12-1.**   4.6 miles.

**12-2.**   Speed 14.5 kts. Engine speed 2200 rpm.

**12-3.**   8.5 miles. 5.7 kts. New ETA 1343.

**12-4.**   Speed 0.3 kts.

**12-5.**   Speed 8.0 kts.

**12-6.**   Position L 41°22.1'N, Lo 71°20.0'W. Speed 15.7 kts.

**12-7.**   Position L 41°16.2'N, Lo 71°26.9'W. ETA 0957. Poor cut with the 0930 LOP on Point Judith.

**12-8.**   On plotted course line but 0.6 mile ahead of 1200 DR. Speed made good 12.9 kts.

**12-9.**   1200–1230 R Fix L 41°29.6'N, Lo 71°10.0'W. Course 077T. ETA 1257.

CHAPTER **13**

# Electronic Aids
# to Navigation

## 13.01  Technical Developments

Electronic aid to navigation began in 1902 when Marconi, many miles at sea, communicated with a shore-based transmitter by the process we now call radio. The value of the new technique was most dramatically demonstrated in the *Titanic* disaster of 1912, and soon afterward shipboard radio installations became required on all commercial vessels.

Early radio equipment was large and heavy and required power far beyond the capabilities of small pleasure craft. These drawbacks gradually disappeared as more efficient circuits and components were developed and new transmitting frequencies were allotted for marine communications. The scientific activities associated with World War II led to rapid developments in radar and in underwater signaling devices subsequently used as depth finders. The demands of war were also responsible for the development of new systems for determining position at sea.

All of these devices required numerous vacuum tubes, and power requirements, while acceptable, were still annoyingly high, particularly for sailing craft. The introduction of solid-state devices or *transistors* again sharply reduced size, weight, and power requirements to the point where they are no longer limiting factors. A certain amount of power must be put into any radio transmitter, regardless of type, since the transmission of signals requires that power be radiated away from the antenna. Most of the other electronic instruments useful to the small-boat skipper can, transistorized, operate for a full boating season on a single set of small batteries.

## 13.02  Radio Waves

Most of the important electronic aids involve the transmission or reception of electromagnetic radiation, commonly known as radio waves. Everyone is familiar with the fact that the electric power available throughout the United States is alternating current at 60 cycles, which means that it changes

255

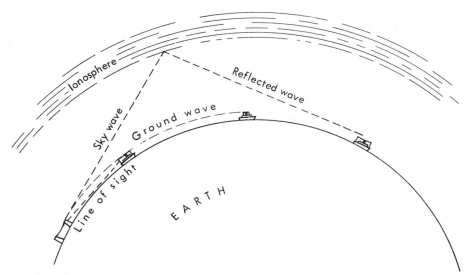

**FIGURE 13-1**    Radio transmission may be by ground wave or by reflected sky wave.

direction, or oscillates, 60 times every second. If the frequency is increased, say one million times to 60,000,000 cycles, and if the generator is connected to an antenna or aerial, a considerable amount of energy will be radiated from the antenna into space. This energy will be in the form of electromagnetic waves, invisible to our eyes, but otherwise very similar to the waves that we call visible light. These waves will travel outward from the antenna at a speed of 186,000 miles per second. In nautical terms this is a speed of 580,000,000 knots.

For many years transmitter frequencies have been specified in *kilocycles* (*kc*) or in *megacycles* (*mc*), the prefixes meaning thousands and millions, respectively. To conform to present worldwide practice, Hertz, the name of the man who first produced and transmitted radio waves, is now used for *cycles*. Thus, kilocycles becomes *kilo-Hertz* (*KHz*) and megacycles becomes *mega-Hertz* (*MHz*). The marine radiotelephone distress frequency can thus be expressed as 2,182,000 Hertz, 2,182 KHz, or 2.182 MHz. Low frequency transmissions, say below 1 MHz, are propagated primarily by a *ground* wave which follows the earth's curved surface, Fig. 13-1. At the higher frequencies long-distance transmissions are achieved through the *sky wave*, which reflects from ionized layers high in the atmosphere to return to earth at great distances. Sky-wave transmission is characterized by a *skip-distance*, within which signals will be rarely if ever heard.

The simplest radio frequency (*rf*) signal is a *CW* or *continuous wave* (Fig. 13-2) where the transmitter produces oscillations at a constant amplitude and frequency. When this oscillation is switched on and off at intervals, a

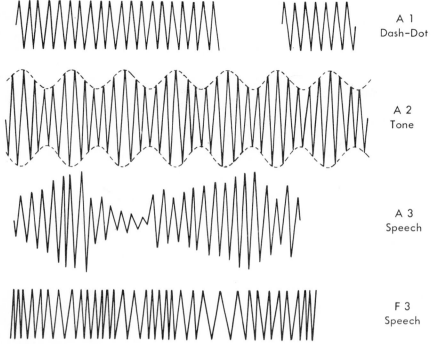

A 1
Dash–Dot

A 2
Tone

A 3
Speech

F 3
Speech

**FIGURE 13-2**  Wave forms of the various forms of radio transmission.

series of *dots* and *dashes* will be produced, and intelligence can be transmitted by coded groups to form letters and numbers. *CW* signals will not be audible as a tone in a receiver unless a *local oscillator* is used to mix a local signal with the incoming oscillations. The local oscillator is sometimes called a *beat frequency oscillator* or *BFO*.

Signals will be received without the need for a local oscillator if a *CW* signal or *carrier wave* undergoes changes in amplitude or is *modulated*. *Amplitude modulation* or *AM* is used in most broadcasting and in some marine radio-telephones. A *frequency modulated* or *FM* signal is produced when the carrier wave is modulated in frequency rather than in amplitude.

The various forms of transmissions, the wave forms of which are shown in Fig. 13-2, are given the following designations:

A1—continuous wave, unmodulated
A2—continuous wave, electronically modulated to produce an audible tone
A3—continuous wave, amplitude modulated by voice or music
F3—continuous wave, frequency modulated by voice or music

## 13.03   Frequency Bands

Each transmitter, of any type, requires a range of frequencies for the transmission of signals. The tremendous demand for communication channels has required the allotment of bands of frequencies to specific uses. Several of these allocated bands are of interest to yachtsmen. The most familiar band is the commercial broadcast, 550-1600 KHz. Besides entertainment, this band carries a considerable amount of weather information of interest to the mariner. A vessel with direction-finding equipment on board may use commercial broadcasting stations for position finding although more exact positions can be established by the use of the lower frequencies emitted by radio beacons, assigned frequencies in the 285-325 KHz band.

A nationwide network of transmitters operating in the 200-400 KHz band broadcasts signals continuously for airplane guidance. Signals from some of these stations near the coast can be used for position finding by boats having radio direction-finding equipment on board. In addition, the air navigation transmitters broadcast weather reports at regular intervals, usually at 15 and 45 minutes after each hour.

The lowest frequency band of interest to small-boat skippers is used for *consol* or *consolan*, position-finding systems operating at 190-200 KHz.

Two frequency bands have been assigned for the use of small-craft radiotelephones. A number of frequencies in the MF band (1600-3500 KHz) are available for A3 or amplitude modulated voice transmissions. A greater number of frequencies within the VHF band (152-166 MHz) can be used for shorter-range voice communication with F3 or frequency modulated signals. Large commercial vessels will carry high-powered equipment operating in frequency bands not assigned to operators of small pleasure craft.

Pairs of frequencies within the MF and VHF bands are set aside for public correspondence transmissions. These are used when a vessel desires to communicate with a telephone connected into the regular land-based telephone system.

Four frequencies have been designated for marine distress calls and direction finding for purposes of search and rescue. These frequencies and their application are:

| | |
|---|---|
| 500 KHz | CW or tone modulated. The LF international distress and calling frequency used nearly exclusively by ships carrying licensed radio operators. This frequency may be used with discretion for radio direction finding in search and rescue situations. |
| 2182 KHz | A2 voice modulated. The MF international distress and calling frequency for ships not carrying a licensed radio operator. The distress signal on this frequency is MAYDAY (13.11). This frequency may be used with discretion for radio direction finding for search and rescue. |
| 8364 KHz | CW or tone modulated. The international survival craft radio distress and direction finding frequency for search and rescue. |
| 156.8 MHz | F3 voice modulated. The VHF international distress and calling frequency. The distress signal on this frequency is MAYDAY (13.11). |

Some Coast Guard and Naval installations monitor one or more of the distress frequencies continuously, with a vigilance varying with the circumstances. The degrees of vigilance are:

Guard—Receiver monitor with transmitter immediately ready
Cover—Receiver monitor with transmitter available
Copy—Receiver monitor with continuous log of receptions
Listen—Receiver monitor with log optional

In addition to the continuous monitors, a good many other stations do part-time surveillance, particularly at the height of the boating season.

## 13.04   Radio Broadcast Receivers

A radio broadcast receiver, perhaps brought on board only for entertainment, can be a useful aid to safe boating. The small, transistorized receivers operate on self-contained batteries and hence may be used for many hours without danger of depleting the main boat battery. Many of these small sets use a highly directional antenna which may permit direction finding, 13.05. The small sets will not establish bearings to the transmitter with the accuracy obtainable with equipment designed specifically for the purpose. There are times, however, when the position information obtainable with a small receiver is a welcome addition to other data.

Much more frequent use will be made of the broadcast receiver to obtain weather information. Safe, comfortable small-boat operation is strongly dependent on the weather and on weather forecasting. Some forecasting can be done from local conditions, but more effective predictions can be made when local observations can be supplemented with data from surrounding areas.

Nearly all commercial broadcasting stations in the United States transmit the latest weather information at frequent intervals. Most of this material is not prepared specifically for marine use, but it does provide useful guides to future conditions. In some popular boating areas special marine weather broadcasts are made on a more limited schedule. These schedules, together with other associated information, are available in a series of *Coastal Warning Facilities Charts*, prepared by the National Weather Service and sold through the Government Printing Office.

Sudden summer-afternoon thunderstorms may be severe enough to present a real hazard to small-boat operations. In most cases a forecast only an hour or so in advance of the storm is sufficient to make preparations for meeting it, or to seek shelter. A radio receiver operating in the AM broadcast band responds well to the electrical discharges which precede and accompany a thunderstorm. With a little experience one can usually distinguish between the discharges of normal summer static and those which grow in number and intensity as a storm develops. Frequently a radio receiver will give an indication of an approaching thunderstorm before local conditions show any visible signs of it. FM receivers do not respond to the random static discharges and so cannot provide the warning obtainable with an AM set.

Continuous weather information is now broadcast from a limited but expanding network of transmitters operated by the National Weather Service,

16.01. All of these transmitters operate with F3 signals at a frequency of 162.55 MHz. Relatively inexpensive receivers, permanently tuned to this frequency, are now available. Permanent tuning is highly desirable at these high frequencies where unskilled manual tuning might cause a signal to go undetected.

## 13.05   Radio Direction Finding

The ground wave from a radio transmitter follows, for the most part, a great circle path, see 13.02, along the earth's surface. This fact permits a determination of the direction from which a radio signal comes, and then, if the location of the transmitter is known, a *line of position* can be established from transmitter to receiver. If the process can be repeated with a second transmitter, two lines of position will be established, with the boat located at the intersection of the two lines.

A

FIGURE 13-3 RDF equipment with directional antennas. (A) Loop antenna. (B) A ferrite loopstick is located inside the raised plastic section. Sensing antenna is at the rear. Courtesy of the Raytheon Company.

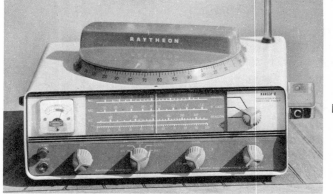

B

*Radio direction finding,* or *RDF,* utilizes a radio receiver equipped with a highly directional antenna. A loop antenna (Fig. 13-3A) has a maximum sensitivity to signals arriving in the plane of the loop and an almost zero sensitivity to signals coming in perpendicularly to this plane. In small-boat RDF receivers the bulky circular loop antenna is usually replaced by a ferrite *loopstick,* (Fig. 13-3B), which also has directional sensitivity although not equal to that of the loop.

When a simple directional antenna is rotated through 360 degrees, the signal strengths will pass through two maxima and two minima. The latter are usually called *nulls* even though they may not be exactly zeros. In practical direction finding the antenna will be set on a null, since this can be located more accurately than the position of a maximum.

As is evident, an RDF receiver using a simple directional antenna can only establish a line of position with an ambiguity of 180 degrees, because there is no way of telling from the loop signal alone which of the two null points is applicable. Usually the position of the vessel is well enough known to rule out one of the nulls as impossible.

### ILLUSTRATIVE EXAMPLE

A ship approaching San Francisco obtains the following bearings from its RDF receiver:

| | | |
|---|---|---|
| Point Reyes | 120° and 300° magnetic | |
| Point Bonita | 080° | 260° |
| SE Farralon Is. | 020° | 200° |

The first observation establishes the vessel on the position line *AB,* Fig. 13-4, this line being drawn through the Point Reyes beacon along a 120-300 degree magnetic bearing. From this observation alone the vessel might be either NW or SE or Point Reyes. The RDF bearing on Point Bonita establishes the line of position *CD,* and this places the ship at point *S,* the only intersection of the two lines of position. In any case there can scarcely be any ambiguity about the ship's position along *CD* because a ship on this line to the East of Point Bonita would be in very restricted water and probably aground. The third bearing from the SE Farralon Island establishes position line *EF* and confirms the position determined from the first two observations.

The 180-degree uncertainty in the reading of a simple antenna can be removed by adding to the signal from the loop a second signal from a nondirectional antenna. This second antenna, which may be just a short rod or whip (Fig. 13-3B) is known as a *sensing antenna.* The sensitivity pattern of a simple loop antenna has two lobes of maximum signal strength and two nulls of minimum strength. When the sensing signal is added, the double response pattern changes to one with a single maximum and a single null.

Several factors besides convenience must be considered in locating an RDF receiver aboard a small boat. Large metal objects and sailboat rigging can reflect incoming radio waves and can thus change the direction from which they appear to come. *The detecting loop should therefore be located as far as possible from interfering metal objects.* The lead between the antenna and the

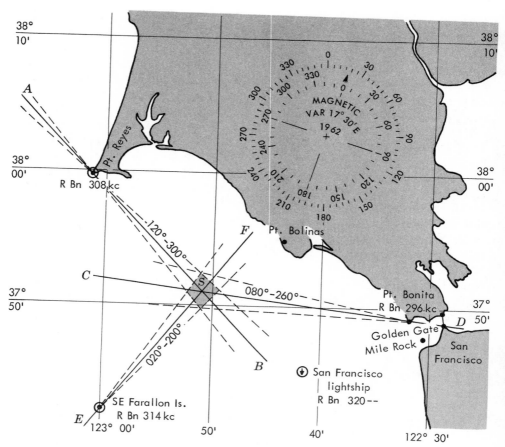

**FIGURE 13-4** Lines of position established by RDF bearings. Each line of position is the midpoint of the broad null whose limits are shown dotted.

receiver must be well shielded so that the lead itself does not form a part of the antenna system. The distance between antenna and receiver should be as small as possible.

When the loop is rotated by hand, extraneous, nondirectional signals may be introduced because the body acts as an antenna. To avoid grossly spurious readings null points must be found by moving the loop by small amounts, withdrawing the hand each time the signal strength is determined. Remote control devices may also be used for moving the loop.

RDF bearings taken between evening twilight and morning twilight may be subject to an error known as *night effect*. Radio-wave transmission may become erratic between sunset and sunrise, particularly at the two twilight periods. This erratic transmission becomes evident by a broad or a shifting null point or by fluctuations in the signal strength. If bearings must be taken under these conditions, several readings should be made in quick succession and then averaged.

RDF receivers may use a loudspeaker, headphones, or an indicating meter as a null detector. Each of these devices contains a powerful magnet which must be kept well away from the ship's magnetic compass. This most important point must be kept in mind when locating the RDF receiver. The magnetic-compass deviation should be checked after an RDF installation, and while it is in operation.

Bearings obtained with an RDF are really the directions of great circles, and in some cases these bearings cannot be plotted directly on a Mercator chart as straight lines. For a ship-transmitter distance of 150 miles or less, the plotting error will be negligible compared to the uncertainty in determining the null point. For greater distances correction factors found in publication *H.O. 205-117, Radio Navigational Aids* may be used to convert RDF bearings to Mercator bearings. *H.O. 205-117*, the electronic equivalent of the Light List for visual aids, is essential for anyone using any of the electronic aids to navigation.

In practice the null points obtainable with small-craft RDF equipment are not infinitely sharp. Each null reading may have an uncertainty of several degrees, leading to corresponding uncertainties in the lines of position. The position lines shown in Fig. 13-4 are thus idealized. In fact each null is more apt to have spreads, as indicated, so that the vessel can only be located within the shaded area and not exactly at point S.

## 13.06    Radiobeacons

In the United States emphasis has been placed on establishing a network of radiobeacons. In this system the radio transmission originates at a lighthouse or other navigational aid. This system requires that an RDF receiver be aboard the vessel, but no transmitting equipment is needed afloat. Fig. 13-5 shows the distribution of radiobeacons along a portion of the coast. Three types of symbols will be noted. The solid circles denote stations providing a radio signal only. The solid circle and cross denotes a radiobeacon combined with an audible signal for *distance finding. Markerbeacons* of very low power, for local purposes only, are indicated by open circles.

Radiobeacons operate in the 285-325 KHz band with AM transmissions. Groups of up to six radiobeacons may operate on a common frequency, sharing transmission times according to a sequence assignment denoted by Roman numerals in the station listings. Thus Ambrose light shares 286 KHz with several other stations, Fig. 13-5. The sequence symbol I indicates that Ambrose transmits during the first minute of each hour, and each sixth minute thereafter. Fire Island Shoal, 286 KHz II, transmits during the second minute of each hour and each sixth minute thereafter. A few beacons transmit continuously instead of on a six-minute cycle.

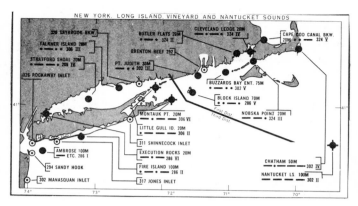

**FIGURE 13-5** Radiobeacons along a portion of the NE coast of the United States. From CG-158, *List of Lights,* Vol. 1, 1970.

Each beacon has a characteristic dot-dash identifying signal which it transmits over a 50-second period. This is followed by a 10-second dash, the continuous signal assisting in making the null adjustment at the RDF receiver.

Distance finding is based on the fact that the reception of a radio signal is practically instantaneous with its emission, while a sound wave requires about 5.5 seconds to travel one nautical mile in air. By determining the time lag between the reception of a radio signal and the arrival of a sound wave that was emitted simultaneously, one can calculate his distance from the source of the sound. This will establish a circular line of position drawn around the radiobeacon as a center. This circle, together with the straight-line determined from an RDF reading on the same station, will fix the ship's position.

Distance finding can only be used within audible range of the transmitting beacon. This distance can be highly variable, particularly in periods of low visibility, owing to the dispersing action of fog on sound waves.

In using synchronized radiobeacons for distance findings, one must understand the coding system so that the timing shall be made between the correct signals. The details of the signals emitted by beacons can be obtained from the *List of Lights* or from H.O. 205-117. A distance-finding station will transmit its characteristic call for a period of 48 seconds, which will be followed by a two-second silent period. The silent period will be ended by a 10-second radio signal and a five-second blast on the fog signal. The mariner will start his watch at the beginning of the radio dash and will stop it when he first hears the fog signal. This time, divided by 5.5, will give him the approximate distance to the beacon in nautical miles.

Waterborne signals have also been used by some stations for distance finding. These signals travel outward from the transmitter at about 0.83 nautical miles per second. Special gear is required to receive and time the underwater signals, which is therefore not used on small craft.

## 13.07     Electronic Fathometers

For centuries the *lead line* has been a most important aid in sailing *on-soundings,* or in areas where depth can be determined with a weight and a line. Although simple in principle, the lead line in practice leaves something to be desired. Reading the depth markers on the line with the rapidity required with even a slowly moving boat is an art during daylight hours. At night lead-line readings are much more difficult. Because of these difficulties, and the fact that a knowledge of depth is most valuable information, electronic depth-finders or fathometers have become one of the most widely accepted aids to small-boat navigation.

In the electronic fathometer an electric circuit generates oscillations at about 200 KHz. These oscillations are fed in short pulses to a *transducer,* usually a crystal of barium titanate, which converts the electric oscillations into mechanical vibrations. The transducer is mounted outside the hull in a watertight case faired to the hull to minimize water resistance, Figs. 13-6A and 13-6B.

The mechanical vibrations set up by the transducer are transmitted to

**FIGURE 13-6**   (A) Recording electronic fathometer displaying a record of bottom reflections and echoes from shallower objects. Courtesy of Apelco. (B) Indicating type of electronic fathometer with the transmitter-receiver unit. Courtesy of Heath Company.

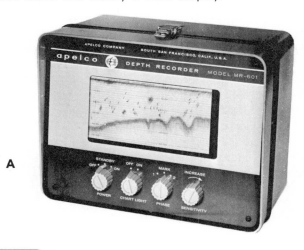

A

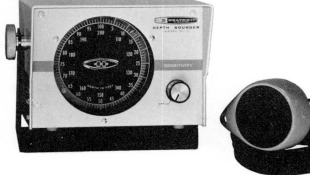

B

the water as a wave motion traveling at about 5,000 feet per second. When this wave reaches the bottom, a small portion of it will be reflected back to the transducer. The latter now reverses its original function and converts the feeble vibrations into an electrical signal which can then be amplified up to a usable level. Electronic circuits measure the time between the departure and arrival of the pulse and display this time on a scale or a chart graduated directly in depth (feet or fathoms). Pulses are sent out at such a rapid rate that there will be an almost continuous display of depths.

Reflection is somewhat dependent on the type of the reflecting material, and in some cases a good guess can be made as to the kind of bottom from the sharpness of the signals displayed. Reflection will take place from any solid object. Schools of fish produce spurious echoes, but these will usually be less marked than the reflections obtained from the bottom. In deep water large angles of pitch and roll may prevent the reception of the reflected signals. This is seldom a problem in depths where the fathometer is of the most value.

## 13.08   Radiotelephone

The radiotelephone is potentially the most valuable and at the same time the most abused electronic device aboard small craft. Frequently the radiotelephone is the only link with shore or with other ships to report disaster and summon assistance. All too often urgent calls must await the completion by thoughtless operators of casual gossip, obscene stories, or even musical selections, all of which are strictly forbidden on the marine bands. Every radio transmitter requires a certain amount of space in the allotted band, and when this space is being used by one transmitter others within its range are excluded. With the present crowding in the marine bands, the use of valuable air space for trivia is inexcusable.

Except for the frequencies allocated to public correspondence (connection to public land-based telephone systems), all marine frequencies are designated only for the purposes of *business, marine operations, and distress calls*. The Federal Communications Commission (FCC) can assess fines for improper use of the marine bands, without requiring court action. Hopefully this power, wisely used, will substantially reduce the large number of violations that have occurred in the past.

A license, obtainable by application to the FCC, is required to operate a shipboard radiotelephone. No examination is required, but the license is restricted to operating the equipment; adjustments and repairs can only be made by the holder of at least a Second Class Radiotelephone Operator's License. This license is issued only after passing a comprehensive examination in the theory and practice of radiotelephone communication.

An equipment or station license is required in addition to the operator's permit. To qualify for a station license, shipboard equipment must meet prescribed standards relating to power input, modulation quality, and carrier frequency stability. Requirements change as advances in electronics become commercially feasible.

A manufacturer can submit samples of his equipment to the FCC for testing. If FCC requirements are met the equipment will be listed as *type acceptable*, which means that its performance will be satisfactory when it is in proper adjustment. Station licenses will not be granted to equipment that is not type acceptable until FCC tests demonstrate that it is capable of satisfactory performance.

When new standards of performance are prescribed, a considerable amount of time is allowed for manufacturers to develop new equipment and make it available for purchase. Purchasers of either new or used equipment should make sure that it is type acceptable and hence is eligible for licensing.

When purchasing equipment it should be kept in mind that regulations require the use of the VHF band whenever this will provide effective communication. Vessels at sea or in remote areas will use the MF band as at present but with considerably improved equipment.

## 13.09   Marine VHF-FM

At the low output power permitted a station in this band, the practical range of a marine VHF station is limited to the *line of sight* distance between the antennas of transmitter and receiver. The reflected sky wave is too weak to be useful or to interfere with a distant station using the same frequency. Effective range may be 10 to 30 miles on a 24 hour basis between a boat and

**TABLE 13-1**
**Designated noncommercial VHF-FM channels available for small-boat radio communication**

| Channel | Frequency Coast | MHz Ship | Points of Communication | Conditions of Use |
|---|---|---|---|---|
| 16 | 156.800 | 156.800 | Coast to ship | Distress, safety, and calling |
| 65 | 156.275 | 156.275 | " " " | Port operation |
| 66 | 156.325 | 156.325 | " " " | " " |
| 12 | 156.600 | 156.600 | " " " | " ", Coast Guard |
| 73 | 156.675 | 156.675 | " " " | " " |
| 14 | 156.700 | 156.700 | " " " | " " |
| 74 | 156.725 | 156.725 | " " " | " " |
| 20 | 161.600 | 157.000 | " " " | " " |
| 15 | 156.750 | None | " " " | Weather, state of sea, time signal, notices to mariners, hazards |
| 17 | 156.850 | 156.850 | " " " | State control |
| 68 | 156.425 | 156.425 | Coast to ship Intership | For small noncommercial boats having limited number of channels |
| 09 | 156.450 | 156.450 | Coast to ship | Commercial and noncommercial |
| 69 | 156.475 | 156.475 | " " " | For marinas, yacht clubs, service to noncommercial vessels |
| 71 | 156.575 | 156.575 | " " " | Same as channel 69 |
| 78 | 156.925 | 156.925 | " " " | Same as channels 69 and 71 |
| 70 | None | 156.525 | Intership | For recreational boats during maneuvers, cruises, rendezvous |
| 72 | None | 156.625 | " | Same as for channel 70 |
| 26 | 161.900 | 157.300 | Coast to ship | Public correspondence |
| 27 | 161.950 | 157.350 | " " " | " " |
| 28 | 162.000 | 157.400 | " " " | " " |

land station and, due to lower antenna heights, only 5 to 15 miles between boats. In the early phases of VHF-FM adoption, many coastal areas will not be adequately served by shore stations. The earliest installations have been placed in busy harbors and along heavily traveled coasts.

The large number of channels available in the VHF band has substantially reduced the congestion that made the MF band almost unusable. This fact alone has made VHF the band of choice for all but long-range voice communications. When Coast Guard shore stations operating in the VHF band are fully installed, small craft will make little use of MF communications.

Channels of particular interest to the operators of small boats are listed in Table 13-1. Three pairs of VHF frequencies are reserved for public correspondence. Additional stations using the same frequencies are expected to provide complete coverage of all major waterways.

## 13.10    MF Marine Band

For many years nearly all marine radiotelephone communication has been conducted in this band. It will continue active for distances beyond the range of VHF-FM, and be greatly improved by changes in equipment that must be made by 1977. Shipboard stations usually operate on five or more pretuned channels selected from the following authorized frequencies:

> Assigned Frequencies in the 2 MHz Marine Band
> 2182 KHz  Calling and distress
> 2670 KHz  Communication with Coast Guard
> 2003 KHz  Intership—Limited coast station—Great Lakes only
> 2142 KHz  Intership—Pacific Coast north of 42° N—days only
> 2638 KHz  Intership—all areas
> 2738 KHz  Intership—all areas except Great Lakes and Gulf of Mexico
> 2830 KHz  Intership—Gulf of Mexico only
> One or two public correspondence channels appropriate for the ship's locale.

The tendency of high frequencies to behave more like visible light, propagating in straight lines while the lower frequencies tend to curve around the earth, has been noted. The effective range of a station operating in the 2 MHz band consequently is generally proportional to its power output, since much of its radiation propagates as a ground wave. Certain characteristics of radio emissions, other than power, can improve the range and the quality of signal detectable by a receiver. Such a characteristic is the single sideband emission.

An amplitude modulation of a continuously generated *carrier wave* by a low frequency oscillation actuated by the voice, in this case, produces sideband emissions, one a corresponding number of cycles above the carrier wave, the other the same number of cycles below the carrier wave, Fig. 13-7. A transmitter operating at 2500 KHz and modulated by a 100 KHz oscillator will thus emit three parts, a *carrier wave* of 2500 KHz and 2600 KHz and 2400 KHz side-

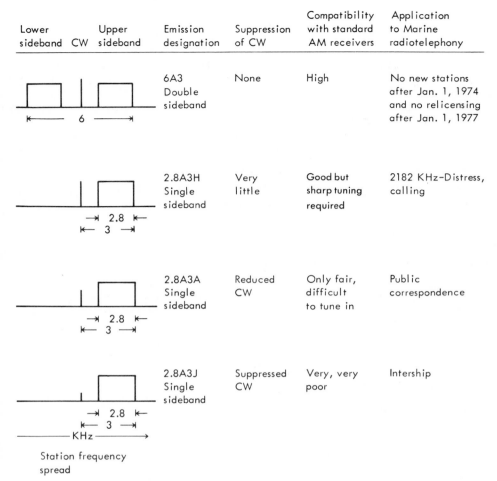

| Emission designation | Suppression of CW | Compatibility with standard AM receivers | Application to Marine radiotelephony |
|---|---|---|---|
| 6A3 Double sideband | None | High | No new stations after Jan. 1, 1974 and no relicensing after Jan. 1, 1977 |
| 2.8A3H Single sideband | Very little | Good but sharp tuning required | 2182 KHz–Distress, calling |
| 2.8A3A Single sideband | Reduced CW | Only fair, difficult to tune in | Public correspondence |
| 2.8A3J Single sideband | Suppressed CW | Very, very poor | Intership |

Station frequency spread

**FIGURE 13-7** Schematic of the energy radiated in the carrier wave and the sidebands from various types of transmitters.

bands. In the usual AM transmitter, most of the power radiated is at the carrier frequency.

The common AM receiver will respond to the entire transmission, carrier and both sidebands, when in fact only one of the sidebands is needed to convey the intelligence. One sideband can be completely suppressed and the carrier completely or nearly so. Now a large fraction of the transmitted power will be in the remaining sideband. A single-sideband receiver will replace the suppressed carrier frequency and thus permit the modulated signal to be made audible. Precise receiver tuning is required, because the carrier frequency must be replaced exactly if high quality reception is to be obtained.

Three types of sideband capability are required of shipborne stations, A3H operation on 2182 KHz only, A3A operation on public correspondence frequencies only, and A3J operation on intership frequencies only, Fig. 13-7. Type acceptable equipment will transmit the proper sideband configuration for each chosen channel, relieving the operator of this selection. Regulations require a licensed VHF station as a prerequisite to a new 2 MHz station license.

## 13.11   Radiotelephone Operation

Before transmitting, every radio operator must monitor for several minutes the channel he expects to use to avoid interfering with other users. Coast Guard stations, public correspondence stations, and some large ships continuously monitor the distress-calling frequencies though pleasure boats are not required to do so.

When a routine message is to be transmitted to another ship or to a Coast Guard station, the originating station must call the desired receiver using that ship's name or the name of the Coast Guard station. Only distress calls may be addressed to "any ship" or "any station". Initial contact is made on 156.8 MHz or 2182 KHz, unless by prior arrangement an intership or ship-to-shore frequency is to be used. After the contact has been made both stations must switch to another mutually acceptable frequency, leaving the calling channel open for other calls or distress signals. The entire body of priority messages only are transmitted on 156.8 MHz or 2182 KHz.

Three types of priority radiotelephone messages are recognized. The distress signal MAYDAY (from the French *m'aider:* help me) indicates that the vessel sending the signal is threatened by serious and imminent danger and requests immediate assistance. In originating a MAYDAY signal, the word MAYDAY is repeated three times, followed by the name of the vessel, all known information as to the vessel's position, the nature of the distress, the nature of the help requested, and any other information which might be of assistance to rescue teams.

The *urgent* signal PAN, pronounced as spelled, indicates that the originating vessel has an urgent message concerning the safety of some other vessel, or some person on board another vessel, which is deemed to demand prompt attention. The transmission form is the same as the distress signal except that it is prefaced by the urgent rather than the distress signal.

The *safety* signal SAYCURITAY, pronounced as spelled, indicates that the originating station has an important message concerning the safety of navigation or an important meteorological warning that is deemed to warrant prompt transmission. The transmission form is similar to that of the other priority transmissions except for the change of prefix.

Some Coast Guard transmitters make use of a distinctive two-tone signal to clear the 2182 KHz channel of all routine traffic for the transmission of a distress signal. When a Coast Guard monitor intercepts a distress signal, the two-tone warning may be sounded on 2182 KHz by the powerful, shore-based transmitter. Anyone hearing this repetitive 1300-2200 Hz tone pattern should refrain from transmitting on 2182 KHz and should monitor this channel with his receiver to determine the nature of the distress call, which will be repeated by the Coast Guard after sounding the band-clearing signal. In general, the range of the Coast Guard transmitter will be much greater than that of a shipboard installation and some skippers, hearing the band-clearing signal may think that they are too distant to cause interference with the distress call. Freak transmissions over abnormally great distances occur frequently, and it is the part of wisdom to refrain from using 2182 KHz until the emergency situation is resolved.

In the great confusion and excitement associated with an emergency afloat, a distress message may be garbled and difficult to understand unless the radio operator knows in advance how to make the transmission. There should be a legible card mounted near the transmitter from which *anyone* can read the following distress message, substituting where necessary.

MAYDAY–MAYDAY–MAYDAY
This is:    (call letters)         Yacht (name)
This is:      "      "              "      "
This is:      "      "              "      "
Position: Latitude and Longitude in degrees, *or* Bearing in degrees true and Distance in miles to a prominent geographic position
Nature of distress: (Fire, foundering, and so forth)
Kind of assistance desired: (Evacuation, take in tow, and so forth)
Number of persons aboard and condition of any injured
Present seaworthiness of the vessel
Description of vessel: Length, rig, cabin arrangement, color of hull, color of decks
Your listening frequency and schedule

PAN and SAYCURITAY calls follow the same outline, except the bearing and distance to the vessel in distress or location of navigational hazard must be given. *The tendency to shout into the microphone must be overcome.* Shouting will only overmodulate, thus reducing intelligibility. Operators should not become impatient because distress messages are lengthy and detailed. When the first MAYDAY is heard by a Coast Guard station, a search and rescue boat, plane, or helicopter will be alerted. The bearing to the distressed vessel will be transmitted from the Coast Guard station to the rescue craft after it has left its port. The distressed vessel may be instructed to transmit at intervals for direction-finding purposes. When information or assistance other than in an emergency is needed from the Coast Guard, switch to 156.6 MHz or 2670 KHz for the body of the message after the initial contact.

Operators hearing a distress call are cautioned to keep off the air unless they are certain they can play an important role in rescue operations.

## 13.12    The Citizen's Band

The Citizen's Band occupies a segment of frequencies between 26.965 and 27.255 MHz in which the FCC has assigned 23 channels. These channels can be used for purposeful, noncommercial communications by people engaged in lawful business or recreation.

Very low powered stations, below 100 milliwatts output, need not be licensed. These are often used by children speaking to each other within a few hundred yards. Licensed stations may emit up to five watts and may erect antennas 20 feet above the structure on which they are mounted.

Operators of small boats often use the Citizen's Band to conduct rendezvous, regattas, contests, and other prearranged activities, when distances do not exceed about five miles. Marinas and yacht clubs use the Citizen's Band for sailing instruction and direction of traffic in a yacht basin.

The Citizen's Band is most effective when used for prearranged contacts. General calls for a response from any station are very apt to go unheard. Under no circumstances should a boatman consider a Citizen's Band radiotelephone a safety communication instrument. It can *not* substitute for marine band radio.

## 13.13   Automatic Pilots

Recent electronic developments have brought automatic piloting equipment within the reach of the small-boat owner. With this equipment on board the navigator determines a desired compass course and sets the automatic pilot accordingly. Electronic circuits then keep the vessel on this course until otherwise instructed.

An automatic pilot undoubtedly relieves the helmsman of what is sometimes an arduous, monotonous duty: that of maintaining a steady course for a long period of time. An automatic pilot does not, however, assume the responsibilities of a lookout, for the electronics has no sensing mechanism for detecting possible collisions and taking steps to avoid them.

As small-boat speeds increase, the time acceptable for a lapse in vigilance of a lookout decreases. A short time away from the wheel can easily stretch out until the robot pilot has put the vessel in a dangerous position. Any operator of automatic piloting equipment will do well to keep in mind at all times the rule governing lookouts.

## 13.14   Small-boat Radar

Radar was developed during World War II to meet the need for a device capable of detecting, in any weather, the approach of high-speed attack airplanes. Since the war many radar techniques have been adapted to television. Improved transmitters and the introduction of transistors have brought size and power requirements within reach of the small-boat owner. Costs have also been reduced sharply, but small-craft radar is still expensive.

As in the electronic fathometer, both transmitter and receiver are on board. The transmitter sends out a rapid series of pulses from a highly directional antenna so that each radio-wave pulse travels outward almost like a short pulse of light from a focused searchlight beam. If there are no obstacles, each pulse will continue to move outward at a speed of 186,000 miles per second, being gradually absorbed by air and attenuated by distance. If there is some solid object, preferably metal, in the path of the pulse, some energy will be reflected back to the antenna where it can be amplified sufficiently to actuate a display tube. The reflected pulses will be displayed on the screen of a tube similar to those used in television receivers.

The most common radar presentation is *PPI* or *plan position indicator*. In *PPI* the series of pulses is transmitted from a slowly rotating antenna which repeatedly scans the entire horizon. An electron beam capable of activating the display-tube screen rotates in synchronism with the antenna and also moves outward from the center of the tube face to produce a series of closely spaced spiral lines. The tube face is thus scanned in such a way that the ship's position is at the center of the screen, the ship's heading is toward the top of the screen, and distances out from the center represent distances from the ship to the reflecting object.

The electron beam scanning the tube face is too feeble to produce a glow unless a reflected signal is picked up by the antenna. Then a bright spot appears, corresponding to those pulses which were intercepted and reflected. Definition on the small screens of shipboard radar is too poor to permit identification of small objects from the shapes of the light spots on the tube. Distant vessels, for example, will appear as nondescript blobs of light, with a size

**FIGURE 13-8** Mercator chart of the eastern end of Long Island Sound with a vessel on course 265T at point S.

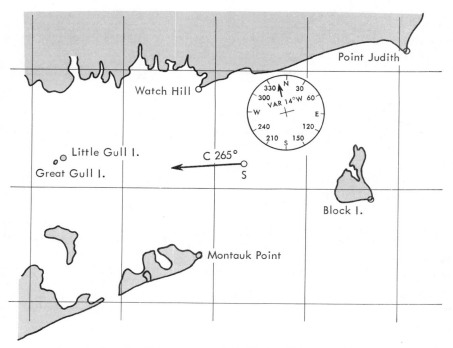

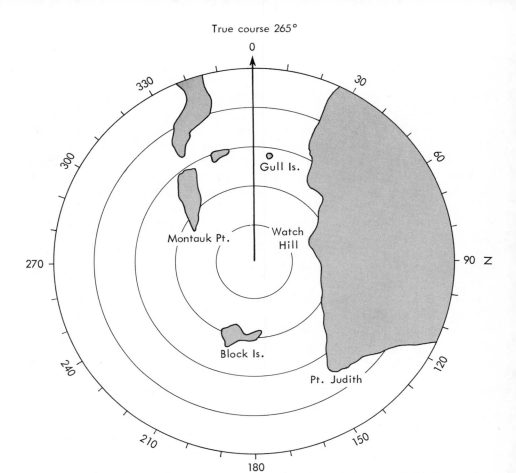

**FIGURE 13-9**  Schematic PPI radar display as seen on a vessel on course 265T at point S, Fig. 13-8.

proportional to the reflecting power of each but with little semblance to distinctive shapes. With practice, however, some skill can be developed in interpreting patterns seen on the screen in terms of the objects producing them; compare Figs. 13-8 and 13-9.

High-powered radar sets may have a range of 100 miles; small-boat equipment is more apt to be limited to 10 miles or less. Maximum range depends upon the height of the antenna and the power available in the pulses, as well as the nature and size of the reflecting object. The average small boat is quite restricted in the first two of these important factors.

An entirely new approach to radar detection replaces the visual presentation on the display tube by an audible signal. A high-frequency radar beam is sent out and is reflected in the usual way. The returning signal is then made to produce an audible tone, whose frequency or pitch is determined by the distance to the reflecting object. The loudness of the tone depends upon the size and the reflecting ability of the distant object. With some practice it is quite easy to distinguish between the pure tone from a metal buoy, the less

FIGURE 13-10   An audible radar unit in
use in fog.

distinct sound from a distant vessel, and the warble from an irregular shoreline.
Figure 13-10 shows the audible system in use aboard ship.

Although the range is restricted to about two miles the audible system
is very useful in small-boat operation during periods of low visibility. Power
drain is low so that the unit can be used on vessels with very limited power
capability. Signal interpretation is more readily attained than is the recognition of radar patterns on a display tube. With the audible system the operator
can also use his eyes in searching for visual supplements to the radar signals.
No small advantage is the low cost of the audible unit when compared to that
of the conventional radar system.

Radar is a valuable aid to safe boat operation because the beams are
readily transmitted through fog and clouds. Radar is not, however, a foolproof
device guaranteed to prevent marine accidents. Witness to this is a number
of collisions between radar-equipped ships. The 1960 International Conference
on Safety of Life at Sea made some recommendations regarding radar*:
". . . it must be recognized that small vessels, small icebergs, and similar floating objects may not be detected by radar." Again, ". . . radar range and bear-

---

* The proposed rules, changes, and recommendations are to be found in Annex B, Final
Act of the Safety of Life at Sea Conference, 1960, dated June 17, 1960.

ing alone do not . . . relieve a vessel of the duty to stop her engines and navigate with caution when a fog signal is heard forward of the beam."

Since radar operation involves the transmission of radio waves, it comes under the control of the Federal Communications Commission. A license for the equipment is required, and the transmissions must meet FCC regulations.

It seems doubtful that radar will become a universal answer to the need for a device readily applicable to most pleasure boats. Several new systems designed to aid navigation in periods of low visibility are under investigation, and some of these are undergoing field trials. The future capabilities of these systems cannot be estimated at the present time.

## 13.15  Loran

Loran, a system of long-range aid to navigation, is another development of World War II. Loran is the only positive, long-distance system of position finding now available. It is an invaluable aid to the ocean cruiser who in bad weather may be several days without an opportunity to obtain a position from celestial observations. Power requirements for loran are moderate because it is not necessary to have a transmitter on board. Special and complex receivers are required, however, and their cost is still high in spite of several price reductions.

A *master* loran transmitting station M (Fig. 13-11) sends out a succession of short pulses of radio waves. Each pulse will be received on board a ship equipped with the proper receiver and will be displayed on the face of a cathode-ray or television-type tube, Fig. 13-12. Each pulse will also be received by a *slave* transmitter S, located at some distance from the master, and this

**FIGURE 13-11**  A master-slave pair of transmitters in the loran system establishes a series of hyperbolic lines of position.

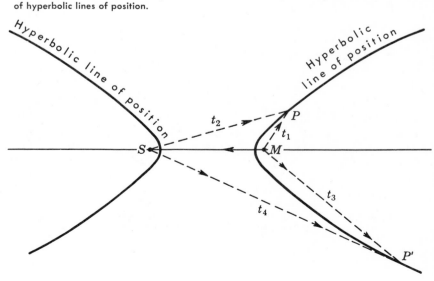

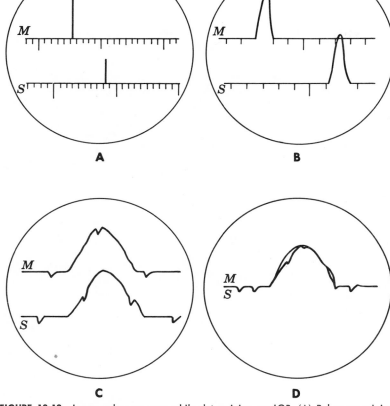

**FIGURE 13-12** Loran pulses as seen while determining an *LOP.* (A) Pulses as originally seen with a slow sweep across the face of the display tube. (B) Pulses expanded by using a fast sweep. (C) Pulses brought into alignment by adjusting delay circuits. (D) Pulses brought into coincidence for measuring the time delay.

pulse will trigger the transmission of a pulse from the slave. The pulse from the slave will also be received by the ship, always at a later time than the pulse from the master. Each master-slave pair transmits at a characteristic frequency and pulse rate designated by 1L1, 1L3, 2H2, 2H3, and so on.

The time interval between the reception of the two pulses on board ship will be 6.18 microseconds (millionths of a second) for each nautical mile of *path difference* from the transmitters to the ship. Although the time between the reception of the two pulses is very short, it can be readily measured by electronic circuits in the loran receiver.

At point $P$ (Fig. 13-11) there will be a time difference of $t_2$-$t_1$ microseconds between the arrivals of the pulses. The same time *difference* will be obtained at some other point, as $P'$, for the two longer transmission times $t_3$ and $t_4$. An infinite number of points will have the same time difference although the individual times will differ. Each value of time difference will define one *hyperbolic* line of position. A single loran measurement will only locate the

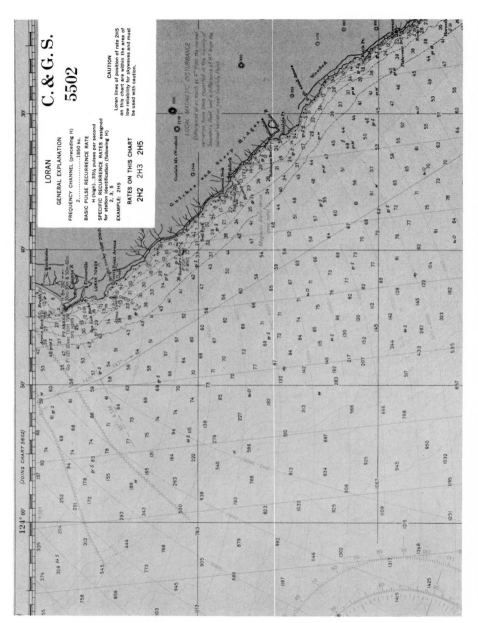

**FIGURE 13-13** A portion of NOS chart No. 5502 showing loran lines of position and the location of a loran transmitter.

278

particular hyperbola on which the ship is located. A second loran reading from another master-slave pair will determine a second hyperbolic line of position. The ship will of course be located at the intersection of the two lines of position.

Loran lines of position are now being added to many general and sailing charts. Fig. 13-13 shows such a chart for the West Coast of the United States, with the position lines originating from the station pairs shown in Fig. 13-14. Each line of position is marked with the transmission characteristics and with the number of microseconds delay associated with that particular hyperbola.

Loran positions are best determined from ground-wave transmissions which proceed directly from transmitter to receiver. Ground-wave signals are generally usable during the day to about 900 miles. At night one-reflection sky waves can be utilized out to perhaps 1,500 miles. Sky-wave reception requires the use of somewhat uncertain corrections to take into account the longer path taken by the reflected waves. At still greater distances two-reflection

**FIGURE 13-14** Loran station-pairs along the West Coast of the United States.

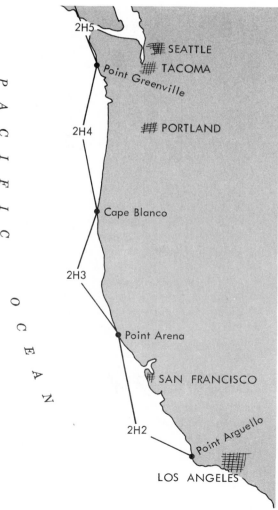

signals may be received, but these are not used for navigation because of the uncertainty of the corrections.

## 13.16    Omega

The omega navigational system is expected to overcome some of loran's limitations. Like loran, measurements are made between signals produced by pairs of transmitters. However, omega operates in the very low-frequency (VLF) band, thus reducing night effects, and the transmitter pairs are separated by thousands of miles. Only eight stations will be required to cover virtually the entire earth. Where loran compares the difference in arrival times of pulses, omega compares the phase difference or difference of arrival times of individual radio waves. Lines of position from two pairs establish a fix, as with loran, with a precision of the order of one mile in the daytime and two miles at night. Unfortunately omega receivers are relatively expensive.

## 13.17    Aeronautical Aids

In many locations navigational aids for aircraft can be used by surface vessels. The most familiar of these is the aircraft radiobeacon, a constantly repeating coded identification signal transmitted in the 200 to 400 KHz band. When such a station can be heard on the water, a bearing can be obtained with considerable precision using a radio direction finder. The skipper planning to make use of aeronautical aids must preplot them on his charts for they are not located on charts prepared for surface navigation. A line of position can then be drawn from the transmitter's location.

*Very high frequency, omnidirectional radio* (*VOR*), usually called *Omni*, is a precise radio direction finding system in which a radio beam is made to rotate 30 times per second in a clockwise direction around its transmitter. When the beam passes magnetic north a nondirectional signal is transmitted. The special shipborne receiver measures the time lapse from the nondirectional signal to the beam's reception. This, in effect, measures the magnetic bearing from the transmitter to the ship, the reciprocal of which is the direction from the ship to the station. Omni receivers are expensive and electronically complex, though their operation is not difficult. Magnetic bearings are displayed on a dial after the receiver makes a number of conversions from the sequence of signals received. Very accurate bearings are obtained, though the high frequencies used limit areas covered.

Even more elaborate is *Distance Measuring Equipment* (DME), a feature many omni stations possess. Here, the shipborne station transmits a short radio signal that is returned by the land station. By measuring the time lapse for the signal's round trip an expression of distance to the *DME* station is obtained. VOR and DME operate in the VHF and Ultra High Frequency (UHF) band, respectively. Consequently, these aids have limited range, but there are many closely spaced stations where air traffic is heavy.

## 13.18    Time Signals

Highly accurate time must be available on board any vessel depending upon celestial observations for determining position. A one-minute error in time can result in a position error of 15 miles, so the celestial navigator requires a knowledge of time to at least one or two seconds. Before the development of modern radio communication, the navigator depended on one or more chronometers, carefully rated ashore and tended with meticulous care while at sea. An adequate chronometer installation is scarcely practical aboard the average small boat.

Radio time signals are a boon to the off-shore navigator. Since a radio signal can make a complete circuit of the earth in only 0.13 second, no correction of the received signals is required for navigational purposes. A large fraction of the navigable waters of the earth are covered by the time signals from two time transmitters operated by the National Bureau of Standards and based on U.S. Naval Observatory time control:

WWV    Fort Collins, Colorado
WWVH    Maui, Hawaii

WWV transmits continuously on carrier frequencies of 2.5, 5, 10, 15, 20, and 25 MHz to provide wide coverage by both ground and sky waves. WWVH transmits continuously on 5, 10, and 15 MHz. Each station emits A2 transmissions with regular voice announcements which can be detected by any radio receiver capable of tuning to the proper frequency.

Occasionally atmospheric conditions give better reception from station CHU in Ottawa, Canada, which transmits A2 signals on 3.330, 7.335, and 14.670 MHz. Other time signals are transmitted by various government stations around the globe so that time can be accurately known in even the remotest location.

The A2 transmissions mentioned are supplemented by regular transmissions of time signals in code, or A1. These are available to, but probably will not be used by, the small-boat navigator.

## 13.19    Medical Advice Afloat

All too often an accident or illness on board a small vessel may be serious enough to require medical advice before reaching port. The exact procedure to be followed depends on the location of the vessel. Practically all governments have a system for giving medical advice by radio, but the details of the arrangements vary. HO 117 should be consulted for a list of stations available for medical consultation.

The U.S. Public Health Service has an arrangement whereby free medical advice can be obtained through the 500 KHz distress channel regularly guarded by the Coast Guard. Messages requesting medical advice may be considered urgent but are not disasters warranting the use of the MAYDAY call on 156.8 MHz or 2182 KHz.

# CHAPTER 14

# Lighting Requirements

## 14.01 Sunset to Sunrise

Too many people use their boats in daylight only, partly through fear of night running with its somewhat increased risk of collision. These people are missing some of the finest experiences of boating. It is futile to try to explain the beauty of a sunset or a sunrise under way, or the isolated joy of running through a cool summer night. These experiences are individual and intimate, but very real and amply reward the effort required to become proficient at nighttime boat operation.

Although the regulations governing boat lighting are complex, thousands of boatmen have mastered them to the point where night running is no more hazardous than sailing in full visibility. Boat lighting must be considered from two viewpoints. On the one hand, one must be sure that his own boat is properly lighted. The requirements are easily determined once and for all from a knowledge of the boat class and the waters in which she is to be operated. Then one only need keep the lights in good order and be sure there is sufficient power to operate them.

On the other hand, the problem of identifying an approaching vessel from the lights is more difficult. One starts with a knowledge of the basic light arrangements and their appearance as seen from various angles. Differences noted in the number, position, and color of lights denoting a vessel's size, type, and heading may necessitate reference to the illustrations in the following sections of this chapter. It is of the utmost importance to identify an approaching vessel from its display of lights. For example, the consequences of mistaking a tug with a barge on a long towing hawser for a group of separate vessels can be serious if a small boat tries to run across between them.

## 14.02 Applicable Rules

Regulations concerning shipborne lights are prescribed by International, Inland, Great Lakes, and Western Rivers Rules. Certain rules are fundamental.

Rule 1 of both International and Inland Rules is typical: "The Rules concerning lights shall be complied with in all weathers from sunset to sunrise, and during such times no other lights shall be exhibited, except such lights as can t be mistaken for the prescribed lights or impair their visibility or distinctive character, or interfere with the keeping of a proper lookout." Another point of agreement is Rule 1 (c) (ix) ". . . the word *visible*, when applied to lights, means visible on a dark night with a clear atmosphere." All prescribed shipborne identification lights shall burn steadily. Flashing and occulting lights are illegal.

Both rules make the same distinction between power-driven vessels and sailing craft. Rule 1 (c) (iii) states, "the term 'power-driven vessel' means any vessel propelled by machinery"; and (iv), "every power-driven vessel which is under sail and not under power is not to be considered a sailing vessel, and every vessel under power, whether under sail or not, is to be considered a power-driven vessel."

Boat lights may be roughly classified as *running* lights, required while under way, and *riding* or *anchor* lights. Running lights may be subdivided into colored *side lights*, always red on the port side and green on the starboard side, and various white *range* lights arranged so as to assist in determining the heading of an approaching vessel.

With one exception, only four different angular openings are specified for boat lights: 112.5, 135, 225, and 360 degrees, corresponding to 10, 12, 20, and 32 points respectively. As with compass bearings, light openings formerly specified in points are now preferably given in degrees. As shown in Fig. 14-1, the combination of two 112.5° (10 point) lights as prescribed for the colored side lights and a 135° (12 point) light as may be prescribed for the stern make a total of 360° (32 points), so that the combination will emit some sort of light in all directions.

**FIGURE 14-1** Standard light apertures of 10, 12, 20, and 32 points. The apertures are usually, but not exclusively, associated with the positions shown.

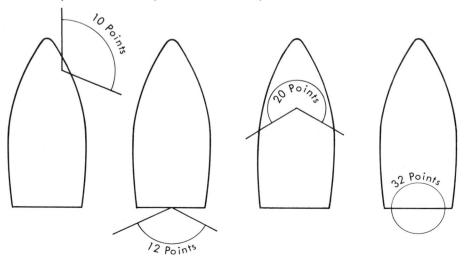

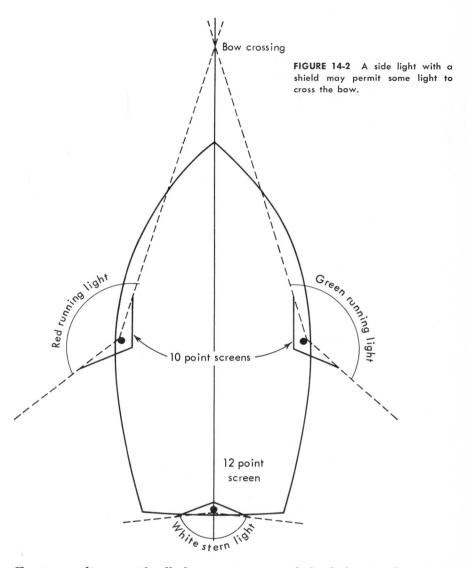

Bow crossing

**FIGURE 14-2** A side light with a shield may permit some light to cross the bow.

Red running light

Green running light

10 point screens

12 point screen

White stern light

Exact compliance with all the requirements of the lighting rules is not always possible. For example, all rules agree in requiring screens to prevent the colored side lights from being seen across the bow on the opposite side. A study of Fig. 14-2 will show that this requirement cannot be precisely fulfilled. The source of light, be it electric or a liquid fuel, cannot be a microscopic point, and hence it must be located somewhat outside the screens as shown. It is then inevitable that some light will cross the bow, and some will be seen more than two points abaft the beam. This is rarely a practical difficulty, but *it must be kept in mind when attempting to evaluate a set of approaching lights.*

Identification is complicated by the fact that certain lighting options are allowed. While lighting on the high seas must conform to International Rules, there are options within these rules. International lighting may be used on inland waters, on the Great Lakes, and on the Western rivers. Lighting under Inland Rules may be used on all inland waters, on the Great Lakes, and on the Western rivers, but not on the high seas.

## 14.03    Required Lighting While Under Way

There is no easy way to learn the required lighting displays. Hard study and a handy reference list for a refresher probably represents the best solution to the problem. The requirements are presented here in a series of diagrams. Each light is characterized by the required angular opening in points, a first-letter abbreviation for the color, and the required visibility in miles. Thus 12W2 designates a 135° (12 point) white light with a required visibility of two miles.

Figure 14-3 illustrates lighting displays for the classes of vessels most commonly used in recreational boating. Some variations in placements are allowed, particularly with respect to height. For example, Inland Rules require only that the 360° (32 point) stern light be higher than the forward lights, either colored or white, and that the 135° (12 point) stern light be as nearly as is practicable at the level of the side lights. Both Rules require power-driven vessels to show a forward range light at least three feet above the colored side lights and at least nine feet above the gunwhale. The nine-foot requirement does not apply to vessels of less than 40 feet.

International Rules permit powerboats under 65 feet loa to use a combination red-green lantern in place of the separate side lights shown in Fig. 14-3. A combination light is acceptable in sail boats only up to 40 feet; above this separate side lights are required.

Neither set of rules prescribes a running light pattern for small boats primarily intended for rowing. These boats are required, however, to have available a white light which shall be displayed when another vessel is approaching. This lighting arrangement is acceptable even if the small boat is under sail but is not to be used when under power.

The small-boat skipper should be able to identify vessels larger than those governed by the regulations illustrated in Fig. 14-3. These large craft develop strong wave patterns which the small boat will do well to avoid, particularly at night. Figure 14-4 illustrates the international requirements for a power-driven vessel more than 150 feet in length. The forward range light must be at least 15 feet lower than the after range light. The 135° (12 point) stern light should be as near to the level of the side lights as is practicable. Power-driven vessels less than 150 feet in length and vessels engaged in towing need exhibit only one of the white range lights but may show two as illustrated.

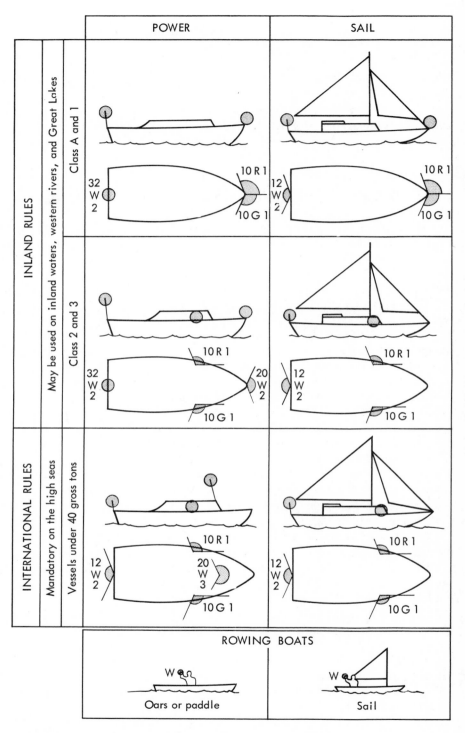

**FIGURE 14-3** Required lighting displays for common classes of pleasure boats.

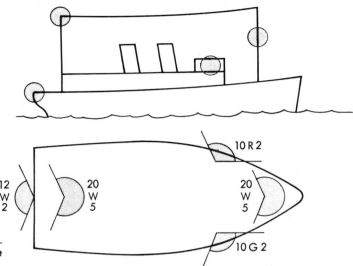

**FIGURE 14-4** Lighting of a power-driven vessel more than 150 feet under International Rules.

A seagoing vessel more than 65 feet in length may be lighted according to Fig. 14-5 while in inland waters. The after 225° (20 point) range light is optional. If carried, this light shall be at least 15 feet higher than, and at least 15 feet aft of the forward range light. As far as is practical the 135° (12 point) stern light shall be at the level of the side lights.

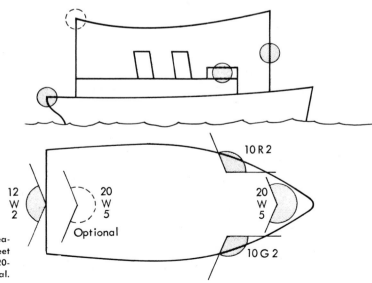

**FIGURE 14-5** Lighting of a seagoing vessel more than 65 feet while in inland waters. The 20-point after range light is optional.

A nonseagoing vessel more than 65 feet in length, excepting ferryboats, will show lights as in Fig. 14-6. The 360° (32 point) after range light must be at least 15 feet higher than the forward range light.

Ferryboats plying inland waters are usually double-ended (Fig. 14-7) and covered by a specific set of lighting requirements. Two pairs of colored side lights are required, used one pair at a time in accord with the direction of motion. The two white range lights are displayed at equal heights. The officer

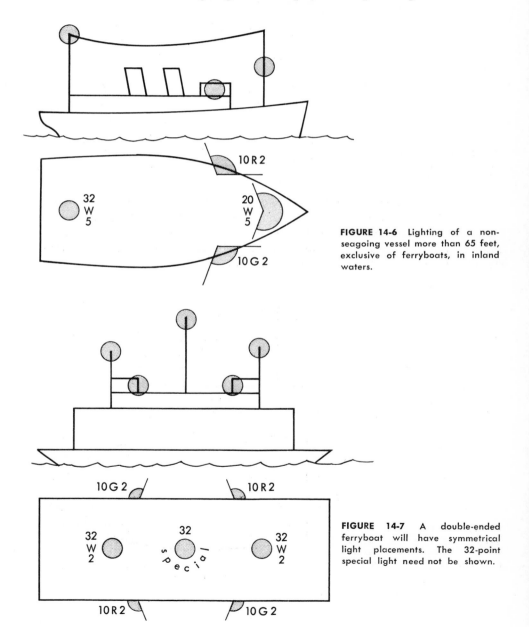

FIGURE 14-6 Lighting of a non-seagoing vessel more than 65 feet, exclusive of ferryboats, in inland waters.

FIGURE 14-7 A double-ended ferryboat will have symmetrical light placements. The 32-point special light need not be shown.

in charge of Marine Inspection may assign to each ferryboat line in his district a distinguishing light of any color, including white. If this special light is displayed, it shall be 360° (32 point) amidships and at least 15 feet above the range lights.

## 14.04   Anchor Lights

The Secretary of the Army, through the Corps of Engineers, may designate certain "special anchorage areas" where vessels under 65 feet in length need not show a distinctive light while at anchor. In all other areas anchor lights must be displayed in accordance with either the International or Inland Rules. The two sets of rules governing anchor lights are essentially the same. Vessels under 150 feet in length (Fig. 14-8) require a single 360° (32 point) white light that is visible two miles. Vessels more than 150 feet in length shall show

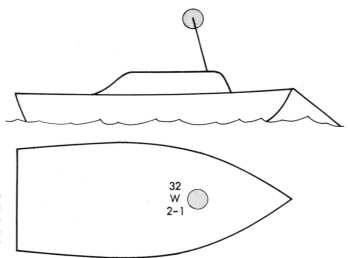

FIGURE 14-8   A vessel under 150 feet at anchor. Under International Rules the anchor light must have a visible range of two miles, while only one mile is required under Inland Rules.

two 360° (32 point) anchor lights (Fig. 14-9), the forward anchor light to be at least 20 feet above the hull, with the after light at least 15 feet lower than the forward light. Each of the two lights shall have a visible range of at least three miles.

## 14.05   Unmaneuverable Vessels

A vessel aground must show the specified anchor lights, and, in addition, must display two red lights in a vertical line separated by not less than six feet under International Rules and three feet under Inland Rules as illustrated,

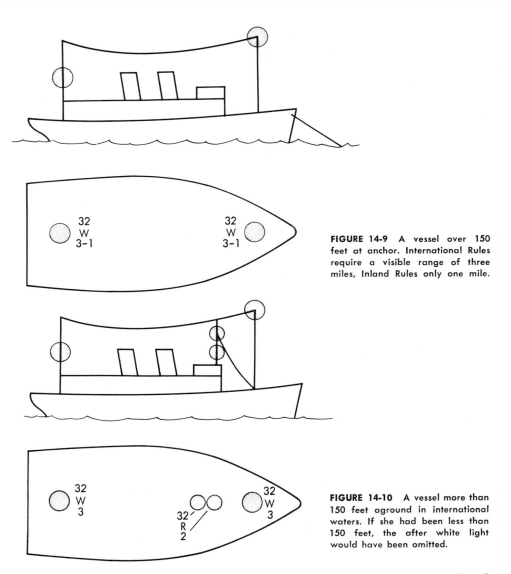

FIGURE 14-9 A vessel over 150 feet at anchor. International Rules require a visible range of three miles, Inland Rules only one mile.

FIGURE 14-10 A vessel more than 150 feet aground in international waters. If she had been less than 150 feet, the after white light would have been omitted.

Fig. 14-10. If the vessel is not hard aground but is not under command and has way on, she must add the regular colored side lights to appear as in Fig. 14-11. The red lights indicate a vessel not under command but constitute neither a distress signal nor a request for assistance.

An unmaneuverable working vessel shall display three vertically arranged lights in the color sequence red, white, red (Fig. 14-12), with each vertical separation at least six feet under International Rules and three feet under Inland Rules. If the vessel has way on, she shall add her regular side lights to the vertical display.

There are provisions for lighting specific types of working vessels that are apt to be found in inland waters rather than on the high seas. Each of the vessels is assumed to be unmaneuverable even though she may be technically

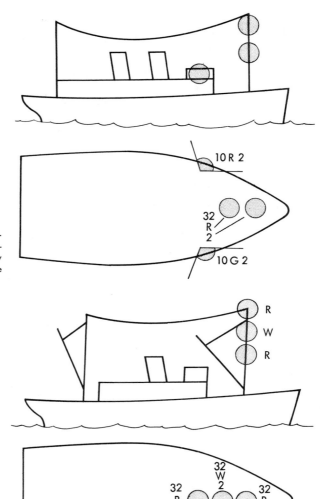

**FIGURE 14-11** An unmaneuverable vessel with way on in international waters. If she had no way on, the side lights would not be shown.

**FIGURE 14-12** An unmaneuverable working vessel with no way on in international waters.

under way. Only a few of the more common examples of these specific lighting requirements can be given here.

Figure 14-13 illustrates the lighting of a vessel and two lighters working on a partially or totally submerged wreck, which may be either fixed or drifting. The white lights at bow and stern of the working vessel shall be at least six feet above the deck. The lower red light shall be at least 15 feet above the deck with the upper red light between three and and six feet above it. Note that only the outer lighter is lighted.

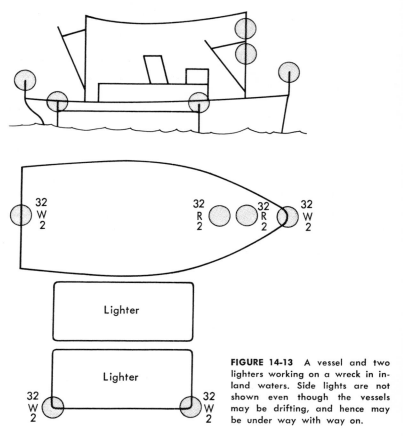

**FIGURE 14-13** A vessel and two lighters working on a wreck in inland waters. Side lights are not shown even though the vessels may be drifting, and hence may be under way with way on.

A dredge is usually held in working position by moorings or by spuds driven into the bottom. Lighting of a moored dredge is shown in Fig. 14-14. All white lights are to be at least six feet above the respective decks. The two vertically arranged red lights on the dredge must be more than three and less than six feet apart with the lower at least 15 feet above the deck.

A suction dredge is under way while working and consequently carries the usual running lights of its class. In addition, it must display two red lights vertically arranged below the forward white range light, and two red lights vertically below the after range light. The stern red lights are unique in that they cover only four compass points, two on either side of dead astern (Fig. 14-15).

One frequently encounters a working vessel moored and engaged in underwater construction such as pipe or cable laying or excavating. Such a vessel is lighted with a vertical display of three red lights with a vertical spacing of from three to six feet. This simple arrangement is not depicted here.

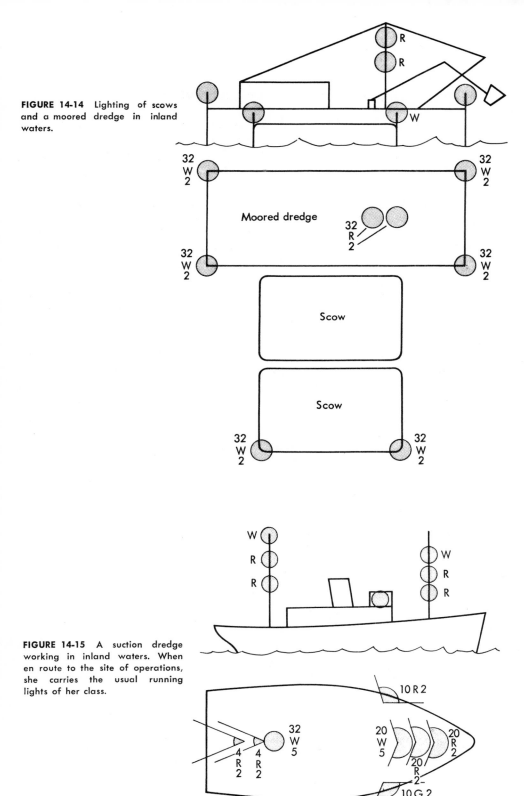

**FIGURE 14-14** Lighting of scows and a moored dredge in inland waters.

**FIGURE 14-15** A suction dredge working in inland waters. When en route to the site of operations, she carries the usual running lights of her class.

## 14.06   Towing Situations—International Rules

Tugs regularly tow barges or scows by a tow line astern, by pushing ahead, or by lashing alongside. These situations present quite different problems to a vessel approaching at night, and so the lights displayed by a tug and its tows must be distinctive. Unfortunately, distinction can only be gained by complexity, and lights under towing situations are far from simple. Recognition is made more difficult by the fact that certain options are allowed.

It is most important, however, to quickly recognize the most frequently encountered lighting combinations, and to have the less common arrays tabulated for easy reference. In particular, it is essential to establish promptly whether or not there is a long tow line connecting a group of vessels which may appear to be proceeding independently.

When a tow is less than 600 feet long, as measured from the stern of the towing vessel to the stern of the last tow (Fig. 14-16) or whenever only one vessel is in tow regardless of the length of the tow, the towing vessel shall carry, in addition to the usual side lights, two white lights near the forepart. These white lights shall be vertically arranged and not less than six feet apart. The towing vessel has an option to display or not an after range light, shown dotted in Fig. 14-16. In addition, the towing vessel must carry either the usual 135° (12 point) white stern light or a small white steering light for the benefit of the tow. Any steering light shown must not be visible forward of the beam. A similar steering light may be carried by all but the last vessel in the tow which must exhibit the regular 135° (12 point) stern light. Each towed vessel must carry the usual colored side lights.

When a tow of more than one vessel exceeds 600 feet, the tug shall add a third white light of similar character to the two vertical white lights required for the shorter tow. All other requirements, including the optional after range light, remain as for the shorter tow.

FIGURE 14-16   Lighting of a stern tow of less than 600 feet in international waters. If the tow exceeds 600 feet, a third white light of similar character must be added to the two shown on the foremast.

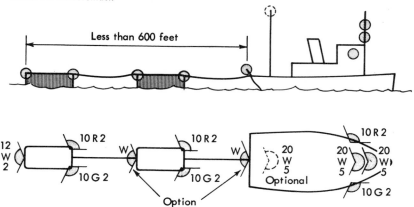

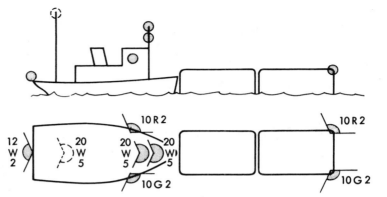

**FIGURE 14-17** A tug pushing a tow in international waters is lighted exactly as for a short stern tow. Colored side lights are shown by the tug and the forward tow.

A vessel pushing a tow or with a tow alongside (Fig. 14-17) is governed by the lighting requirements for a short stern tow. The most forward of the vessels being pushed shall display the usual colored side lights.

The two-light or three-light vertical array is characteristic of almost all towing arrangements. Note that the after range light, if used, must be above the vertical forward group.

## 14.07   Towing Situations—Inland Rules

A minor distinction is made between vessels under 150 feet and those 150 feet or more in length. Though there are a variety of options, the features distinguishing a tow are two or three vertically arranged white lights for stern tows (Fig. 14-16) and two similarly arranged lights for tows alongside or pushed ahead. The vertical lights may be amber if the tows are pushed (Fig. 14-17). When vertical lights are in the forward part of the towing boat, they are 225° (20 point) lights. When in the after part of the vessel, they are either 360° (32 point) or one 360° (32 point) and two 135° (12 point) lights combined with three vertical 225° (20 point) lights forward. When only one vertical array is used, a white light forward or aft must form a central range with one of the vertical lights except on towing vessels under 150 feet in length and on a pushing tow (Fig. 14-18 A and B). No other white lights may be displayed by a towing vessel, but she must carry the usual side lights.

Barges or scows being pushed ahead shall display the usual colored side lights on the leading vessel only. If two or more are being pushed abreast, the appropriate colored side light shall be shown on the outer side of each outer, leading vessel. A barge towed alongside shall display an appropriate colored side light if the corresponding light on the towing vessel is obscured (Fig. 14-19 A and B).

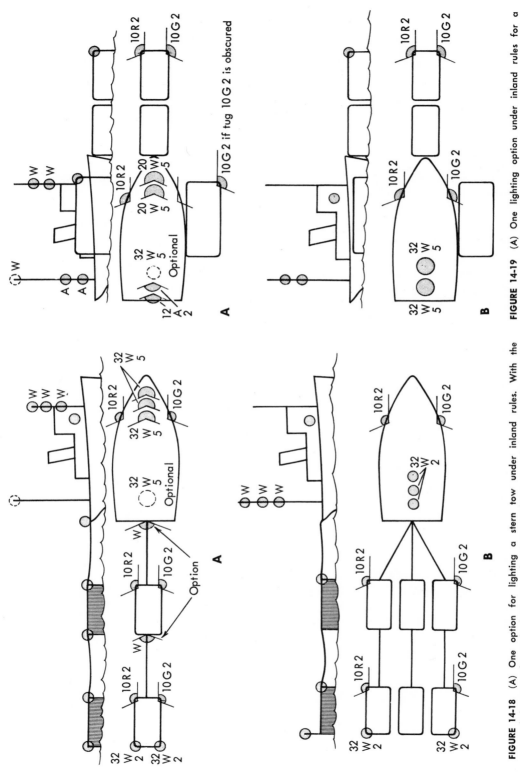

**FIGURE 14-18** (A) One option for lighting a stern tow under inland rules. With the towing light array forward, there are suboptions involving the after range light and the stern light. (B) There are no suboptions when the tug elects to display the towing lights aft.

**FIGURE 14-19** (A) One lighting option under inland rules for a tow alongside or ahead. The amber lights are a unique requirement. (B) When the towing lights are displayed aft, there are no suboptions.

## 14.08   Special Lighting Requirements

The preceding sections have emphasized the lighting requirements of the International and Inland Rules. Other regulations apply to larger vessels on the Great Lakes and on the Western rivers. Small craft using these waters are lighted under international or inland conventions according to the schedule shown in Fig. 14-3.

Special lighting arrays for towed vessels are required in certain prescribed areas. These special requirements do not apply to the towing vessel, so the distinctive vertical array of two or three white lights still serves to distinguish a tow. One of the prescribed areas is the Gulf Intracoastal Waterway and some connecting waters, where the rules governing towed vessels in Western rivers are to be followed. Another set of rules applies to the waters around New York harbor, including the Hudson River and Lake Champlain, East River, Long Island Sound, and Narragansett Bay.

Fishing vessels when engaged with nets, lines, or trawls (not sportsfishing) in international waters must carry two 360° (32 point) lights, an upper green over a lower white, at least four feet apart. A 225° (20 point) five-mile white light (the standard range light) is optional for such vessels.

Insofar as possible, the special vessels operated by the United States Government must conform to the lighting requirements for other vessels. In some cases, however, the unique construction of these vessels prevents a lighting display in strict accordance with general rules. A submarine, for example, carries the usual colored side lights and a single white 225° (20 point) masthead light instead of the two white range lights regularly required for vessels more than 150 feet long. A submarine's stern light may be located as much as 150 feet forward of the stern. This display may be easily mistaken for that of a small, readily maneuverable powerboat. To assist in recognition, United States submarines are authorized to display in addition an amber-colored rotating light producing 90 flashes per minute, visible for three miles at all points of the horizon. The amber light shall be located approximately six feet above the white masthead light.

Specific exemptions or waivers of lighting requirements are granted to particular vessels. USN exemptions are published in the *Federal Register* and in *Notices to Mariners*. Coast Guard exemptions are published in Part 135 of Title 33 of the *Code of Federal Regulations*. When their operations require, as in time of war, all government vessels are exempt from the regular rules. The exemptions apply only to the penalties normally levied for failure to display the proper lights. In the event of a collision, an improperly lighted vessel must be found at fault, since nothing in the basic law exempts even government vessels from the lighting requirements.

## 14.09    General Considerations

All of the rules governing lighting specify required distances of visibility without giving any clues as to the sizes of the light sources needed to attain the specifications. Obviously the density of the colored glass used in the side lights will have a great effect on the size of light source required. Some general statements can be made about white light sources.

On an absolutely clear night the required candlepower of a white light source will increase approximately as the square of the distance of required visibility. On a clear night of average visibility the required candlepower will increase even more rapidly than this because of absorption by the atmosphere. Thus if a 2 *CP* bulb is visible for 1 mile, a range of 3 miles will require $3 \times 3 \times 2 = 18$ *CP*, and it would be the part of wisdom to install a standard 21 *CP* bulb.

Electric power is at a premium on board small boats, particularly sailboats, but it is poor economy to skimp on the size of either running or anchor lights. These lights are intended to prevent collisions and any added visibility assists in this prevention. Table 14-1 lists the current consumption of some of the common sizes of bulbs used in boat lighting. The visibility distances given in Column 2 must be considered as approximate values only.

**TABLE 14-1**

**Characteristics of Standard Automobile Light Bulbs**

| Candle Power | Miles | 6 volts | | | 12 volts | | |
|---|---|---|---|---|---|---|---|
| | | Bulb No. | Base | Amp. | Bulb No. | Base | Amp. |
| 1 | — | 51 | Min | 0.2 | 53 | Min | 0.12 |
| 2 | 1 | 55 | SC | 0.4 | 57 | SC | 0.24 |
| 3 | 1 | 63 | SC | 0.6 | 67 | SC | 0.4 |
| 6 | 2 | 81 | SC | 1.0 | 89 | SC | 0.6 |
| 6 | 2 | 82 | DC | 1.0 | 90 | DC | 0.6 |
| 15 | 2 | 87 | SC | 1.9 | 1003 | SC | 0.9 |
| 15 | 2 | 88 | DC | 1.9 | 1004 | DC | 0.9 |
| 21 | 3 | 1129 | SC | 2.6 | 1141 | SC | 1.3 |
| 21 | 3 | 1130 | DC | 2.6 | 1142 | DC | 1.3 |
| Search | — | 4535 | — | 5.0 | 4435 | — | 2.5 |

Searchlight bulbs are included in Table 14-1 because a strong, focused beam is sometimes of great help in locating a buoy or other navigational aid. Searchlights are not required, and in fact all rules are emphatic in forbidding the careless use of intense lights. Inland Rules: "Sec. 80.34 . . . Flashing the rays of a searchlight or other blinding light onto the bridge or into the pilot house of any vessel under way is prohibited. . . ."

All rules agree in forbidding the display of any light that might be confused with those prescribed, Sec. 14.02. To implement this requirement, penalties of license revocation or fines up to $500 may be imposed.

A considerable mental effort is required to convert a pictorial representation of prescribed lighting into the patterns that will actually be seen on an approaching vessel. The reader is urged to study the diagrams carefully and, by the aid of any study devices he finds useful, to work out the patterns expected as various types of vessels approach from a variety of angles. As boat speeds have increased, the time available for identification and for planning a course of action has shortened. Two vessels, each having a speed of 15 knots, may converge with a relative speed of 30 knots. In this not uncommon situation, side lights visible for only one mile will be in view for only *two minutes* before collision.

A skipper is, of course, particularly concerned when both colored lights of an approaching vessel are visible, because this indicates the distinct possibility of collision. He must then extract as much information as possible from the relative positions of all lights displayed so as to establish accurately the course relative to his own. Throughout the identification great care must be taken to avoid confusing lighted vessels with lighted aids to navigation, or with lights on shore.

## 14.10   Day Signals

Vessels engaged in certain specific occupations are required to exhibit characteristic *day signals* during daylight hours. The display of a day signal does not confer on that vessel any special privileges, but it does serve to distinguish a vessel usually incapable of taking any evasive action to avoid collision. Under Inland Rules day signals are prescribed for vessels engaged in specific tasks. Both rules also prescribe day signals for vessels not under command, for whatever reason.

**TABLE 14-2**

**Day Signals—Inland Rules**

| Situation | Day Signal |
|---|---|
| Moored dredge working | Two red balls |
| Self-propelled dredge under way and dredging | Two black balls |
| National Ocean Survey vessel under way and surveying | Three shapes: a green ball above a white diamond above a green ball |
| National Ocean Survey vessel at anchor and surveying | Two black balls |
| Coast Guard buoy tender at work | Two orange and white vertically striped balls |
| Vessel over 64 feet anchored in fairway | One black ball |
| Fishing vessel under way and fishing—tending nets, trolling, or oyster dredging | An empty basket, as a bushel basket, hoisted in the rigging |
| Skin or scuba diving | Red flag with white diagonal |

Day signals are made by hoisting on a vertical line one or more colored *shapes*. These shapes are fabric covered frames in the form of balls, cylinders, cones, and other easily distinguishable forms, usually two feet or more in their principal dimensions. The entire list of day signals is a formidable one; fortunately for identification purposes, one seldom needs to know the exact meaning of a signal. It is usually sufficient to remember that a vessel flying a day signal should be approached with caution, or better, given a wide berth.

A few of the more commonly encountered day signals are given in Table 14-2.

CHAPTER **15**

# Electricity Afloat

## 15.01   More Power To You

Ashore the demands for electrical energy are rising rapidly in all the nations of the world. In the United States electric power consumption has been doubling about every 10 years, and there is no evidence that the demand is tapering off, though it eventually must do so. Some of the increased demands come from population increases, but the larger portion is due to the ever-increasing number and variety of electrically operated devices that come to be looked on as necessities of life.

The increased demands for power have extended to shipboard until many craft have almost all of the electrical appliances that are found in the modern home, as well as those that are peculiar to life afloat. Ashore we take electricity for granted, using it freely and frequently forgetting to turn off lights and other devices when they are no longer needed. Ashore the power is available and at a cost that is not prohibitive.

When a boat is not tied up, with land-based power available, it must be electrically self-sufficient at all times. Electric power is the lifeblood of all engine-driven craft. A power failure can leave a boat without propulsion, without lights, and without means to communicate its plight to sources of aid. Modern marine installations provide substantial amounts of power afloat, but the supply is nevertheless strictly limited. Unnecessary use of electricity on board is a luxury that can never be afforded.

Land-based electric power is universally generated as alternating current (AC), because of the convenience that this offers for changing voltages by means of transformers. In an AC system the direction of current flow changes back and forth at a frequency determined by the speed of the generators. A frequency of 60 complete cycles per second or 60 Hertz (60 Hz) has been adopted by almost all commercial power companies. In a commercial power system the generators are left running at all times to maintain voltage on the distribution network. No method of storing AC energy is available, so isolated systems as in a car or a small boat use the direct current, or DC storage capability of a battery. Storage batteries on board form the only reservoir of electrical energy available between periods of direct power generation.

## 15.02    The Lead-Acid Storage Cell

Although research has been extensive, no economically feasible storage cell has been found to replace for mobile use the lead-sulphuric acid combination developed about 1870 by Planté. A lead-acid cell consists of a negative electrode of a spongy form of lead and a positive electrode of lead peroxide ($PbO_2$) immersed in a dilute solution of sulphuric acid. When an external circuit is completed between the electrodes or *plates*, a current will flow from the positive electrode * or *pole* to the negative pole, with the circuit being completed by a flow through the acid *electrolyte*, Fig. 15-1.

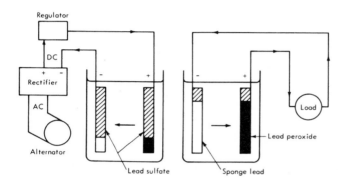

**FIGURE 15-1** (A) An external source charging a discharged lead-acid storage cell. (B) A fully charged cell supplying current to an external load.

While current is flowing through the battery, chemical energy stored there is being converted into electrical energy. Sulphuric acid is extracted from the electrolyte to form lead sulphate ($PbSO_4$) at each of the plates. When a DC supply of sufficient voltage and proper polarity is connected, Fig. 15-1, the direction of current flow through the cell will be reversed. Lead sulphate will be converted to lead and lead peroxide and sulphuric acid will reenter the solution. Charging is complete when all of the lead sulphate has been converted. Further current flow will not increase the energy stored in the cell but will only break down the water in the cell into its components oxygen and hydrogen, which will bubble off from the cell as a highly explosive mixture. Some gases will be generated throughout the charging cycle, so each cell must be provided with an escape vent, and the cells must be installed in an area with adequate ventilation.

A fully charged lead-acid cell will develop a potential difference of 2.06-2.14 volts, the exact value depending on the acid concentration and the temperature. During discharge the voltage gradually decreases to about 1.6 volts at

* The flow actually consists of electrons moving out from the negative pole, but custom refers to a fictitious positive charge flowing in the opposite direction.

the end of the useful power cycle. For all but the most precise calculations, each cell may be considered to deliver a voltage of 2.0 volts. Any desired voltage can be obtained by connecting individual cells in series. Note that the energy-storing capacity of a cell increases with its size, but the voltage remains at 2.0.

It is important to be able to determine accurately the charge state of a storage cell. Specific gravity of the electrolyte has been found to be a more useful charge indicator than has the cell voltage. The solution commonly in use in lead-acid batteries consists of 4 volumes of concentrated sulphuric acid to 11 volumes of water. This solution has a specific gravity 1.280 times that of water. As the cell discharges and acid enters the plates, the specific gravity will drop to about 1.150 at complete discharge. These specific gravities are readily measured with a *hydrometer,* an inexpensive instrument with a graduated float. In specifying specific gravities, the decimal point is frequently neglected. Thus one refers to a specific gravity of "twelve eighty" or "eleven fifty".

The capacity of a cell to store energy depends on the total amounts of lead and lead peroxide available for conversion by the discharge. Thick, bulky electrodes are undesirable, so a typical high-capacity cell electrode consists of an assembly of thin plates with the active chemicals pasted on grids of a lead-antimony alloy. The two types of plates will be interleaved with each other and will be kept from electrical contact by insulating *separators.* Each positive-negative plate assembly will be mounted in a case of acid-proof material such as hard rubber. A space below each set of plates allows for the accumulation of some sludge or sediment which might otherwise bridge across the electrodes and short circuit the cell.

## 15.03    Storage Battery Installations

Lead-acid storage cells are most commonly assembled in groups of 3, 4, or 6 to form batteries of 6, 8, or 12 volts. For many years 6-volt systems were in general use, but they have now been largely replaced by 12-volt installations. The 8-volt batteries are commonly connected in groups of four to provide 32 volts for larger vessels with heavy power demands. Still larger vessels may have a battery bank of 16 large individual cells.

The rate at which electrical energy is consumed is measured in watts, and the total energy consumption is then obtained by multiplying the rate in watts by the time of consumption in hours. The number of watts being consumed is obtained by multiplying the number of amperes flowing by the system voltage.

$$\text{watts} = \text{amperes} \times \text{volts}$$
$$W = I \times V \qquad \text{15-1}$$

The total energy consumed over a period of T hours is

$$\text{watt-hours} = V \times I \times T \qquad \text{15-2}$$

For a given system voltage V will be relatively constant at 6, 12, or 32 volts, and so a measure of a battery's ability to deliver energy will be given by the product of I × T, known as *ampere-hours*. A battery is thus said to have a capability of, say 80 ampere-hours, which is to say that the battery should be capable of supplying 1 ampere for 80 hours, 8 amperes for 10 hours, and so on. In practice somewhat more energy can be obtained from a battery at the lower rates and with intermittent use than is available at a high discharge rate.

A battery installation should be made only after a careful assessment of present and future power needs. It is almost impossible to overestimate the amount of battery capability that would be desirable. Power demands usually increase faster than anticipated, and the ability of a battery to deliver energy will decrease with age. Space limitations on board may prevent the installation of as much battery capability as would be desired.

Storage batteries are heavy. Made primarily of lead, filled with a liquid heavier than water, and assembled into a heavy protective case, a 12-volt battery will weigh about 0.8 pounds per ampere-hour. Six-volt units will weigh a little more than half this, perhaps as much as 0.45 pounds per ampere-hour. For ease in handling and to aid in installation in small quarters, it may be desirable to power a 12-volt system with two 6-volt units connected in series. The split-unit installation has the added advantage of requiring one replacement of only half of the system in case a single cell develops a fault.

Duplicate battery banks should be installed whenever it is possible. One common practice is to use one bank for essential services such as engine starting and navigation lights, assigning the second bank to some of the less important uses which provide only fringe benefits. Appropriate switches must be provided in a duplicate installation to permit a reversal of the battery roles and to insure flexibility in the charging connections.

Batteries must be installed where they are accessible for inspection and servicing. Cable terminals should be checked occasionally, and the electrolyte level must be maintained above the top of the plates by replacing the water that has been lost by evaporation and electrolysis. Neglect will seriously shorten the life of even the highest quality battery.

Batteries must not be installed in any location, as deep down in a bilge, where they may be submerged. Seawater in contact with the battery fluid will lead to the production of hydrochloric acid, whose corrosive properties will be added to those of the already present sulphuric acid. Widespread damage to the hull and its installations can quickly follow the mixing of battery contents with the bilge water.

Battery life is shortened by exposure to high temperatures. This is only one of the reasons why marine batteries should not be located close to the engines. Contact with fuel vapors should also be avoided. A loose cable clamp can easily lead to an arc that is quite capable of igniting any vapors that may be present. For the same reason great care should be taken to avoid dropping tools or other metal objects across the battery terminals. The resulting short-circuit can easily produce a destructive arc and may lead to a disastrous fire.

Wherever they are located, batteries must be securely strapped down with corrosion-resistant fastenings. Weights of this magnitude can do serious hull or machinery damage if they should come loose in a seaway. The breakage of a cable connection because of battery movement could have serious consequences even if there was no major hull damage.

Lead-acid batteries should always be installed in lead-lined, acid-proof compartments. Escaping gas bubbles from each cell will carry minute droplets of the electrolyte along with them, to be deposited on surrounding surfaces. The corrosive acid will attack wood and metal parts and in time will render them useless as strength members. Frequent inspections should be made of the members supporting the batteries to be sure that no spilled acid has destroyed the structural integrity. All joints in the lead box liner should be closed by lead burning and not by soft solder. Lead is one of the few metals that can resist attack by sulphuric acid. The tin component of soft solder is not acid resistant and will be quickly eroded.

## 15.04 Battery Maintenance

Automobile batteries are frequently shamefully neglected, but a failure can usually be overcome by using another car and a pair of jumper cables to get the engine and the generator running. Such services are scarcely to be expected at sea, where the safety of the vessel may well depend on a functioning battery. Some owners purchase expensive, heavy-duty batteries designed specifically for marine service. With proper maintenance these units will give satisfactory service for many years. Abuse can, however, shorten the useful life to a single season. There is a tendency to use the expensive units as long as possible, and it can happen that they are kept on board just one season, or even just one cruise too many. An alternative practice followed by many is to purchase standard automobile-type batteries and to discard them after only one season. This routine is acceptable if one resists the temptation to take a chance on a second season, and then perhaps another, until a failure occurs.

Electrolyte levels must be checked regularly, on a schedule suited to the type of batteries installed. Electrolyte levels are maintained by adding only water that has been purified by distillation or by passage through an ion-exchange column. Lead-acid cells are sensitive to impurities, particularly the iron and chlorine that are found in many common tap waters. Fill but do not overfill each cell. Any excess should be promptly wiped up with a rag that is to be discarded. *Never add acid to a battery.* A low specific gravity is the result of a loss of acid into the plates and not from the cell itself.

A lead-acid battery should never be left in a discharged state. A long discharge period tends to fix the sulphuric acid in the plates so that subsequent charging currents will only partially restore them to the charged condition. A discharged battery is also susceptible to damage by freezing. As shown in Table

15-1 the electrolyte in a discharged battery freezes at a distinctly higher temperature than does the fluid in a fully charged cell.

**TABLE 15-1**

**Freezing Points of Battery Electrolytes**

| Specific Gravity | Freezing Point, °F |
|---|---|
| 1.280 | −96 |
| 1.250 | −61 |
| 1.200 | −16 |
| 1.150 | + 5 |
| 1.100 | +18 |

Just below the freezing point the solution is a soft slush, but this can change to a hard, destructive solid at still lower temperatures. On subsequent thawing the electrolyte may leak out from cracked cells and cause destructive corrosion. When a battery is to be unused for several weeks or months, as after fall decommissioning, it should be removed from the boat and stored where it will not be subjected to temperature extremes. It should be lightly charged at least once a month to compensate for some charge leakage that will take place even with no electrical load. Battery life will be prolonged if it is kept at full charge rather than be allowed to go through a series of charge-discharge-charge cycles.

## 15.05   Battery Charging Devices

In normal use the shipboard battery will be charged by a DC generator or by an alternator driven by the main propulsion engine or engines. For many years DC generators provided the charging current, but these are now largely supplanted by alternators. The AC thus produced is *rectified* or converted to DC before being supplied to the battery, Fig. 15-1. In either charging system a voltage regulator will be interposed between the charging source and the battery. The voltage regulator serves two functions. First, it responds to the increased battery voltage as full charge is approached and reduces the charging rate to prevent battery damage from an overcharge. Second, it disconnects the battery from the charging circuit when the voltage of the latter drops below that of the battery. Without the latter function the entire battery charge might be dissipated back through the charging generator as soon as the propulsion engine slowed or was stopped.

Voltage regulators are carefully adjusted at the factory to properly program the charging rate. These adjustments should not be changed without a thorough knowledge of the details of regulator operation. Accurate meters will be needed to monitor the performance of the regulator as the adjustments are changed.

Alternators have several distinct advantages over DC generators. Alternators are simpler, more trouble-free, and come to charging voltage at relatively slow engine speeds. During idling or slow-speed trolling, an alternator will continue to provide charging current where a DC generator might be unable to do so.

Either type of charger is usually driven by a Vee belt from a pulley on the engine crankshaft. The tension in this belt must be carefully adjusted. Too much tension will lead to rapid, excessive wear of the alternator bearings. A slack belt may slip and fail to drive the alternator at proper speed. A considerable amount of power is required to drive either an alternator or a generator. A 40-ampere charging rate in a 12-volt system means an electrical power output to the battery of more than $12 \times 40 = 480$ watts. Since 746 watts is the electrical equivalent of 1 horsepower, the driving belt must deliver to the alternator $480/746 = 0.64$ horsepower, without allowing for any losses in the generating system itself.

At dockside, with commercial AC power available, the most efficient battery charging is done with transformer-rectifier units. Only charging units with an isolating transformer (Fig. 15-2) should be used on shipboard to insure

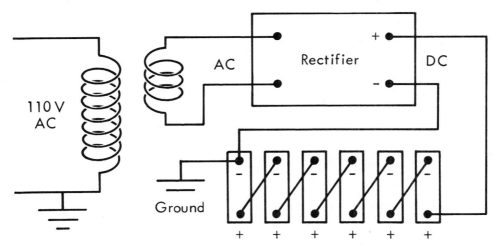

**FIGURE 15-2** Six cells in series on charge from a commercial power line. The isolation transformer prevents a current flow between the two grounds.

that the "hot" side of the AC line does not get connected to the grounded side of the boat system. For most purposes AC charging units with rates of 5-10 amperes are sufficient. An overnight charge with one of these chargers will put 50-100 ampere-hours into a battery, a charge sufficient for starting the propulsion engine. "Quickcharging" at rates of 100 amperes or more is not recommended, unless the pressure of time is all-important. At high rates the diffusion of electrolyte into and out of the plates is incomplete, and so the energy stored may be considerably less than that acquired by the same charge delivered at a slower rate. At very high rates the battery temperature may rise to an undesirable level.

## 15.06    Power Priorities on Board

Each skipper should permit the use of electric power-consuming devices in strict accord with the known energy reserves in the battery system. Some items will be absolutely essential to the operation of the vessel, some will be desirable but not indispensable, and some will be for convenience only.

Top priority must always go to the starting of the propulsion engine. Once this is running, battery charge will be regained unless there is a failure in the charging system. If the engine cannot be started, and if there is no engine-driven auxiliary charger on board, battery charge can only go downhill. Running lights, power-driven horns, bilge pumps, and the radiotelephone are critical items. With the latter inoperative, signals for assistance will be limited to visual ranges, which are apt to be inadequate.

Table 15-2 lists typical power requirements for some of the equipment commonly found on board. Several of the values listed in the table will require modification in individual cases, depending on the size of the item installed.

**TABLE 15-2**

**Typical Power Requirements**

| Function | Watts | Current Drain at 6 volts | 12 volts | 32 volts |
|---|---|---|---|---|
| Starter | 800 | 130 | 65 | 25 |
| Ignition | 12 | 2.0 | 1.0 | 0.3 |
| Bilge Pump | 40 | 6.7 | 3.3 | 1.3 |
| Running Lights (each) | 10 | 1.7 | 0.8 | 0.3 |
| Receive | 10 | 1.7 | 0.8 | 0.3 |
| Radiotelephone Standby | 20 | 3.3 | 1.7 | 0.6 |
| Transmit | 70 | 11.7 | 5.9 | 2.2 |
| Anchor Windlass | 500 | 83 | 42 | 16 |
| Eng(in)er Room Blower | 50 | 8.3 | 4.2 | 1.6 |
| Horn | 50 | 8.3 | 4.2 | 1.6 |
| Searchlight | 30 | 5.0 | 2.5 | 1.0 |
| Cabin Light (each) | 25 | 4.2 | 2.1 | 0.8 |
| Pressure Water | 60 | 10.0 | 5.0 | 1.9 |
| Shower Pump | 60 | 10.0 | 5.0 | 1.9 |
| Electric Head | 100 | 16.7 | 8.3 | 3.1 |
| Depth Sounder | 20 | 3.2 | 1.7 | 0.6 |
| Radar | 200 | 32 | 17 | 6.2 |
| Refrigerator | 120 | 20 | 10 | 3.7 |
| Television | 140 | 23 | 12 | 4.4 |

For example, the 70 watts allocated to the radiotelephone in the "transmit" mode corresponds to the demands of what is listed as a 35-watt set. The latter figure is only the amount of power supplied to the final amplifier tube in the transmitter; the total power requirement will be about twice this figure. The power required by an anchor windlass will vary widely with the amount of pull required. The amount allocated in Table 15-2 is about the maximum requirement for boats 30-45 feet loa.

The total energy drain from a battery will be the product of the current and the time it is flowing. Some of the essential power is required for only short periods of time, while some other less important uses may go on for extended periods. Thus for a 12-volt system:

| One anchor light for 10 hours | $10 \times 0.9 =$ | 9 ampere-hours |
|---|---|---|
| Television for 3 hours | $3 \times 12 = 36$ | |
| 5-minutes radio transmission | $5/60 \times 6 =$ | 0.5 |
| 1-minute engine start | $1/60 \times 67 =$ | 1.1 |

Note the relatively low power requirement for engine ignition listed in Table 15-2. A gasoline engine that is running will operate for many hours with a disabled charging system, using battery power alone. A diesel engine requires no ignition power at all.

## 15.07   Electrical Distribution Systems

An adequate and well-maintained wiring and switching system is essential to insure that electric power is delivered to its utilization point with a minimum of loss. Connections are necessarily made with an assortment of lugs, clamps, and springs, each exposed to the corrosive action of salt-bearing air and subject to engine vibration and hull pounding in heavy weather. The low-voltage circuits may carry relatively heavy currents, requiring switches to carry considerably greater currents than would be the case for similar functions ashore. When a switch interrupts a heavy current, an electric arc capable of igniting combustible vapors may be struck.

Copper is the metal most commonly used to conduct electric currents with a minimum of loss due to the resistance of the conductor itself. A famous relation known as Ohm's Law states that the voltage across any part of a DC circuit is proportional to the current flowing through the circuit. That is

$$V = R \times I \qquad \text{or } R = \frac{V}{I} \qquad \text{or } I = \frac{V}{R} \qquad\qquad 15\text{-}3$$

where R is the resistance in ohms, V is in volts and the current I is in amperes. Table 15-3 lists resistance values for some of the sizes of copper wire commonly used on board.

TABLE 15-3

**Characteristics of Copper Wire**

| Wire Gage No. | R, ohms/foot | Safe Current Capacity Amperes | Breaking Strength Pounds |
|---|---|---|---|
| 0 | 0.00010 | 120 | 2900 |
| 2 | 0.00016 | 90 | 1900 |
| 4 | 0.00026 | 70 | 1200 |
| 6 | 0.00041 | 50 | 750 |
| 8 | 0.00065 | 35 | 480 |
| 10 | 0.0010 | 25 | 300 |
| 12 | 0.0016 | 20 | 200 |
| 14 | 0.0026 | 15 | 120 |

Ohm's Law is very simple to apply and is useful in determining the size of wire required to properly supply various utilities.

## ILLLUSTRATIVE EXAMPLE

Consider an anchor windlass located 20 feet from the 12-volt battery. Assume that the windlass motor has a resistance of 0.115 ohms and that a current flow of 80 amperes is required to break out the anchor. Compare the situations if the wiring system consisted of (a) No. 14 gage copper and (b) No. 2 gage copper.

(a)  The complete circuit will require 2 × 20 = 40 feet of wire
Resistance of 40 ft. of No. 14 copper 40 × 0.0026 = 0.104 ohms
Total circuit resistance 0.104 + 0.115 = 0.219 ohms
Maximum possible current flow 12/0.219 = 55 amperes
This current is insufficient to break out the anchor
Furthermore almost half of the power taken from the battery will be lost in the wiring, which will be raised to an unsafe temperature

(b)  Resistance of 40 ft. of No. 2 copper 40 × 0.00016 = 0.00064 ohms
Total circuit resistance 0.00064 + 0.115 = 0.10464 ohms
Maximum possible current flow 12/0.10464 = 120 amperes
Here sufficient power is available at the windlass, and no dangerous amount of heat will be generated in the wires

The safe current capacities listed in Table 15-3 are based on safe temperature rises in concealed conductors from which heat can not readily escape.

All shipboard wiring must have adequate mechanical strength as well as the necessary low electrical resistance. A small load such as a colored side light could be carried by a small wire without excessive loss, but such a wire would be fragile and easily damaged. For mechanical strength no wire smaller than No. 14 gage is recommended for shipboard wiring, except for short lengths inside of fixtures. Stranded conductors are preferred over single solid wires, since the former is less likely to be broken by vibration.

All wiring shall be run as high as practicable above the bilges. Metal conduit and the metal-armored cable used in house wiring are not recommended because of the danger of trapping moisture therein. All wires should be secured at appropriate intervals by clamps or cleats made of material that is not subject to deterioration by rusting. Two wires should be run to each point of power utilization. Even though one side of the circuit is a common ground, the ground must not be used to carry any working current.

Circuit-control switches and either fuses or protective circuit breakers should be mounted on an enclosed switchboard. Switches outside the enclosure, especially those in the main circuits handling heavy currents should be enclosed vapor-proof designs to prevent the ignition of any flammable vapors by an arc formed at the switch contacts. Well-designed circuit breakers are preferred to fuses for circuit protection against overloads. Spring clips and any other type of fuse contact must be kept scrupulously clean and tight. Corrosion at this point can increase the local resistance and lead to localized heating to the point where the fuse will melt and open an otherwise intact circuit.

## 15.08    Electrical Grounds

Any extensive system of electrical conductors can serve as an electrical *ground* or reference point from which electrical potentials are measured. The most extensive ground is the earth itself. One point of an electrical distribution system may or may not be tied to ground. One side of all commercial 110-volt AC power lines is grounded and will be tied to some of the buried service pipes entering each building. On board a vessel the engine and its associated piping will form a ground, and one side of the DC system (usually the negative) will be connected to it. The vessel ground will be in more or less good contact with the external water ground by way of the propeller shaft and couplings, through-hull fittings and pipelines.

The vessel's ground system must not be used as a current-carrying part of the electrical distribution system. The process of electroplating, or the electrical deposition of metals, is well known. Electric currents are equally capable of deplating or removing metals selectively when they are in a circuit containing conducting liquids. Currents flowing through a ground system can rapidly produce electrolytic corrosion with serious weakening of some of the metal structures. Hence the requirement that two wires forming a complete circuit be run to each point of power utilization, even though one side of the circuit is maintained at ground potential by a connection at the battery.

When 110-volt power is brought on board, the greatest care must be taken to avoid painful or lethal contacts with it. No dangerous shocks will be received from a 6-volt or a 12-volt DC system, and 32 volts is probably also safe for everyone. The 110-volt AC supply is quite another matter. With one side of the system grounded, any contact with the other or "hot" side can lead to serious consequences. Any connection between a vessel and dockside power should be made only with the approved three-wire connectors that carry a separate ground wire as well as the two power conductors. Every 110-volt device brought on board should have its exposed metal parts grounded, either through an external connection or through a three-wire attachment cord. Particular attention should be paid to the condition of any portable electric tools used on board. Your life may well depend on the integrity of the ground connection to these devices.

## 15.09    Protection Against Lightning

A lightning stroke consists of an electrical discharge from a cloud, at a potential of many tens of thousands of volts, to another cloud of opposite polarity or to the earth. Currents of several thousand amperes may flow for a short period of time, releasing an energy estimated to range as high as that from the explosion of a pound of TNT.

Ashore most of the lightning strikes will take place to high objects such as towers or trees, but a direct strike to earth may occur if no easier path is available. Strikes to sharp points as on a lightning rod are more probable than to smooth, rounded surfaces. When a good conducting path is available, the electrical discharge will flow harmlessly to ground. In a high resistance circuit, such as that presented by a living tree, most of the electrical energy will be discharged into the conductor itself, which may be shattered as a result.

A vessel on the relatively smooth surface of the water may well provide the easiest path for a lightning discharge to ground, and so it must be protected against the destructive effects of a strike. A wooden mast for example is a poor electrical conductor that would be shattered by a strike. For protection, a grounding conductor whose resistance is not greater than that of No. 8 gage copper wire (Table 15-3) should terminate in a sharp point at least six inches above the masthead. The conductor should lead downward in as straight a line as possible to a large conducting area below the waterline. The metal keel of a sailboat will provide a satisfactory ground, as will a large copper plate that may have been installed to improve radio performance. Metal standing rigging such as shrouds and stays can serve as grounding conductors but must be connected to the underwater ground by heavy cable. All connections in the grounding circuit must be carefully made to insure the necessary low resistance.

A radio antenna should be equipped with an approved type of lightning arrestor or with means for providing a solid ground during an electrical storm. Any coil, such as an antenna loading coil or a spirally wound conductor, will present a high resistance to a lightning discharge and must be bypassed with a straight grounding wire.

Any metallic fitting of appreciable size that is aloft, such as sail slide tracks, should be tied to the main ground by as straight line conductors as possible.

Not all discharges of atmospheric electricity take place with the dramatic suddenness of a lightning strike. A charged cloud will be surrounded by an intense electric field that may extend for a considerable distance from the cloud itself. At some distance from the main charge, the charge may leak to ground slowly rather than being discharged in a single large pulse. The slow discharge will favor sharp points, and at night a blue glow known as St. Elmo's fire may be seen at the tips of the conductors carrying the discharge current. A characteristic hissing noise will accompany the slow discharge, and the field may be intense enough to cause hair on the crew members to stand erect. If the discharge is taking place to a collapsible radio antenna, it should not be lowered but left erect to serve as a discharge point. A dangerous strike is not apt to follow the hissing discharge, but prudence suggests that the vessel, if under way, move away from the high-field area.

CHAPTER **16**

# Boats Under Sail

## 16.01 An Ancient Art

Man discovered early in his boating experience that a large surface exposed to the wind could be used as a means of propulsion. The earliest record of a sailing craft appears to date around 6000 B.C. For many centuries after this, sailors did little more than spread sails of papyrus, linen, or canvas before a favorable wind. When the wind became unfavorable, sails were lowered in favor of oars, usually pulled by slaves.

*Square-rigged* vessels, capable of sailing directly before the wind or at most a few degrees from it, were commonly used in offshore voyages well into the nineteenth century. These long voyages with heavy cargos took advantage of the tendency of the trade winds to blow rather steadily both in amount and direction. As coastwise trading developed, the superior maneuverability of the *fore-and-aft* rig became increasingly evident. The number of square-riggers began to decline until today they are essentially museum pieces. *Sprit* rigs and *lateen* sails still are used to some extent, but modern pleasure-boat sailing is dominated by the fore-and-aft rig.

The confirmed powerboat man, or *stinkpotter,* may well inquire as to why he should know of the arts of the sailor, or *ragman.* In the first place, some appreciation of the capabilities and limitations of sailing craft will give the powerboater a better feeling for the problems confronting the sailor. In addition, some knowledge of sail may be invaluable to a skipper caught offshore with a disabled power plant. Properly handled, even a jury rig will suffice to produce directed motion and bring home an otherwise helpless vessel.

## 16.02 Types of Sailing Craft

In earlier days the *catboat* was regularly seen; today the type is represented primarily by sailing dinghies, although some of the larger sizes are popular in some local areas. The catboat rig (Fig. 16-1), has a single mast stepped well forward, a large *mainsail* bent to a boom that extends back at least to the

313

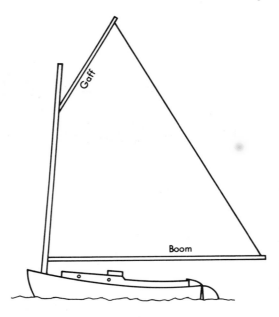

Gaff

Boom

FIGURE 16-1 A gaff-rigged catboat, typically 20-28 feet loa. Note
the heavy unsupported mast.

transom, and an outboard rudder. An occasional catboat carries a small forward sail or *jib,* but these are not typical of the species. The catboat rig is
simple because there is only one sail to tend. She does not sail well to windward, however, and in the larger sizes, the heavy sail is hard to handle.

Because of its better performance to windward, the *sloop* has largely replaced the catboat. In the sloop a single mast is stepped at about 30 percent of
the distance from stem to transom. A large mainsail is standard, with a single
headsail or jib selected to suit the existing wind conditions. As the aerodynamics
of sail action becomes better understood, there is a tendency to increase the
size of the headsail relative to that of the main.

When a single mast is stepped a bit farther aft, at say 40 percent of the
stem-transom distance, the sloop becomes a *cutter.* More canvas can now be
hoisted in the *foretriangle,* or the space forward of the mast. Cutters regularly
carry two foresails, but in other respects are quite comparable to sloops,
Fig. 16-2.

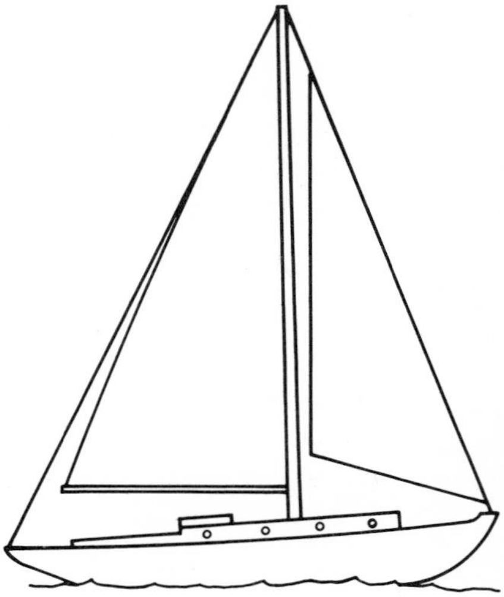

FIGURE 16-2 Sloop with a Marconi mainsail. Shown is a masthead rig because the forestay runs
clear to the truck of the mast.

Sloop or cutter rigs can be put on any hull form from a flat-bottomed skiff to the 12-meter sloops now used in competition for the America's Cup. Except in the smaller sizes, a typical sloop will have a round bilge and a stern that tapers back to the transom. There will be a considerable overhang both fore and aft, making the loa perhaps 30 percent greater than the lwl. This shape is in sharp contrast to the almost vertical stem and transom of the typical catboat.

In a *ketch* rig (Fig. 16-3A) the mainmast is stepped about as in the sloop, with a small *mizzen* mast aft, but forward of the rudder post. The mizzen sail of a ketch will have an area up to about 60 percent of the area of the main. In a *yawl* rig (Fig. 16-3B) the mizzen mast is usually stepped abaft the rudder post, which reduces the area of the mizzen to about 25 percent of the area of the main.

FIGURE 16-3   (A) Ketch rig, mizzen mast forward of the rudder post. (B) Yawl rig, mizzen mast abaft the rudder post. Each boat has set a jib, main, and mizzen. (C) Schooner, mainmast abaft the foremast.

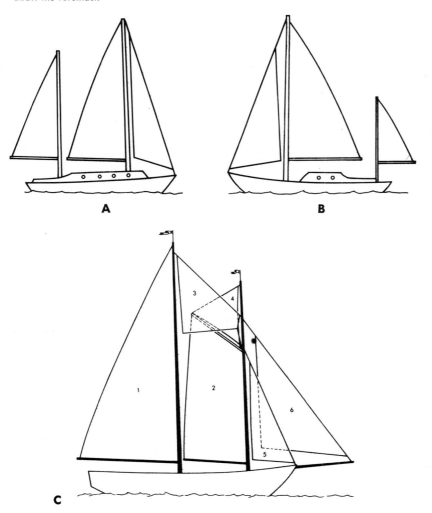

The divided rig of ketch or yawl adds complications to the rigging and the handling of sails. On the credit side, a given sail area is more easily handled when it is in two pieces, or conversely, a given crew can handle a larger area of sail if it is divided into two parts. In heavy weather either of these two rigs can take off the main completely and sail under jib and mizzen with a good balance of effort fore and aft. If a sloop or cutter drops her main, she will lose balance, because most of the driving force will be well forward, on the jib.

When the mainmast is stepped at about 60 percent of the stem-transom distance, with a smaller foremast, we have a *schooner*, Fig. 16-3C. This design apparently originated in Scandinavia, but it was brought to its ultimate development in the United States. As sizes increased, more masts were added, a trend which culminated in the construction of one "seven-master." Today one rarely sees more than a two-masted schooner.

Many sail combinations are available to a schooner. Sail handling is somewhat complicated by the mass of rigging, but one can set a sail combination to work effectively in almost any weather condition.

## 16.03   Leeway and Heel

A boat of any shape will sail *downwind*, or almost in the direction of the prevailing wind. When a boat sails at an angle to the wind, there will be a considerable force on the sails tending to move the boat sidewise, in addition to the force component that drives the hull forward. The side, or lateral force, will give the boat an excessive side slippage, or *leeway*, unless steps are taken to reduce it. In addition, the lateral force will cause the vessel to heel, a tendency which must be countered by buoyant forces developed on the submerged portions of the hull, or by *ballast*, located deep down in the structure.

Leeway is reduced by presenting a large underwater area to a sidewise motion, while the forward area is kept small to reduce the resistance to the desired forward motion. In a *keel boat* the large, longitudinal surface is obtained with a deep, thin keel below the hull, Fig. 16-4A. This keel will be faired into a rounded bilge to form the typical wineglass shape of a keel boat. The keel may be made of iron or lead, putting ballast deep in the water. As we have seen, this massive weight lowers the center of gravity of the boat, providing a powerful righting force opposing the tendency to capsize. In some designs the keel will be made of wood, and *inside* ballast will be placed deep inside the hull.

Alternatively, leeway can be reduced by a *centerboard* (Fig. 16-4B), consisting of a relatively light metal plate or board which can be raised or lowered as occasion demands. In small sizes the centerboard may become a *daggerboard*.

A *centerboarder* must attain most of her stability against capsizing by hull design, since the righting force of a heavy keel is missing. Centerboarders have a distinct advantage over keel boats in shoal water sailing. In general the

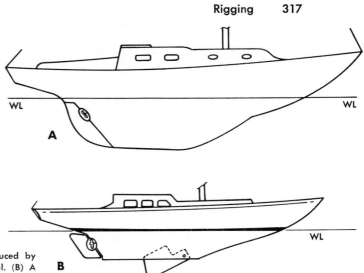

**FIGURE 16-4** (A) Leeway is reduced by the side resistance of a deep keel. (B) A shallow keel is supplemented by an adjustable centerboard.

draft of a keel boat will be significantly greater, for equal-size hulls. In addition, a grounding in a centerboarder can be relieved by pulling up the board; the grounded keel boat must await the rising tide or be towed free.

## 16.04   Rigging

The classical catboat was equipped with a short, heavy mast with enough inherent strength to withstand the forces imposed on it by a large mainsail. Wind speeds increase with height above the water, so modern designs have tended toward taller and taller masts, with weight aloft reduced to a minimum. These tall, slender masts must be supported by *standing rigging*, usually consisting of plow steel or stainless steel cables. Lateral strength is achieved by a system of *shrouds*, running down from the mast over *spreaders* to *chainplates* fastened solidly to the hull, Fig. 16-5.

Longitudinal strength is obtained from a system of *stays*. A *forestay* or *jibstay* will run from the stem or the bowsprit to a point well up the mast. In a *masthead* rig this forward stay will be secured to the very top of the mast, called the *truck*. The *permanent backstay* will run from the truck to the transom. Auxiliary stays may be added to stiffen particular sections of the mast.

The tensions in shrouds and stays must be carefully adjusted, usually by means of *turnbuckles*. Tremendous forces can be easily exerted by turnbuckles, and great care must be taken in making the adjustments so that large, distorting forces are not introduced into both mast and hull.

When sailing in a brisk wind, the forces in the standing rigging become extremely large. Any rigging failure will almost certainly be followed by a mast failure, a major disaster. Frequent inspection of all parts of the standing rigging for signs of corrosion or other incipient failures is well worthwhile.

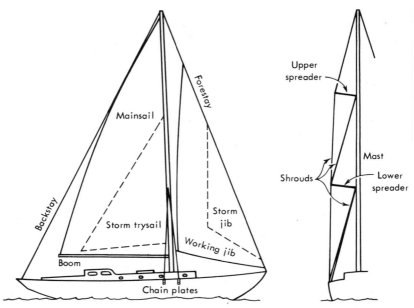

**FIGURE 16-5** Typical standing rigging and working sails on a masthead sloop. Dotted lines show storm sails.

## 16.05 Sails and Their Parts

Because of the higher wind velocities aloft, it is advantageous to carry as large an area of canvas as high as possible. This is accomplished in the *gaff-headed sail*, Fig. 16-1, by adding a second spar or *gaff*, which stretches the *head* of a four-sided sail in the same way that the *foot* of the sail is stretched along the *boom*. The added weight and complexity of the gaff rig tend to offset its advantages. Modern designs favor the three-sided sail known as *jib-headed, Bermuda*, or *Marconi*.

The parts of a triangular sail are named in Fig. 16-6. The luff of a mainsail is held to the mast by slides or hoops. Similar slides hold the foot to the boom. When the sail is hoisted by the main *halyard*, the *luff* is stretched taut. A fullness is created by sewing together strips or *cloths* to permit the sail to belly out as it fills with wind. The position of the boom, and hence of the *clew* of the mainsail, is controlled by the mainsheet, which is a rope and not a piece of cloth. Blocks may be needed on the mainsheet to obtain the force needed to *trim* or bring in the boom in a brisk wind.

The luff of a staysail or jib is *hanked* to the forestay with snap hooks or shackles. A working jib may be attached to a boom, to a short spar known as a *jib club*, or it may be used *loose-footed*. Modern Genoa jibs or simply *Genoas* extend well aft of the foretriangle and overlap the main. Genoas are always used loose-footed.

In light air a boat sailing with the wind, or nearly so, may hoist a spinnaker. These are the big balloonlike sails which delight the photographer, but which require constant attention if they are to be kept full and drawing. A

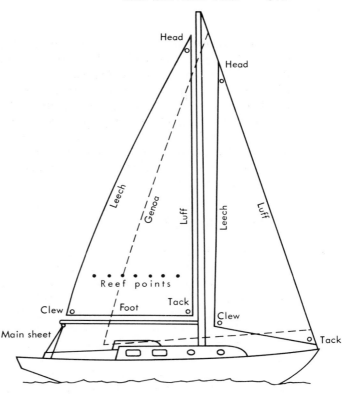

FIGURE 16-6 Names of the various parts of the sails on a Bermuda-rigged sloop. Note the overlap between the big Genoa (dotted) and the mainsail. Usually the main will have more than one set of reef points.

properly set spinnaker can provide a tremendous amount of drive, but it can easily foul on various parts of the rigging. The tack of a spinnaker is held out from the boat by a *spinnaker pole,* the sheet from the loose-footed clew is led well aft.

Table 16-1 lists typical values of relative sail areas for a cruising sloop, expressed as percentages of the mainsail area. Values for a boat designed primarily for racing may deviate substantially from these values.

**TABLE 16-1**

**Relative Sail Areas**

| Sail | Relative Area (%) |
|---|---|
| Mainsail | 100 |
| Trisail (storm main) | 45 |
| Storm jib | 22 |
| Working jib | 65 |
| Genoa | 85 |
| Large Genoa | 150 |
| Spinnaker | 300 |

Before the advent of synthetic fabrics the finest sails were made of Egyptian cotton. Cotton sails required careful handling, mildewed rapidly when stored wet, and were relatively bulky. Most sails today are made of the synthetic Dacron. This material has little stretch so that a sail is unlikely to be distorted by excessive tension. Dacron does not absorb moisture, and sails made of it may be stored wet without injury, although it can not be considered good practice to do so. The high-tensile strength of the fibers permits a reduction in weight without loss of strength. Spinnakers are usually made of nylon instead of Dacron. Nylon is somewhat stronger for a given weight, and the stretch of nylon does no harm in a spinnaker. Sailcloth weights range from less than one ounce per square yard for a light spinnaker or *drifter* to 12-14 ounces for a large main or a storm trisail.

## 16.06   Sailing Off the Wind

Sailing *off* or *before* the wind means that the wind is coming from directly aft, or very nearly so. It is the easiest point of sailing to understand. All sails are set so that their surfaces are about perpendicular to the wind; direct pressure on the after surfaces forces the boat forward. In a fore-and-aft rig sailing off the wind (Fig. 16-7A), the sails are put in proper position by *starting* or paying out the sheets. The boom and the clew of the mainsail will swing wide of the boat. Similarly the clew of the jib will be well outboard when sailing off the wind.

When the wind is not directly aft, but slightly off the quarter, as shown, both sails will fill and draw. If the wind hauls aft, the jib, being partly shielded by the main, will collapse and may suddenly swing to the other side as the

**FIGURE 16-7**   (A) Position of working sails when running. In light air the jib may be held out to weather with a pole, as shown by dotted lines. She is then sailing *wung out*. (B) Greater drive sailing off the wind is obtained by setting a spinnaker.

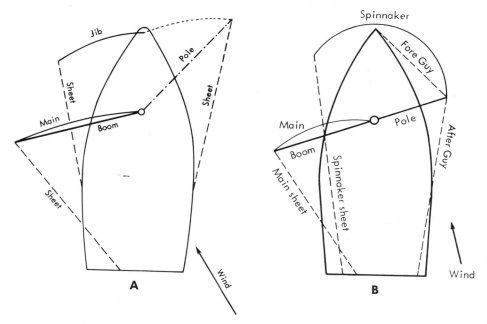

wind catches the front rather than the after surface of the sail. This is a danger signal, for if the wind continues to shift in the same direction, the main will also suddenly swing to the other side, producing an *accidental gybe*.

Any sudden shifting of the mainsail as the direction, or *eye* of the wind passes across the stern, is known as a *gybe*. A *controlled gybe* is a quick and convenient way of changing course when running before a light or a moderate breeze. In a controlled gybe the mainsheet is hauled in or *trimmed* until it has brought the boom amidships where the sheet is held securely. The stern of the boat is then brought through the eye of the wind until it is coming well over the other quarter. The mainsheet is then started slowly, allowing the wind to carry the boom forward to the proper position for running. The boom must be under the control of the sheet at all times during this maneuver.

In an uncontrolled gybe, which is usually caused by inattention on the part of the helmsman, the wind shifts across the stern until it blows on the forward face of the mainsail, forcing it sternward. Since the mainsheet was well started, there will be lots of slack line as the boom comes amidship. In a brisk blow the boom swinging across the cockpit is quite capable of killing a crewman or knocking him overboard. Boom and sail will continue around until the slack in the sheet is taken up on the other side. If any part of the mainsheet system fails as the slack is taken up, the boom will continue forward into the shrouds, probably smashing them and itself in the process. The extent of the damage will depend on the wind velocity. Except in the lightest breeze, an uncontrolled gybe is a spectacular and a highly dangerous performance.

Running in a heavy wind is a dangerous point of sailing because of the danger of a gybe. A *preventer* may be rigged from the end of the boom to hold it forward, but constant vigilance is the best gybe preventer. When the jib collapses, a prompt change of course is indicated to keep the wind well on the proper quarter.

A spinnaker, Fig. 16-7B, may be carried when the wind is well aft of the beam. The spinnaker pole, carrying the tack of the sail, is maintained nearly perpendicular to the wind direction by adjusting the after and forward guys. To keep the sail full and drawing, the spinnaker sheet must be tended almost constantly by a skilled hand. If the wind draws forward toward the beam, there will be an increasingly large lateral force in addition to that producing forward drive. Under this condition an improperly handled spinnaker can overpower the boat and lead to a knockdown. Alternatively, the spinnaker and its rigging can become incredibly tangled with the forward standing rigging. Sometimes hours of hazardous work aloft are required to clear a badly fouled spinnaker.

## 16.07    Reaching

A boat sailing with the wind about abeam (Fig. 16-8) is *reaching*. Reaches may be classified as *broad*, *beam*, or *close* as the wind shifts progressively to-

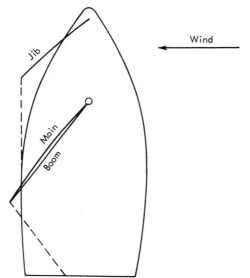

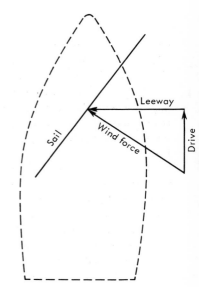

**FIGURE 16-8** On a reach both main and jib sheets are trimmed inboard from the running position.

**FIGURE 16-9** Part of the wind force on an angled sail produces forward drive and part produces leeway.

ward the bow. If the sails are left broad off in proper position for running, a beam wind will catch both surfaces. There will be much fluttering of canvas but little or no forward drive. There will be none of the consequences of a gybe, because the forward edge of each sail is rigidly held to either mast or forestay. To obtain forward drive the sheets must be trimmed until the flutter disappears. As the sail is trimmed, the flutter gradually disappears. The leading edge or *luff* retains the flutter longest, hence a fluttering sail is said to be *luffing*.

On this point of sailing, with the mainsail well sheeted in, the force on the after side will have two components. One component will drive the boat forward (Fig. 16-9), while the other produces leeway and heel.

The situation at the jib is somewhat more complicated. Wind caught by the jib will be deflected into the slot between the sails, and with the proper trim the air rushing through this narrow opening will create a suction on the forward face of the main. This suction will act to pull the boat forward, just as suction at the top surface of an airplane wing creates a lift that is larger than the force of pressure from below. As the jib is trimmed in harder the slot narrows until the jib begins to direct the airstream against the forward surface of the mainsail. When the main is thus *backwinded*, suction is reduced and drive decreases.

If a boat is headed too close to the wind for a given set of the sails, they will begin to flutter along the luffs. Luffing reduces forward drive and should be eliminated, either by easing the boat to a course farther off the wind or by trimming the sails a little flatter. Changes in wind direction may require rather frequent adjustments of the sheets to keep the sails drawing well without luffing.

On a reach the boat must be sailed a few degrees closer to the wind than the desired course. Leeway from the side thrust on the sails is only partially prevented by the keel or centerboard. Only experience with a particular boat will teach the helmsman the amount of allowance that must be made for leeway.

Side pressure will also produce a considerable heel while reaching in a brisk breeze. This is an exhilarating point of sailing, but if heel becomes excessive, there is danger of a *knockdown,* which is a heel of 90 degrees. A knockdown puts mast and sail in the water and presents some difficulties, if not dangers. In a small boat some heel can be counteracted by having the crew *hike,* which is to lean out over the weather rail. On larger boats where hiking has less effect, excessive heel is reduced by sailing the boat a little closer into the wind (*heading up*) or by starting the sheets slightly. If excessive heeling continues, the sail area must be reduced by *reefing* or by changing sails.

## 16.08    Close-hauled

A well-designed boat will sail within about 45 degrees of the wind by *strapping down,* or trimming all sails hard in toward the line of the keel, Fig. 16-10. In this condition she is sailing *close-hauled, hard on the wind,* or simply *on the wind.* A ship sailing as close to the wind as possible, with every sail full, but not attempting to make a particular course, is sailing *full and by.*

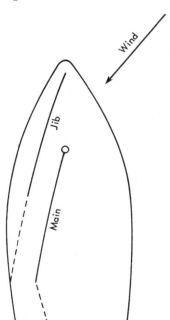

**FIGURE 16-10** A sloop close-hauled on the starboard tack. The jib shown slightly overlaps the main. A large Genoa may extend as far aft as the clew of the main, greatly increasing the slot effect.

As the sails are trimmed in going from a reach to close-hauled, less of the force goes into forward drive and more into producing leeway. Close-hauled the boat will gain ground to windward, but she may be sluggish and will not make the speed obtainable when she is sailed slightly farther off the wind. It is frequently worthwhile to sail somewhat more off the wind to maintain speed or *footing*, rather than to sacrifice speed to gain position to windward.

Because of the large force producing leeway and heel, the helmsman sailing close-hauled must be extremely alert to avoid a knockdown in a strong wind or a sudden puff. If a knockdown is averted by *heading up* too much or too long in a strong puff of wind, all way may be lost. With the boat dead in the water, rudder action is lost so there is no longer any control of the boat's heading. A puff of wind may then strike hard and suddenly from sufficiently abeam to produce a knockdown, and with rudder action lost there is no way of parrying by heading up. To avert this danger, *a sailboat should have steerage way on at all times*.

Sheets should not be permanently secured or *belayed* to cleats because it may be imperative to release them quickly to avoid a knockdown. Starting the sheets, especially the main, will instantly annul the effects of a strong puff. The boat will quickly *stand up* as the wind meets the sails at a more acute angle. As with heading up, however, the boat will lose way rapidly, and the sheets must be quickly retrimmed to keep her moving and thus retain control of the direction in which she is sailing.

It is prudent to *shorten sail* when frequent parrying is required to avoid excessive heel or a knockdown. The jib may be replaced by one of a smaller size, or may be removed completely. If the boat continues to be hard pressed, the main must be reefed. In older days reefing was always accomplished by lashing the lower portion of the sail into a bundle on top of the boom. A row of short pieces of line, or *reef points*, were put into the sail parallel to the foot by the sailmaker, Fig. 16-6. Double and sometimes triple sets of reef points were usually provided so that the main could be drastically shortened in a heavy blow. *Roller reefing* gear has recently become more popular as it has been made available in larger and larger sizes. In roller reefing a crank-driven gear mechanism rotates the boom so that the sail is wound around it much like a window-shade roller. Even in a heavy sea one man can pay out the main halyard to lower sail as he simultaneously winds the lower part of the sail around the boom.

## 16.09   Tacking

No sailboat can proceed directly into the wind, so a series of *tacks* or *boards* must be used if the course to be made good is close to the wind. One will sail close-hauled or perhaps on a close reach for a convenient distance and will then *come about* on the other tack. In coming about the bow of the boat passes through the eye of the wind, and all the sails may swing over to the other side with considerable clatter; but there will be none of the devastating effects that may accompany a gybe.

The helmsman alerts the crew for a change in tack by the cry "ready about." When all is in readiness, the helmsman will cry "hard-a-lee" and will start to bring the boat's head up toward the wind. With sufficient crew on board, one man will trim the mainsheet as the boat heads up, in order to keep her sailing as long as possible. As soon as the wind comes in over the opposite bow, the mainsheet will be started until the desired point of sailing is attained. A working jib will swing over to the new tack without attention, but a large overlapping Genoa must be *walked around* the mast and shrouds by a crew member as the boat comes up into the wind. Boats may be tacked without trimming the mainsheet as described, but the simpler maneuver is somewhat less seamanlike.

In coming about a boat passes through a point where all forward drive is lost, with both sails luffing as they head directly into the wind. At this point the boat must have sufficient way on to provide steerage so that she will continue on around to the new tack. If steerage is lost, the boat will remain headed directly into the wind where she is said to be *in stays* or *in irons*. While in stays a boat is vulnerable to a sudden puff of wind from abeam, so she must be gotten to footing again at once. When caught in stays, she will actually begin to move backward because of the wind pressure directly on the bow. There will then be some rudder action, but it will be in the opposite direction to that associated with forward motion. The helmsman puts the rudder, say to port, which with the backward motion will throw the bow to starboard. If now the jib is forcefully pushed to port, it will assist in turning the boat off the wind, whereupon the sails can be trimmed and the rudder put over to starboard. Now drive by the sails will halt the backward motion and start her forward on a port tack. If this is not the tack desired, another attempt to come about can be made when she is judged to be moving with sufficient speed.

## 16.10   Heavy-weather Sailing

The definition of heavy weather must be very flexible, for the effect of wind and sea will depend largely on the size and type of boat involved. Conditions that will send small, open day-sailors to cover may be only smart sailing weather to a heavy cruising boat. Auxiliaries only about 20 feet loa have been sailed single-handed across the Atlantic, and during the passage they have weathered storms of considerable strength. Properly handled, a well-built boat in good condition can survive weather that will exhaust the crew from the constant battering, seasickness, and the situation's general tension.

As wind and sea rise, sail must be reduced by removing the jib and reefing the main. Sailing into the wind now may cause too much pounding and strain on hull and crew. Sailing with the seas abeam is extremely uncomfortable and may be dangerous; excessive rolling may dip the end of the boom into the water. Although neither of the authors has experienced the events to which this leads, such conditions are obviously very serious, for the boat will try to pivot about the buried boom and sail and may suffer a knockdown in the process. The chance of catching the boom can be reduced by carrying it high and parrying the biggest seas on the forward quarter.

If the boat continues to be hard-pressed under reefed main alone, the time has come to set the storm sails. The storm jib is simply a small sail hanked to the jib stay in the usual way. The storm trisail is a small sail set high on the mainmast, Fig. 16-6. Since the boom is not used with the trisail, it will be brought amidships and lashed down securely. The loose-footed trisail is sheeted well aft with a double sheet arrangement similar to that used with a Genoa.

Careful consideration now must be given to the future course of action. The original sailing plan is of secondary importance: the chief concern now is the comfort and safety of the crew and the vessel. It is tempting to run for shelter, but this may not be the preferred course of action.

Harbors to windward now are out of the question; boat and crew would suffer too much damage beating into the seas to reach there. Harbors to leeward are acceptable if they can *surely* be entered with the weather at least as bad as that being experienced. Remember that under storm conditions boat performance may be so reduced that maneuvers that are simple in mild weather become impossible. If there is any question about entering a leeward harbor, it should not be attempted. A good boat and crew will survive if they have sea room, but may not if they run aground on a beach or are carried onto a rocky shore.

On a run to leeward the helmsman must be constantly on the alert to prevent *broaching*. Each overtaking sea must run squarely under the stern, and any tendency to yaw must be counteracted immediately. This will be easier to do than with the usual power cruiser because of the smaller target presented by the sailboat transom and because of the more deeply buried rudder. Every effort should be made to avoid a gybe even though there is no boom outboard with the storm trisail.

If the storm continues to rise so that it becomes increasingly difficult to avoid broaching, it will be necessary to *heave-to*. In heaving-to the helmsman watches for the most favorable, or perhaps the least unfavorable, condition of wind and sea and *quickly* brings the boat's head into the wind. Both jib and trisail are sheeted in hard, and the tiller is lashed somewhat to leeward, the best point being determined by trial and error. The boat will now start to sail into the wind, but as soon as she makes a little way, rudder action will head her up, and way will be lost. She will lie reasonably quietly, losing surprisingly little headway. She can now look after herself without constant attention from the crew. The latter will do well to go below and attend to their own needs for food and warmth, for even worse conditions may lie ahead.

In a long hard blow the seas may rise to a point where lying hove-to is no longer safe. The boat may be tossed about so violently as to threaten destruction. Under these conditions there is nothing left but to *run for it*. As the name suggests, this means running before the wind, either with bare poles or with a small amount of jib set to provide an orienting and steering force well forward. To run safely she must run slowly, so that the seas do not break directly over her but rush past on either side. A big sea anchor, heavy lines, or anything available must be streamed astern to reduce headway.

Tending either helm or sea anchor will be heavy work which should be relieved regularly, for each of these jobs requires prompt, positive action to avoid broaching. An assignment to either of these two duties should not exceed 30 minutes. A well-built, well-found boat will survive even these extreme conditions. If the crew can persist, the boat can be brought safely through even very severe gales.

# CHAPTER 17
# Weather
# Forecasting

## 17.01   Information and Observation

Some of the somber discussions of the preceding chapters may suggest that the sailor risks his life from storm every time he leaves his mooring. In fact, severe storms are so rare and weather reporting so thorough that there is little excuse for the weekend cruiser to be out in extreme weather. The accuracy of weather forecasting improves rapidly as the time between forecast and fulfillment shortens, permitting on Friday afternoon a rather complete prediction of weekend conditions. Long-range forecasting is improving, but it still leaves much to be desired, so any plans for an extended cruise must include the possibility of encountering disagreeable, even dangerous conditions.

An increasing number of small boats are making relatively long passages from various ports on the East Coast of the United States to the Bahamas or to one of the islands in the West Indies. Each of these vessels will be at sea for times well beyond those for which any accurate weather forecast will be valid. Skippers making such passages may choose a time of year that will minimize the chance of encountering either a hurricane or a strong winter storm. However, even with this choice he will be dealing with probabilities, not certainties, and he should prepare accordingly.

Weather forecasting depends on combining local observations with information received from surrounding areas. The use of storm-tracking planes and the development of satellites instrumented for meteorological observations have greatly increased the amount of available information. Much of this information is transmitted regularly by commercial radio stations, which several times each day broadcast the weather forecasts prepared by the National Weather Service. In most boating areas these general forecasts are supplemented by special marine broadcasts with special bulletins if deteriorating weather conditions warrant.

Special mention should be made of the rapidly expanding network of radio transmitters operated by the National Weather Service, which is a part of the National Oceanic and Atmospheric Administration (NOAA). Each of

328

the stations in the network operates on a frequency of 162.55 MHz with FM transmission. This frequency is higher than those assigned to the commercial FM band, and hence it will not be accepted by the ordinary FM receiver. A considerable number of special FM receivers permanently tuned to the 162.55 MHz weather stations are now available. The VHF-FM band is almost free of interference from static, but it has a limited range—perhaps 50 miles under favorable circumstances. As the number of transmitters continues to grow, most of the coastal waters of the United States will be covered by the signals.

Each NWS transmitter operates continuously 24 hours a day with taped messages repeated every five to seven minutes. Tapes are updated every two to three hours as new information is received. When severe weather conditions are anticipated, routine transmissions are interrupted for special advisories.

Most of the boating hazards associated with bad weather come from disregarding authoritative information rather than from lacking it. It is common to see all sorts of small boats leaving shelter in the face of marginal or deteriorating conditions. Most of these craft do not get into serious trouble. On the other hand, there are too many cases in which swamped, capsized, or disabled boats are towed to safety by the Coast Guard or by other rescue vessels. Each boatman should know the expected weather patterns and should act prudently in accordance with this knowledge.

Man has had unlimited opportunities to study weather patterns, yet few have observed with care, and fewer yet have understood the meaning of what they have seen. The recognition of weather signs and their translation into future probabilities have been the subject of many books. Here, we can do no more than point out some of the basic factors, common conditions, and simple clues, which if properly interpreted can supplement information obtained by radio from professional forecasters working with data from large areas of the earth.

## 17.02    Insolation

In the last analysis the changing environmental conditions we call weather result from the large-scale interchange of energy between land, sea, air, and water vapor. The tremendous energy content of a hurricane is well known; less obvious, but of much greater importance, is the continuous exchange of energy between liquid and gaseous water.

Practically all of the energy received on earth comes from our sun. Rays from the sun travel through empty space with little energy loss, and only a small fraction of the available energy is absorbed by the earth's atmosphere. The surface of the earth, on the other hand, either land or water, absorbs a large fraction of the solar energy falling on it. This process of heat transfer to the earth is known as *insolation*.

On a hot summer day, with equal insolations the temperature of land surfaces will rise well above the surface temperatures of adjacent water areas. In the first place, land surfaces absorb more and reflect less solar energy than water. In addition water has a very large *heat capacity*, a characteristic which enables it to absorb relatively large quantities of energy with little rise in temperature. The heat capacity of land is relatively low. Finally, wave motions will mix the warm, upper-water layers with cooler, deeper layers to reduce the surface temperature.

As the sun goes down in the afternoon and insolation decreases, the hot land surfaces will radiate energy to the air above them. The air will be heated, will expand, and rise. As the hot air rises, it will pull in underneath itself the cooler air from over the water, thus creating the well-known *onshore* breeze of the late afternoon, Fig. 17-1A.

During the night both land and sea will radiate energy, with the land cooling more rapidly because of its lower heat capacity. By morning the sea may be warmer than the land, a situation that will produce an *offshore* breeze by a reversal of the afternoon conditions, Fig. 17-1B.

When heat absorbed by the earth is radiated to the air above, the lower layers receive the most energy and hence become warmer than the air at higher altitude. This leads to the well-known decrease in air temperature with altitude above the earth's surface. The rate at which temperature decreases with altitude is known as the *lapse rate*. Lapse rates are somewhat variable, and there may actually be an *inversion*, where for a time temperature may increase with increasing altitude. An average lapse rate of about 3.3° F for each 1,000 feet of altitude will obtain in most cases. This lapse rate will continue through the *troposphere* up to altitudes of 35,000-50,000 feet. Here, in the *tropopause*, temperatures are relatively constant as altitude increases. At extreme altitudes, in the *stratosphere*, temperature has little meaning, because there is little matter out there with which to define a temperature. This region has no immediate significance for us since surface weather is generated primarily in the troposphere.

**FIGURE 17-1** (A) An onshore breeze is formed by air rising over the heated land area. (B) A morning offshore breeze is the result of an uplift over the warmer water.

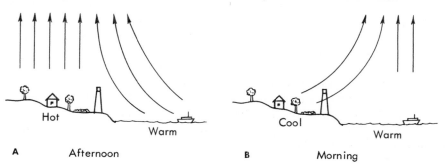

## 17.03    Humidity

Except for man-made impurities our atmosphere is composed primarily of oxygen, nitrogen, and argon, which are gases under normal conditions, and water, which may be present as a gas, liquid, or solid. All free air contains some water, but on a clear day we are not aware of it because it is all in the gas phase and is, therefore, invisible. Clouds consist of water vapor which has *condensed* out of the gas phase to form many tiny droplets. This condensation usually takes place around minute dust particles which are found throughout our atmosphere. A further condensation of the minute droplets into larger drops leads to rain or some other form of *precipitation* when the drops become too large to remain suspended. Fog, the bane of the boatman's existence, is essentially a cloud formed at the surface of the earth instead of at high altitude.

Air can contain any amount of water in gas form, up to a certain limit determined by the temperature. When air contains as much water as it can hold, it is said to be *saturated*, or to have a *relative humidity* of 100 percent. Air containing one half of the saturation amount of water has a relative humidity of 50 percent, and so on. The amount of water held at saturation increases with the temperature.

When a quantity of air is heated, the relative humidity will decrease because the amount of water vapor then present will be a smaller fraction of the capacity. Conversely, cooling air will raise its relative humidity. If the cooling continues to the saturation point, vapor will begin to condense to a liquid which will separate from the air as precipitation. The temperature at which condensation occurs is known as the *dew point*. The dew point will depend on the amount of water vapor originally present in the air before it was cooled. Condensation will also take place when sufficient moisture has been added to an air mass at constant temperature.

The mariner is interested in the difference between the temperature actually existing and the temperature of the dew point, because this difference can be used to estimate the chance of future fog formation. This temperature difference, known as the *dew point difference*, can be determined in a variety of ways.

A *hair hygrometer* will give an indication of the relative humidity. This instrument is based on the fact that blond human hair stretches as the relative humidity increases and shrinks as the surrounding air dries. A hair hygrometer is not a precision instrument, but when carefully constructed, it has a sufficient accuracy for present purposes. With a knowledge of the relative humidity, the dew point difference can be determined from tables or from a curve, Fig. 17-2. Strictly, a different curve should be used for each air temperature, but the single curve illustrated will suffice for all ordinary boating conditions.

### ILLUSTRATIVE EXAMPLE

Assume a relative humidity of 72 percent as measured with a hair hygrometer. How close are conditions to the dew point?

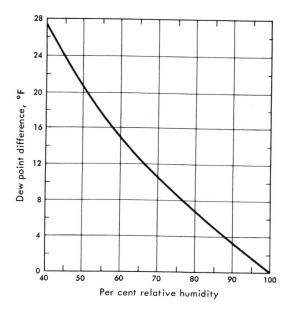

**FIGURE 17-2** The relation between relative humidity and dew point difference.

We enter the baseline of Fig. 17-2 at 72 and move up vertically until we reach the curve. Moving over horizontally until we cut the vertical scale, we find a dew point difference of 9° F. If the present air mass cools 9° F, we thus reach the dew point, and fog may be expected.

Relative humidity is determined more accurately with a *wet-bulb and dry-bulb thermometer,* or by a *sling psychrometer,* Fig. 17-3. Either of these two instruments consists of two thermometers, one an ordinary dry bulb which measures air temperature. The other has a cotton tube or wick surrounding the bulb. When the wick is wet with *fresh* water, evaporation will cool the wet bulb, which will then read less than the dry bulb. With a low relative humidity, evaporation will be rapid, and the difference between the readings of the two thermometers will be large. If the relative humidity is 100 percent, there will be no evaporation, and the readings will be equal. The wet bulb will never read higher than the dry. The sling psychrometer is merely a design in which the two thermometers are whirled rapidly before reading to insure maximum rate of evaporation.

**FIGURE 17-3** A sling psychrometer for measuring relative humidity.

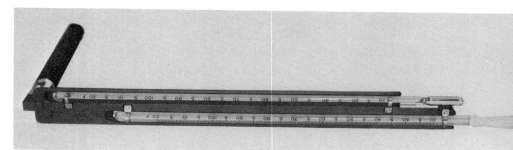

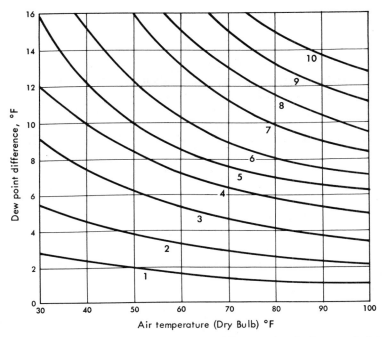

**FIGURE 17-4** Curves for determining dew point differences directly from wet-bulb and dry-bulb thermometer readings. Each curve corresponds to a given difference between the readings of a dry-bulb and a wet-bulb thermometer. This difference must be carefully distinguished from the dew point difference on the vertical scale.

Tables or curves may be used to determine the dew point and the dew point difference from the wet- and dry-bulb readings. Figure 17-4 may be used to obtain the dew point difference directly.

### ILLUSTRATIVE EXAMPLE

Assume sling psychrometer readings of: dry bulb 72° F, wet bulb 67° F. How close are conditions to the dew point?

The dry-bulb wet-bulb difference is $72 - 67 = 5°$ F. We enter the baseline of Fig. 17-4 at 72 and move vertically upward until we reach curve 5. Moving horizontally from this point to the left-hand scale, we find a dew point difference of 7.5° F. The interpretation of this value is as before.

## 17.04   Radiation Fog

Condensation of water droplets onto surfaces that have been cooled to or below the dew point produces dew. The mariner is more interested in condensation where the droplets remain suspended in the air to form *radiation fog*. This type of fog is less frequently encountered than some others, but the mariner should learn to recognize it, because it provides some valuable forecasting information.

On a clear night the surface of the earth, both land and sea, will radiate heat to the air above and to the depths of space. Temperatures of the earth's surface and of the air layers immediately above it will drop rapidly, possibly reaching the dew point by midnight or a bit later. At this point, water vapor will condense into droplets which remain suspended to produce fog. The only difference between fog and a cloud is the altitude at which they are formed.

A strong breeze will prevent the formation of radiation fog by a violent mixing of the lower, cold layers of air with the warmer, upper layers, thus preventing cooling to the dew point. A gentle breeze will mix only a few hundred feet, producing a fog which is thin from the aviator's viewpoint, but which is thick enough to obscure vision at the mariner's level.

On land radiation fog is known as *ground fog*. Since the coldest air is the heaviest, it will flow down into the lowest areas to form fog first, thus giving rise to the feeling that the fog hugs the ground.

Radiation fog disappears, lifts, or burns off when the sun warms the earth the next day. As heat is absorbed by the earth, it is radiated to the lower fog layers. When these warm above the dew point, the liquid droplets return to the invisible vapor state, and the fog disappears progressively from below upwards.

Radiation fog is characterized by:

(1) Clear skies, probably due to remain for the next 12-18 hours at least.
(2) Gentle winds offering no threat to a small boat.
(3) Short duration. Radiation fog will disappear by noon, usually several hours earlier. This is in contrast to other fog types which may persist for several days.

## 17.05    Wind Strengths

Wind speeds are commonly measured either in mph or in knots. A measure known as *wind force* is known as the Beaufort scale after the admiral who developed it. Table 17-1 lists the comparative scales together with a brief description of the accompanying sea conditions and the expected wave heights. The listed sea and wave conditions can be only approximate, because the actual conditions will depend on other factors such as the length of time the

**TABLE 17-1**

**Wind and Sea Relations**

| Wind Speed (knots) | Wind Force Beaufort | Description | Wave Hgt. (feet) | Sea Conditions |
|---|---|---|---|---|
| 0–1 | 0 | Calm | | Smooth, mirrorlike |
| 1–3 | 1 | Light air | ¼ | Small ripples |
| 4–6 | 2 | Light breeze | ½ | Small wavelets, smooth crests |
| 7–10 | 3 | Gentle breeze | 2 | Wavelets, some crests break, foam |
| 11–16 | 4 | Moderate breeze | 4 | Small waves, some foamy crests |
| 17–21 | 5 | Fresh breeze | 6 | Moderate waves, many foamy crests |
| 22–27 | 6 | Strong breeze | 10 | Large waves, spray |
| 28–33 | 7 | Near gale | 14 | Streaks of foam, spindrift |
| 34–40 | 8 | Gale | 18 | Higher, longer waves, spindrift |
| 41–47 | 9 | Strong gale | 22 | Breaking crests, spray |
| 48–55 | 10 | Storm | 27 | Sea all white, curling crests |
| 56–63 | 11 | Storm | 30 | Very high waves, low visibility |
| 64– | 12 | Hurricane | | Indescribable confused seas |

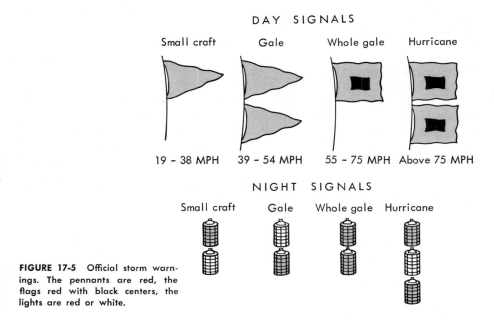

FIGURE 17-5 Official storm warnings. The pennants are red, the flags red with black centers, the lights are red or white.

wind has been blowing and the *fetch*, or the unobstructed distance exposed to it.

When a prediction of heavy weather has been made by the NWS, the appropriate storm signal will be displayed at various Coast Guard stations, yacht clubs, and other designated locations. The small-boat skipper should both learn where these signals are displayed in his locality and look for them before leaving port. Storm signals are displayed in one of four degrees of severity.

*Small-craft advisory:* One red pennant by day; one red light vertically over one white light at night, Fig. 17-5. Displayed when the forecast calls for winds up to 33 knots (38 mph) or when sea conditions dangerous to small-craft operation, or both, are predicted.

*Gale warning:* Two red pennants vertically displayed by day; one white light vertically above one red light by night. Displayed when the forecast calls for winds of 34-47 knots (39-54 mph).

*Storm warning:* One square red flag with a black center by day; two vertically arranged red lights by night. Displayed when winds ranging 48-63 knots (55-73 mph) are forecast.

*Hurricane warning:* Two square red flags with black centers displayed vertically by day; one white light between two red lights, vertically arranged, by night. Displayed when winds of more than 64 knots (74 mph) are forecast.

Storm signals are not displayed for a transient disturbance, such as a summer thunderstorm, even though the winds might be expected to reach gale force. When storm signals are displayed, it is evidence that a prolonged and widespread disturbance has been forecast.

## 17.06   Cold Front

The sun's rays are not spread uniformly over the surface of the earth, because of its curvature and the tilt of the axis, Fig. 17-6. With this uneven heating large air masses may acquire quite different temperatures. The line separating a cold-air mass from a warm mass is called a *front*. A front may be *stationary*, but in general, differences in atmospheric pressure will cause one air mass to advance into the other. A moving front is named after the advancing mass. Thus a *cold front* refers to a situation in which a cold-air mass is forcing its way into a mass of warmer air.

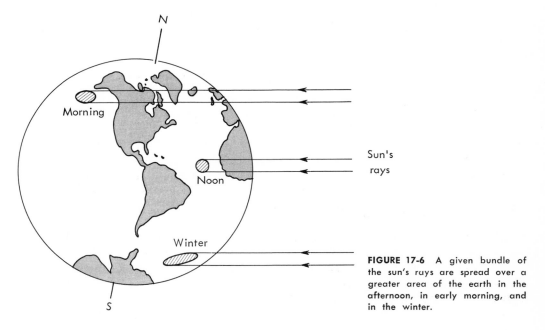

FIGURE 17-6   A given bundle of the sun's rays are spread over a greater area of the earth in the afternoon, in early morning, and in the winter.

Cold air, being heavier, will drive itself as a wedge underneath the lighter warm air, Fig. 17-7. Several forces act to make the frontal surface of separation rather steep as shown. This steep surface forces warm, moist air rapidly upward, causing it to cool. When the lifted air is cooled to the dew point, clouds will form as the water vapor condenses. These clouds will be *cumulus:* clouds with a vertical structure rather than a horizontal layering. Cold-front cumulus clouds may have quite flat bases as they abruptly reach the altitude of the dew point.

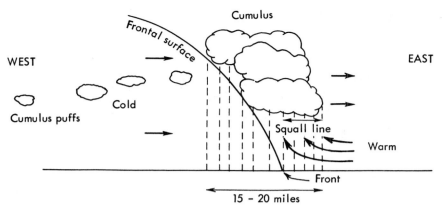

**FIGURE 17-7** The advance of a cold air mass. The steep frontal surface pushes warm moist air violently upward.

The violent upthrust at the front may leave a region of low pressure beneath into which warm moist air will rush, frequently at very high velocity. This produces a confused, turbulent wind pattern just ahead of the front. This region of turbulence, known as the *squall line*, has been experienced by all boatmen just prior to a frontal passage. The squall line will be promptly followed by violent showers or thundershowers from the rapidly condensed moisture in the lifted air.

A typical line squall may last for 20-30 minutes as the front moves past at perhaps 20-30 knots. Note that this is the velocity with which the front is advancing; wind velocities in the squall may be much higher. This is not sufficient time to kick up a violent sea, but the confused wind patterns and the high velocities may present a threat to small boats. A squall line appears as a long line of dark, ominous-looking clouds, with cumulus heads towering to great heights. The rumble of thunder will usually accompany the squall.

Small boats will do well to seek shelter when this display is seen. Sailboats cannot hope to sail effectively with the turbulent winds in a heavy squall. All sail should be lowered and secured until the squall has passed.

Cold-front passage will be marked by an abrupt drop in temperature, the end of heavy rainfall, and the appearance of isolated cottonlike cumulus clouds indicative of fair weather. There will be an abrupt shift of the wind at the frontal passage, usually from the south or southwest into the northwest.

## 17.07  Warm Front

When the push is behind a mass of warm air, it will ride up and over a wedge of the retreating colder, heavier air. The slope of a warm front wedge is much gentler than that of a cold front, which permits a warm front to announce its coming many hours in advance, Fig. 17-8.

The thin front edge of the advancing warm air may be at an altitude of 30,000 feet perhaps 800 miles in advance of the ground-level portion of the

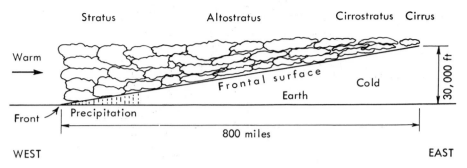

**FIGURE 17-8** Advancing warm air rises slowly along a frontal surface. Clouds precede the actual front by hundreds of miles.

front. Temperatures at the high altitude will be well below freezing so that all of the moisture in the leading edge will be frozen into tiny ice crystals. These ice crystals produce the high *cirrus* clouds which are sometimes so thin as to be almost invisible from the ground.

As the warm front advances at perhaps 15-20 knots, the warm-air wedge thickens, and the clouds become heavier and lower. Cirrus clouds will be followed by *cirrostratus, altostratus,* and *stratus,* in succession. The use of the word stratus in each of the cloud forms indicates a horizontal layering rather than the vertical structure of a cumulus. Warm-front clouds cover large areas, but the winds lack the violence associated with a cold front.

Rain may start falling 6-10 hours before the frontal passage. Rain will be steady, less violent than the downpour that accompanies a cold-front squall, and can be expected to continue until the front passes. As the front passes, there will be an abrupt wind shift, typically from the northwest to the south-west or south.

Warm fronts are, then, associated with a protracted spell of disagreeable weather seldom dangerous to small craft. In contrast, a cold front carries heavy winds and rain, but is soon past.

## 17.08   Uplift Thunderstorms

A thunderstorm need not be associated with a cold-front passage; any process by which large masses of moist air are thrust upward will serve. On a very hot day, for example, the land surfaces may reach extreme temperatures. The resulting heating and expansion of the air sets up strong vertical currents. Moist air will be carried rapidly to high altitudes where it will condense to liquid or even freeze to fall as hail in addition to the drenching rain.

Uplift thunderstorms usually occur in the late afternoon or early evening when heating is maximum. These storms will be relatively small, isolated events in contrast to the line of storms accompanying a cold front. When the frontal storm passes, there will be a drop in temperature as the cold air moves in.

Conditions after an uplift thunderstorm will be about as hot and humid as before.

Each thunderstorm type has high winds blowing in a confusion of directions and is equally dangerous to small craft. Powerboats should prepare for a heavy blow or should seek shelter; sailboats should douse all canvas before the first blast to await clearing with bare poles.

A less violent uplift may produce clouds and perhaps brief showers without a thunderstorm's extreme conditions. An island mass the size of the Hawaiian Islands, for example, is large enough to produce a vertical uplift from the heating of the land. Moisture-laden air moving in from the oceans will be carried aloft to condense and produce the frequent, short rains typical of tropical islands. Island masses may sometimes be detected from the high-altitude cloud cover at distances well beyond the range of direct sighting of the land.

The Western mountain ranges in the United States give a strong vertical uplift to the moisture-laden air coming from over the Pacific. Frequent precipitation will occur on the western side of the ranges while the eastern slopes will be almost deserts, being exposed to air that has already deposited all of its moisture.

## 17.09    Cloud Identification

Clouds are observed in such an infinite variety of forms that exact classification is for the expert. The small-boat sailor cannot hope, and does not need to make, precise cloud identification. It is, however, quite feasible to learn enough of the basic types to make a good estimate of cloud origins, and thus to make some forecast of future developments.

We have already referred to the basic classification of *cumulus* for clouds with vertical development, and *stratus* for clouds composed of horizontal layers. Combined forms will usually be seen, and the combinations will be reflected in the names. When a cloud is a potential or actual source of precipitation *nimbus-* or *nimbo-* may be added to its designation.

Clouds with an essentially horizontal development may be classified according to their heights as *low* or $L$ (below 7,000 feet), *middle* or $M$ (between 7,000 and 20,000 feet), and *high* or $H$ (above 20,000 feet). Strongly developed cumulus clouds may extend into all of these regions. To simplify reporting, cloud types are coded according to an international agreement. Some of the standard types are illustrated in Fig. 17-9 with their code designations.

Isolated *cumulus* clouds, $L1$, Fig. 17-9, are usually seen after the passage of a storm. They have little vertical development and are indicative of fair weather.

One of the many forms assumed by *stratocumulus* clouds is illustrated by $L4$. These clouds, formed by a spreading and intensifying of the isolated cumulus, may occur as long, heavy rolls or gray bands covering a large portion of the sky. Still heavier cloud cover may follow.

L4

LI

L7

L9

M3

**FIGURE 17-9** Cloud patterns with International type-designations. Descriptions are given in the text. Courtesy of National Weather Service.

M6

H4

H8

H9

**FIGURE 17-9** (Cont.)

Heavy, broken masses of cumulus, called *fractocumulus*, L7, indicate the imminent approach of bad weather. Wind and heavy rain can be anticipated.

A well-developed *cumulonimbus* or thunderhead, L9, will be accompanied by strong turbulence and heavy rain. The photograph shows a flat base where the rising air is cooled to the dew point.

A typical middle cloud formation, *altocumulus*, M3, is shown covering a large portion of the sky at an almost constant altitude. This pattern usually changes slowly, but it may thicken and be followed by precipitation.

Another type of *altocumulus*, M6, is formed from a heavy cumulus cover.

This type of cloud should be watched closely as it may lead to worsening weather.

A typical *cirrus* cloud, *H*4, tends to become denser and to lower, eventually leading to precipitation.

A cirrus cloud has thickened to form a *cirrostratus, H*8, covering a large portion of the sky.

A relatively thick development at high altitude produces a *cirrocumulus* cloud, *H*9. The flecks of cloud interspersed with open sky give this type the name *mackerel* sky. This cloud type is apt to be well in advance of approaching precipitation.

Cloud types should be studied and classified at every opportunity, ashore or afloat, and associated with past and subsequent weather patterns. There is rarely a lack of material for study.

## 17.10    Barometric Pressure

We live at the bottom of an ocean of air, and as a consequence we must support the weight of the air above us. We are not conscious of this pressure because all of the body cavities are exposed to the same pressure. Hence our bodies are not exposed to a collapsing pressure as an empty, evacuated container would be.

Atmospheric pressure is measured with some sort of a *barometer*. In the crude mercury column instrument illustrated in Fig. 17-10, the open end of an evacuated tube is dipped into a dish of mercury. Atmospheric pressure acting on the free surface will force mercury up the tube until the upward force is just balanced by the weight of the mercury in the column. As the pressure changes, the height of the column which it will support will also change, and so this

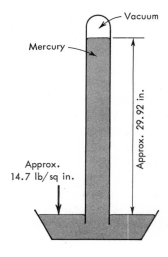

Vacuum

Mercury

Approx. 29.92 in.

Approx. 14.7 lb/sq in.

**FIGURE 17-10** A simple mercury barometer. Atmospheric pressure on the exposed surface forces mercury up into the evacuated tube.

height can be used as a measure of the pressure. This normal atmospheric pressure at sea level, about 14.7 pounds per square inch, will support a mercury column 29.92 inches or 76.0 centimeters high.

Mercury columns provide the most accurate means of measuring atmospheric pressure, and so it is customary to express all readings in either inches or centimeters. Professional meteorologists prefer to express atmospheric pressure in *millibars,* a pressure unit such that 29.92 inches of mercury equals 1,013.2 millibars, or mb.

Every boat used for extensive cruising should carry a good barometer, and while under way it should be read at regular intervals. A good barometer can provide valuable information on local conditions which, when combined with radio reports of distant conditions, will give a good insight into future prospects.

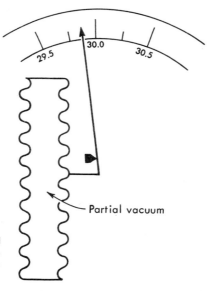

FIGURE 17-11  In    an    aneroid barometer the position of the bellows changes with changes in atmospheric pressure.

Small-boat barometers are almost always *aneroids,* Fig. 17-11. A partially evacuated metal bellows expands and contracts with changes in atmospheric pressure. A system of multiplying levers converts the slight bellows movements into motions of a pointer across a scale. Temperature changes will also cause the bellows to change its volume and hence the instrument must be carefully temperature compensated if its readings are to depend on pressure only. A shipboard barometer must be of good quality if its readings are to be useful.

Trends in barometric pressure are of greater significance in forecasting than a single isolated reading. A recording barometer, or *barograph,* provides a continuous record of atmospheric pressure on a paper chart attached to a revolving drum. A reliable barograph can relieve a crew of the duty of reading and recording the barometer at regular intervals.

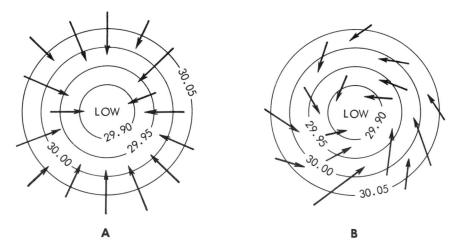

**FIGURE 17-12** (A) An idealized low-pressure area on a stationary earth, showing the inflow of air across the isobars. (B) On a rotating earth the inflow tends to line up along the isobars. The latter are idealized here for simplicity.

## 17.11   Low-pressure Systems

In the temperate zone a variety of meteorological conditions may combine to produce an area of low barometric pressure, which may have a diameter of from 200 to 1,000 miles. Air from the surrounding high-pressure areas will flow into the low in an attempt to equalize pressures. On a stationary earth the inward movement would be directly across the lines of equal pressure or *isobars*, Fig. 17-12A. In the Northern Hemisphere the earth's rotation will deflect the inward flow into a counterclockwise spiral motion called a *cyclone*, Fig. 17-12B. Rotation in the Southern Hemisphere will be clockwise.

Some of the air spiraling inward will be lifted, to cool and condense water vapor into precipitation. A cyclone is thus frequently accompanied by rain, almost always by clouds. A cyclonic system will generally move from west to east with perhaps a northerly or southerly component at perhaps 20-25 knots. Winds near the center of the low may be considerably greater than this speed of advance, so small-boat skippers will do well to keep track of these disturbances.

One of the first signs of an approaching low is a falling barometer. Pressure will drop, slowly at first, and then more rapidly as the center nears. When the center passes, the barometer will begin to rise.

The center of a low can be roughly located from the peripheral wind direction. If one faces into a cyclonic wind, the center of the low will be slightly more than 90 degrees around to his right. This is the origin of the old saying, "Face the wind and the storm center will be in your right hip pocket." There will be an abrupt change in wind direction as the center of a low passes, the exact sequence depending on the position of the observer with respect to the center. A study of Fig. 17-12B will show some of the possibilities.

## 17.12    High-pressure Systems

When a region of high pressure exists, the air contained in it will start to flow outward to equalize the pressure with the surroundings. As in a low, the earth's rotation will act to change the radial outflow to a spiral motion. In the Northern Hemisphere the outward spiral from a high will be clockwise; in the Southern Hemisphere it will be counterclockwise. The high-pressure system, or *anticyclone*, may extend over many hundreds of miles. The system will generally move at 10-15 knots. The prevailing direction of movement in the United States is toward the east, with either a northerly or southerly component.

An anticyclone may bring brisk but not gale winds. Precipitation is not associated with a high. In a high any vertical air flow will be downward as air from aloft tends to keep the high filled. As this air descends, it will warm, clouds will disappear as the dew point is passed, and the weather will be generally fine. The barometer will rise as the system approaches, steady, and then fall slightly as the system moves on.

A study of Fig. 17-13 reveals the sequence of wind directions to be expected with the passage of a high. The circular motion will bring in air from great distances to affect the local temperature. Thus a high located to the west will bring in masses of air from the north, and a cooling trend is to be expected. Conversely a southerly flow will be associated with a high that has moved on to the east. This pumping action is intensified in the region between a well-developed high and a low because the effects of the two counter-rotating systems will be additive.

**FIGURE 17-13**    An idealized (A) and an actual (B) high-pressure system on a rotating earth.

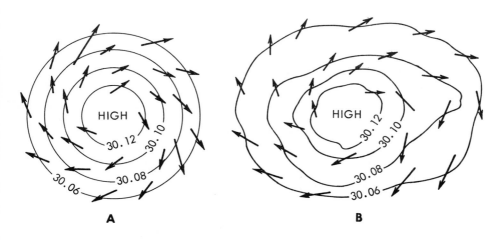

## 17.13   Cyclones

The development of a low-pressure system deserves more consideration, because it carries a threat of disagreeable, even dangerous weather. In particular, a cyclonic system may well develop at the line of demarcation between a cold-air and a warm-air mass.

We have previously pictured a front as a rather smooth surface separating two masses of air at different temperatures. This smooth separation is seldom observed. In particular there may be intrusions of one air mass into the other. Again, at one point the warm mass may be the more energetic, producing a warm front; at another point the cold air may be the aggressor, as a result of local pressure variations.

Figure 17-14 shows an intrusion with warm and cold fronts which has developed into a cyclonic disturbance. A wedge of warm air with SW winds is shown pushing into a cold-air mass, forming a warm front. On the western side of the wedge a cold front has formed as cold air pushes underneath. Note that in the diagram the fronts are designated by the symbols used by the NWS on its official maps.

As the warm, moist air is pushed from behind, it will be squeezed upward and cooled. The system will be a cyclone because the winds will have a generally counterclockwise rotation around the vertex of the two fronts. Barometric pressure will be lowest at this point.

The two fronts shown in the diagram are actually the lines of separation of the air masses at the earth's surface. North of the vertex there is an *occluded* front formed by warm air that has been pushed up out of contact with the

**FIGURE 17-14** The formation of a cyclonic disturbance around an advancing mass of warm air penetrating into a cold air mass.

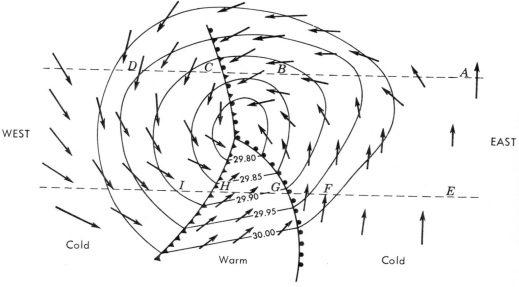

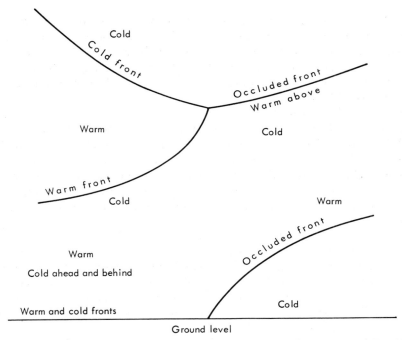

Cold

Cold front

Occluded front
Warm above

Warm

Cold

Warm front

Cold

Warm

Occluded front

Warm

Cold ahead and behind

Warm and cold fronts

Occluded front

Cold

Ground level

**FIGURE 17-15** A plan view and a vertical section of the cyclonic system of Fig. 17-14. A goodly portion of the warm air has been pushed aloft to form an occluded front.

earth by underlying cold air. The occluded-front line shown represents the points at which the warm air is closest to the ground, Fig. 17-15.

In a well-developed cyclone the typical lowering stratus clouds of a warm front will precede the front itself by many hours. Gentle warm-front rains may fall as the cloud deck lowers, and the isolated skipper may think that there is nothing ahead but a simple warm-front passage. In fact, he may be faced with some very nasty weather, the exact situation depending on his location with respect to the center of the disturbance.

## 17.14   Cyclonic Passage

Consider the sequence of events experienced by a vessel at point $A$ as the cyclonic disturbance of Fig. 17-14 moves due east. Initially the winds will be gentle, generally out of the south. Light cirrus or high cirrostratus clouds will cover a large portion of the sky. As the system advances the winds will shift successively from S to SE, E, and NE. This shift in a counterclockwise direction is known as *backing*. As the winds back, with little change in velocity, the cloud deck will lower, and at about $B$ the steady, gentle rain of a warm front will start to fall. The barometer has been dropping steadily as the system approached, but the drop was not precipitous. At point $C$, the trailing edge of the occluded warm-air mass, the rain may be heavy for a short time. It will not, however, approach the violence of a thunderstorm. Now the barometer will tend to be steady or to rise slightly, and at $D$ the skies will clear except for scattered fair-weather cumulus puffs. The wind will probably hold in the NW for at least 12 hours.

Now consider a vessel at $E$. As at $A$, winds are gentle from the south, cloud cover is high cirrus or cirrostratus. With the advance of the system, winds will shift slightly clockwise, or *veer*. At about $F$ warm-front rain will begin to fall, preceded by a lowering of the cloud deck. The barometer has been dropping slightly but steadily as the system advanced. At $G$ the wind will veer rather suddenly into the SW as the warm front passes. In a strong system there may be a distinct rise in temperature as the warm sector arrives at our point of observation.

With the arrival of the warm sector, rain may cease and the skies may tend to clear because of the increased capacity of the warm air to hold moisture. Better weather may seem to be ahead, but soon the dark, turbulent clouds of a squall line appear in the west. At $H$ all of the violence of a cold-front passage descends on the vessel. After 30 minutes or so the wind veers abruptly into the NW, the skies clear, and the barometer shows a definite tendency to rise. Better weather is ahead at last.

Although the picture presented here has been simplified, the actual sequence of events will differ only in detail. In general, the system will not pass directly from west to east, and the warm-front intrusion may have a different orientation than that illustrated. These variations will act to shift all wind directions somewhat from those given in the example. If the structure of a cyclonic disturbance is kept in mind, the sequence of events in any actual situation can be readily anticipated.

Note that the right hip-pocket rule can be used to good advantage throughout the passage of the system to locate the center of the disturbance. With this knowledge the weatherwise skipper can be prepared for future events well ahead of their arrival.

## 17.15   Advection Fog

Fog will be formed whenever air at the earth's surface is cooled below the dew point or when moisture is added to surface air to bring its relative humidity to 100 percent. If the dew point happens to be below the freezing point, 32° F, *frost* or *rime* may also be formed. The latter two forms of precipitation are of little interest to the average recreational boatman.

Radiation on a clear night has already been mentioned as one process by which air may be cooled to produce fog. *Advection,* or the horizontal movement of air masses, is a more common source of fogs which may be of much greater duration than those produced by radiation cooling. Two types of advection cooling and one method for adding moisture can be distinguished:

(1) The movement of cold air over a warm body of water: Evaporation of liquid water into vapor proceeds rapidly from a warm body of water, which will, therefore, have above itself air at a relatively high humidity. If now a cold-air mass moves in and mixes, the moisture-laden air may be cooled below its dew point to produce fog. This process does not depend on radiation cooling at night and warming by day, so advection fog produced by mixing may persist for many hours or days until more favorable wind conditions are established.

Perhaps the best example of this type of fog formation occurs as the Gulf Stream flows to the north and east along the East Coast of the United States. Water in the Gulf Stream is several degrees warmer than the surrounding waters, and the air above the stream will have a high relative humidity. As cooler air blows in and across the stream, a persistent advection fog can be formed.

As winter approaches, the water areas of the Arctic, because of their high heat capacity, are warmer than the land. Air moving from the land over the water will cause a persistent advection fog known as *Arctic smoke*.

(2) Warm, moist air may move into a cold area and be cooled below the dew point. This is the most common type of fog encountered in small-boat operation. This type of advection fog is best formed with winds of 3-12 knots. It may be of some comfort to the small-boat skipper to know that he will not simultaneously encounter heavy fog and high winds.

The famous California fogs are an example of this type of advection process. Warm, moist air from the Pacific moving eastward, encounters a cold southward-flowing current just off the California coast. Mixing and fog formation occur just offshore and may roll inland. At certain times of year the land surfaces may be cool enough to bring the incoming Pacific air down to the dew point, with the usual result.

Hundreds of fishermen have lost their lives because of advection fogs formed on the Grand Banks east of Newfoundland. Here the warm water of the Gulf Stream, flowing NE, meets the cold, south-flowing Labrador Current. As these two flows meet and mix, dense advection fog is formed. Advection fog thus formed may persist for weeks. The August 1963 pilot chart of the North Atlantic (Fig. 10-6) indicates fog 40 percent of the time on the Grand Banks.

(3) Fog also may form when moisture is added to a mass of air at a constant temperature. The best example of this is associated with the passage of a warm front. Gentle rain originating in the warm, uplifted air may fall into the lower, colder air, increasing its moisture content to the dew point. The raindrops may dissipate into the smaller droplets of fog, so the sailor at sea level experiences a dense fog rather than the rain taking place at higher alti-

tudes. This type of fog may persist as the warm front slowly passes. The heavier rains associated with the actual frontal passage will clear up warm-front fog.

## 17.16    Tropical Cyclones

The term *tropical cyclone* refers to those storms originating near the equator and moving generally northward, leaving a broad swath of destruction in their wake. Technically these storms are cyclones because of the counterclockwise spiraling winds around a low-pressure center. Tropical cyclones are enormously more powerful than the cyclonic storms of the midlatitudes. Known as hurricanes in the Atlantic, typhoons in the Pacific, tropical cyclones are the most destructive storms known to man.

The exact mechanism which leads to the formation of a tropical cyclone is not known. They originate over water as a small, low-pressure area which grows in size and intensity. Rain falls in incredible amounts, winds may reach 150 knots at the center, and may be at hurricane force (greater than 65 knots) 100 miles from the center. The hurricane winds are the result of an intense barometric pressure gradient, which may reach 2 inches in 150 miles. Sea-level pressures of less than 26.20 inches have been recorded at the center of intense storms.

When well established, the tropical cyclone will move in a path that can be only poorly predicted. In general, Atlantic hurricanes form in the West Indies, move northwesterly toward the Florida coast, and then veer to the northeast as they move up the coast toward New England. Tropical cyclones eventually dissipate their fury in the cool air of Canada or the Maritime Provinces. Typhoons in the western Pacific also tend to have a northwest to northeast course as they move against the coasts of Japan. There are many variations to the general pattern, and little reliance can be placed on long-range trajectory predictions. Modern methods of airplane tracking and satellite observations provide vastly better information than was available a few years ago.

A tropical hurricane usually moves forward at 20-30 knots, with many variations. The center may remain almost stationary for several hours or may suddenly speed up well above its average rate.

As with any low-pressure disturbance, the location of the hurricane center can be determined by the right hip-pocket rule. This knowledge may be of considerable importance; it will establish the vessel either in the right hand or "dangerous" semicircle or in the left hand or "navigable" semicircle. The words "dangerous" and "navigable" are relative; any point in the path of a tropical cyclone is dangerous and not necessarily navigable. There is, however, an advantage in being on the left-hand side of an advancing hurricane in the northern hemisphere. As an example, consider a hurricane with 100 knot winds moving forward at 25 knots. On the right side (as viewed from behind looking in the direction of progress), the two velocities will add since the storm as a whole is moving in the same direction as the spiraling winds. Because of this velocity addition, a stationary object will be subjected to winds of 125 knots. On the left side the two velocities will subtract, to produce an effective velocity of only 75 knots. This is still an extremely dangerous wind, but much to be preferred to 125 knots.

Radio reports are now the best advance notice of an advancing tropical cyclone. The first observable evidence will be the development of a long-wave-length groundswell in open waters. This swell was originally formed at the center of the disturbance and moved ahead much faster than the speed of the storm itself. A swell that has a long period, perhaps as long as 15 seconds from crest to crest, should be viewed with suspicion.

Cirrus clouds may precede the storm center by 1,000 miles, frequently appearing as long tails extending out from the storm center. As the storm approaches, the cloud cover thickens with heavy stratified layers. This cloud sequence is seen in other situations, so it does not uniquely predict a tropical cyclone.

The barometer may not give a positive indication until the storm center is within 200-300 miles. Then the pressure drop is definite and at an increasing rate as the center nears. Very close to the center the pressure drop may be precipitous. This drop will be followed by an equally rapid rise as the storm moves on.

Winds will begin to rise when the storm center is 300-400 miles away. These winds will be gusty at times, but between squalls they will take on the typical spiral of a low. When this pattern is established, the right hip-pocket rule can be utilized.

The storm is composed primarily of the moist, warm air of its tropical origin. This air is responsible for the temperature and humidity increases, and the general feeling of oppression that is noticeable as the center approaches.

Wind velocities increase as the center nears. At the very center or eye of the storm, there is a small area where the wind velocities are very low. The seas here are beyond description, with enormous waves making up from all directions. Even worse things may be in store, for the wind will suddenly pick up again from the opposite direction. This sudden reversal can add to the confused seas as it will oppose any directional tendency set up by the previous winds.

The anatomy of a tropical cyclone is well known, and some diagnostic signs can be given to alert the small-boat skipper to approaching danger. It is meaningless, however, to give suggestions for boat handling in a storm of this magnitude. If caught out in a tropical cyclone, the fate of a small boat and its crew will be determined by things other than seamanship.

## 17.17   Marine Weather Service on the Great Lakes

Tropical cyclones are most unlikely on the Great Lakes, but the relatively small areas (by ocean standards) and shallow depths lead to some hazardous conditions peculiar to these waters. Any wind on an enclosed lake will be offshore at some portion of the circumference. These offshore winds can be deceptive, since they may be accompanied by smooth water out to one to two miles. Farther out the steep, breaking seas characteristic of shallow water develop as the wind takes effect. A strong continuous blow may actually lower the water level at one end of a lake to a point where the danger of running aground is seriously increased. Winds on the lakes may suddenly change direction, creating confused seas that are difficult for a small boat to cope with and making a return to harbor a dangerous undertaking.

During the spring and summer months thunderstorms and the passage of squall lines are the most common and dangerous hazards on the lakes. A sharp, regular lookout from the south around to the northwest should be maintained for the appearance of the distinctive clouds of a thunderstorm. Visual observations should be supplemented by noting the pattern of static discharges on an AM radio, a very useful indicator of thunderstorm activity.

The National Weather Service has developed a series of special advisory radio broadcasts for the Great Lakes area. These broadcasts should be monitored regularly before leaving port and when under way. When bad weather is forecast, do not delay a return to port. A sudden storm may preclude entrance into a safe harbor just at the time shelter is most needed.

Weather advisory broadcasts for the Great Lakes consist of plain language transmissions and special forecasts given in the *Mafor* (*Ma*rine *For*ecast) code. Each Mafor broadcast is preceded by a brief weather summary in plain language giving the positions of the major features on the weather map that may affect the lake region within 24 hours. Small craft, gale, and storm warnings, if applicable, will be given in plain language.

The Mafor coded transmissions follow a strict sequence:

| Information Transmitted | Range | Example |
|---|---|---|
| Keyword indicating a marine forecast | — | Mafor |
| Day of month | 0-31 | 16 |
| Time (Greenwich Mean) for start of forecast | 0-24 | 12 |
| Name of lake or seaway | — | Superior |
| A group indicator (now always 1) | — | 1 |
| Forecast period (hours) coded | 0-9 | 3 |
| Wind direction coded | 0-9 | 4 |
| Wind speed, knots coded | 0-9 | 3 |
| Forecast weather coded | 0-9 | 5 |
| Maximum wave height during forecast period | — | 10-15 |

The example given would be broadcast as:

Mafor 1612 Superior 13435 Waves 10-15 feet. The information is decoded by reference to the following tables:

**TABLE 17-2**

**Mafor Coding**

| Forecast period, hours | Wind direction | Wind speed, knots | Forecast weather |
|---|---|---|---|
| 0–0 | 0–calm | 0– 0–10 | 0–Good visibility (over 3 miles) |
| 1–3 | 1–NE | 1–11–16 | 1–Icing possible (23–32°F) |
| 2–6 | 2–E | 2–17–21 | 2–Icing probable (below 23°F) |
| 3–9 | 3–SE | 3–22–27 | 3–Mist (visibility up to 3 miles) |
| 4–12 | 4–S | 4–28–33 | 4–Fog (visibility less than ⅝ mile) |
| 5–18 | 5–SW | 5–34–40 | 5–Drizzle |
| 6–24 | 6–W | 6–41–47 | 6–Rain |
| 7–48 | 7–NW | 7–48–55 | 7–Snow, or rain and snow |
| 8–72 | 8–N | 8–56–63 | 8–Squalls |
| 9–Occasionally | 9–Variable | 9–64 + | 9–Thunderstorms |

The example given would be decoded as: Forecast for the 16th day of the month starting at 1200 hours Greenwich Mean Time (E.S.T. 0700). For Lake Superior during the first 9 hours, south winds 22-27 knots, drizzle, waves 10-15 feet.

A complete Mafor broadcast may include several coded groups covering a number of time intervals and applying to a variety of lake areas.

# APPENDIX I
# Glossary

Most of the nautical terms used in the text have been defined as they occur. For more ready reference these, together with other terms frequently encountered, have been collected in the glossary. Many of these terms have local variations in meaning. An attempt has been made to give what is believed to be the most common meaning, without an elaborate discussion of variants.

| | |
|---|---|
| *abaft* | To the rear of; toward the stern; behind. |
| *abeam* | To the side of; at right angles to the keel line. |
| *aboard* | On or within a ship or boat. |
| *abreast* | Alongside of. |
| *adrift* | Loss of mooring or fastenings—opposite of *secure*. |
| *aft* | Near the stern. |
| *after* | Toward the stern and applied to everything abaft the midsection. |
| *aground* | Touching the bottom; to have run the vessel onto a shoal or rock, lodging it there. |
| *amidships* | In or toward the middle of a ship or boat in either length or breadth. |
| *athwartship(s)* | Across the ship, at right angles to the keel. |
| *back* | A wind shift counterclockwise, opposite to *veer*. |
| *backfire flame arrestor* | A device to prevent the escape of flame from the carburetor when engine backfires. |
| *backstay* | Part of rigging, a wire from the mast to the after portion of vessel. |
| *bail* | To dip water from a boat. |
| *ballast* | Heavy material placed low down in a boat or on her keel to maintain trim and improve stability. |
| *batten* | A thin strip of wood put in a pocket in a sail to improve the sail's shape. |
| | Strips of wood bridging seams or joints between wooden members. |

| | |
|---|---|
| *batten down* | To secure hatches (strictly: securing with strips of wood). |
| *beam* | (1) A vessel's greatest width measurement; (2) A transverse structural member underneath deck or roof. |
| *beam ends* | Used in reference to a vessel on her side, *i.e.*, on the ends of her beams. |
| *bear* | To have a direction with respect to the vessel. |
| *bearing* | The direction of an object from the boat. |
| *bed down* | To fasten down a fitting or the superstructure to the deck. |
| *bedding compound* | Viscous sealing substance placed under deck attachments. |
| *before* | In front of. |
| *belay* | (1) Make fast or secure a line; (2) Stop. |
| *below* | (1) To go down or to a lower level; (2) At a lower level. |
| *bend* | To fasten by knotting one rope to another. |
| *berth* | (1) A slip, place where a boat moors; (2) Sleeping accommodations on board, bunk. |
| *bight* | (1) A shallow bay; (2) A *u*-shaped bend in a rope; the middle part of a rope. |
| *bilge* | Externally, the underbody from the keel to the turn where the bottom joins the side; internally, the lowest part adjacent to the keel or keelson. |
| *bilge water* | The water in the bilges. |
| *binnacle* | The mount and housing for the compass. |
| *bitt* | A post or casting (not a cleat) to which mooring lines are made fast. |
| *bitter end* | The inboard end of the anchor rode, "the last extremity." |
| *block* | A structure containing one or more sheaves (pronounced shivs) or pulleys over which rope or wire rope are run. |
| *bollard* | An upright, piling, or column, usually on a pier or seawall, for mooring vessels. |
| *boom* | The movable horizontal spar used to extend the foot, or lower edge, of a fore-and-aft sail. |
| *bow* | The forward part of the vessel's sides where they converge to meet the stem. |
| *broach-to* | To come to lie broadside to the waves, a dangerous situation in a seaway. |
| *bulkhead* | A partition separating compartments. |
| *buoy* | An anchored float used to mark a channel or mooring. |
| *burgee* | A small, triangular or swallow-tailed flag. |
| *butt* | The end of a plank. |
| *butt block* | A backing of hard wood spanning a butt joint to which both planks are fastened. |
| *butt joint* | The joining of two planks end-to-end. |
| *capsize* | To turn over. |

| | |
|---|---|
| *carry away* | To break loose a piece of gear or a line. |
| *carvel* (*carvel built*) | The method of side and bottom planking in which planks are laid edge to edge producing a smooth surface. |
| *cast off* | To let go a line made fast to a mooring or untie a knot. |
| *catboat* | A single-masted, fore-and-aft rigged vessel having the mast stepped very far forward and usually carrying only one large sail. |
| *caulk* | To fill seams with cotton or oakum. |
| *ceiling* | Sheathing on the inside of the hull, not necessarily overhead. |
| *centerboard* | A large metal or wooden plate let down through a slot in the keel to increase resistance to leeway in a sailing craft. |
| *chart* | (1) A nautical map; (2) To draw course and bearing lines on a chart. |
| *chine* | The line at the intersection of the bottom and sides of a flat- or vee-bottom boat. |
| *chine log* | The longitudinal framing member at the chine to which both the bottom and side are fastened. |
| *chock* | (1) The wooden or metal fitting through which mooring lines are led; (2) A wooden wedge driven under shoring timbers supporting a boat on shore. |
| *clamp* (*paired*) | A full length longitudinal framing member at the top and inside the frames but below the deck beams, if any. |
| *clear* | (1) To arrange with authorities for a vessel's departure for a foreign port; (2) To disentangle a line. Opposite to a *foul* line. |
| *cleat* | (1) A wooden or metal fitting (not a bitt) having one or two horns to which a line is secured, made fast, or belayed; (2) To make a line fast to a cleat; (3) A wooden strip acting as support for a shelf or similar structure. |
| *clew* | The after lower corner of a fore-and-aft sail. |
| *clinker* (*clinker built*) | A method of side and bottom planking in which an edge of each plank overlaps the adjacent plank; lap strake planking. |
| *close aboard* | Near, close to. |
| *close-hauled* | Having the sails trimmed in to the greatest extent for sailing as close to the wind as possible. |
| *coaming* | The board on edge around a cockpit or hatch to keep water on deck from running below. |
| *cockpit* | A relatively small space, lower than general deck level. |
| *companionway* | The access to the below decks by way of the companion ladder. |
| *counter* | That portion of a boat's stern overhanging the water from the waterline to the transom. |
| *cradle* | A framework of timbers in which the boat is hoisted or moved about on shore. |

*cuddy*  A small living space in the forepeak of an otherwise open boat.

*cutter*  A single-masted, fore-and-aft vessel carrying two head sails or in which the mast is stepped more than one third the vessel's length abaft the stem.

*davit (dā' vĭt)*  Single or paired curved arms used to hoist or lower small boats, anchors, ladders, and the like.

*dead ahead*  Squarely ahead of the boat.

*deadrise*  The rise of a boat's bottom above a horizontal line from the keel to the chine.

*dinghy (ding' gĭ)*  A small open boat.

*double-ender*  A boat coming to a point at both bow and stern like a canoe—that is, having no transom or round stern.

*douse*  To lower quickly, as a sail.

*draft*  The depth of water from the surface to the bottom of a boat's keel: A vessel has a draft of four feet.

*ebb*  The receding flow of water back to the sea after high tide.

*even keel*  To be trimmed to ride level with respect to the designed waterline.

*fastening*  A bolt, screw, rivet, or nail used to hold the wooden members of a boat together.

*fathom*  A unit of length equal to six feet.

*fender*  A soft cushion hung over the side of a vessel to prevent chafing.

*fid*  A tapered hand tool used to open the lay of rope in splicing, to enlarge holes in canvas, and the like.

*fish*  To mend a broken spar, oar, and the like by binding on a splint.

*flare*  (1) Describes upward and outward curve of the topsides; (2) A hand-held or Roman candlelike torch used for a distress signal.

*flood*  The flow of water toward the shore accompanying a rising tide.

*floor (floor timber)*  An athwartships framing member resting on the keel and fastened to the frame at each end.

*flush deck*  Describes a deck unbroken by raised cabin, continuous, except for hatches, and the like, stem to stern.

*fly*  The dimension of a flag from the halyard to the free end.

*following sea*  An overtaking sea, waves catching up, slapping the stern or even coming aboard over the stern.

*fore*  A prefix denoting *in front of.*

*fore-and-aft*  Lengthwise, in distinction from athwartships.

| | |
|---|---|
| *forward* | Toward the fore part of a vessel; as, to go forward, he is forward. |
| *foul* | (1) Tangled, dirty; opposite to *clear* and *clean;* (2) To foul the anchor: Anchor line wrapped around the anchor. |
| *founder* | To fill with water and sink. |
| *frame* | The skeletal structure of a boat, that which supports and stiffens the skin. |
| *frames* | The transverse members, ribs, to which bottom and sides are fastened. |
| *freeboard* | The vertical distance from the water to deck level, usually stated from the point of least freeboard. |
| *furl* | To roll and securely bind a sail to a boom, mast, or stay. |
| *gaff* | The spar to which the head (upper edge) of a four-sided fore-and-aft sail is laced. |
| *galley* | The kitchen aboard ship. |
| *garboard* (*garboard strake*) | The plank next to the keel. It is fastened along its lowest edge to the keel, also to each frame. |
| *grapnel* | An anchor with four or five arms and flukes; a grappling iron or grab hook. |
| *grounding* (*going aground*) | The act of running a vessel onto the bottom. |
| *ground tackle* | Anchors, cables, and other gear used to secure a vessel at anchor. |
| *gybe* | With a fore-and-aft rigged sailboat, a change of course which swings the stern across the direction from which the wind is blowing. |
| *hatch* | An opening in the deck and its cover. |
| *haul* (*haul out*) | (1) To bring a boat ashore on a railway or with a lift; (2) Pull: Haul on a line. |
| *hawser* | A large mooring or towing line. |
| *head* | (1) The forward part of a boat, including the bows and stem; (2) The edge of a square sail or the top point of a triangular sail; (3) The toilet room. |
| *heave* | (1) To haul, pull with great effort; (2) To throw: To heave a line; (3) To rise and fall: The sea heaves. |
| *heave-to* | To bring a sailing vessel nearly into the wind, after sails trimmed hard in, foresails backwinding aftersails. |
| *helm* | Steering mechanism including the rudder, tiller or wheel, and any connections. |
| *hoist* | Dimension of a flag along the staff or halyard; to raise. |

| | |
|---|---|
| *hull* | The body of a vessel including the frame and its covering; bottom, topsides, and deck. |
| *inboard* | Inside the bulwarks. Toward the centerline; toward the inside, as an inboard engine; move inboard. |
| *kedge* | (1) To move a vessel by carrying an anchor out in a small boat and then hauling up to it; (2) Strictly a small anchor used for kedging. By usage, a traditionally shaped anchor. |
| *keel* | The main longitudinal structural member extending from stem to stern along the center of the bottom of a boat. |
| *keelson* (*kĕl' s'n*) | An internal, longitudinal member extending along the centerline over the keel. |
| *ketch* | A two-masted, fore-and-aft rigged vessel carrying the larger sail on the foremast. |
| *knee* | A corner brace or strengthening member having two arms, making an angle. Knees are installed where topsides join the transom and the like. |
| *knot* | A unit of speed, one nautical mph. |
| *labor* | To roll and pitch excessively and make progress with difficulty. |
| *lap strake* | Clinker built; a method of planking in which the edge of one plank overlaps the adjoining plank. |
| *lay* | Put, put yourself; the direction in which rope strands run. |
| *lay to* | To heave-to, put head into the wind. |
| *lay up* | To put up or store a boat or supplies. |
| *lee* | (1) The sheltered or down-wind side: The lee of an island; (2) Pertaining to the down-wind side or an object on the down-wind side: The lee shore or lee rail; opposite to the *weather side*. |
| *lee shore* | The shore onto which the wind is blowing. |
| *leeward* (*lū' ērd*) | (1) Pertaining to the down-wind direction; as, the leeward direction; opposite to *windward*; (2) Toward the lee; as, sailing to leeward of the buoy. |
| *leeway* (*lē' wā'*) | A down-wind movement; the lateral movement of a ship caused by the wind when sailing close to the wind. |
| *let go* | To release, cast off, drop. To let go moorings, anchor, or sheets. |
| *lie to* | To remain nearly stationary with head to windward or by trimming sail in order to sail very slowly to windward. |
| *limber* | A notch or hole in a floor timber through which bilge water runs to the lowest part of the bilge. |

*line*    All rope and cordage used aboard a boat.

*loa*    A boat's length from the foremost point of the stem to the aftermost part of the hull.

*locker*    Any storage compartment aboard a boat.

*log*    (1) An apparatus for measuring the speed and distance of a boat's progress through the water; (2) A recordbook of courses sailed, occurrences, and observations kept by the master of each ship.

*Lubber (Lubber's) Line*    The index or indicator marking the keel line on a compass or pelorus.

*lwl*    The boat's length at the waterline when in proper trim.

*make fast*    To fasten, attach, or tie. To make a line fast to a cleat.

*mast*    A vertical, fixed spar used to suspend sails or flags.

*outboard*    Outside the bulwarks or away from the center line.

*painter*    A line at the bow of a small boat used to make fast to a wharf or large boat.

*pay*    To smear tar or seam compound. To pay seams.

*pay out*    To slacken, allow to run out. To pay out anchor line.

*pitch*    The longitudinal rocker motion of a boat caused by wind and waves.

*pitch*    The angular slope of propeller blades.

*port*    (1) The left side of a boat when facing forward; (2) A harbor.

*quarter*    The after part of a boat's side.

*rabbet*    A groove or recess cut into one member to receive the end or edge of another in joining parts, as the garboard to the keel.

*raised deck*    Describes a design in which a portion of the deck is higher than the rest; a broken deck, opposed to flush deck.

*reach*    To sail with the wind direction anywhere from slightly forward of the beam to slightly abaft the beam or on the beam.

*reef*    To reduce the sail area.

*rode*    A rope anchor line.

*Samson post*    A strong pillar through the deck to which mooring and towing lines are made fast.

*schooner*    A two or more masted, fore-and-aft rigged vessel carrying the largest sail, mainsail, on the aftermost mast.

| | |
|---|---|
| *scupper* | An opening in the bulwarks or system of drainage pipes in the cockpit through which water can flow overboard. |
| *sea* | The description of the waves: There was a high sea. |
| *sea anchor* | A parachutelike drag towed in a seaway to reduce drift. |
| *seams* | The crevice or line between the edges of adjoining hull or deck planks. |
| *sheave (shĭv)* | Grooved wheel in a block, pulley, or spar. |
| *secure* | (1) Safe, beyond danger; (2) To seize, make fast, or confine. |
| *sheer* | The deck or gunwale line as seen from the side. |
| *sheer strake* | The topmost plank of the boat's side, the upper edge of which describes the sheer as seen from the side. |
| *sheet* | A line used to trim, adjust a sail with respect to the wind's direction. |
| *shelf* | One of a pair of internal structural members, extending the length of the vessel immediately below the deck beam. |
| *shroud* | Standing rigging supporting a spar athwartships. |
| *skeg* | A deepening extension of the after portion of the keel to which the rudder is sometimes attached. |
| *slip* | (1) A vessel's berth between piers; (2) To let go moorings and stand out to sea. |
| *sloop* | A single-masted, fore-and-aft rigged vessel with one headsail or in which the mast is stepped in the forward third of the vessel's length. |
| *sound* | To measure the depth. To sound the tanks with a dipstick or sound the depth of water with lead and line. |
| *spar* | Mast, boom, gaff, and other sticks and poles that support sails and flags. |
| *spring line* | A line used at a dock to keep the vessel from moving ahead or astern. |
| *starboard* | The right side of a vessel when facing forward. |
| *stay* | Standing rigging supporting the mast in a fore-and-aft direction. |
| *stem* | Timber from forward end of keel up to deck level. |
| *stern* | The after portion of a vessel, specifically the region abaft the rudder post. |
| *stove* | Smashed in from the outside. |
| *strake* | One course of side or bottom planking from stem to stern though more than one piece may be used. |
| *stringer* | An inside fore-and-aft structural member attached to the frames usually close to the waterline level. |
| *strip planking* | Planking of narrow pieces that are glued and edge fastened. |
| *tack* | (1) The direction of a vessel's sailing with respect to the |

wind. The starboard tack when the wind blows from the starboard side and port tack when the wind blows from the port side; (2) To come about: From the starboard tack to the port tack; (3) The forward lower corner of a fore-and-aft sail.

*tackle (tă′ kl)*    Blocks and line used to increase a man's pulling power or make the direction of pull more convenient.

*taffrail*    The rail around a vessel's stern.

*taffrail log*    A distance-measuring device attached to the taffrail.

*tiller*    A lever put into the rudder-head by which it is turned and the vessel steered.

*topsides*    The vessel's sides between waterline and rail.

*transom*    The flat or slightly curved stern of a square-ended boat.

*trim*    (1) The state in which a vessel floats; (2) To make a vessel ride on an even keel by shifting ballast or cargo; (3) To change the set of a sail by pulling in the sheet.

*veer*    A wind shift clockwise—opposite to back, as the wind veers from southwest to west.

*warp*    (1) A mooring line; (2) To move a vessel by pulling on her warps.

*watch*    A tour of duty, usually four hours, on board ship. Five watches and two two-hour *dogwatches* daily provide a rotation of the time of duty.

*way*    Movement of a vessel through the water.

*weather*    (1) To successfully endure foul weather: To weather a storm; (2) Describes the windward side: Weather rail, opposite to *leeward*.

*weigh*    Lift up: To weigh anchor.

*well found*    Fully equipped or fully tried and approved.

*whip*    To wind a binding of small cordage around other parts such as the ends of rope.

*windward*    (1) Describes the direction from which wind blows: Windward side; (2) A direction toward the wind: Sailing to windward.

*work*    A vessel or its parts work when structural members loosen and move against each other.

*yaw*    To deviate off course.

*yawl*    A two-masted, fore-and-aft rigged vessel in which the after or mizzen mast is stepped abaft the rudder post and carries less than 20 percent of the total sail area.

# Coast Guard
# Districts-Reports

Written reports to the Coast Guard should be addressed to the *Commander* of the nearest Coast Guard District. Accident reports are required by the Federal Boating Act of 1958, Section 13 (c):

> In the case of collision, accident, or other casualty involving a motorboat or other vessel subject to this Act, the operator thereof, if the collision, accident, or other casualty results in death or injury to any person, or damage to property in excess of $100, shall file with the Secretary of the Department within which the Coast Guard is operating, unless such operator is required to file a accident report with the State under section 3 (c) (6) of the Federal Boating Act of 1958, a full description of the collision, accident, or other casualty, including such information as the Secretary may by regulation require.

Other reportable items include:
1) Malfunctioning or displaced aids to navigation;
2) Errors or omissions on National Ocean Survey charts;
3) Significant deviations from tabulated tide and current data.

### COAST GUARD DISTRICTS AND ADDRESSES OF DISTRICT COMMANDERS

| No. | Address | Waters of Jurisdiction |
|---|---|---|
| First .......... | J. F. Kennedy Federal Building<br>Government Center<br>Boston, Massachusetts 02203<br>PHONE: 223-3634 | Maine, New Hampshire, Massachusetts, and Rhode Island to Watch Hill. |
| Second ........<br>(WR) | Federal Building, 1520 Market Street<br>St. Louis, Missouri 63103<br>PHONE: MArket 2-4604 | Mississippi River System, except that portion of the Mississippi River south of Baton Rouge, Louisiana, and the Illinois River south of Joliet, Illinois. |
| (SR) | 1600 Hayes Street, Suite 304<br>Nashville, Tennessee 37203 | |
| (ER) | 550 Main Street, Rm. 4020-A<br>Cincinnati, Ohio 45202 | |
| (NR) | P. O. Box 693<br>Dubuque, Iowa 52001 | |

| No. | Address | Waters of Jurisdiction |
|---|---|---|
| Third (NA) | Governors Island, Building 104, Rm. 101<br>New York, New York 10004<br>PHONE: 264-3311 | Rhode Island from Watch Hill, Connecticut, New York, New Jersey, Pennsylvania and Delaware, not including the Chesapeake and Delaware Canal. |
| (SA) | c/o USCG Base Gloucester<br>King & Cumberland Streets<br>Gloucester, New Jersey 08030 | |
| Fifth | Federal Building, 431 Crawford Street<br>Portsmouth, Virginia 23705<br>PHONE: 393-6081 | Maryland, Virginia, North Carolina, District of Columbia, and the Chesapeake and Delaware Canal. |
| Seventh | 51 Southwest First Avenue<br>Miami, Florida 33130<br>PHONE: 350-5011 | South Carolina, Georgia, Florida to 83° 50′ W. and Puerto Rico and adjacent islands of the United States. |
| | Commander, Greater Antilles Section<br>U. S. Coast Guard<br>San Juan, Puerto Rico<br>PHONE: 722-2174 | Immediate jurisdiction of waters of Puerto Rico and adjacent islands of the United States. |
| Eighth | Room 333, Custom House<br>New Orleans, Louisiana 70130<br>PHONE: Express 2411 | Florida from 83° 50′ W. thence westward, Alabama, Mississippi, Louisiana, and Texas. |
| Ninth (ER) | New Federal Office Building<br>1240 East 9th Street<br>Cleveland, Ohio 44199<br>PHONE: 522-3131 | Great Lakes and St. Lawrence River above St. Regis River. |
| (CR) | U. S. Post Office Bldg., Rm. 207<br>Federal & Jefferson Streets<br>Saginaw, Michigan 48605 | |
| (WR) | 2420 S. Lincoln Memorial Drive<br>Milwaukee, Wisconsin 53207 | |
| Eleventh | Heartwell Building, 19 Pine Avenue<br>Long Beach, California 90802<br>PHONE: 437-2941 | California, south of latitude 34° 58′ N. |
| Twelfth | Appraisers Building, 630 Sansome Street<br>San Francisco, California 94126<br>PHONE: 556-9000 | California, north of latitude 34° 58′ N. |
| Thirteenth | Alaska Building, 618 Second Avenue<br>Seattle, Washington 98104<br>PHONE: MAin 4-2902 | Oregon, Washington, and Idaho. |
| Fourteenth | 677 A la Moana Boulevard<br>Honolulu, Hawaii 96813<br>PHONE: Honolulu 588-840 | Hawaii and the Pacific Islands belonging to the United States west of longtitude 140° W. and south of latitude 42° N. |
| Seventeenth | FPO Seattle, Washington 98771 | Alaska. |

# Calculating the Effect of Current

The movement of a boat *over the bottom*, which is to say relative to fixed objects, is the sum of any movement due to her own efforts through oars, engine, or sails, and any movement of the water through which she passes. This relation may be written as:

$$\text{Boat to Bottom} = \text{Boat to Water} + \text{Water to Bottom}$$

where the word *movement* or *speed* is to be understood throughout. The plus sign used in the expression does not mean the simple addition of numbers. Due regard must be taken to the directions as well as the numerical values of the two movements or speeds that are to be added.

Predicted values of tidal currents (speeds of water to bottom), based on past experiences, are to be found in the *Tidal Current Tables*. Although the predicted values are good values on the average, abnormal weather conditions may lead to quite different current values at a particular time. Furthermore, that which we call current includes the effects of wind on the superstructure. Boats differ greatly in their response to wind, which requires that each skipper must learn his own boat's performance under a variety of conditions.

If a boat starts from a known position (fix), the effect of current can be determined by comparing a later DR position with a second fix obtained at the end of the run. When conditions are reasonably constant, the *set* (direction) and *drift* (amount) of the current can be applied to a future DR point to obtain an EP. When most of what we call current is due to wind, conditions are not apt to remain constant with a change of course because the boat will present a different area to the wind as the course is changed.

Four different situations are of interest:

1. To determine the set and drift caused by an unknown current. Figure A-1 shows a course line running from a 1030 Fix to a 1206 DR, and also a 1206 Fix. Current has, then, moved the boat from the expected 1206 DR to the known 1206 Fix. Set is found to be 220° *T* by transferring the direction of the current line to the nearest compass rose shown on the chart. The distance 1206 DR– 1206 Fix is found to be 2.4 miles by comparing the charted distance with the

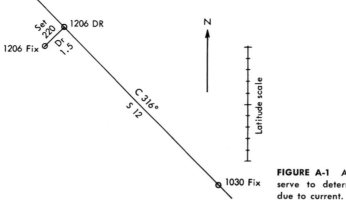

FIGURE A-1 A DR and a fix serve to determine set and drift due to current.

latitude scale. This displacement took place in $1206 - 1030 = 1$ h 36 m or 96 m so:

$$\text{Drift} = \frac{2.4 \times 60}{96} = 1.5 \, \text{knots}$$

Set and drift are marked on the illustration in accordance with the usual conventions.

2. To determine an EP and the track and speed made good, knowing current. Let us consider the effect of the previously determined current on a course of 075° $T$. Figure A-2 shows the situations at 1305 and 1520. The drift of 1.5 knots was effective for $1520 - 1305 = 2$ h 15 m $= 135$ m, and so the boat was moved off course a total of $135 \times 1.5/60 = 3.4$ miles. This distance can now be plotted in the direction of 220° $T$ from the 1520 DR to give the 1520 EP as shown. A measurement along the 1305 Fix-1520 EP line gives an estimated distance made good of 24.4 miles at 079° $T$. The estimated speed made good is $24.4/2.25 = 10.8$ knots.

3. Knowing current, to find the course that must be steered to make good a

FIGURE A-2 The displacement caused by the current is laid off from the DR to obtain an EP and an estimate of the course and the speed made good.

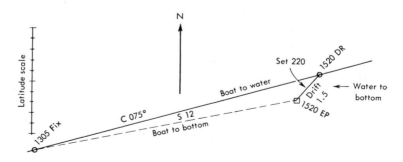

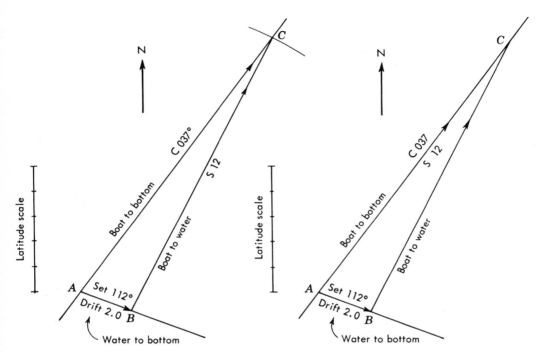

**FIGURE A-3** Boat speed and current are added geometrically to obtain the course to be steered and the speed that will be made good.

**FIGURE A-4** Geometrical addition is used to determine the course and speed that must be maintained to make good a desired course and speed.

particular course. Consider a boat making 12 knots desiring to make good a course of 037° *T* in the presence of a 2-knot current with a set of 112° *T*. A line of indefinite extent is drawn in the direction to be made good, 037° *T*, Fig. A-3. At some convenient point, *A*, a current line of 2 miles is laid off along 112° *T* to determine point *B*. From *B* an arc of 12-mile radius is drawn, intersecting the desired course line at *C*. The direction of *BC* = 028° *T* is the direction to be steered. A measurement of *AC* gives 12.3 knots as the speed made good.

4. Knowing current, to find the course and speed that must be maintained to make good some desired course and speed over the bottom. Reconsider situation 3 with the added requirement that a speed of 12 knots is to be made good along a course of 037° *T*. As before lay off an 037° *T* course line, Fig. A-4, and at *A* draw the 2-mile current line to *B*. A distance of 12 miles is now laid off along the desired course line to establish point *C*. The direction of *BC* = 027° *T* gives the course to be steered, and the length of *BC* = 11.7 knots gives the speed that must be maintained to make good 12.0 knots.

# APPENDIX IV

# Special Piloting Methods

We have seen how a position can be established (fix) from cross bearings on two objects of known positions. Position can also be determined from two consecutive bearings on a single object if there is a straight run of known distance between the two observations.

With the boat on a steady course at constant speed, a relative bearing is taken on a distant, fixed object. The helmsman endeavors to maintain course and speed, and at some later time a second relative bearing is taken on the same object. The distance traveled between the two observations can be determined from the elapsed time and a speed curve, or from log readings. From these data the distance off from the sighted object can be calculated from a trigonometric solution of the triangle involved. By plotting the calculated distance on the *LOP*, a running fix is obtained. Only a few special cases, where the solution can be simply obtained with no knowledge of trigonometry, will be considered here.

1. *Bow and Beam Bearings,* probably the most frequently used pair of observations, require a knowledge of the times at which the distant object had relative bearings of 045° and 090° (abeam).* The distance off from the sighted object at the time of the second observation will then be equal to the distance run between the two observations.

Figure A-5 illustrates the situation for a boat making 9 knots on a course of 010° *T*. Buzzard Point Light was observed to have a relative bearing of 045° at 2334 hours, and 090° at 2355. The time between the observations was 21 minutes, so the distance traveled during this time was 21 × 9/60 = 3.15 or 3.2 miles. The boat was 3.2 miles off the Light at 2355.

A line of position is established by a line through the sighted object at an angle of 090° with the course line (280° *T* in the present case). The distance run (3.2 miles) laid off along the *LOP* will give a running fix. The position will be a running fix because it was determined from one valid *LOP* and information involving the boat movement.

---

* Relative bearings are usually measured clockwise from the ship's heading. In the special cases considered here the relative bearings will be taken in either direction from the heading.

368

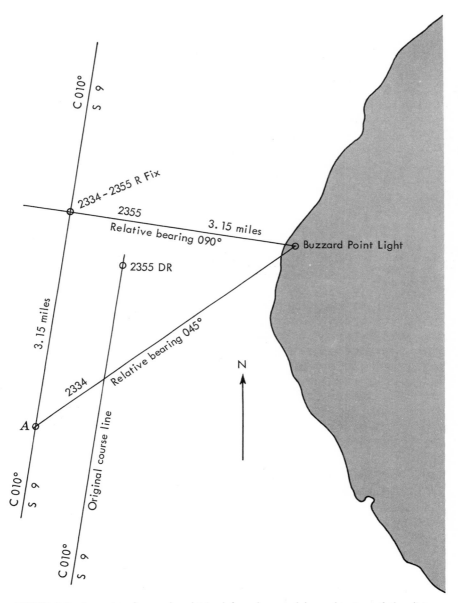

C 010°
S 9

2334-2355 R Fix

2355

Relative bearing 090°

3.15 miles

Buzzard Point Light

2355 DR

3.15 miles

Relative bearing 045°

2334

N

A

C 010°
S 9

Original course line

C 010°
S 9

**FIGURE A-5** A running fix can be obtained from bow and beam bearings if the distance run between the two observations is known.

A course line can now be drawn through the running fix at 010° *T*. The first observation on the light was made at point *A*, 3.2 miles back on the course line from the running fix. Customarily point *A* is not plotted since a knowledge of it does not contribute to the determination of the running fix nor of the subsequent course line.

Essentially the same relations hold if the first observation is made at a relative bearing of 090°, with the second at 135°. With this sequence of ob-

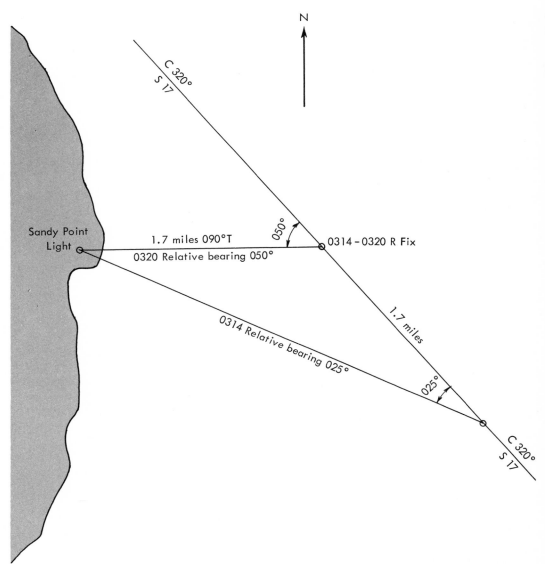

**FIGURE A-6** A running fix can be obtained from a knowledge of the distance run while doubling the relative bearing on a distant object.

servations, the running fix will be established for the time of the first observation rather than the second.

2. Another useful case is known as *Doubling the Angle off the Bow*. The first observation on a distant object is made at any convenient relative bearing of less than 045°, the second when the relative bearing is exactly twice the first value. As before speed and course are held as constant as possible between the observations. Under these conditions the distance off at the time of the second observation is equal to the distance run between the observations.

Figure A-6 illustrates the method for a boat making 17 knots at 320° *T*. At 0314 the relative bearing of Sandy Point Light was 025°. The double angle, 050°, was observed at 0320. During the elapsed time of 6 minutes, or 0.1 hours, the boat traveled 1.7 miles. The boat was, therefore, 1.7 miles off Sandy Point Light at 0320.

The true bearing of the second observation can be readily determined from the relative bearing and the true course. In the example cited this will be 320 − 050 = 270° *T*. The reciprocal bearing, 270 − 180 = 090° *T* can be drawn from the object sighted. The running fix will lie on this line of position at the calculated distance from the object. The course line can now be drawn through the running fix. If desired the entire construction can be made, as shown.

3. Observations made at 022.5° and 045° are a special case of doubling the angle off the bow. All of the relations described in Case 2 hold. In addition, the distance off when the sighted object is abeam (the closest approach) will be 0.7 of the distance run between the two bearings.

4. When observations are made at relative bearings of 026.5° and 045°, the distance off when the object is abeam will be equal to the distance run between the two observations.

Special relations can be worked out for other pairs of angles. The four cases given will suffice for most purposes.

# APPENDIX V

# Compass Compensation

Excessive deviation in a small-boat compass can be reduced, if not eliminated, by the adjustment of two compensating magnets. Details of the method of adjustment will vary with the exact details of the compass construction, but the general principles will apply to all. One compensating magnet (sometimes a pair), usually marked E-W will produce a magnetic field exactly parallel to the lubber line of the compass. A second compensating magnet, or pair, marked N-S, will produce a field at right angles to the lubber line.

When the vessel is headed due magnetic north or south, the moving magnets attached to the compass card will be aligned with the lubber line. In either of these two positions, a movement of the E-W compensator will have little or on effect on the position of the compass card, since this field is now merely adding to or subtracting from the earth's field without changing its direction. In this position, however, the compass card will be influenced by the position of the N-S compensator.

Conversely, when the ship is headed either 090M or 270M, a movement of the E-W compensator will change the position of the card, while the N-S compensator is ineffective. These relationships lead to the prescribed sequence of operations for compensating the compass.

Select an area that will be relatively undisturbed by traffic and where bearings can be taken on some fixed object, preferably two to three miles distant.

1. Sight the distant object and swing the ship until the bearing as read on the compass card has the value calculated from the chart for a heading of 000M. The compass card will now be aligned with the magnetic meridian, but if there is deviation present the lubber line will not coincide with the zero of the compass card.

Remove half of the deviation by adjusting the N-S compensator.

2. Put the boat on a heading of about 090, and adjust the heading until the bearing of the distant object has the value calculated from the chart. Again

the compass card zero will lie along the magnetic meridian, but the lubber line will not be exactly on 090 if there is deviation. Remove half of the deviation by moving the E-W compensator.

3. On a heading of 180, remove half of the remaining deviation with the N-W compensator.

4. On a heading of 270, remove half of the remaining deviation with the E-W compensator.

The adjustment cycle should be repeated at least once, since later adjustments may have a slight effect on the earlier ones. When the deviation has been reduced to acceptable values, obtain data for a deviation table in the usual way.

APPENDIX **VI**

# Morse Code Characters

### INTERNATIONAL MORSE CODE

| | | | | | |
|---|---|---|---|---|---|
| A | • — | M | — — | Y | — • — — |
| B | — • • • | N | — • | Z | — — • • |
| C | — • — • | O | — — — | 1 | • — — — — |
| D | — • • | P | • — — • | 2 | • • — — — |
| E | • | Q | — — • — | 3 | • • • — — |
| F | • • — • | R | • — • | 4 | • • • • — |
| G | — — • | S | • • • | 5 | • • • • • |
| H | • • • • | T | — | 6 | — • • • • |
| I | • • | U | • • — | 7 | — — • • • |
| J | • — — — | V | • • • — | 8 | — — — • • |
| K | — • — | W | • — — | 9 | — — — — • |
| L | • — • • | X | — • • — | 0 | — — — — — |

# Index

**A**

Accident reporting, 44, 131
Admiralty courts, 39
Aeronautical aids to navigation, 280
Aids to navigation:
    buoys, 156-161
    charts, 182-190
    coast pilot, 175
    daymarkers, 168
    electronic, 260-280
    Intracoastal Waterway, 169, 190
    lighted, 160-168
    light list, 156, 169
    tidal current tables, 174
    tide tables, 173
Alcohol:
    at anchor, 68
    on board, 153
    as galley fuel, 136
    in seasickness, 148
    in shock, 152
Algae, 26
Amber light, 121
    on submarine, 297
Anchor:
    bend, 98, 106
    requirements, 55, 97
    rode, 96
    types, 95
Anchoring, 99
Aneroid barometer, 343
Antenna:
    lightning protection and, 312
    radar, 274
    RDF, 261
Anti-cyclone, 345
Anti-fouling paint, 26
Anti-freeze solution, 37
Arctic smoke, 349

Artificial respiration, 149
Atmospheric pressure, 342
Audible signaling equipment, 54
Audible signals, 119-123
Automatic pilot, 272
Azimuth circle, 213

**B**

Backfire flame arrestor, 50
Backing with a single screw, 73
Ballast, 16
Barnacles, 26
    and speed, 230
Barometric pressure, 342
Beam ends, 84
Bearing:
    circle, 213
    conversions, T, M, and C, 212-220
    plotting, 238, 244
    reciprocal, 233
    relative, 234
Bearings:
    bow and beam, 368
    cross, 232
    doubling the angle, 370
Beating to windward, 3, 323, 324
Beaufort scale, 334
Bedding compound, 29
Bend:
    carrick, 104, 106
    sheet, 104, 106
Bermuda rig, 318
Bight (rope), 102
Bilge ventilation, 22, 38, 50, 135
Binnacle, 208
Bitter end, 101
Bleaching wood, 25

Bleeding in shock, 151
Boarding inspection, 46
Boathook, hazard of, 77
Bottled gas, 136-138
Bowline, 105
Boxing the compass, 115
Breaking waves, 81
Broaching, 84, 326
Buoys:
　audible signals, 160
　character of, 157
　lateral system, 156
　lighting patterns, 161
　mooring scope, 158
　ocean, 168
　sizes, 158
　visible range, 162
Burdened vessel, 122
Burning paint, 27
Burns, treatment of, 152

C

Carburetor, 34
Cardinal compass points, 115
Carrick bend, 104, 106
Carrier wave, 257
Carvel planking, 6
Catamaran, 19
Catboat, 313
Caulking, 28
Centerboard, 316
Center of:
　buoyancy, 14
　gravity, 14
Chafing gear, 30, 101
Chart:
　coastal warning facilities, 259
　compass rose, 192
　distance measurement on, 193
　labels, 244
　projections, 178-184
　sources of, 179
　training, 193
　types, 187-190
Chine, 17
Cleating, 101
Clinker-built, 6
Close-hauled, under sail, 323
Clothing, 59
Cloud formations, 339-342
Clove hitch, 106
Coastal warning facilities chart, 259
Coast chart, 187
Coast Guard:
　accident reporting, 44, 131
　approved equipment list, 51

Coast Guard (Cont.)
　buoyage responsibility, 155
　district offices, 363, 364
　insignia, 60
　inspection, 46
　passengers for hire and, 48
　pilot rules, 40
Coast pilot, 175, 176
Code flags, 65
Coded audible signals from aids, 168
Cold front, 336
Collision risk, 116
Command authority, 139
Compass:
　bearing, 116, 233
　card, 204
　compensation, 372, 373
　construction, 201-204
　conversion of readings, 212
　deviation, 208
　installation, 209
　rose, 192
　variation, 207
Corrosion:
　acids, 305
　aluminum, 10
　electrolytic, 311
　engine, 31
　fastenings, 11
　submerged engine, 36
Course line, 240
Course plotting, 238-240
Cross bearings, 233
Cross signals, 120, 123
Cruising range, 2
Cumulus clouds, 336
Current, tidal, 173-175
　calculating the effect of, 365-367
Cutter rig, 314
Cycloidal wave, 80
Cyclone, 344, 346-348
　tropical, 350, 351

D

Damping fluid, compass, 201
Danger sector, 122
Danger signal, 120
Day signals:
　occupation, 299
　distress, 145-147
Dead reckoning (DR), 241
Deadrise, 17
Deep-water lighted structure, 167
Depth finder, 238
Deviation, 206, 208-222
　compensation for, 372, 373
Dewpoint, 331-333

Diesel fuel, 35, 135
Dinghy:
  and man overboard, 142
  in running inlets, 86
  towing, 112
Dismasting, 12
Displacement, 12
Displacement hull, 13
Distance finding from radiobeacon, 264
Distance off by bearings, 368-371
Distance, speed, and time, 225
Distress signals:
  aircraft, 147
  radio bands for, 258
  radiotelephone form for, 270
  submarine, 147
  visual, 145-147
Dockbound, 80
Docking:
  approach, 75-79
  leaving, 79
Dock lines, 93
Documentation, 47
Drift due to current, 247
Drogue, 83
Dry rot, 22

E

Earth:
  magnetic field, 198
  size, 180
Electric:
  energy calculations, 303, 308
  wiring, 309, 310
Electrolysis, 10-12, 311
Electronic aids to navigation, 260-280
Energy from the sun, 329
Engine:
  ignition, 32
  maintenance, 31
  salvage, 36
  storage, 37
  winterizing, 37
Epoxy resin, 9
Equipment:
  audible signaling, 54
  Coast Guard approved, 50
  firefighting, 53
  flotation, 51
  optional, 55
  type acceptable, 267
Estimated position (EP), 241
Everdur, 12
Eye splice, 110

F

Fastenings, 11
Fathometer, electronic, 265
Federal Boating Act of 1958, 40, 45
Fetch of the wind, 335
Fire extinguishers:
  classes, 53
  placement, 138
  testing, 53
Fix:
  by cross bearings, 233
  running, 368-371
Flag etiquette, 62-65
Flame arrestor, 54
Flare, signal, 146
Flotation equipment, 51
Fog:
  advection, 348
  ground, 333
  lookout, 128
  radiation, 333
  signaling equipment, 54
  signals, 126
  speed in, 127
Food poisoning, 152
Fore-and-aft sails, 124, 313
Foretriangle, 314
Foul-weather clothing, 60
Freeboard, 132
Frontal system, 336
Fuel:
  galley, 135-137
  oxidation, 35
Fueling precautions, 133-135

G

Gaff-headed sail, 318
Gale warning, 335
Galley safety, 135-138
Garbage disposal, 67
Gasoline:
  fueling, 133-135
  in the galley, 136
  gum formation in, 35
General charts, 187
Gimbals:
  compass, 202
  galley stove, 137
Glass in hull construction, 9
Glossary, 354-362
Glued-strip planking, 8
Great circle, 180
  charts, 184
  properties, 186
Great Lakes charts, 190

Grounding, 144, 145
Grounding, electrical, 311
   during fueling, 135
Ground tackle, 94
Gybe, 125, 321

# H

Harbor charts, 190
Heading, 201
Heave-to, 83, 326
Heavy-weather operation, 82, 84, 87, 88
Heel:
   when aground, 144
   definition, 13
   under sail, 316
High-pressure system, 345
High seas:
   applicable rules, 40, 113
   boundaries, 41
   lighting rules, 283-306
   rudder signals, 119, 120
Hull construction:
   aluminum, 10
   ferro-cement, 11
   fiberglass, 9
   steel, 10
   wood, 5-8
Hull speed, 19, 20
Humidity, 331-333
   measurement, 332
Hurricane warning, 335
Hydrometer, 303
Hygrometer, 331

# I

Ignition system, 32
Illness at sea, 147-153, 281
In irons, 325
Inland-international boundary lines, 40
International:
   code flags, 65
   Morse code, 374
Intracoastal Waterway:
   aids, 169
   charts, 190

# K

Kedge anchor, 95
Kedging, 145

Kerosene in the galley, 135
Ketch rig, 315
Knockdown, 16, 323
Knot (rope), 102-106
   speed, 225

# L

Labels on chart plots, 244
Lambert projection, 184
Lapse rate, 330
Lapstrake hull, 6
Latitude, 180
   and nautical mile, 181
   parallels of, 181
Lead line, 238
Leeway, 316
Life preservers and vests, 51
Life ring with man overboard, 140
Light list, 156
   abbreviations from, 169
   excerpts from, 170-171
Lighted structure, deep-water, 167
   fog signals from, 168
Lighthouses, 166
   fog signals from, 168
Lighting requirements, 283-300
   at anchor, 289
   towing, 294, 295
   while under way, 285-288
   while unmaneuverable, 289-292
Lightning protection, 311
Lights:
   angular openings, 283
   bulb sizes, 298
   candlepower-range, 298
   height-range, 163
Lightships, 166
   fog signals from, 168
Line of position, 233
   advanced, 242
   hyperbolic, 276
Liquid petroleum (LPG) in the galley, 136-138
Loading:
   and accidents, 132
   formula, 133
Log:
   maintenance, 66
   radio, 67
   sailing, 66
   speed, 227
   taffrail, 227
Longitude, 180
   meridians of, 180
Long splice, 108
Loop antenna, 261
Loopstick, 261

Loran, 276-278
Low-pressure system, 201
Lubber line, 201

**M**

Mafor code, 352, 353
Magnetic field, 198
   of the earth, 199
Mahogany, 6
Man overboard, 88, 132, 140-143
Marconi rig, 318
Marine surveyor, 21
Mayday radio call, 258, 271
Medical advice afloat, 281
Mercator projection, 182
Millibar, 343
Mizzen, 315
Modulation of radio waves, 257
Mooring:
   at a dock, 93
   permanent, 92
   picking up a, 79
Morse code, 374
Motorboat, classes of, 49
Motorboat Act of 1940, 40
Multihulls, 19
Mouth-to-mouth resuscitation, 149
Mushroom anchor, 92, 93

**N**

Nail-sick, 11
Napier diagram, 220
National Ocean Survey (NOS) charts, 179
Nautical mile, 181, 229
Navy, United States:
   insignia, 60
   oceanographic publications, 179
Notices to mariners, 176
Numbering requirements, 46

**O**

Oakum, 28
Offshore breeze, 330
Omega navigation system, 280
Onshore breeze, 330
Operating license, 47
Operator error in accidents, 131
Optical bearing beacon, 164

Overloading, 132
Overtaking signals, 123

**P**

Paint:
   anti-fouling, 26
   removers, 27
   toxicity, 26
Passengers for hire, 48
Passing signals, 120
Paying, seam, 29
Pelorus, 214
   deviation with, 217
   and relative bearings, 234
Period:
   of lighted aid, 162
   of roll or pitch, 16
Pilot charts, 187
Pilot rules, 40, 113
Pitchpole, 85
Planing hull, 13
Planking, 6-8
Plimsoll mark, 132
Plotting positions, 239
Points and degrees, 116
Points of sailing, 124, 320-324
Polyconic projection, 184
Polyester resin, 9
Polymerization, 9, 23, 24
Porpoising, 13
Position determination by:
   bearing and distance, 237
   cross bearings, 232
   soundings, 237, 238
Position plotting, 239
Power-driven vessel, defined, 283
Preventer, gybe, 321
Privileged vessel, 122
Projections, sphere to plane, 181-185
Propeller:
   cavitation, 69
   dimensions of, 69
   handedness, 70
   hazards of, 140
   side thrust, 72
   slip, 74
Public Health Service, United States:
   insignia, 60
   medical advice afloat, 281

**Q**

Quarantine buoy, 159
Quarterdeck, 62

**R**

Radar:
  audible signal, 275
  and lookout, 276
  visual display, 274
Radio:
  broadcast receiver on board, 259
  Citizen's Band, 271, 272
  direction finding (RDF), 260-262
  distress frequencies, 258, 270
  emission types, 257
  frequency bands, 257
  list of navigational aids, H.O. 205-117,
    263
  surveillance by CG and USN, 258
Radiobeacons, 263
Radiotelephone:
  MF band, 268
  operating procedure, 270
  priority messages, 270
  single sideband, 268
  type acceptable, 267
  VHF band, 267
Rank precedence, 62
Reaching under sail, 322
Reciprocal bearing, 233
Reefing, 323
Relative bearing, 116
Relative humidity, 331
Responsibility of command, 130
Resuscitation, 149
  and heart massage, 150
Rhumb line, 181, 186
Rigging, sailboat, 317
Right-of-way, 119-126
Righting moment, 14
Roll, 13
Rope:
  deterioration, 30
  materials, 90
  nomenclature, 102
  strength, 91
Rudder action, 70
Rules of the Road, 40, 113
  in low visibility, 126
  for sailboats, 125
Running fix, 242
  from bearings, 368-371
Running inlets, 85
Running lights, 283

**S**

Safety belts, 139
Sail types, 318, 319
Sailboat types, 313-315

Sailing charts, 187
St. Elmo's fire, 312
Salutes, 62
Schooner rig, 316
Scope of:
  anchor, 99
  buoy mooring, 158
  permanent moor, 92
Sea anchor, 83
Seacock, winterizing, 38
Seam compound, 29
Seasickness, 148
Seizing, rope, 105
Service grades, 60
Set due to current, 247, 365-367
Setting anchor, 99
Sewage disposal, 67
Shadowpin, compass, 204, 221
Shaft alignment, 32
Sheet bend, 104, 106
Shock, 151
Shoes on board, 59
Short splice, 108
Signals:
  audible, 120
  duration, 121
  engine reversed, 121
  in fog, 126, 127
  passing, meeting, overtaking, 120-123
  required equipment, 48-50, 54
  sources, 48-50
Signal display, occupational, 299
Signal flare, 56, 146
Skin diver's flag, 147
Slack water, 246
Sloop rig, 314
Small-craft advisory, 335
Small-craft chart, 190
Sounding datum, 191
Squall line, 336
Square-rigger, 312
Specific gravity, battery, 303
Speed curve, 229, 232
Speed, time, and distance, 225
Spring line, 77, 94
Stability, 13-15
Standing part (rope), 102
Standing rigging, 317
Steerageway, 70
Steering outboards, 71
Stimulants afloat, 148
Storage battery:
  charging, 306
  construction, 302
  freezing point, 306
  installation, 304
  maintenance, 305
Storm warning, 335
Sunburn, 150, 151
Swinging ship, 213, 214

**T**

Tacking under sail, 324
Tank:
  diesel fuel, 36
  gasoline, 35
  installation, 134
  winterizing, 37
Temperature inversion, 330
Teredo, 26
Terminology, marine, 58
Thunderstorms, 311, 338
Tidal currents, 172
  excerpts from tables, 174
Tides, 171, 172
  excerpts from tables, 173
Time signals, 281
Time, speed, and distance, 225
Tonnage, kinds and measurement, 12, 47
Towing techniques, 111, 112
Towing while aground, 145
Trailer safety, 153-154
Trimaran, 19
Trim tabs, 13
Trip line, anchor, 96
Tropical cyclone, 350, 351
True bearing, 116
Tugboat lighting, 294-296
Turns:
  single screw, 73
  twin screw, 75
Typhoon, 350

**U**

Ultraviolet light:
  compass damping fluid, 202
  eye irritation, 151
  nylon, 91

Ultraviolet light (*Cont.*)
  sunburn, 150
  varnish, 25
Under way, definition, 127
Uniforms, 60
Urgent radiotelephone signals, 170

**V**

Variation:
  in compass conversions, 212-220
  source, 207
  shown on charts, 192
Varnish, 25

**W**

Warm front, 337
Wave length, ocean waves, 81
Weather, 328-353
  broadcasts, 328
  on Great Lakes, 352
  warning displays, 335
Weighing anchor, 100
Wheel bearing, trailer, 154
Whipping rope end, 101
Whistle blasts, definition, 121
Winterizing, 37
Wooding, 27

**Y**

Yaw, 18
Yawl rig, 315

# ABBREVIATED RULES—WHISTLE SIGNALS

(See Sections 7.04, 7.05, 7.06, 7.07, 7.08, 7.09, 7.10)

A privileged vessel has the "right of way" over a burdened vessel.

In a **head-on** meeting situation, neither vessel has the "right of way." Both vessels must alter course to starboard to avoid collision.

In a **crossing** situation, the privileged vessel is to starboard and forward of a line 22½° abaft the burdened vessel's starboard beam.

A privileged vessel must maintain course and speed (unless the burdened vessel cannot or will not avoid a collision).

In a crossing situation, the burdened vessel must maneuver so as to cross under the privileged vessel's stern.

In an **overtaking** situation, the privileged vessel is overtaken by the burdened vessel.

Under International Rules, whistle signals are sounded when a course change or maneuver is undertaken to avoid a collision.

Under Inland Rules, whistle signals are sounded to indicate **intent** in passing situations.

In fog and periods of low visibility, only fog signals are given, except on the Great Lakes, where passing signals are given in all weather conditions.

A response to a whistle signal is not required by the International Rules unless the indicated maneuver is considered dangerous to either vessel, in which case the **danger signal** (five short blasts) is given. A response is required by all other rules: when in agreement, the very same whistle signal; when danger is considered to exist, four or more short rapid blasts.

# WHISTLE SIGNALS—JURISDICTIONAL SIGNALS

| Situation | Rule | Maneuver or Intent | Signal |
|---|---|---|---|
| Meeting | International | "I am changing my course to starboard." | 1 short blast |
| | | "I am changing my course to port." | 2 short blasts |
| | Inland | "I intend to keep to the right so that we may pass port side to port side." | 1 short blast |
| | | "I intend to keep to the left so that we may pass starboard side to starboard side." | 2 short blasts |
| | Great Lakes | Course changes as under International Rules in all weathers and require a response. | |
| | Western Rivers | Intent as under Inland Rules, ascending vessel signals first, but the descending vessel is privileged. A descending tow is privileged over a crossing vessel and indicates her intent to continue course. | 3 short blasts |
| Crossing | International | Privileged vessel: "I will maintain course and speed." | not required |
| | | Burdened vessel: "I will alter course to pass under privileged vessel's stern." | not required |
| | Inland | Privileged vessel: "I intend to maintain course and speed." | 1 short blast |
| | | Burdened vessel: "I intend to pass under the privileged vessel's stern." | 1 short blast |
| | Great Lakes | Same as Inland | |
| Overtaking | All | Burdened (overtaking) vessel: "I am altering my course to starboard," or "I intend to pass on your starboard side." | 1 short blast |
| | | Burdened vessel: "I am altering course to port," or "I intend to pass on your port side." | 2 short blasts |